SHINE
SHINE
CHIRP
CHIRP

There is one period during each da
that is my favorite time...The hour
between 10 and 11 in the morning.
The reason is that everything alwa
seems so refreshing and delightful a
that hour. But because of looming
deadlines, I usually end up sleeping
through it...That refreshing and
delightful feeling...what was it like
again?

—Masashi Kishimoto, 2006

岸本斉史

Author/artist Masashi Kishimoto was born in 1974 in rural Okayama Prefecture, Japan. After spending time in art college, he won the Hop Step Award for new manga artists with his manga **Karakuri** (Mechanism). Kishimoto decided to base his next story on traditional Japanese culture. His first version of **Naruto**, drawn in 1997, was a one-shot story about fox spirits; his final version, which debuted in **Weekly Shonen Jump** in 1999, quickly became the most popular ninja manga in Japan.

一楽
ラーメン一楽

NARUTO VOL. 33
The SHONEN JUMP Manga Edition

This graphic novel contains material that was originally published in English in **SHONEN JUMP** #71-72. Artwork in the magazine may have been slightly altered from that presented here.

STORY AND ART BY MASASHI KISHIMOTO

Translation/Mari Morimoto
English Adaptation/Deric A. Hughes & Benjamin Raab
Touch-up Art & Lettering/ Inori Fukuda Trant
Design/Sean Lee
Editor/Joel Enos

Editor in Chief, Books/Alvin Lu
Editor in Chief, Magazines/Marc Weidenbaum
VP, Publishing Licensing/Rika Inouye
VP, Sales & Product Marketing/Gonzalo Ferreyra
VP, Creative/Linda Espinosa
Publisher/Hyoe Narita

NARUTO © 1999 by Masashi Kishimoto. All rights reserved. First published in Japan in 1999 by SHUEISHA Inc., Tokyo. English translation rights arranged by SHUEISHA Inc. The stories, characters and incidents mentioned in this publication are entirely fictional.

No portion of this book may be reproduced or transmitted in any form or by any means without written permission from the copyright holders.

The rights of the author(s) of the work(s) in this publication to be so identified have been asserted in accordance with Copyright, Designs and Patents Act 1988. A CIP catalogue record for this book is available from the British Library.

Printed in the U.S.A.

Published by VIZ Media, LLC
P.O. Box 77010
San Francisco, CA 94107

SHONEN JUMP Manga Edition
10 9 8 7 6 5 4 3 2 1
First printing, December 2008

THE WORLD'S
MOST POPULAR MANGA

www.viz.com

RATED
T
FOR
TEEN

PARENTAL ADVISORY
NARUTO is rated T for Teen and is recommended for ages 13 and up. This volume contains realistic and fantasy violence.
ratings.viz.com

www.shonenjump.com

SHONEN JUMP MANGA EDITION

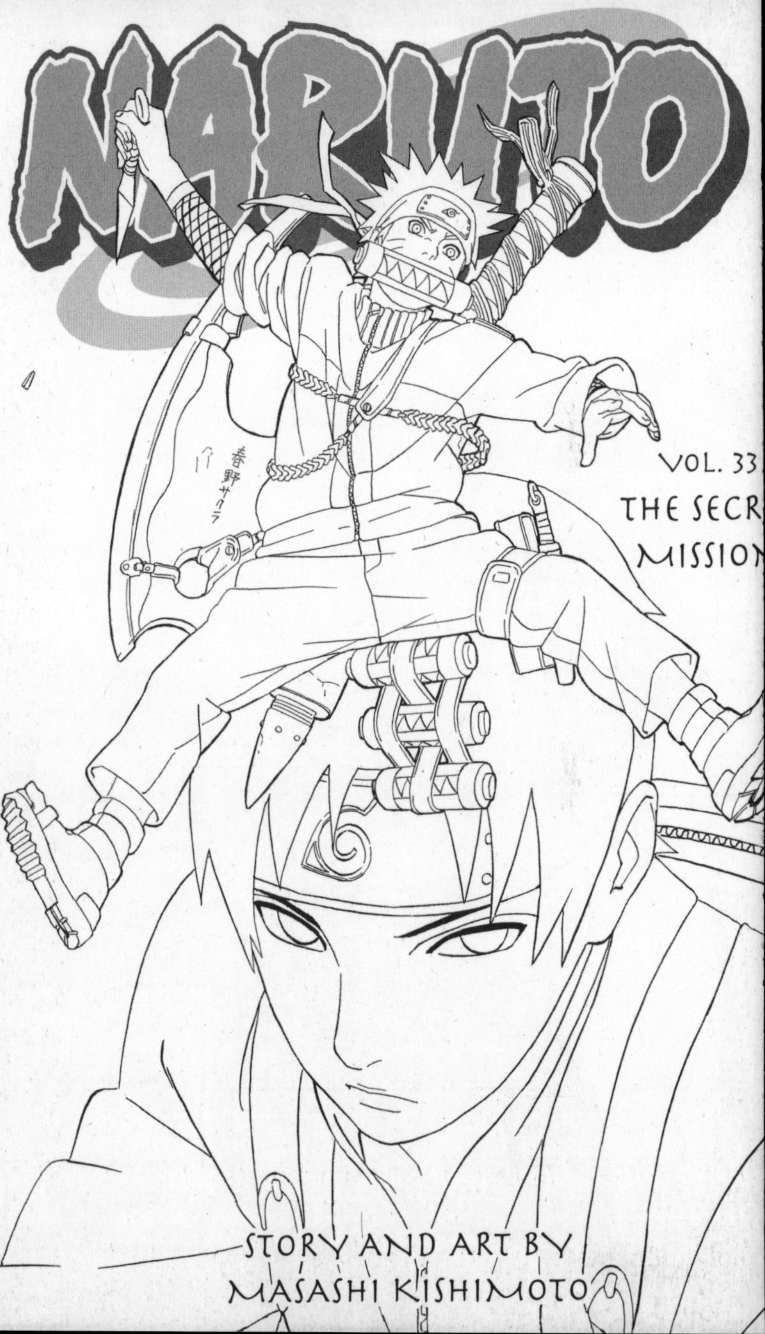
NARUTO
春野サクラ

VOL. 33

THE SECR

MISSION

STORY AND ART BY

MASASHI KISHIMOTO

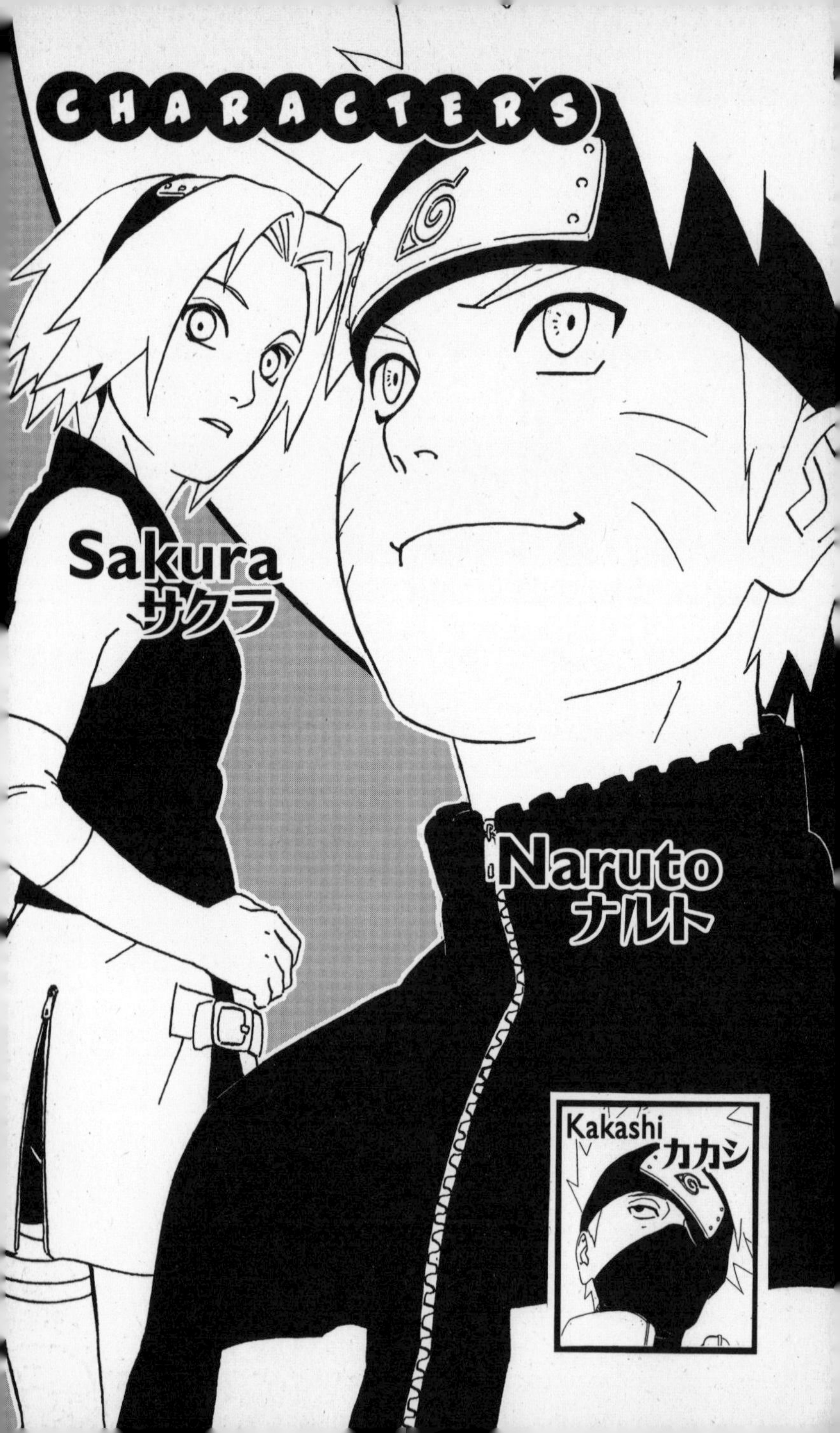
CHARACTERS
Sakura
サクラ
Naruto
ナルト
Kakashi
カカシ

Sai サイ
Tsunade 綱手
Danzo ダンゾウ
Yamato ヤマト
Orochimaru 大蛇丸
Kabuto カブト

The Story So Far…

Against all odds, Uzumaki Naruto, the student least likely to graduate from the Ninja Academy in the village of Konohagakure, becomes a ninja along with his classmates and closest friends, Sasuke and Sakura. During the Chûnin Selection Exams, however, the turncoat ninja Orochimaru launches *Operation Destroy Konoha,* forcing Naruto's mentor, the Third Hokage, to sacrifice his own life to stop the attack and save the village.

Further tragedy follows when Sasuke succumbs to the lure of Orochimaru's power. Though Naruto fights valiantly to stop Sasuke from joining up with their worst enemy, he ultimately fails. After Sasuke flees with Orochimaru, Naruto vows to rescue his friend someday…

In the interim, two years pass and Naruto and his comrades once again confront the mysterious Akatsuki organization. But intelligence gained during that battle leads the new Team Kakashi to a secret rendezvous with an Akatsuki spy who turns out to be none other than the ever-duplicitous Kabuto! Unbeknownst to our heroes, the whole event takes place under the watchful snake eyes of Orochimaru…!

NARUTO

VOL. 33
THE SECRET MISSION

CONTENTS

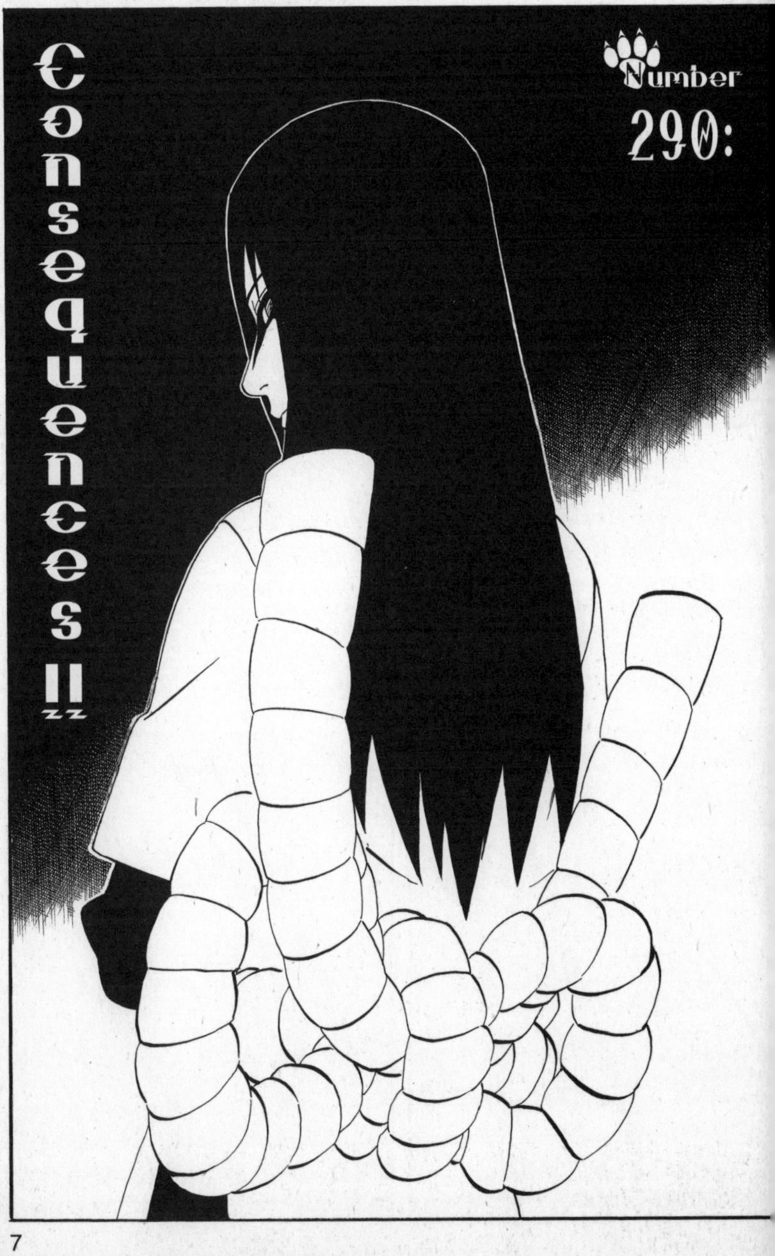
Number 290:
Consequences II

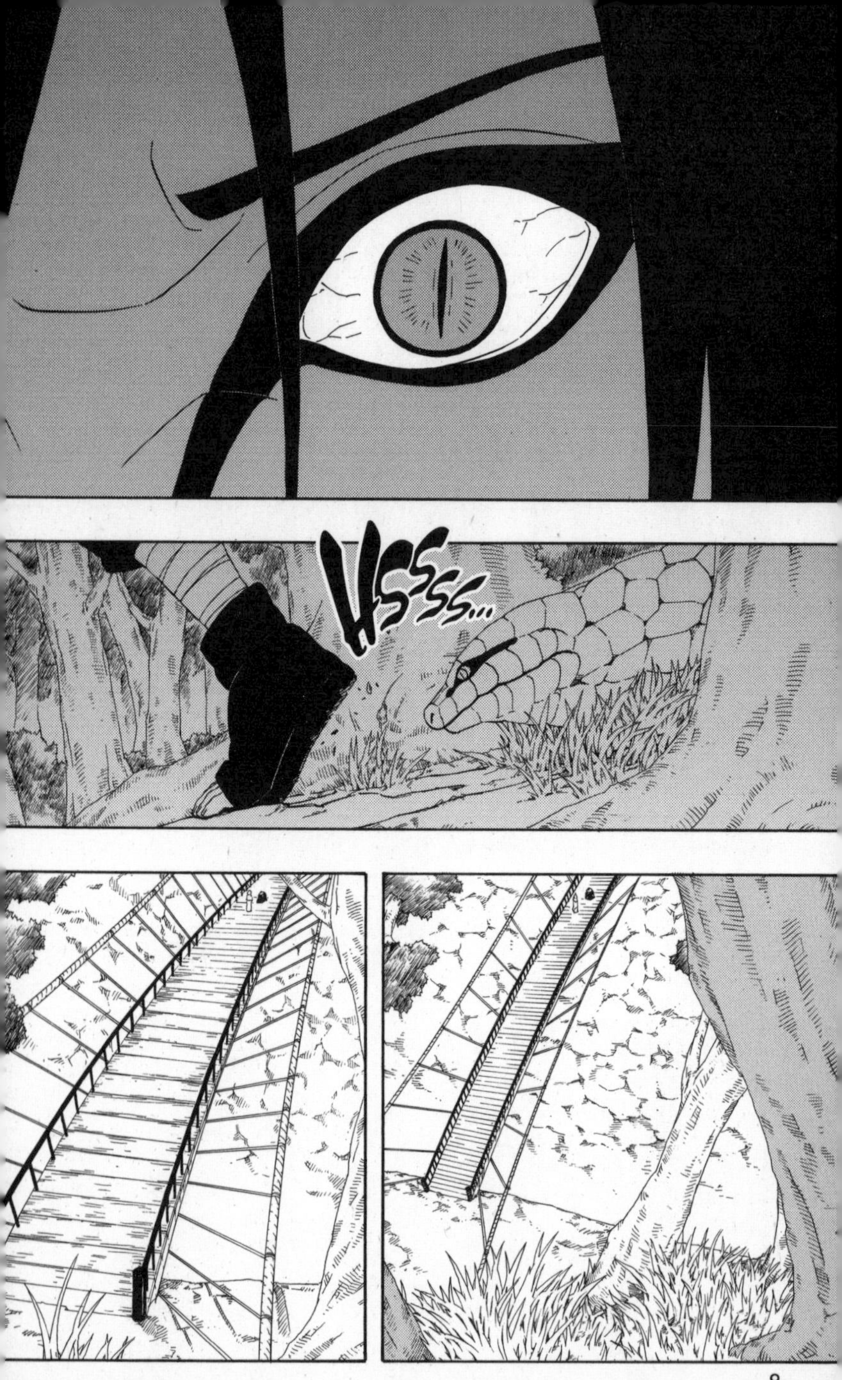
HSSSS...

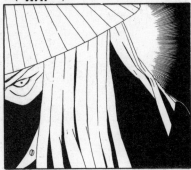

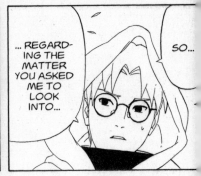

READ THIS WAY

SO...
...REGARDING THE MATTER YOU ASKED ME TO LOOK INTO...
...
THERE ARE STILL A FEW MORE THINGS I WANTED TO ASK HIM...
...BUT THE LONGER WE KEEP TALKING, THE GREATER THE CHANCE I MIGHT SLIP UP...
EVEN AFTER OROCHIMARU TRANSFERS BODIES, HE PUTS A PROTECTIVE JUTSU ON THE CELL SPECIMENS FROM THE OLD HOST BODY...
...SO I HAVE **NOT** BEEN ABLE TO ANALYZE THEM.
HOOSH
I SEE...
...

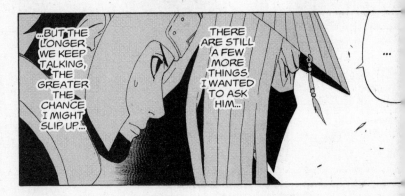

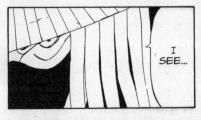

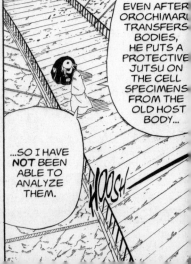

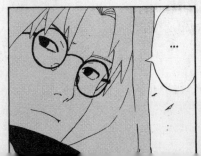

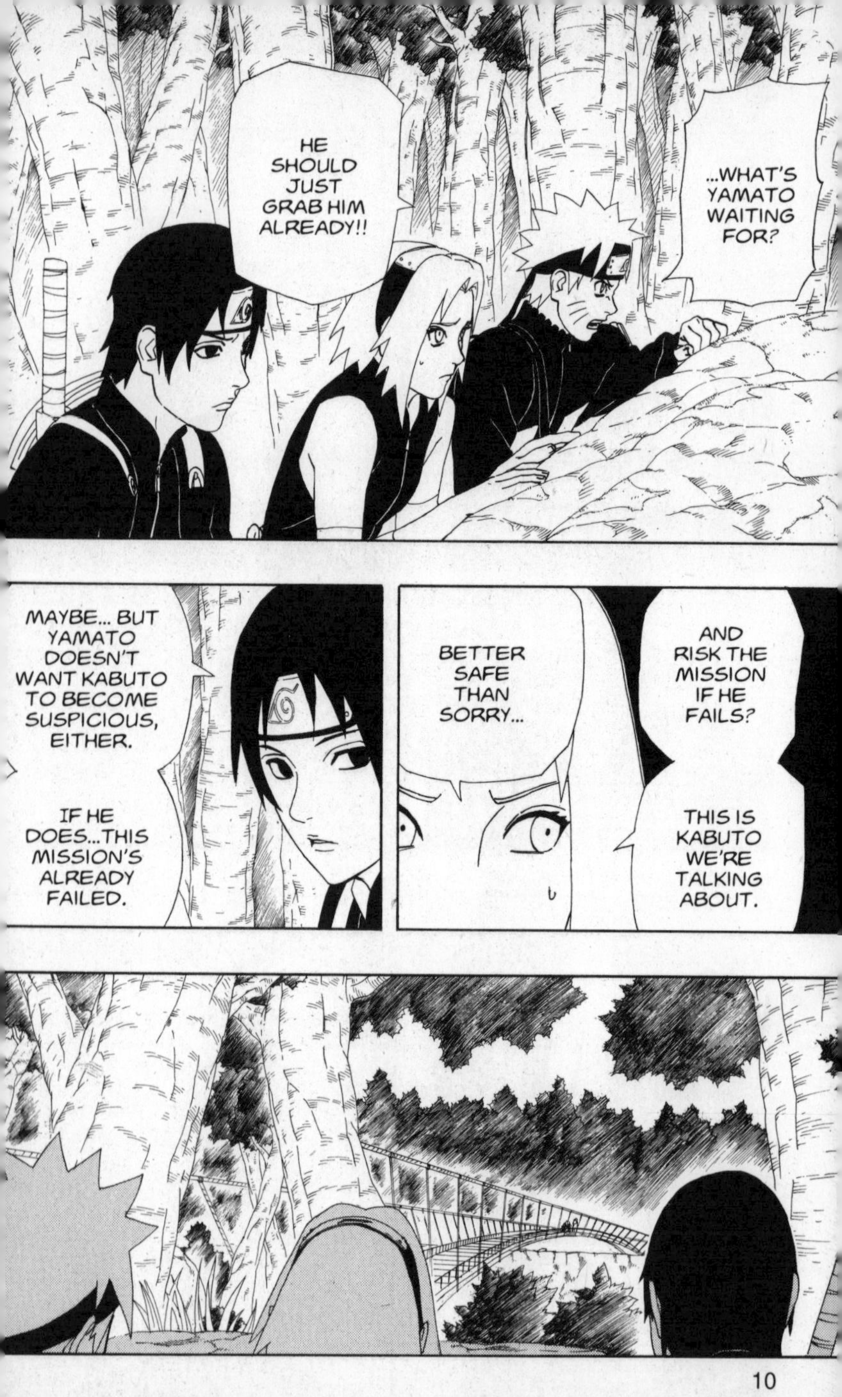
...WHAT'S YAMATO WAITING FOR?
HE SHOULD JUST GRAB HIM ALREADY!!
AND RISK THE MISSION IF HE FAILS?
BETTER SAFE THAN SORRY...
THIS IS KABUTO WE'RE TALKING ABOUT.
MAYBE... BUT YAMATO DOESN'T WANT KABUTO TO BECOME SUSPICIOUS, EITHER.
IF HE DOES...THIS MISSION'S ALREADY FAILED.

READ THIS WAY

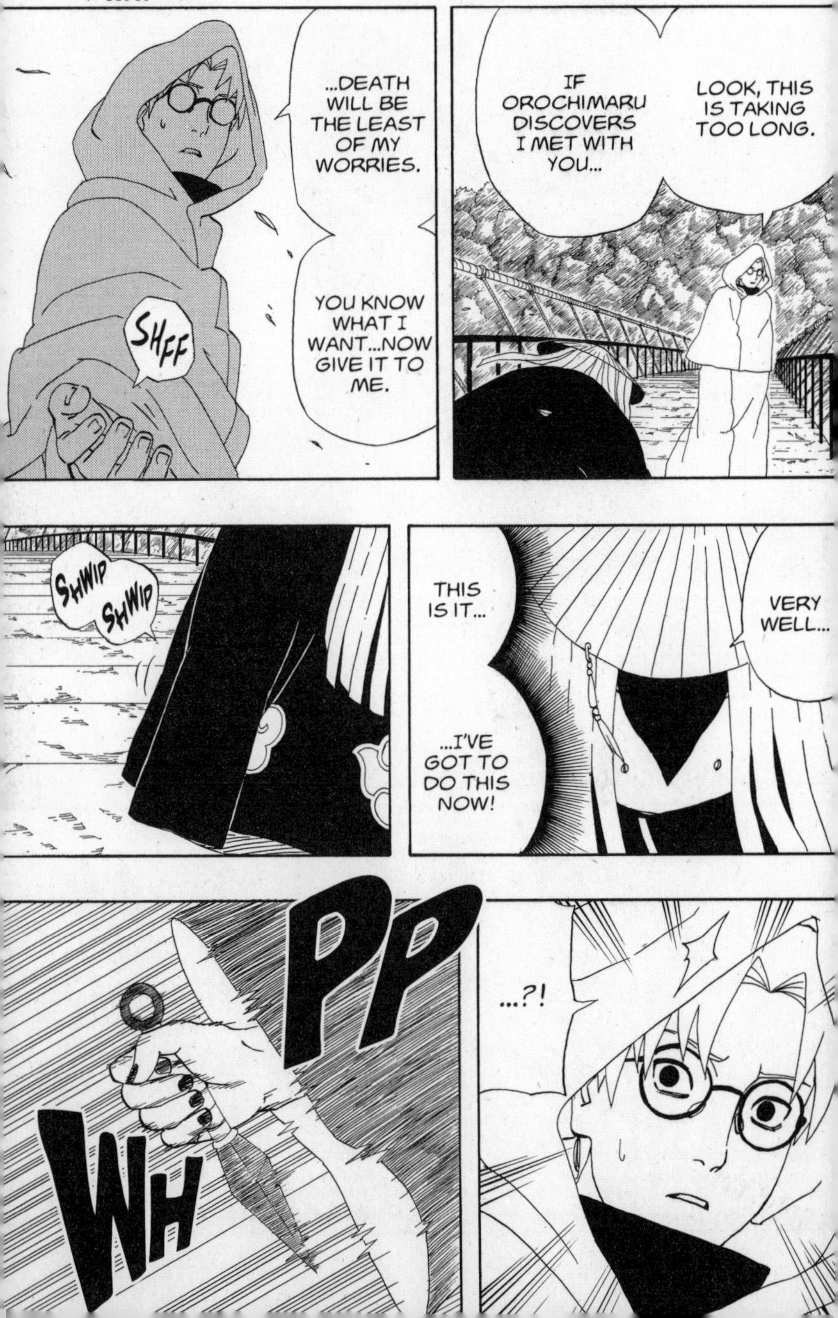

LOOK, THIS IS TAKING TOO LONG.
IF OROCHIMARU DISCOVERS I MET WITH YOU...
...DEATH WILL BE THE LEAST OF MY WORRIES.
YOU KNOW WHAT I WANT...NOW GIVE IT TO ME.
SHFF
VERY WELL...
THIS IS IT...
...I'VE GOT TO DO THIS NOW!
SHWIP SHWIP
...?!
WHPP

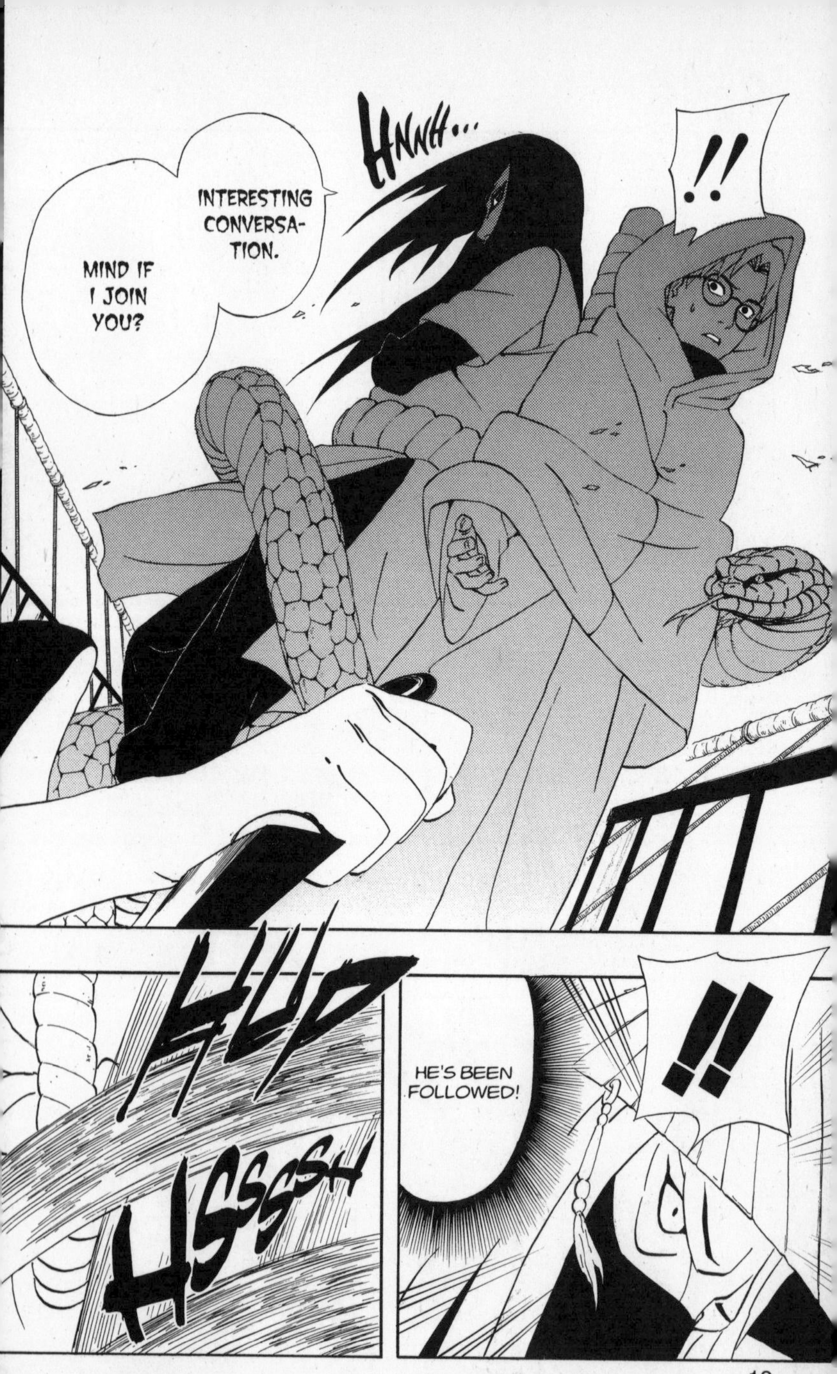
!!
HNNH...
INTERESTING CONVERSA-TION.
MIND IF I JOIN YOU?
!!
HE'S BEEN FOLLOWED!
HUP
HSSSH

READ THIS WAY

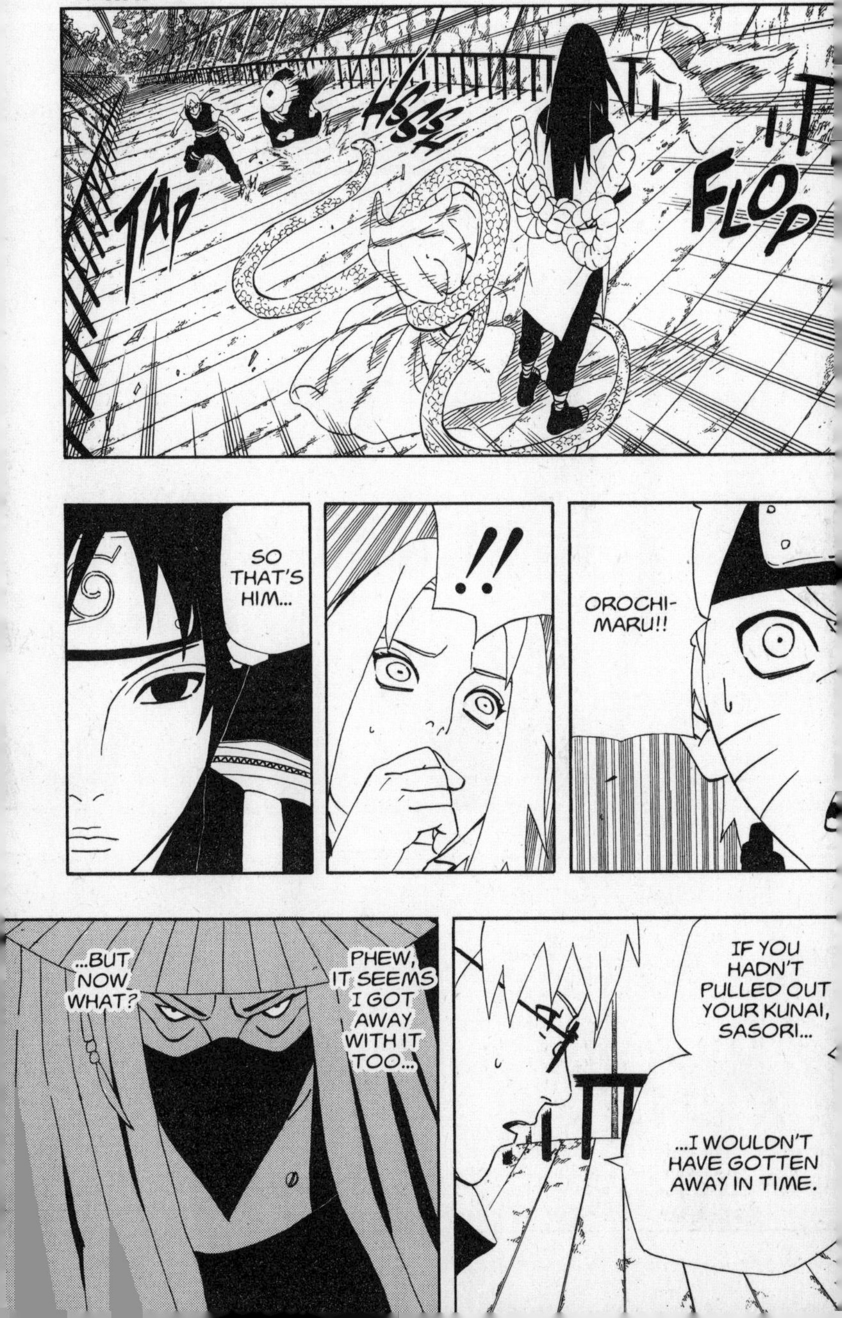
FLOP
HSSH
TAP
OROCHI-MARU!!
!!
SO THAT'S HIM...
IF YOU HADN'T PULLED OUT YOUR KUNAI, SASORI...
...I WOULDN'T HAVE GOTTEN AWAY IN TIME.
PHEW, IT SEEMS I GOT AWAY WITH IT TOO...
...BUT NOW WHAT?

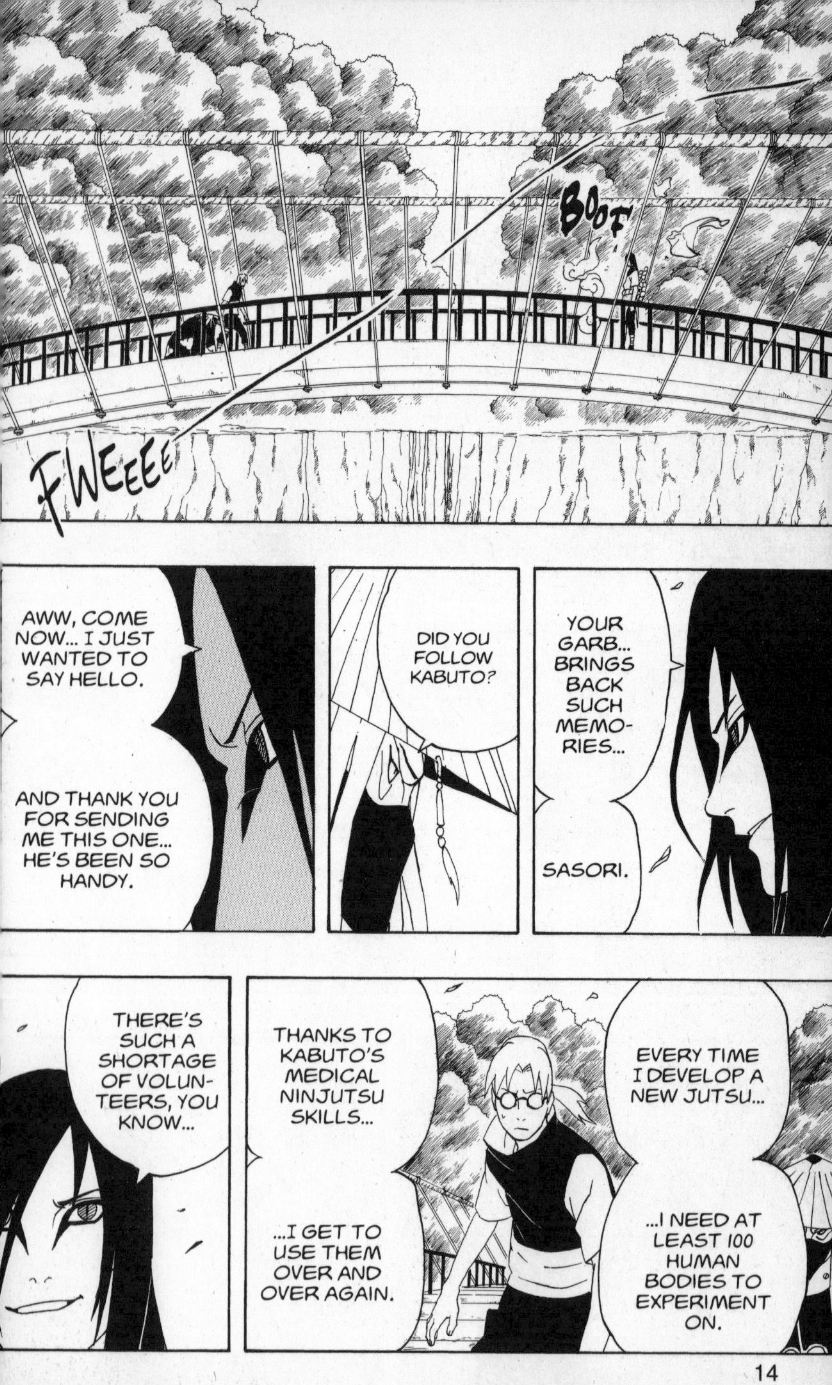
BOOF
FWEEEE
YOUR GARB... BRINGS BACK SUCH MEMORIES...
SASORI.
DID YOU FOLLOW KABUTO?
AWW, COME NOW... I JUST WANTED TO SAY HELLO.
AND THANK YOU FOR SENDING ME THIS ONE... HE'S BEEN SO HANDY.
EVERY TIME I DEVELOP A NEW JUTSU...
...I NEED AT LEAST 100 HUMAN BODIES TO EXPERIMENT ON.
THANKS TO KABUTO'S MEDICAL NINJUTSU SKILLS...
...I GET TO USE THEM OVER AND OVER AGAIN.
THERE'S SUCH A SHORTAGE OF VOLUNTEERS, YOU KNOW...

READ THIS WAY

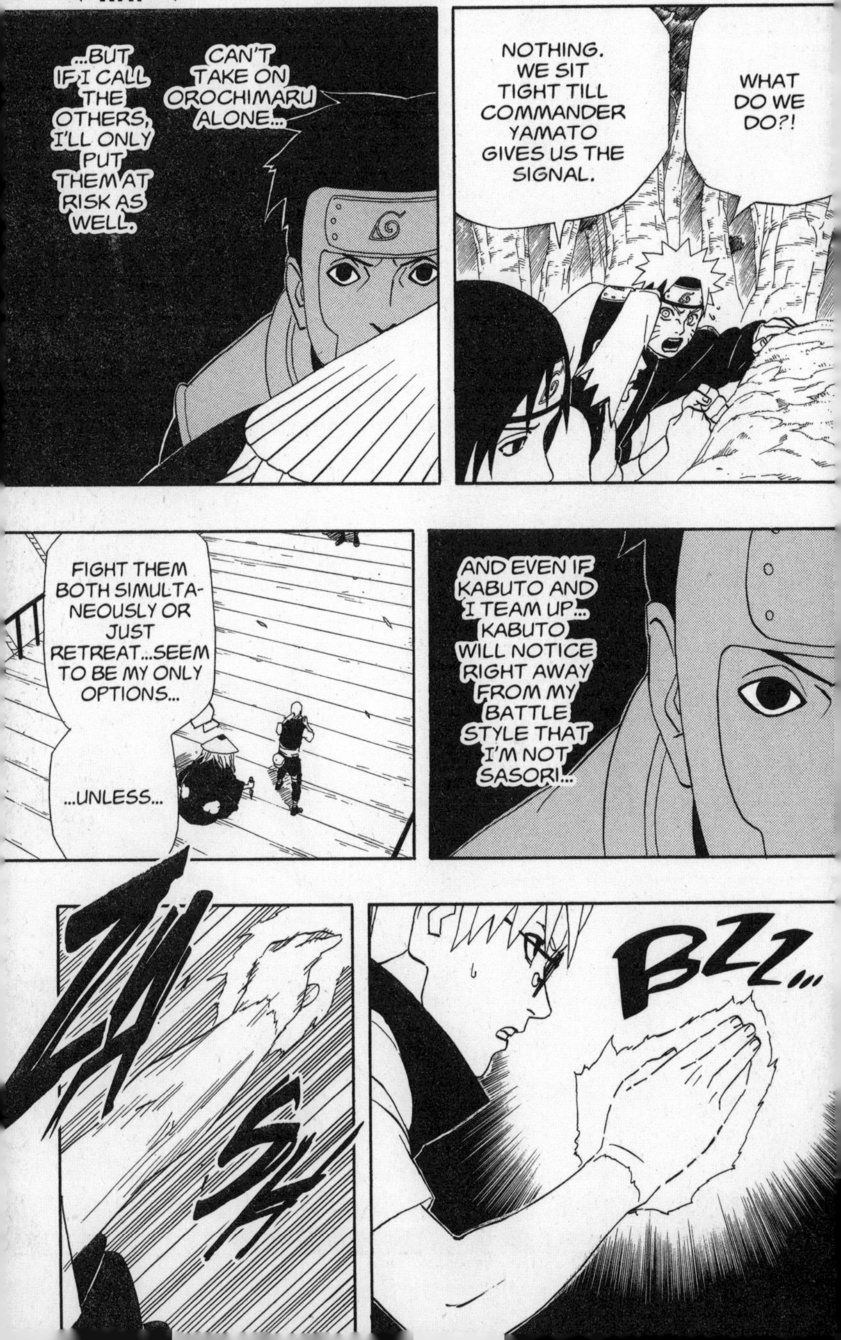
WHAT DO WE DO?!
NOTHING. WE SIT TIGHT TILL COMMANDER YAMATO GIVES US THE SIGNAL.
CAN'T TAKE ON OROCHIMARU ALONE...
...BUT IF I CALL THE OTHERS, I'LL ONLY PUT THEM AT RISK AS WELL.
AND EVEN IF KABUTO AND I TEAM UP... KABUTO WILL NOTICE RIGHT AWAY FROM MY BATTLE STYLE THAT I'M NOT SASORI...
FIGHT THEM BOTH SIMULTANEOUSLY OR JUST RETREAT...SEEM TO BE MY ONLY OPTIONS...
...UNLESS...
BZZ...
ZWSH

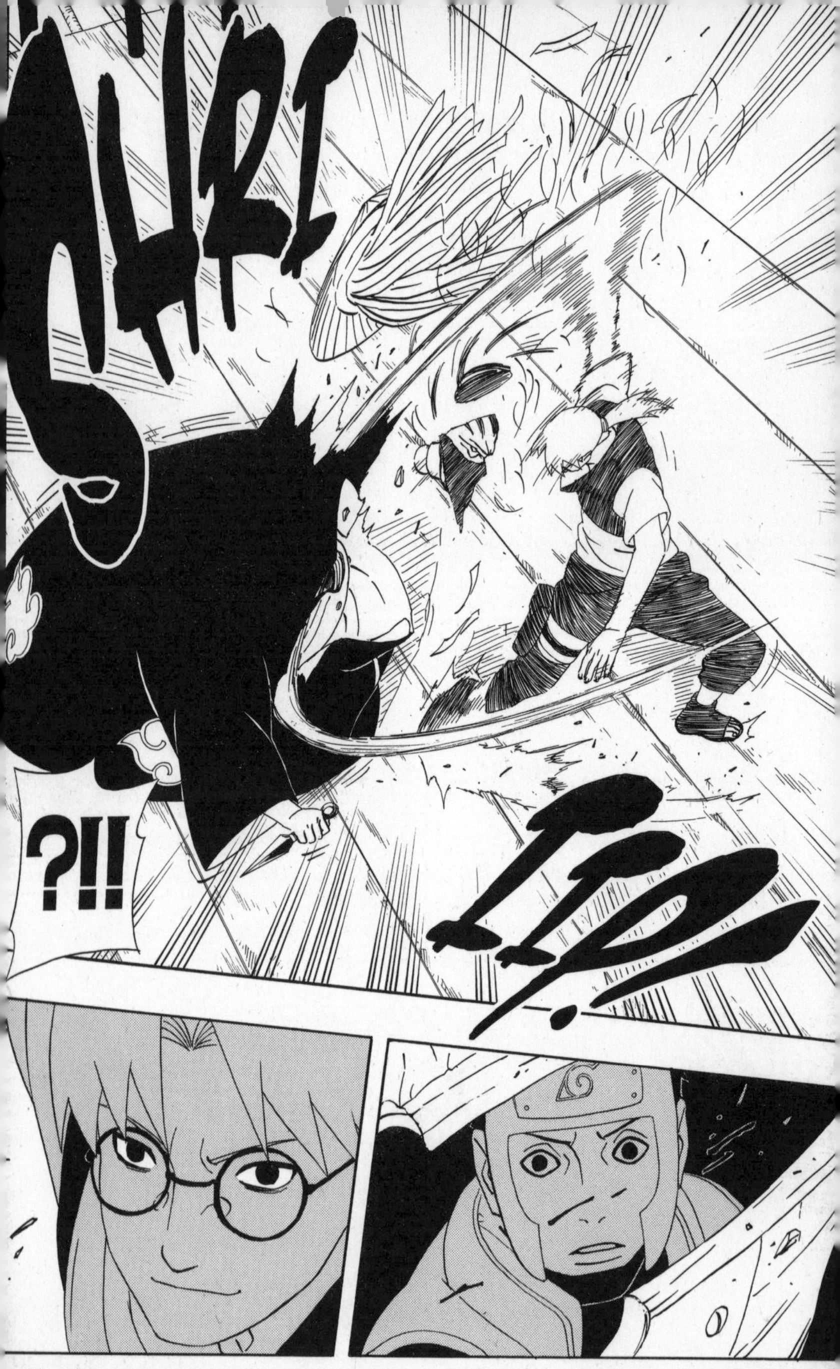
?!!

READ THIS WAY

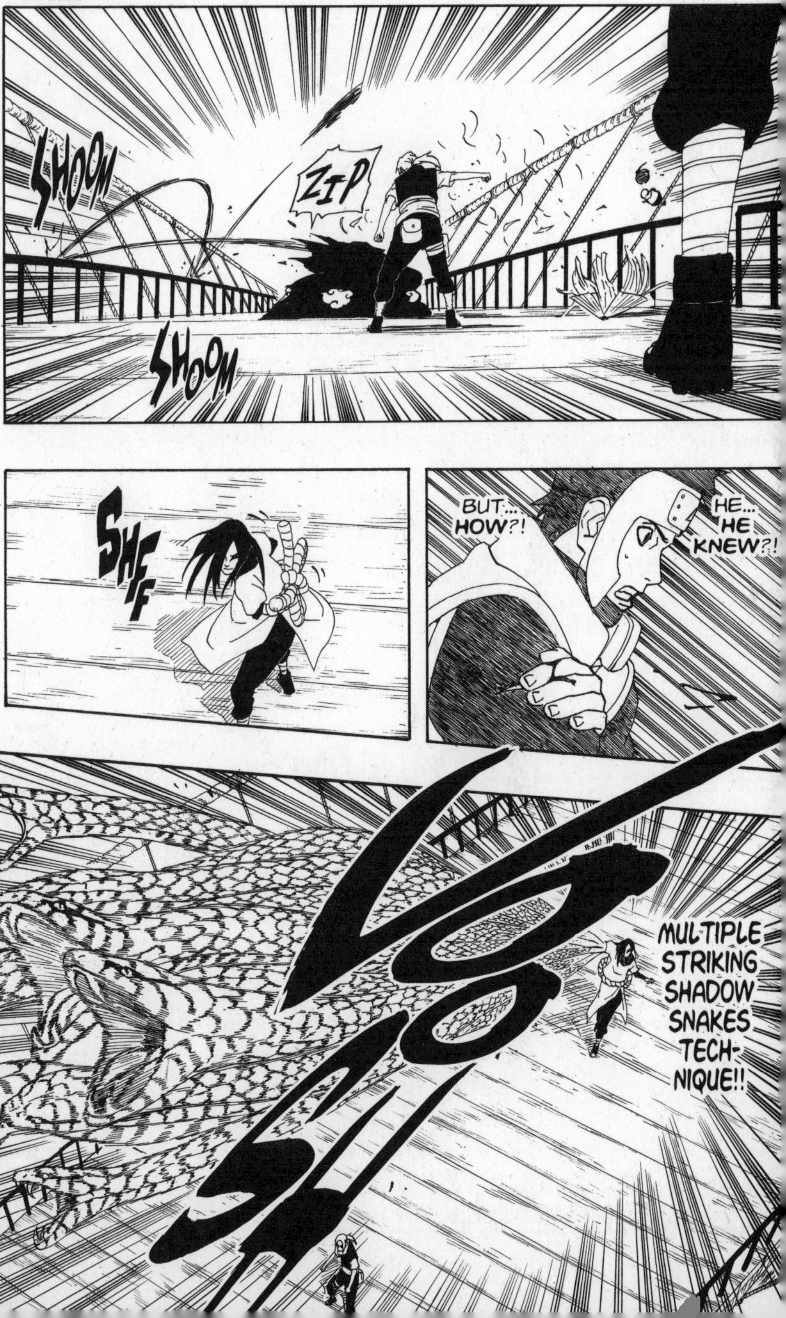
ZIP
SHOOM
SHOOM
HE... HE KNEW?!
BUT... HOW?!
SHFF
MULTIPLE STRIKING SHADOW SNAKES TECH- NIQUE!!

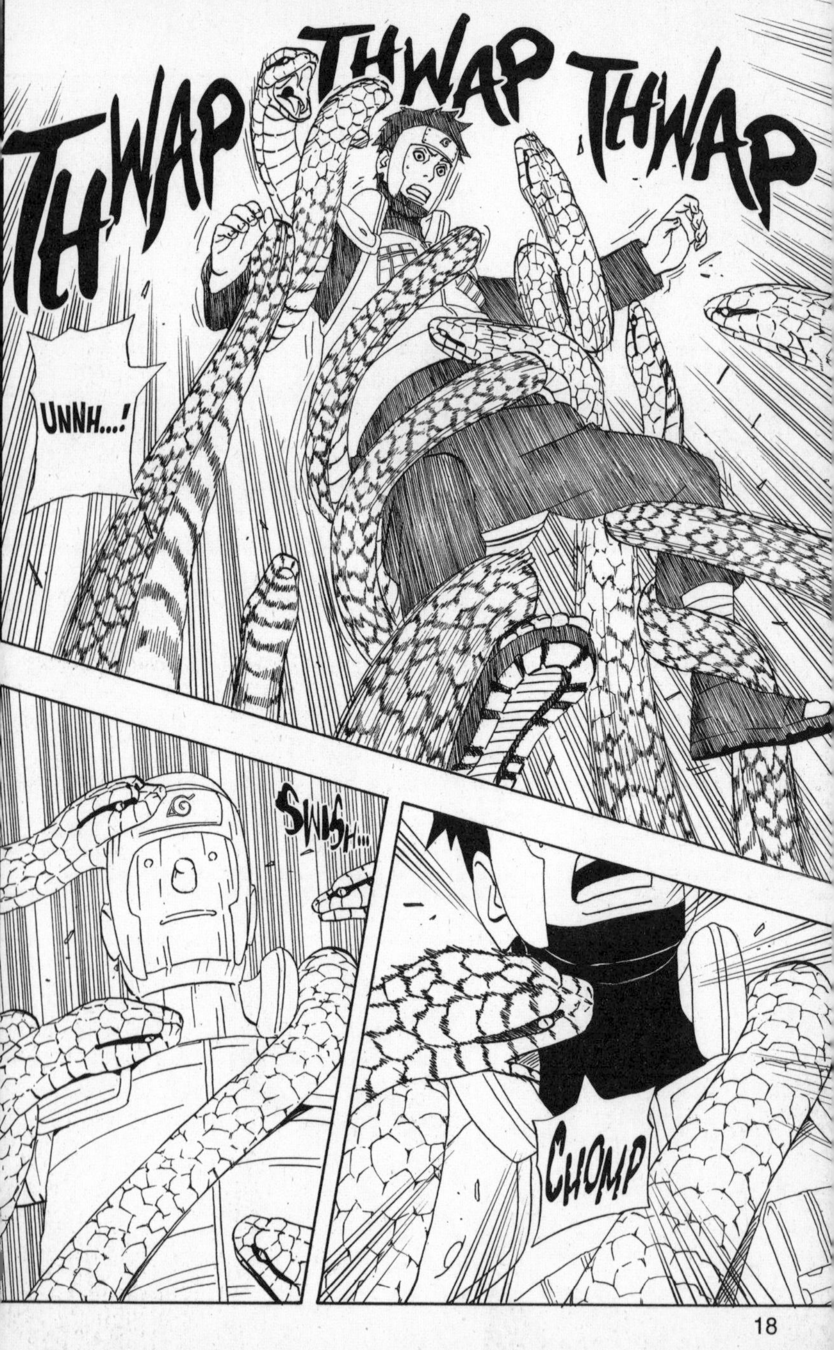
THWAP THWAP THWAP
UNNH...!
CHOMP
SWISH...

READ THIS WAY

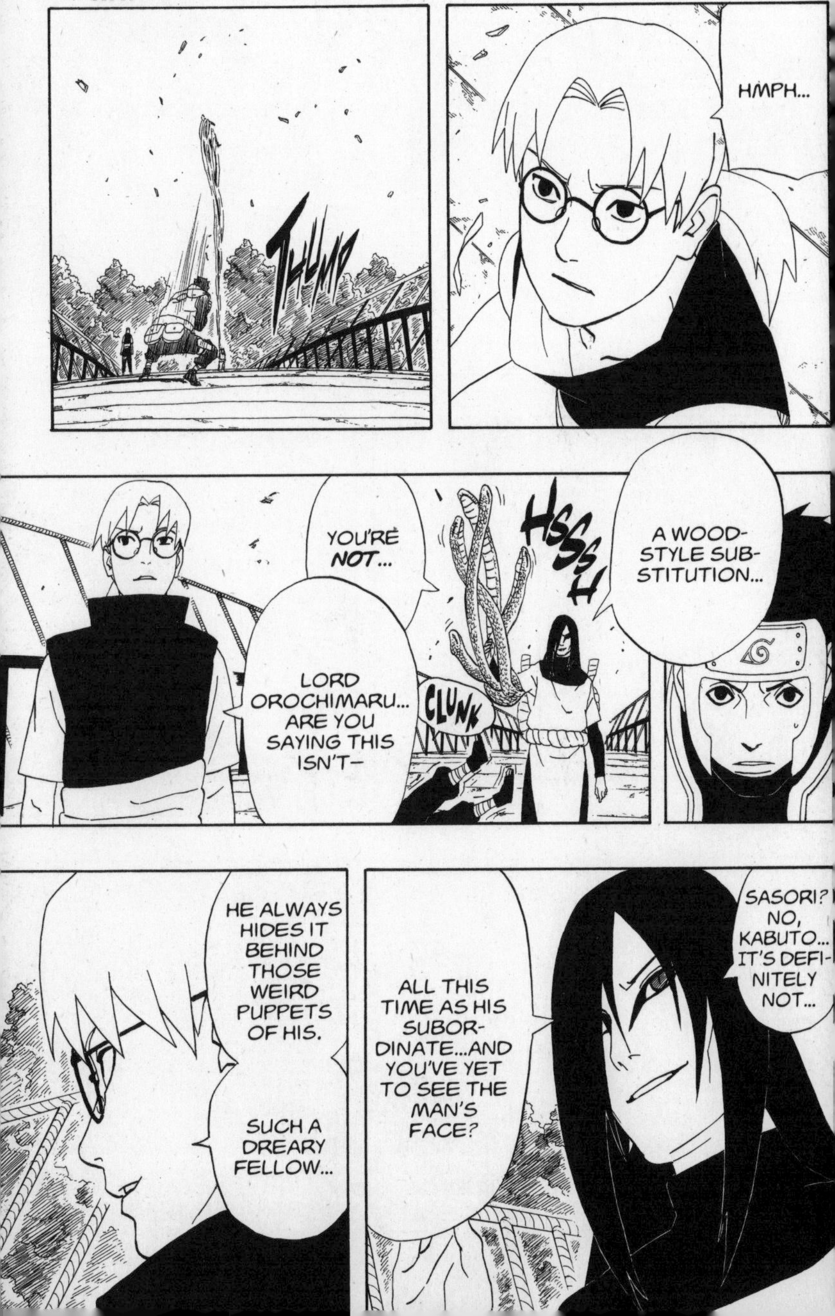
HMPH...
THUMP
A WOOD-STYLE SUBSTITUTION...
HSSSH
YOU'RE *NOT*...
LORD OROCHIMARU... ARE YOU SAYING THIS ISN'T—
CLUNK
SASORI? NO, KABUTO... IT'S DEFINITELY NOT...
ALL THIS TIME AS HIS SUBORDINATE...AND YOU'VE YET TO SEE THE MAN'S FACE?
HE ALWAYS HIDES IT BEHIND THOSE WEIRD PUPPETS OF HIS.
SUCH A DREARY FELLOW...

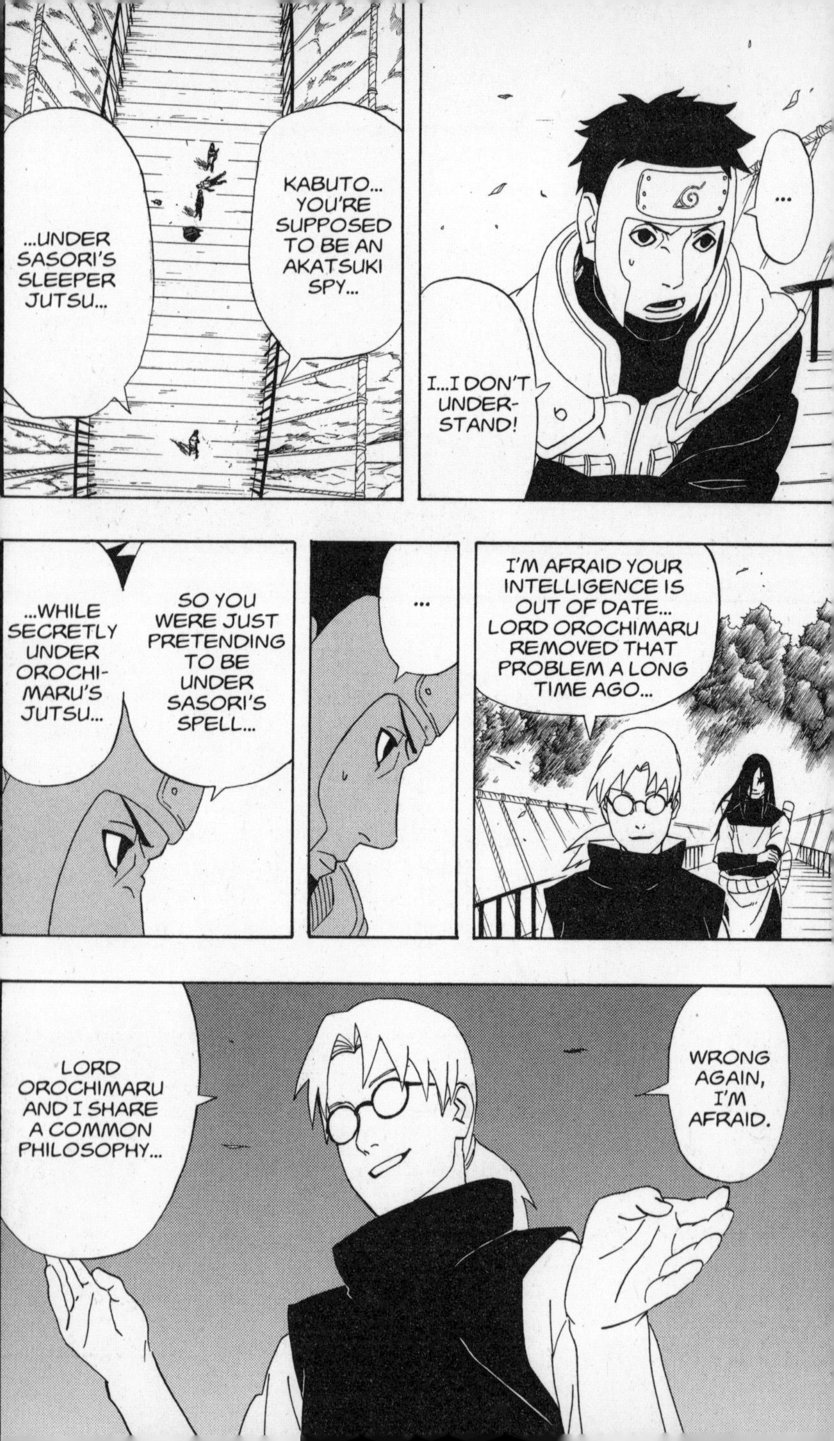
...
I...I DON'T UNDERSTAND!
KABUTO... YOU'RE SUPPOSED TO BE AN AKATSUKI SPY...
...UNDER SASORI'S SLEEPER JUTSU...
I'M AFRAID YOUR INTELLIGENCE IS OUT OF DATE... LORD OROCHIMARU REMOVED THAT PROBLEM A LONG TIME AGO...
...
SO YOU WERE JUST PRETENDING TO BE UNDER SASORI'S SPELL...
...WHILE SECRETLY UNDER OROCHIMARU'S JUTSU...
WRONG AGAIN, I'M AFRAID.
LORD OROCHIMARU AND I SHARE A COMMON PHILOSOPHY...

READ THIS WAY

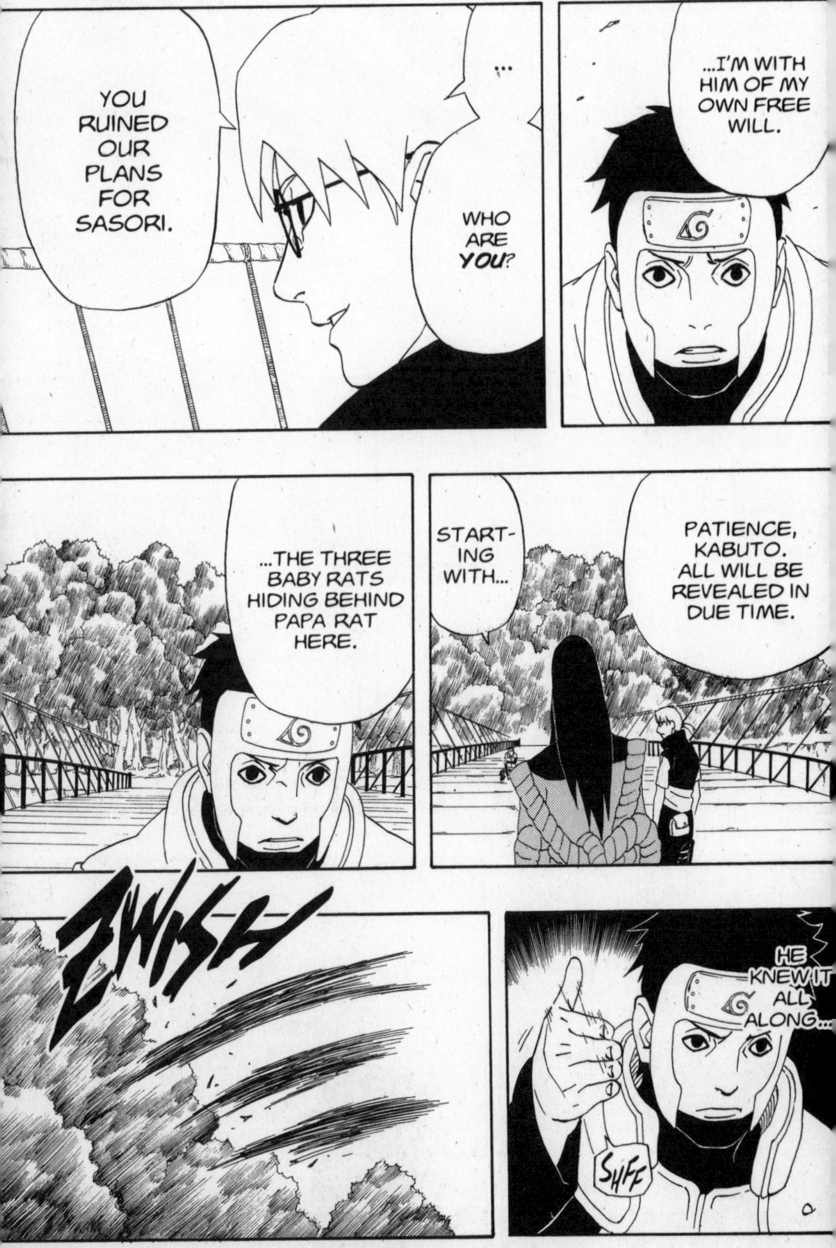

...I'M WITH HIM OF MY OWN FREE WILL.
...
WHO ARE *YOU*?
YOU RUINED OUR PLANS FOR SASORI.
PATIENCE, KABUTO. ALL WILL BE REVEALED IN DUE TIME.
STARTING WITH...
...THE THREE BABY RATS HIDING BEHIND PAPA RAT HERE.
HE KNEW IT ALL ALONG...
SHFF
ZWISH

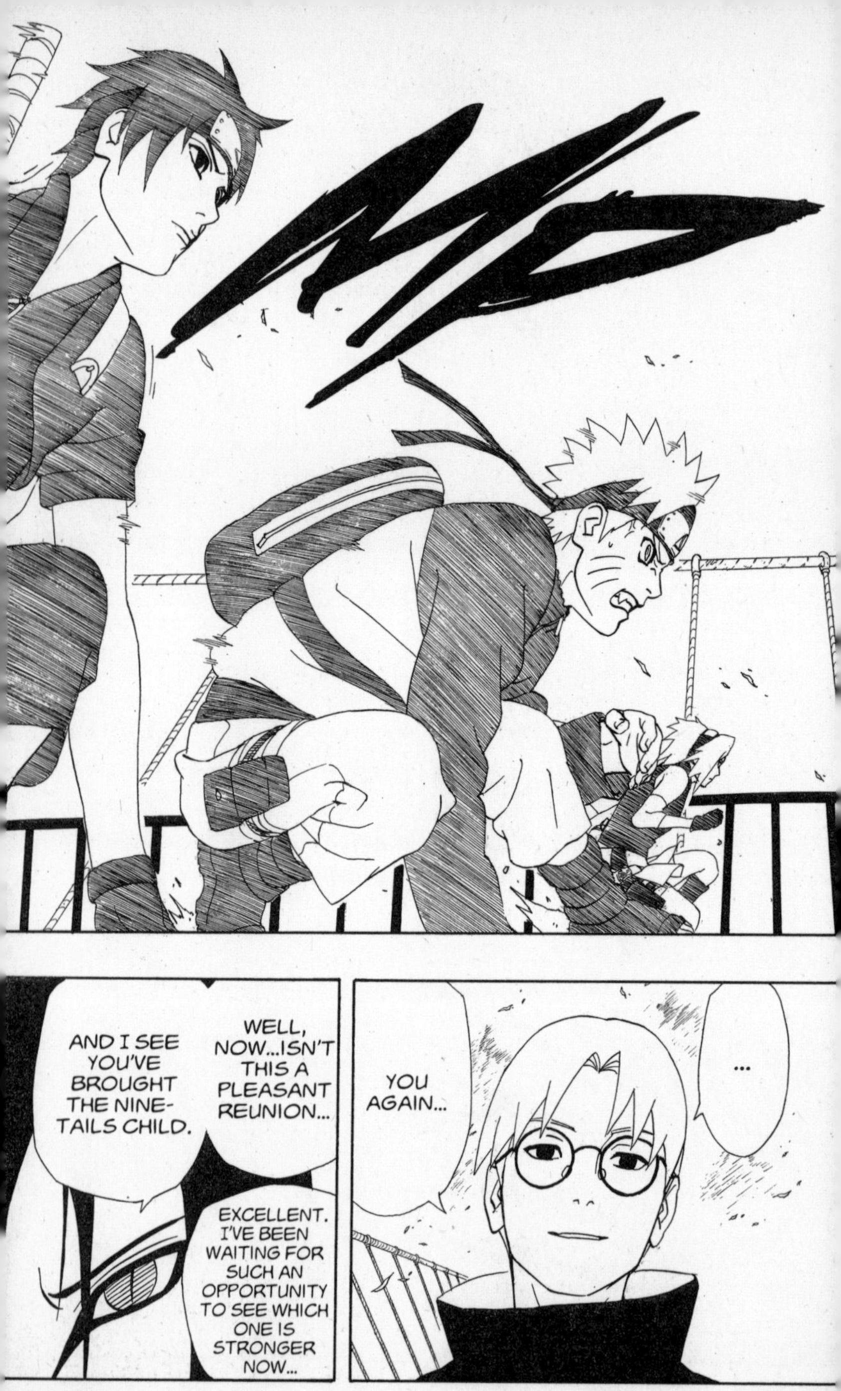
...
YOU AGAIN...
WELL, NOW...ISN'T THIS A PLEASANT REUNION...
AND I SEE YOU'VE BROUGHT THE NINE-TAILS CHILD.
EXCELLENT. I'VE BEEN WAITING FOR SUCH AN OPPORTUNITY TO SEE WHICH ONE IS STRONGER NOW...

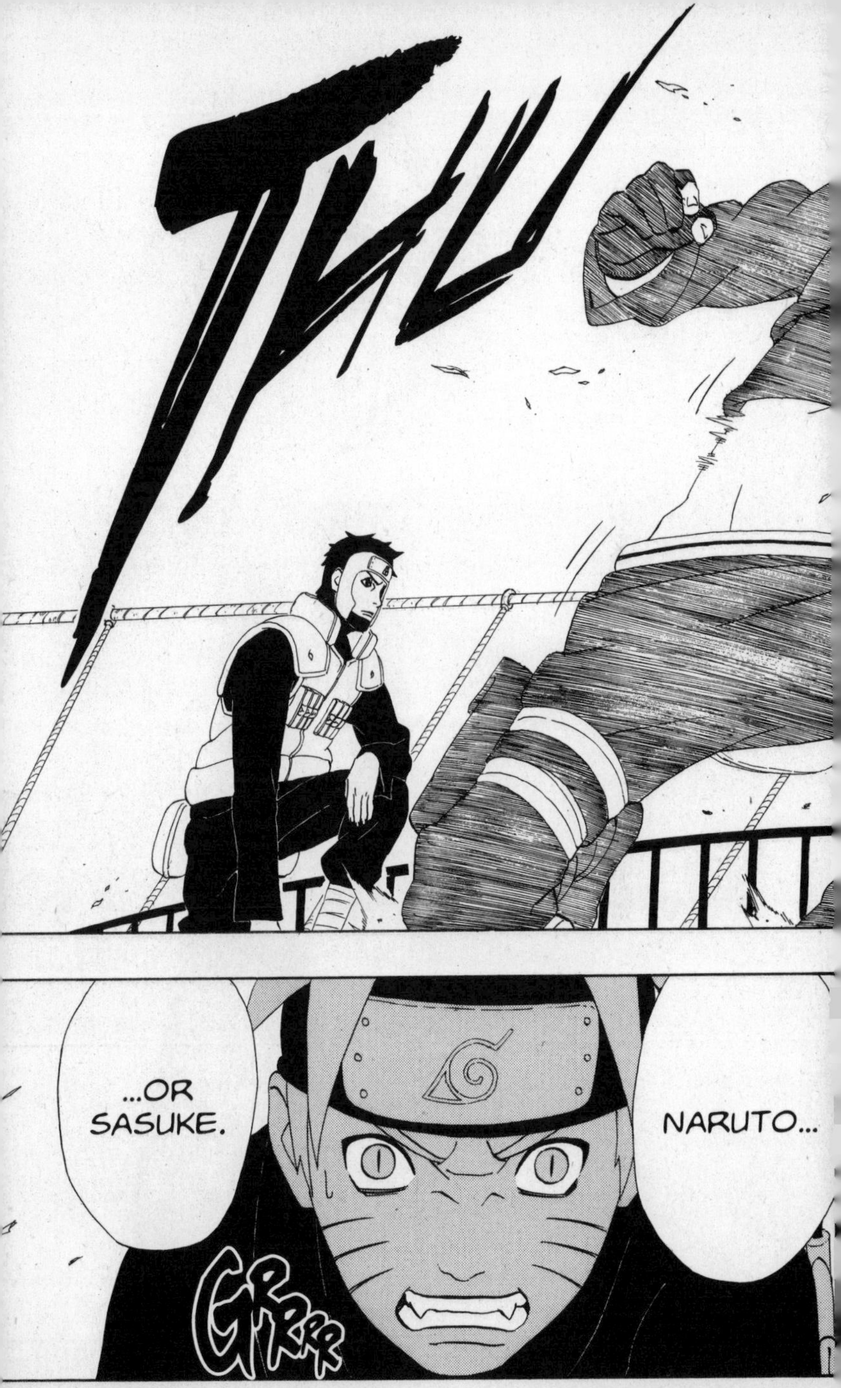
NARUTO...
...OR SASUKE.

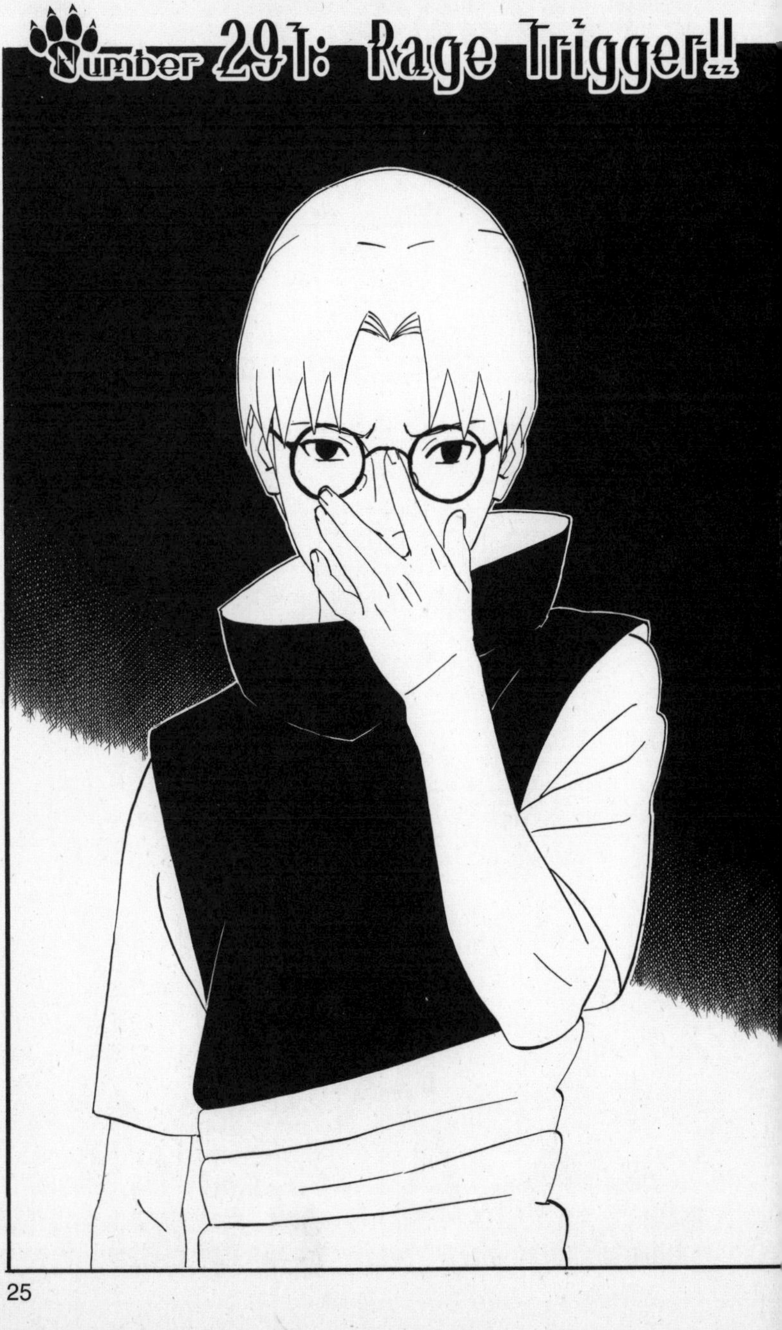
Number 291: Rage Trigger!!

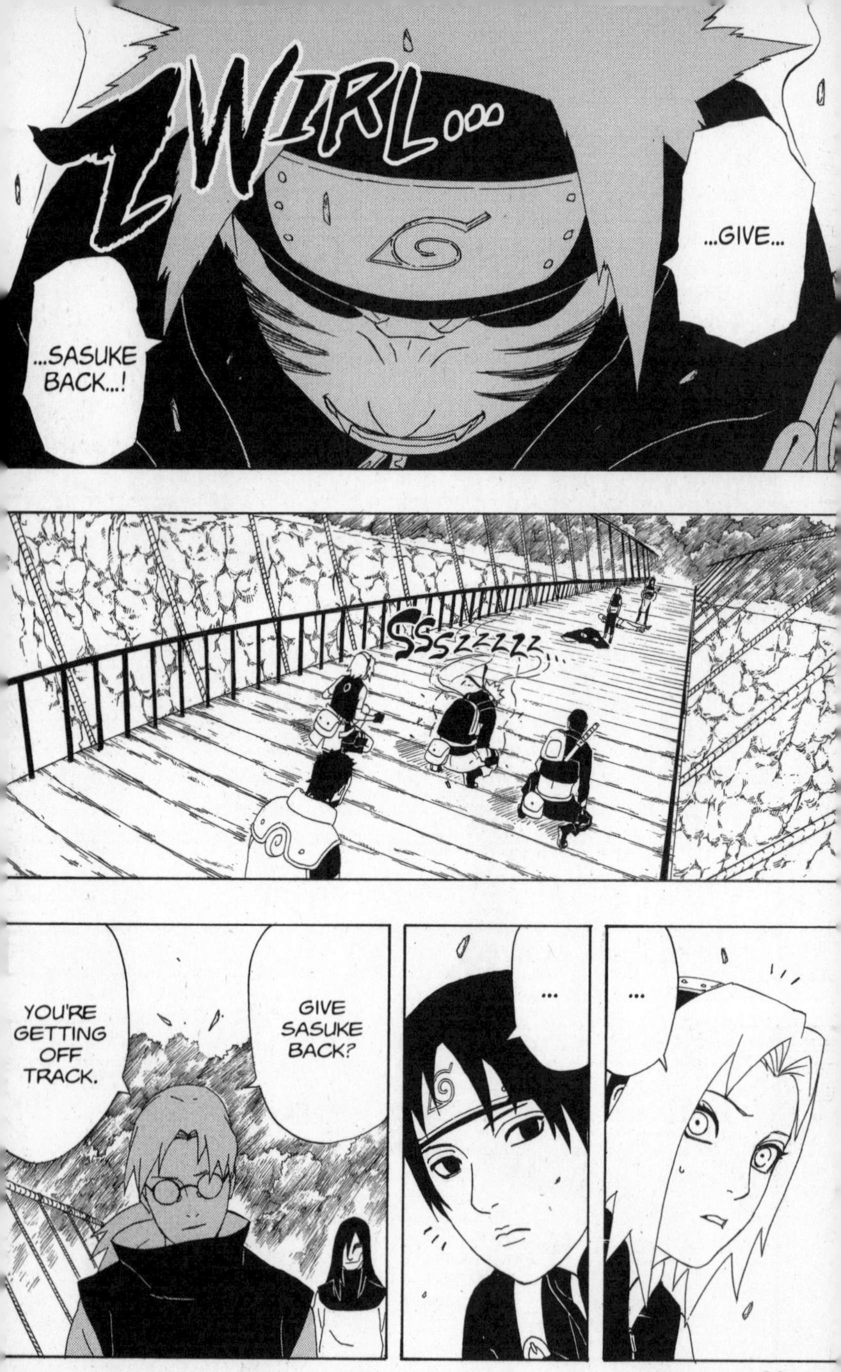

ZWIRL...
...GIVE...
...SASUKE BACK...!
SSSZZZZZZ...
...
...
GIVE SASUKE BACK?
YOU'RE GETTING OFF TRACK.

READ THIS WAY

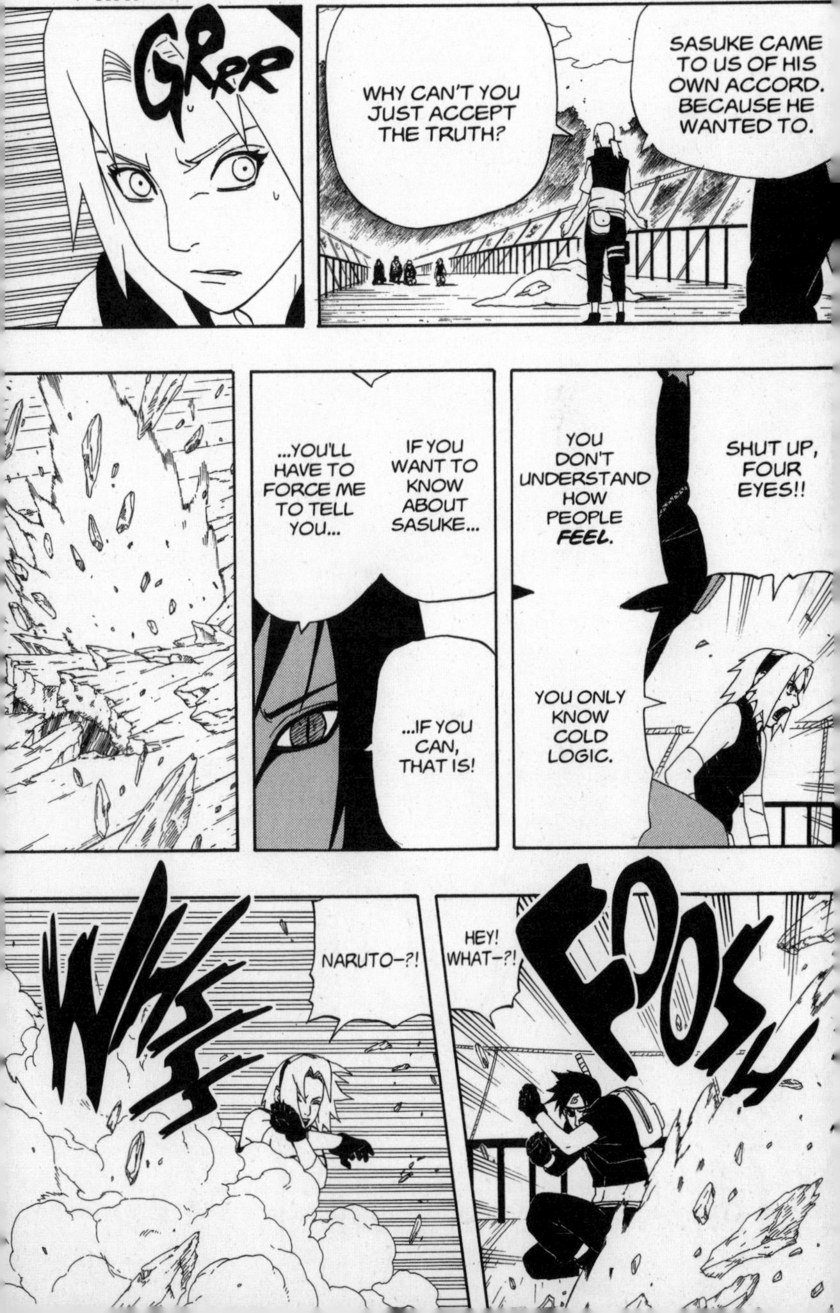
SASUKE CAME TO US OF HIS OWN ACCORD. BECAUSE HE WANTED TO.
WHY CAN'T YOU JUST ACCEPT THE TRUTH?
GRRR
SHUT UP, FOUR EYES!!
YOU DON'T UNDERSTAND HOW PEOPLE **FEEL**.
YOU ONLY KNOW COLD LOGIC.
IF YOU WANT TO KNOW ABOUT SASUKE...
...YOU'LL HAVE TO FORCE ME TO TELL YOU...
...IF YOU CAN, THAT IS!
FOOSH
HEY! WHAT–?!
NARUTO–?!
WHSH

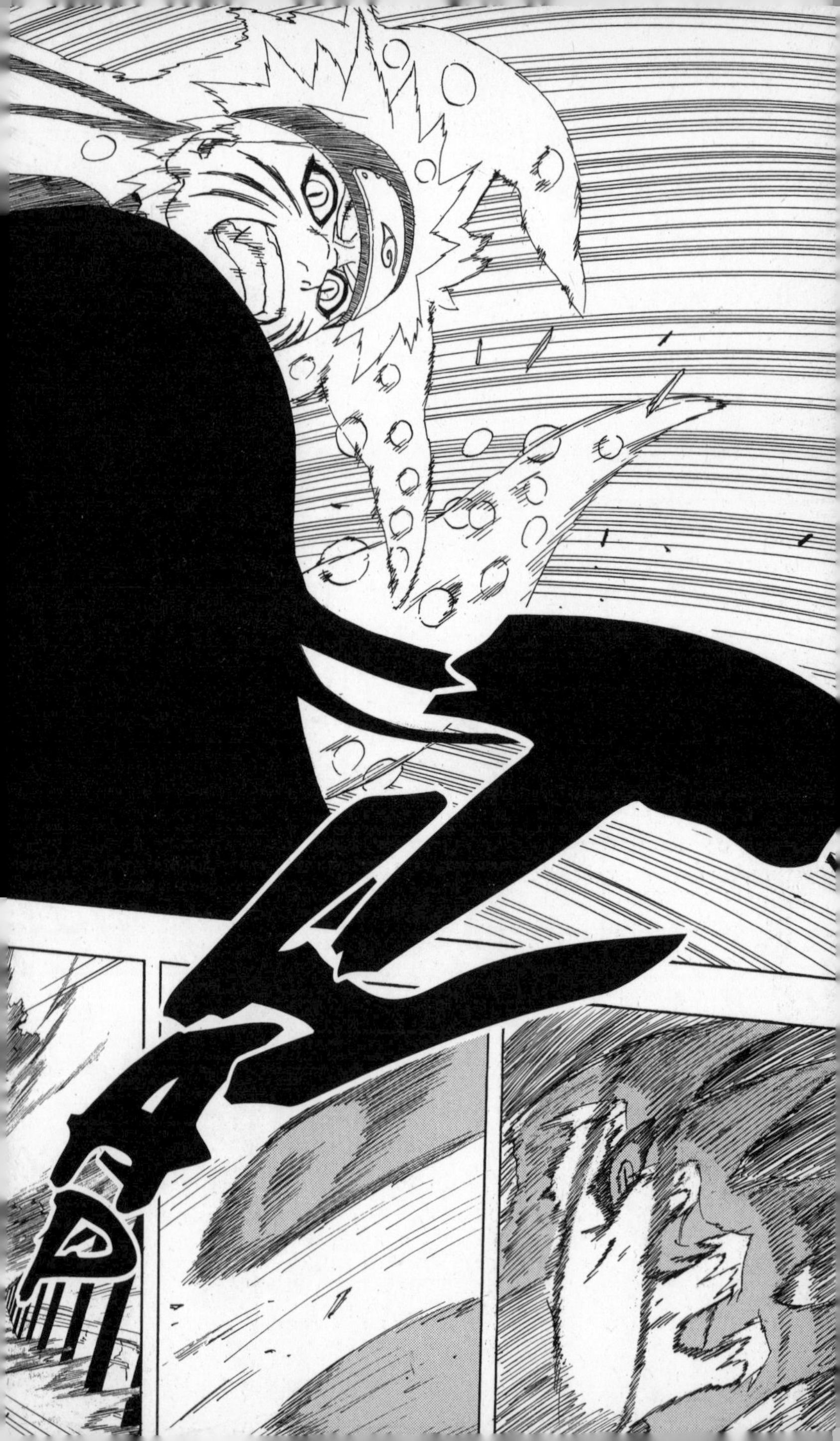

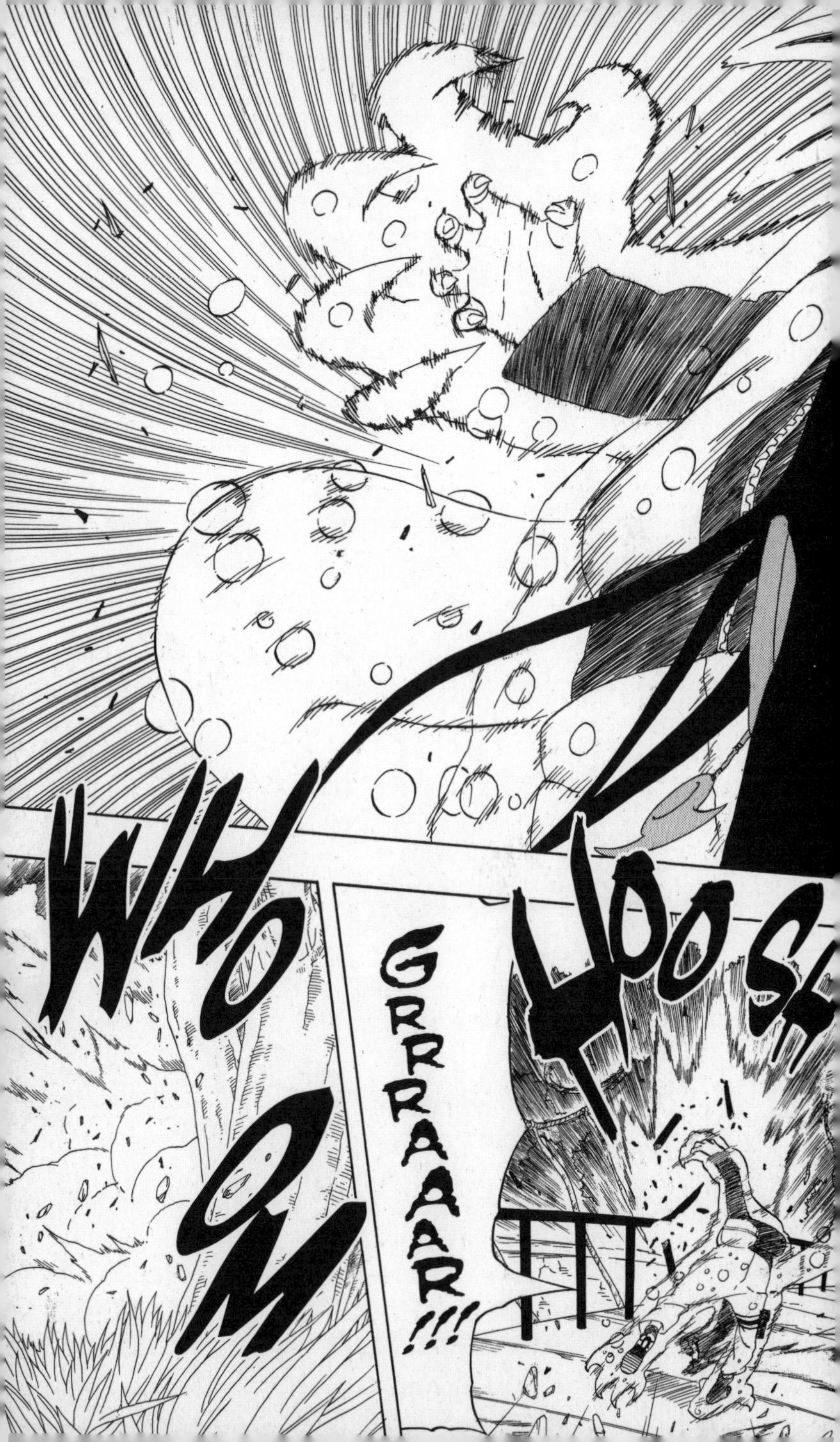
GRRRAAAAR!!!
WHOOSH
WHOOM

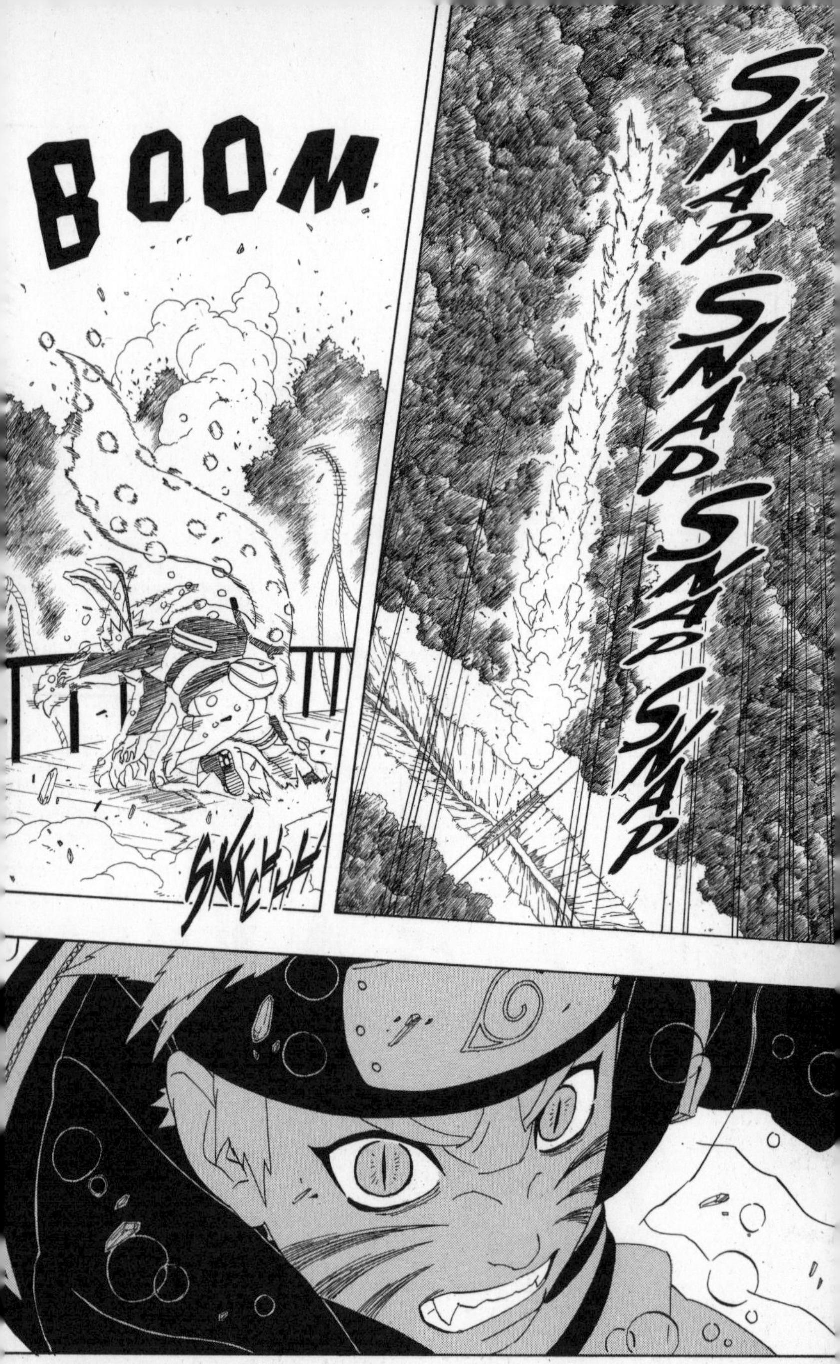
SNAP SNAP SNAP SNAP
BOOM
SKKLLL

READ THIS WAY

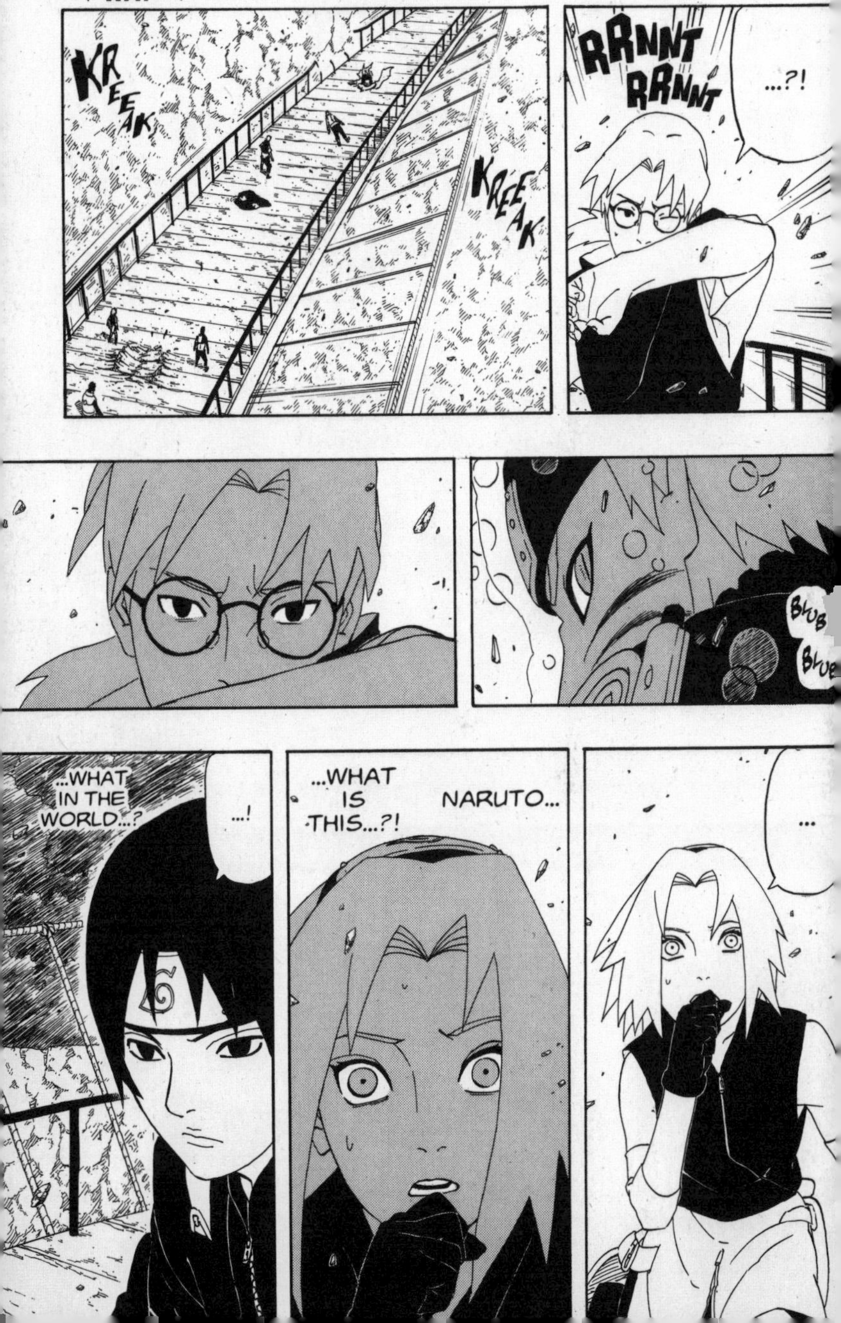
RRNNT
RRNNT
...?!
KREEAK
KREEAK
BLUB
BLUB
...
NARUTO...
...WHAT IS THIS...?!
...!
...WHAT IN THE WORLD...?

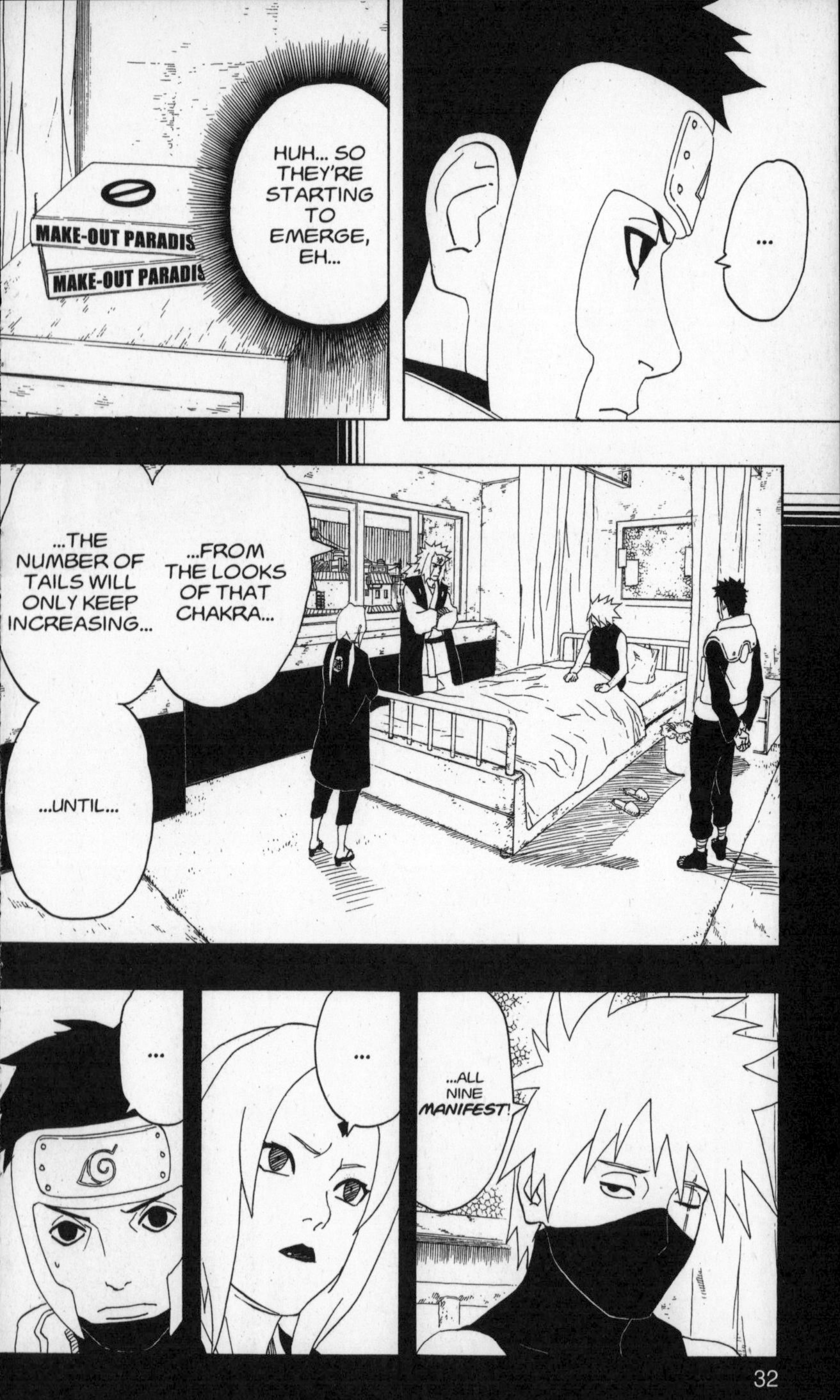
...
MAKE-OUT PARADIS
MAKE-OUT PARADIS
HUH... SO THEY'RE STARTING TO EMERGE, EH...
...FROM THE LOOKS OF THAT CHAKRA...
...THE NUMBER OF TAILS WILL ONLY KEEP INCREASING...
...UNTIL...
...ALL NINE *MANIFEST*!
...
...

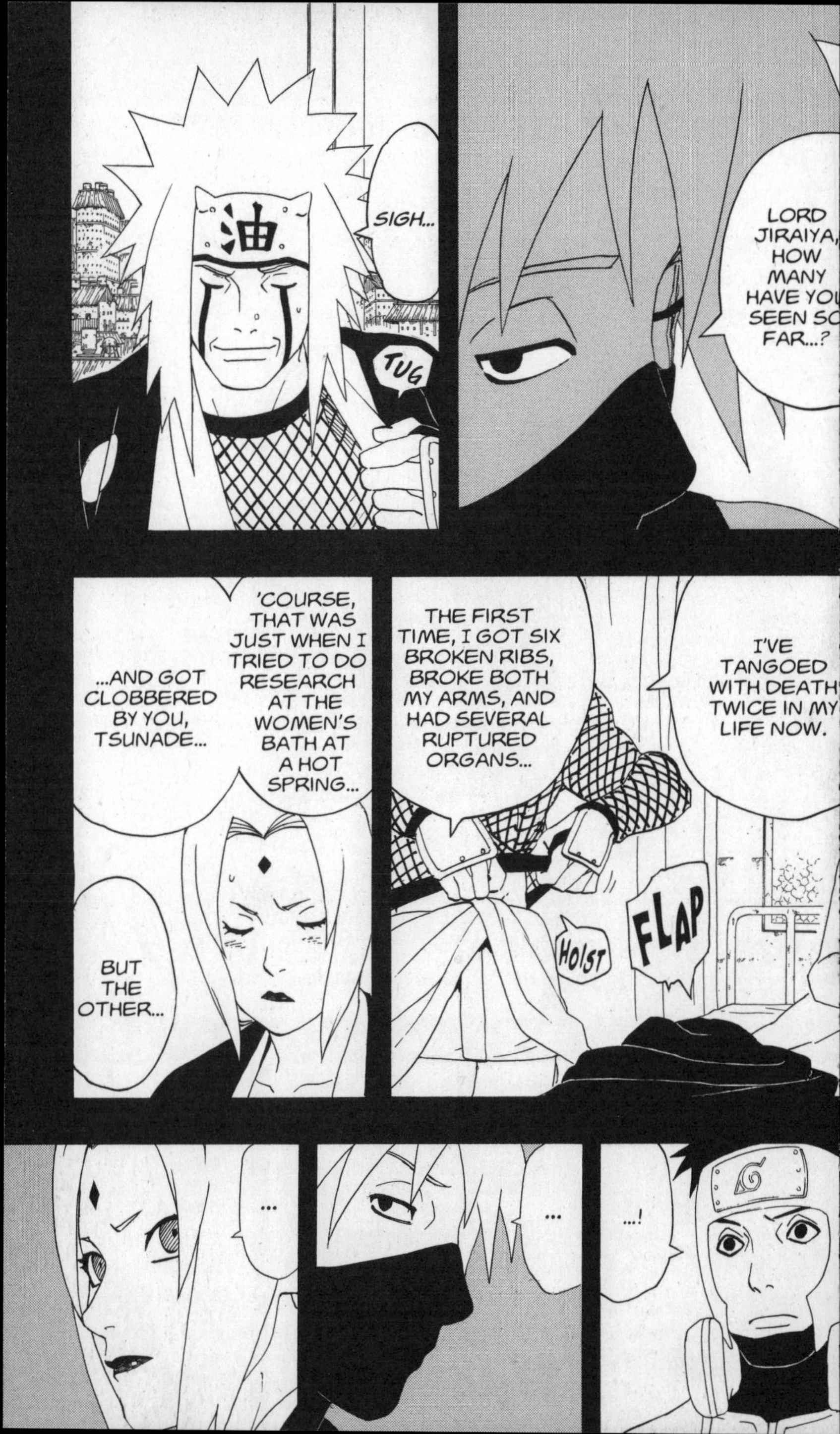
LORD JIRAIYA, HOW MANY HAVE YOU SEEN SO FAR...?
SIGH...
TUG
I'VE TANGOED WITH DEATH TWICE IN MY LIFE NOW.
THE FIRST TIME, I GOT SIX BROKEN RIBS, BROKE BOTH MY ARMS, AND HAD SEVERAL RUPTURED ORGANS...
HOIST
FLAP
'COURSE, THAT WAS JUST WHEN I TRIED TO DO RESEARCH AT THE WOMEN'S BATH AT A HOT SPRING...
...AND GOT CLOBBERED BY YOU, TSUNADE...
BUT THE OTHER...
...!
...
...

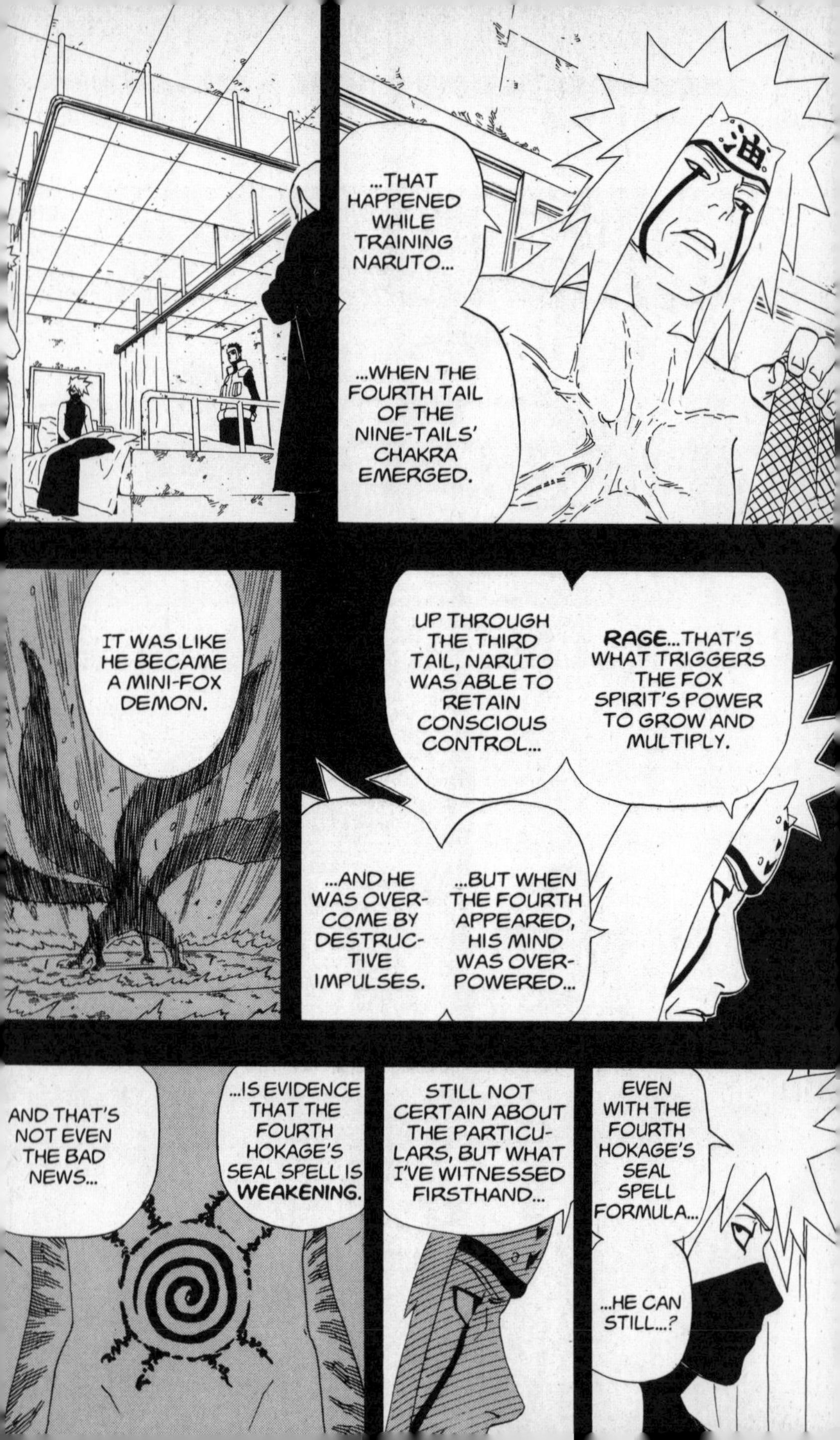

...THAT HAPPENED WHILE TRAINING NARUTO...
...WHEN THE FOURTH TAIL OF THE NINE-TAILS' CHAKRA EMERGED.
RAGE...THAT'S WHAT TRIGGERS THE FOX SPIRIT'S POWER TO GROW AND MULTIPLY.
UP THROUGH THE THIRD TAIL, NARUTO WAS ABLE TO RETAIN CONSCIOUS CONTROL...
...BUT WHEN THE FOURTH APPEARED, HIS MIND WAS OVER-POWERED...
...AND HE WAS OVER-COME BY DESTRUC-TIVE IMPULSES.
IT WAS LIKE HE BECAME A MINI-FOX DEMON.
EVEN WITH THE FOURTH HOKAGE'S SEAL SPELL FORMULA...
...HE CAN STILL...?
STILL NOT CERTAIN ABOUT THE PARTICU-LARS, BUT WHAT I'VE WITNESSED FIRSTHAND...
...IS EVIDENCE THAT THE FOURTH HOKAGE'S SEAL SPELL IS **WEAKENING**.
AND THAT'S NOT EVEN THE BAD NEWS...

READ THIS WAY

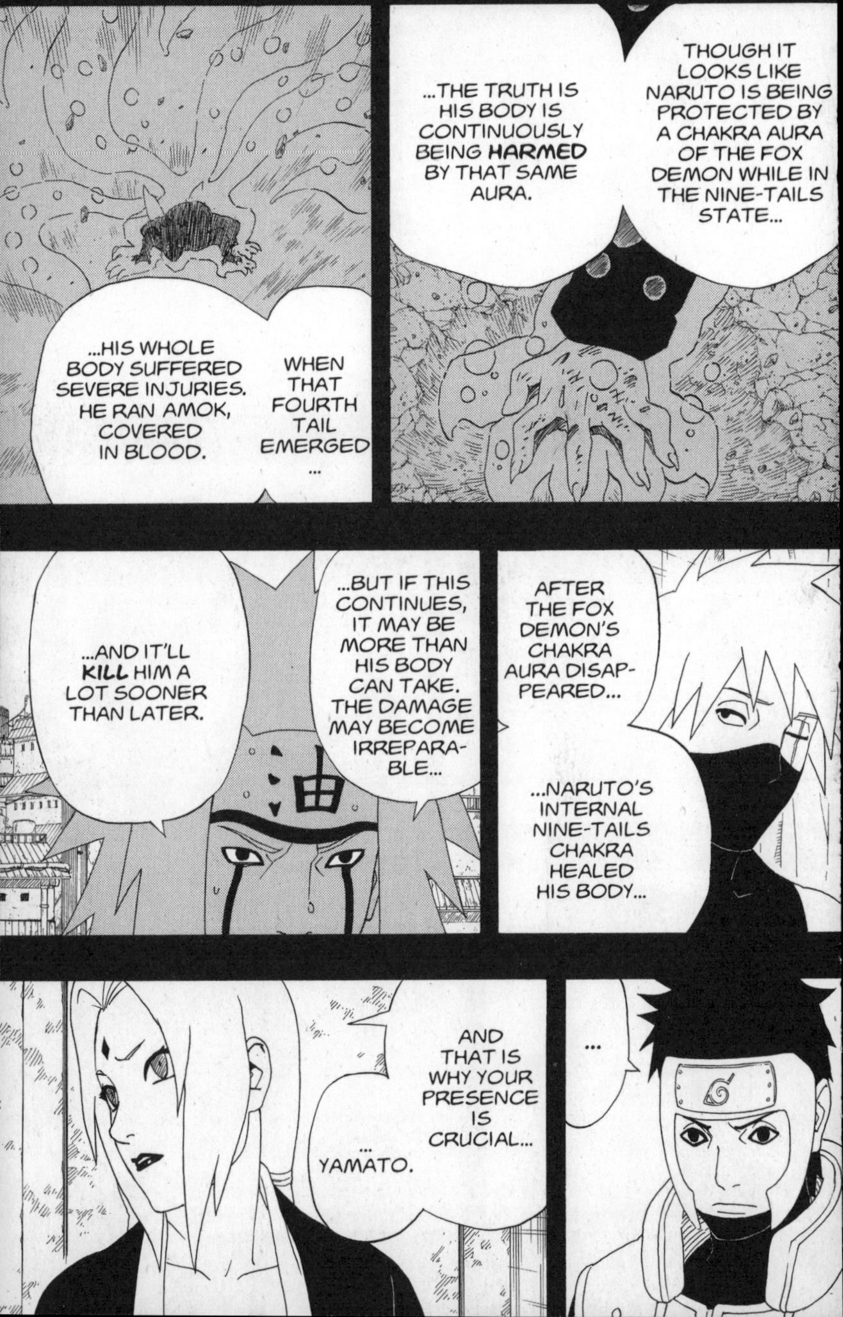
THOUGH IT LOOKS LIKE NARUTO IS BEING PROTECTED BY A CHAKRA AURA OF THE FOX DEMON WHILE IN THE NINE-TAILS STATE...
...THE TRUTH IS HIS BODY IS CONTINUOUSLY BEING **HARMED** BY THAT SAME AURA.
WHEN THAT FOURTH TAIL EMERGED...
...HIS WHOLE BODY SUFFERED SEVERE INJURIES. HE RAN AMOK, COVERED IN BLOOD.
AFTER THE FOX DEMON'S CHAKRA AURA DISAP-PEARED...
...NARUTO'S INTERNAL NINE-TAILS CHAKRA HEALED HIS BODY...
...BUT IF THIS CONTINUES, IT MAY BE MORE THAN HIS BODY CAN TAKE. THE DAMAGE MAY BECOME IRREPARA-BLE...
...AND IT'LL **KILL** HIM A LOT SOONER THAN LATER.
...
AND THAT IS WHY YOUR PRESENCE IS CRUCIAL...
... YAMATO.

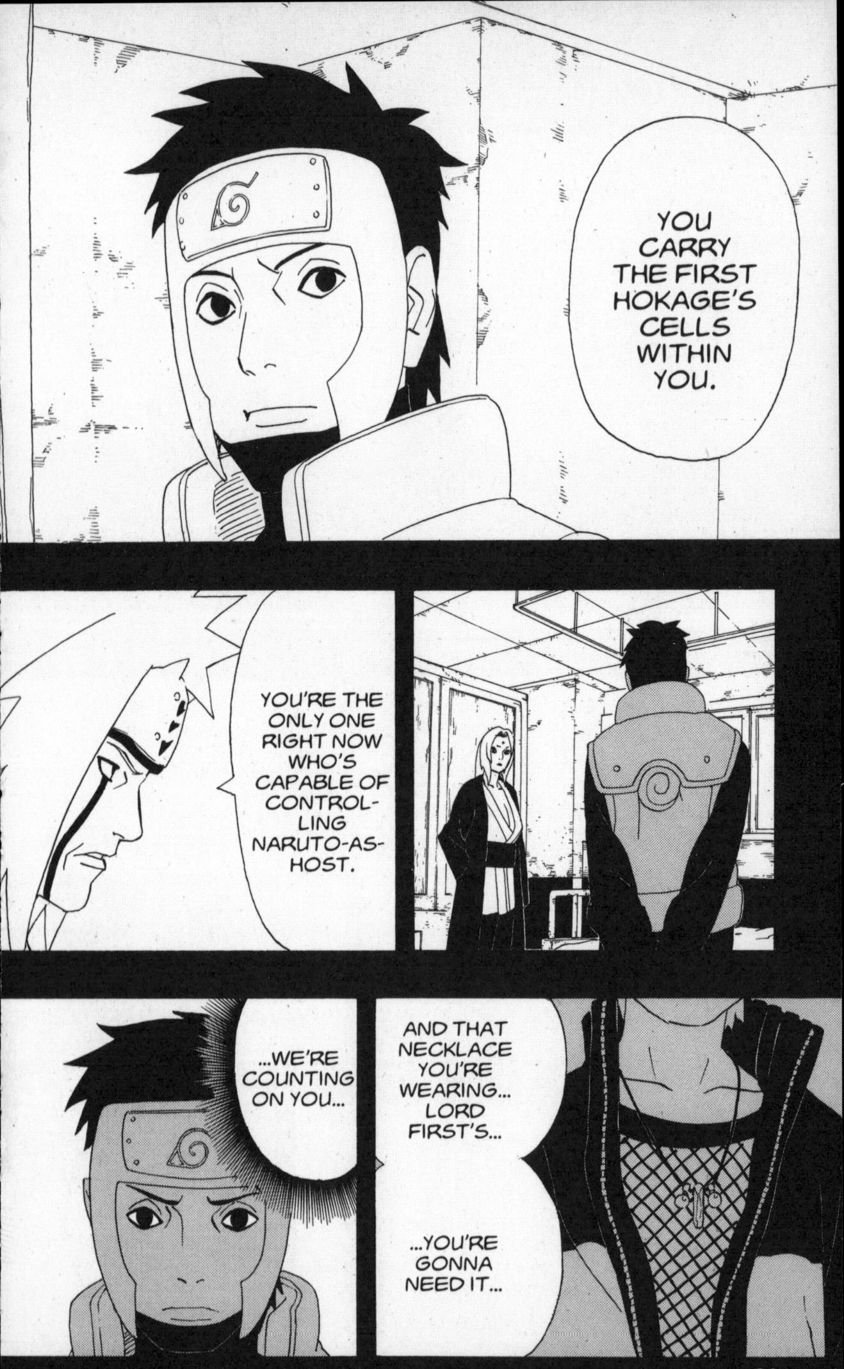
YOU CARRY THE FIRST HOKAGE'S CELLS WITHIN YOU.
YOU'RE THE ONLY ONE RIGHT NOW WHO'S CAPABLE OF CONTROL-LING NARUTO-AS-HOST.
AND THAT NECKLACE YOU'RE WEARING... LORD FIRST'S...
...YOU'RE GONNA NEED IT...
...WE'RE COUNTING ON YOU...

READ THIS WAY

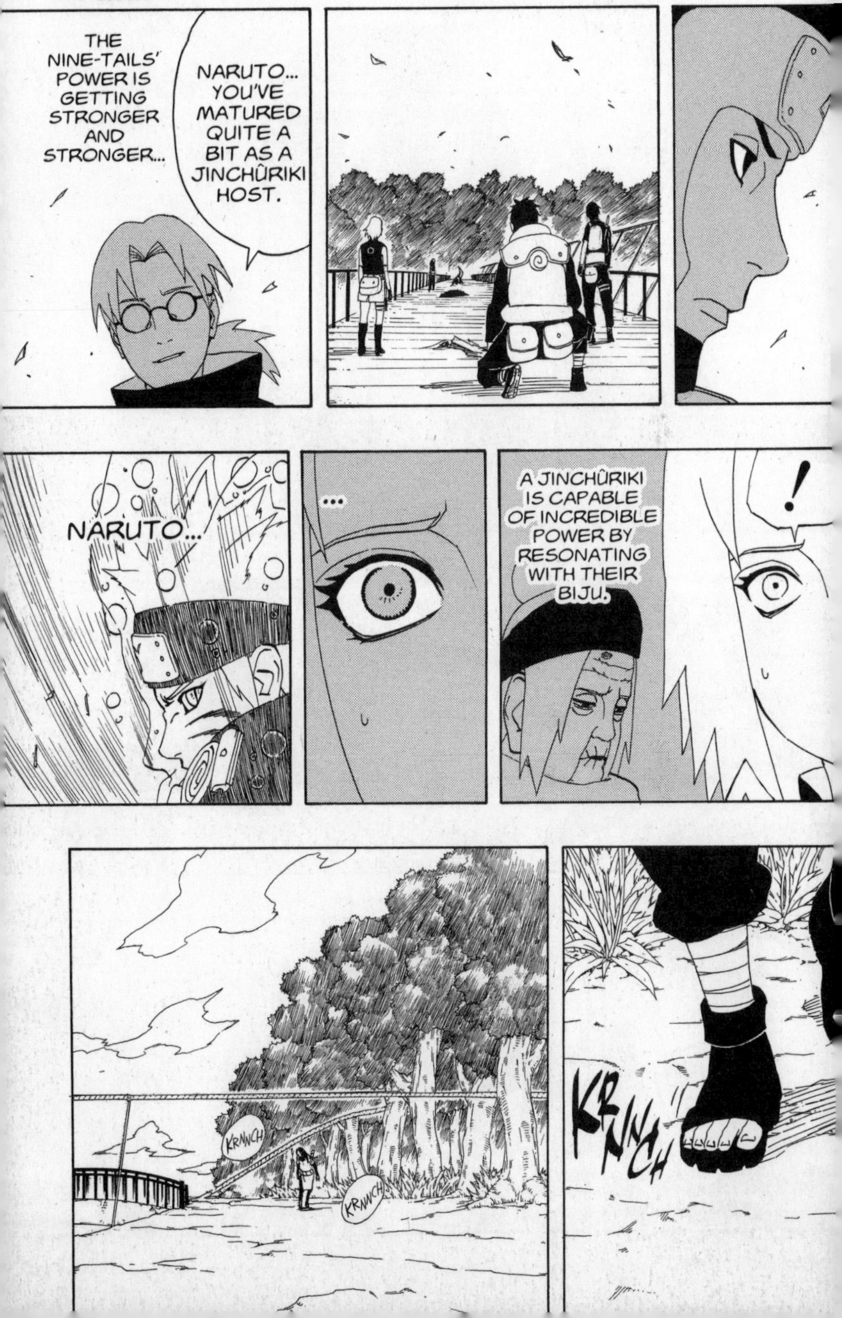
NARUTO... YOU'VE MATURED QUITE A BIT AS A JINCHÛRIKI HOST.
THE NINE-TAILS' POWER IS GETTING STRONGER AND STRONGER...
!
A JINCHÛRIKI IS CAPABLE OF INCREDIBLE POWER BY RESONATING WITH THEIR BIJU.
...
NARUTO...
KRNNCH
KRNNCH
KRNNCH

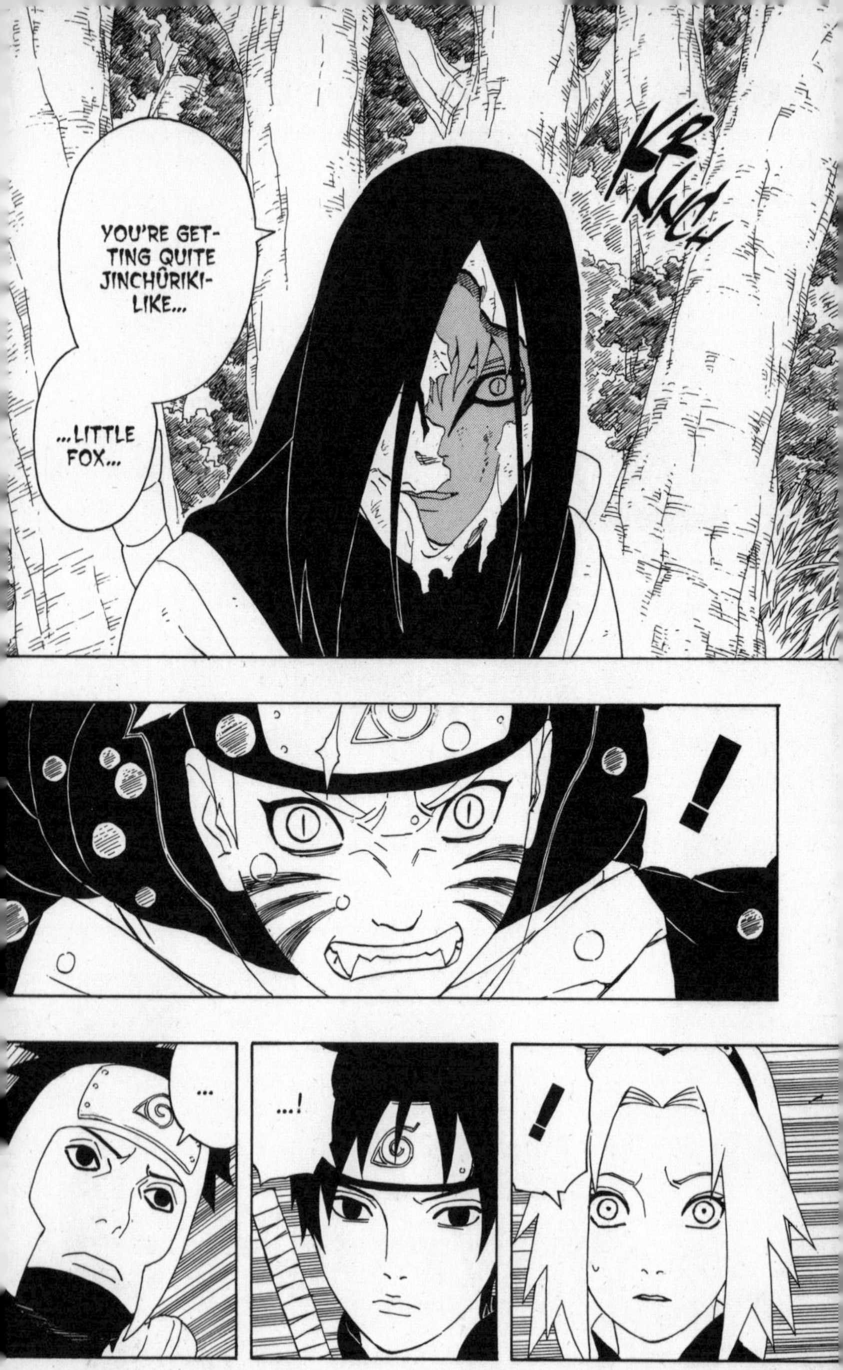
KRNNCH
YOU'RE GETTING QUITE JINCHŪRIKI-LIKE...
...LITTLE FOX...
!
!
...!
...

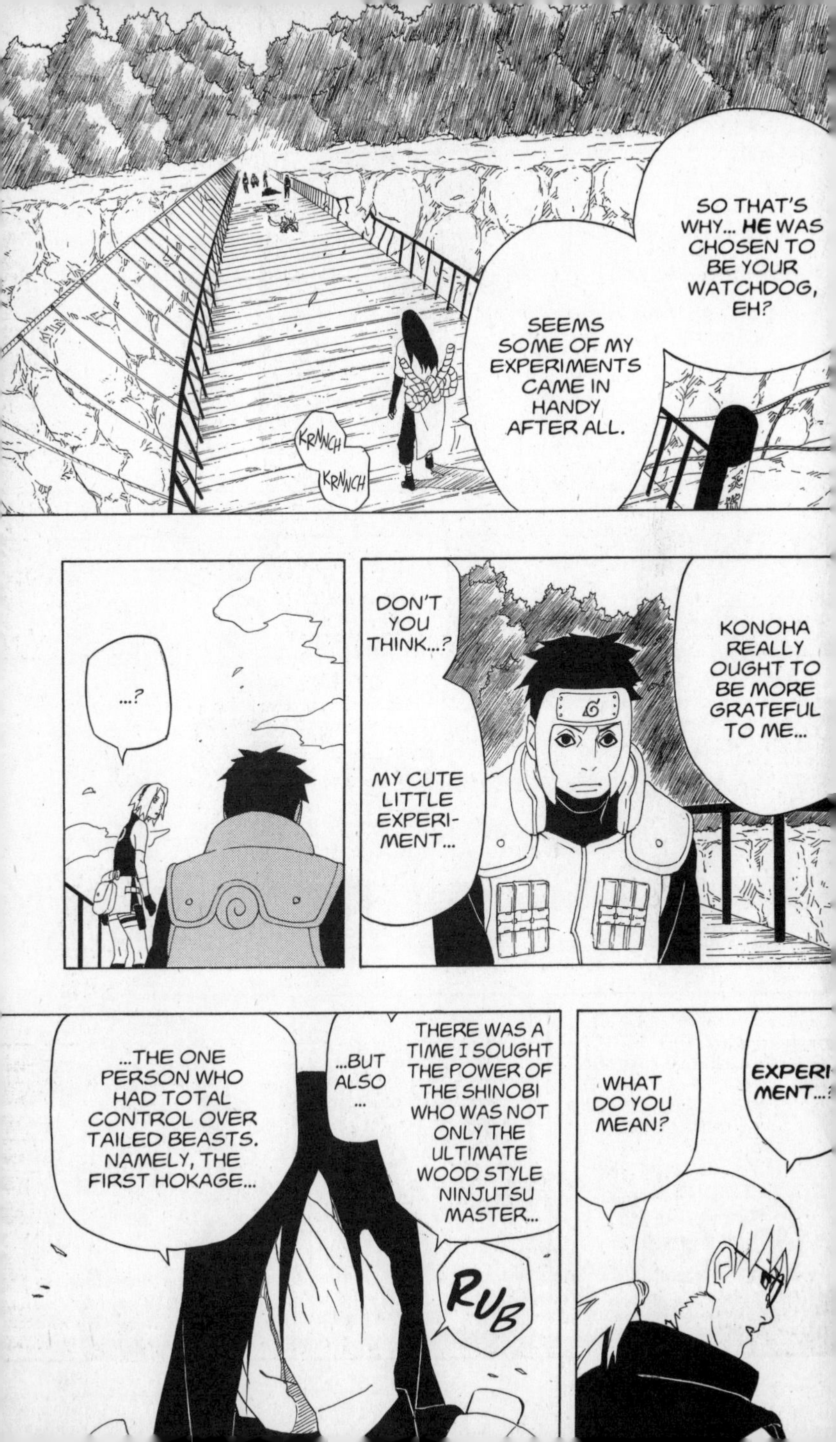
SO THAT'S WHY... HE WAS CHOSEN TO BE YOUR WATCHDOG, EH?
SEEMS SOME OF MY EXPERIMENTS CAME IN HANDY AFTER ALL.
KRNNCH
KRNNCH
KONOHA REALLY OUGHT TO BE MORE GRATEFUL TO ME...
DON'T YOU THINK...?
MY CUTE LITTLE EXPERI-MENT...
...?
EXPERI-MENT...?
WHAT DO YOU MEAN?
THERE WAS A TIME I SOUGHT THE POWER OF THE SHINOBI WHO WAS NOT ONLY THE ULTIMATE WOOD STYLE NINJUTSU MASTER...
...BUT ALSO ...
...THE ONE PERSON WHO HAD TOTAL CONTROL OVER TAILED BEASTS. NAMELY, THE FIRST HOKAGE...
RUB

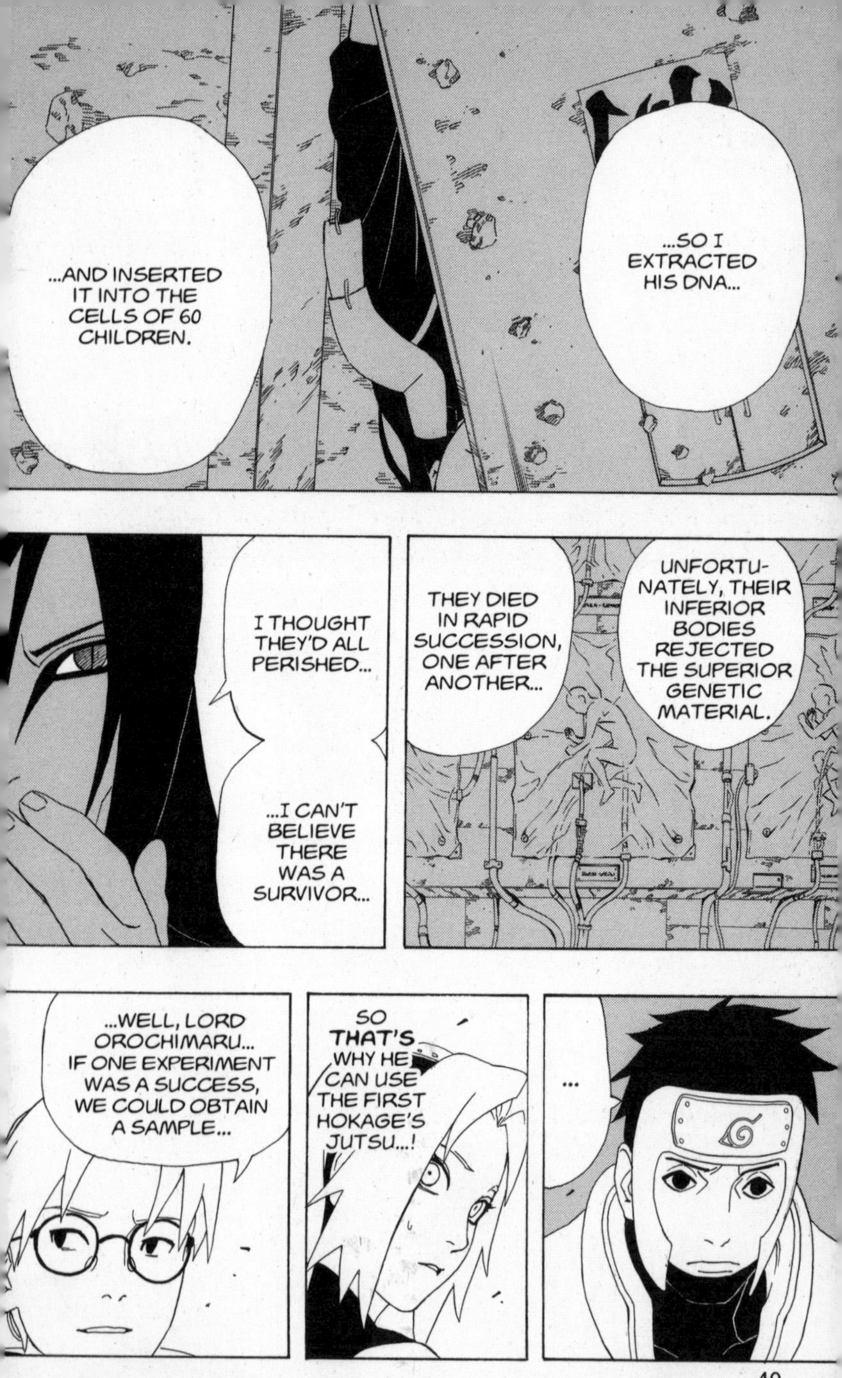
...SO I EXTRACTED HIS DNA...
...AND INSERTED IT INTO THE CELLS OF 60 CHILDREN.
UNFORTUNATELY, THEIR INFERIOR BODIES REJECTED THE SUPERIOR GENETIC MATERIAL.
THEY DIED IN RAPID SUCCESSION, ONE AFTER ANOTHER...
I THOUGHT THEY'D ALL PERISHED...
...I CAN'T BELIEVE THERE WAS A SURVIVOR...
...
SO **THAT'S** WHY HE CAN USE THE FIRST HOKAGE'S JUTSU...!
...WELL, LORD OROCHIMARU... IF ONE EXPERIMENT WAS A SUCCESS, WE COULD OBTAIN A SAMPLE...

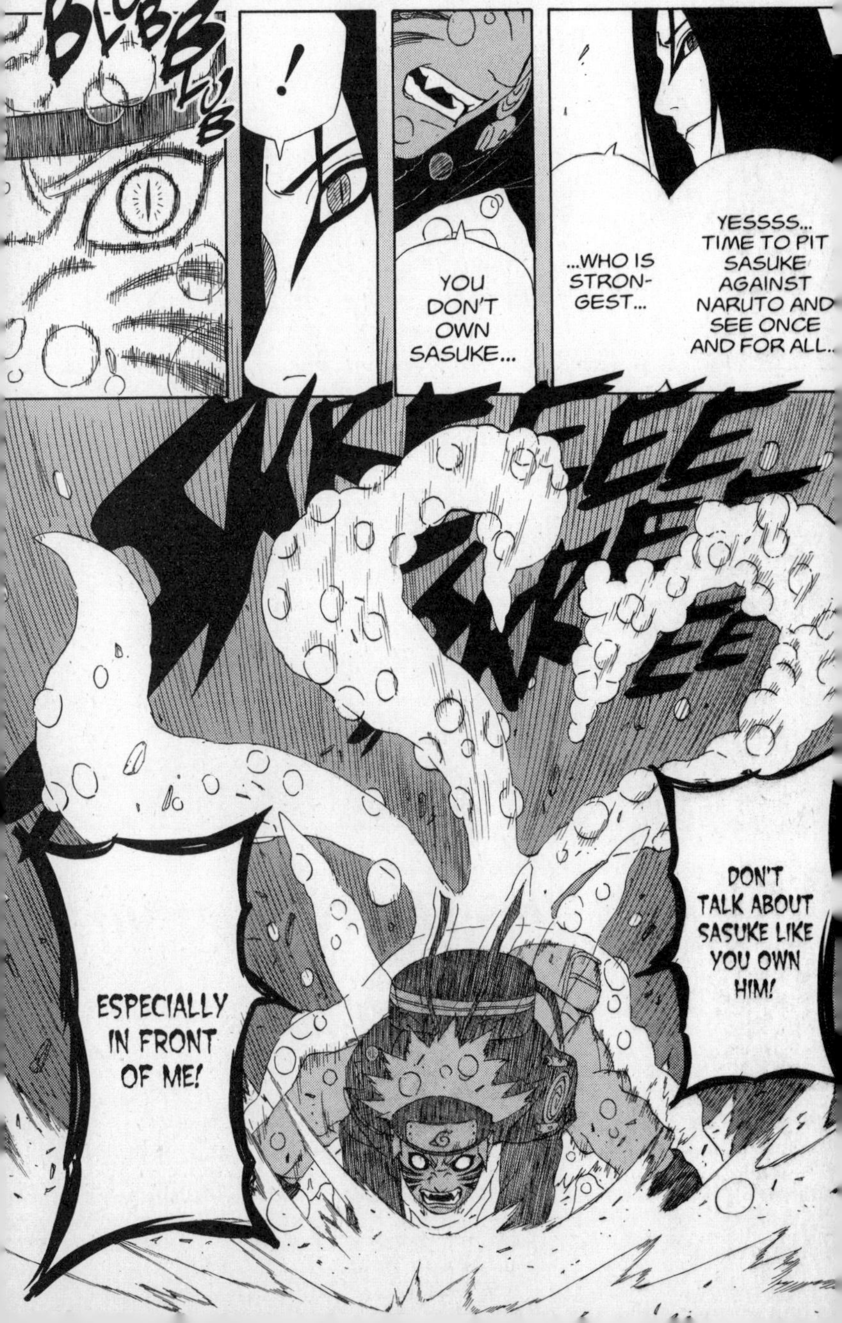
YESSSS... TIME TO PIT SASUKE AGAINST NARUTO AND SEE ONCE AND FOR ALL..
...WHO IS STRONGEST...
YOU DON'T OWN SASUKE...
!
BLUB BLUB
DON'T TALK ABOUT SASUKE LIKE YOU OWN HIM!
ESPECIALLY IN FRONT OF ME!

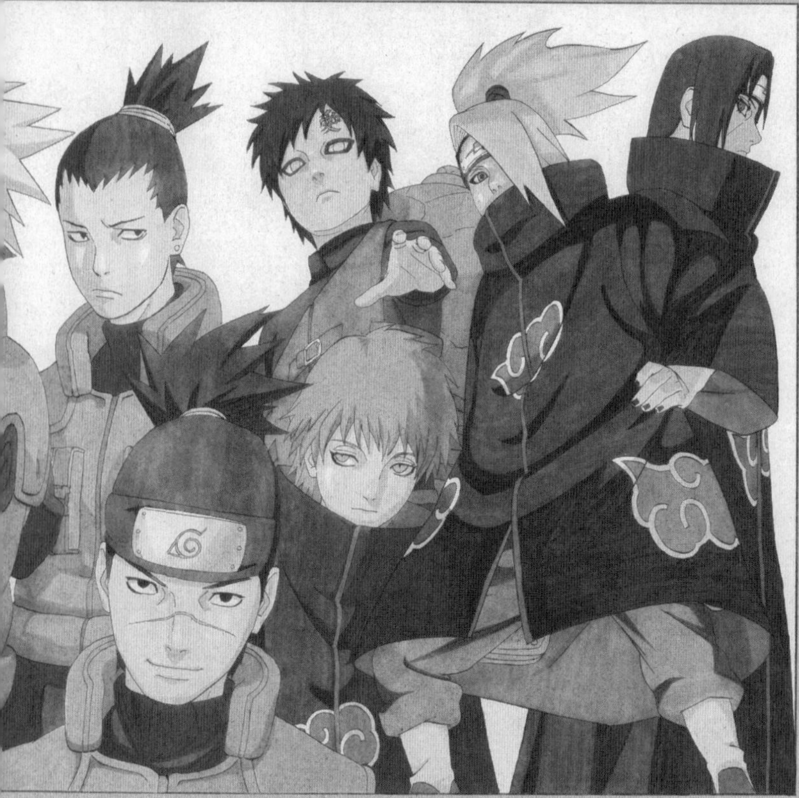

CHARACTER POPULARITY SURVEY!!

3th Place/ Iyuga Hinata	1,048 votes	19th Place/ Kankuro	519 votes	25th Place/ Shiranui Genma	230 votes
4th Place/ akushi Kabuto	829 votes	20th Place/ Might Guy	503 votes	26th Place/ Aburame Shino	226 votes
5th Place/ nuzuka Kiba	677 votes	21st Place/ Sarutobi Asuma	449 votes	27th Place/ Haku	168 votes
6th Place/ emari	671 votes	22nd Place/ Tenten	395 votes	28th Place/ Tayuya	164 votes
7th Place/ amanaka Ino	662 votes	23rd Place/ Gekko Hayate	283 votes	29th Place/ Tsunade	161 votes
8th Place/ ock Lee	640 votes	24th Place/ Orochimaru	237 votes	30th Place/ Kimimaro	148 votes

(This poll conducted in Japan.)

Number 292: The Third Tail...!!

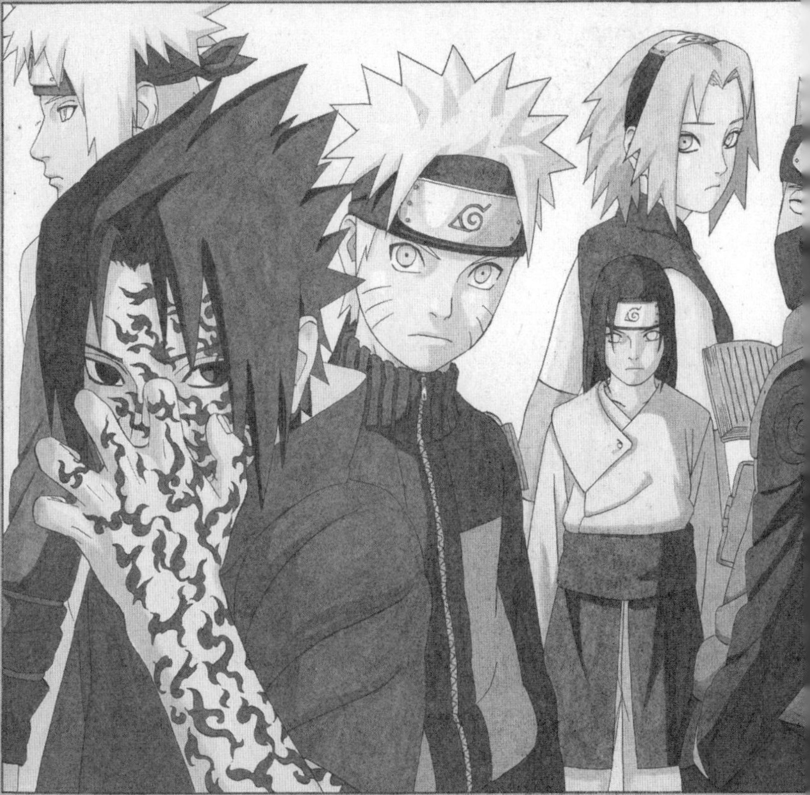

THE RESULTS OF THE SIXTH

1st Place/Uchiha Sasuke	3,242 votes	7th Place/Gaara	1,934 vote
2nd Place/Hatake Kakashi	2,916 votes	8th Place/Hyuga Neji	1,785 vote
3rd Place/Deidara	2,555 votes	9th Place/Fourth Hokage	1,458 vote
4th Place/Uzumaki Naruto	2,283 votes	10th Place/Nara Shikamaru	1,409 vote
5th Place/Umino Iruka	2,232 votes	11th Place/Uchiha Itachi	1,369 vote
6th Place/Sasori	1,949 votes	12th Place/Haruno Sakura	1,359 vote

NARUTO

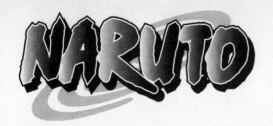

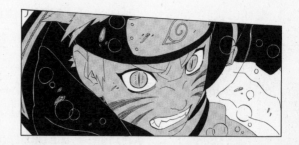

READ THIS WAY

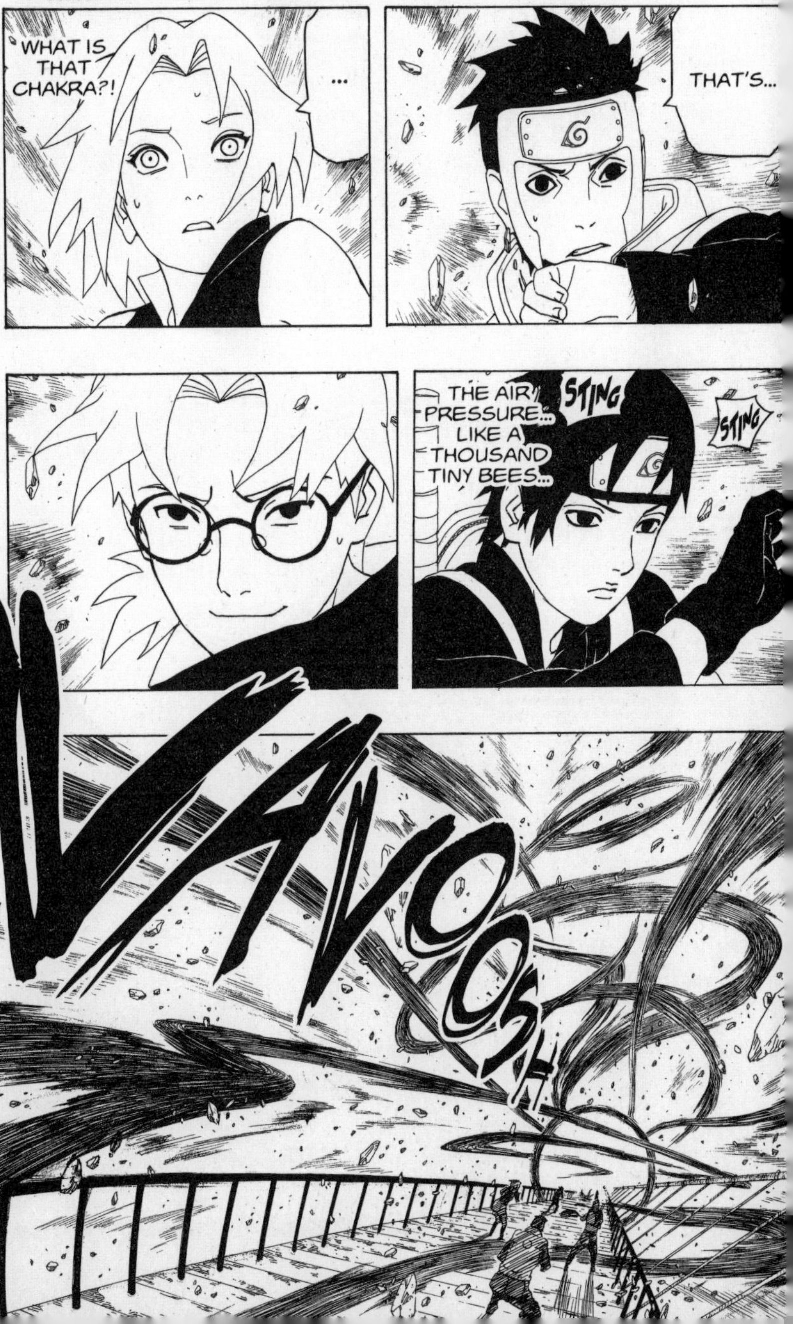
THAT'S...
...
WHAT IS THAT CHAKRA?!
STING
STING
THE AIR PRESSURE... LIKE A THOUSAND TINY BEES...
VWOOSH

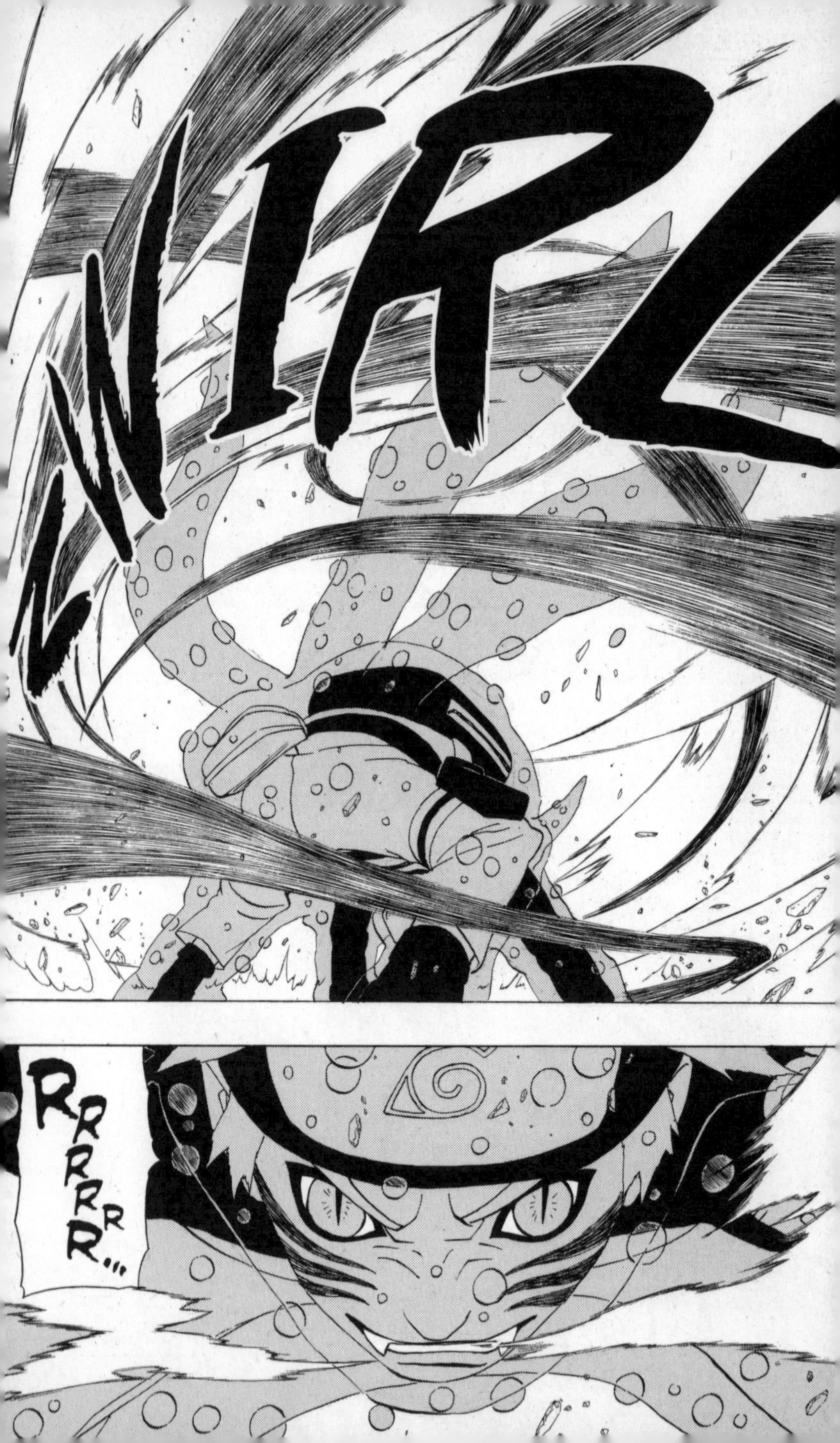
ZWIRL
RRRRRR...

READ THIS WAY

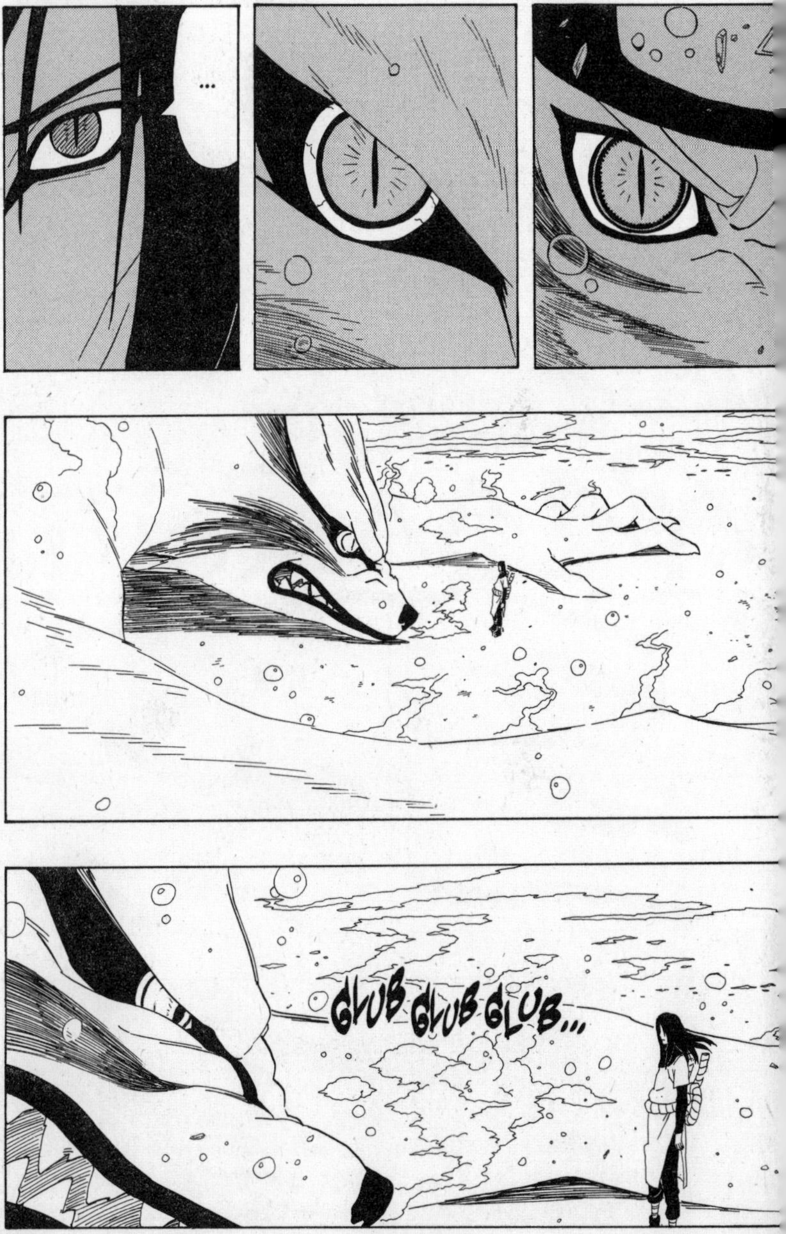
...
GLUB GLUB GLUB...

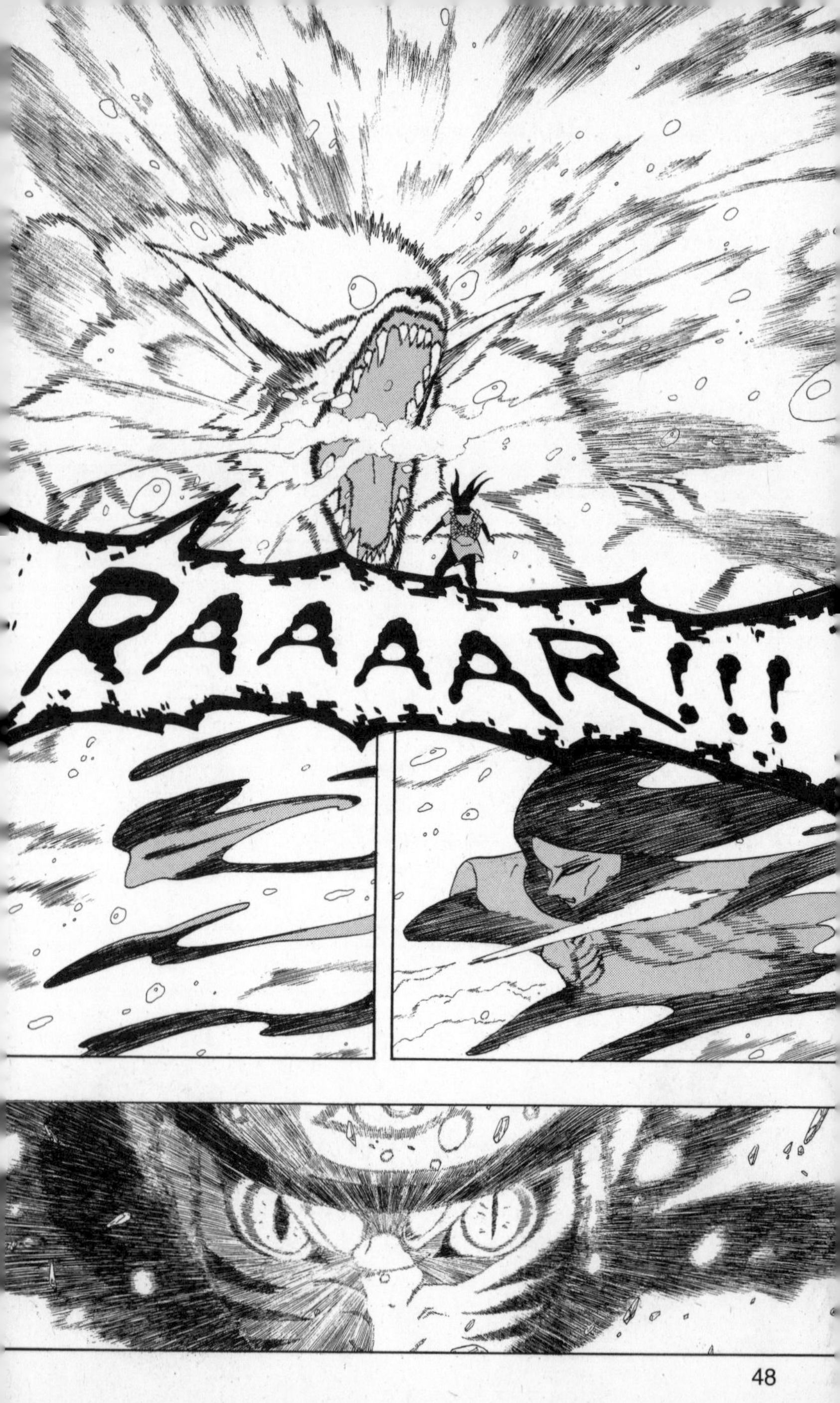
RAAAAR!!!

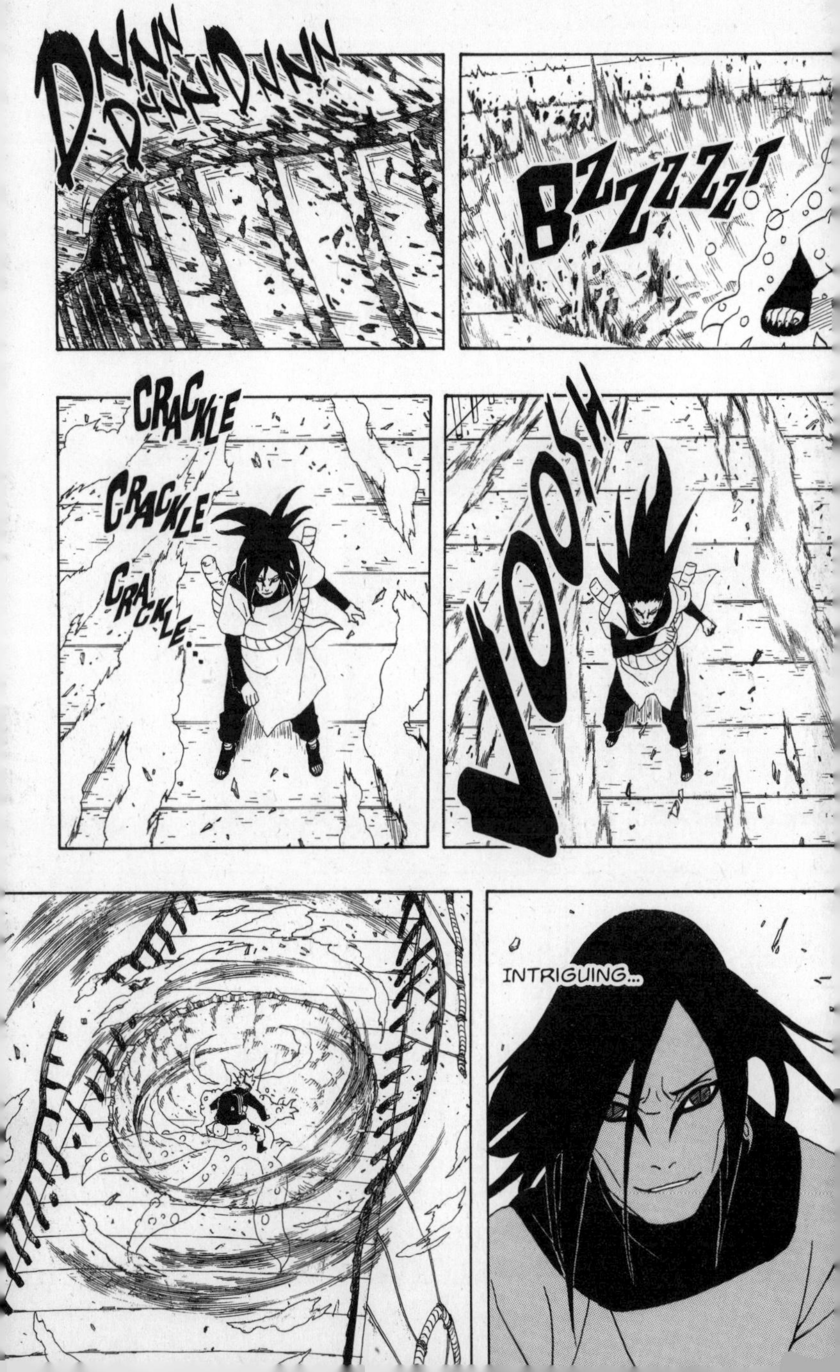
BZZZZZT
DNNN DNNN DNNN
VOOOM
CRACKLE
CRACKLE
CRACKLE...
INTRIGUING...

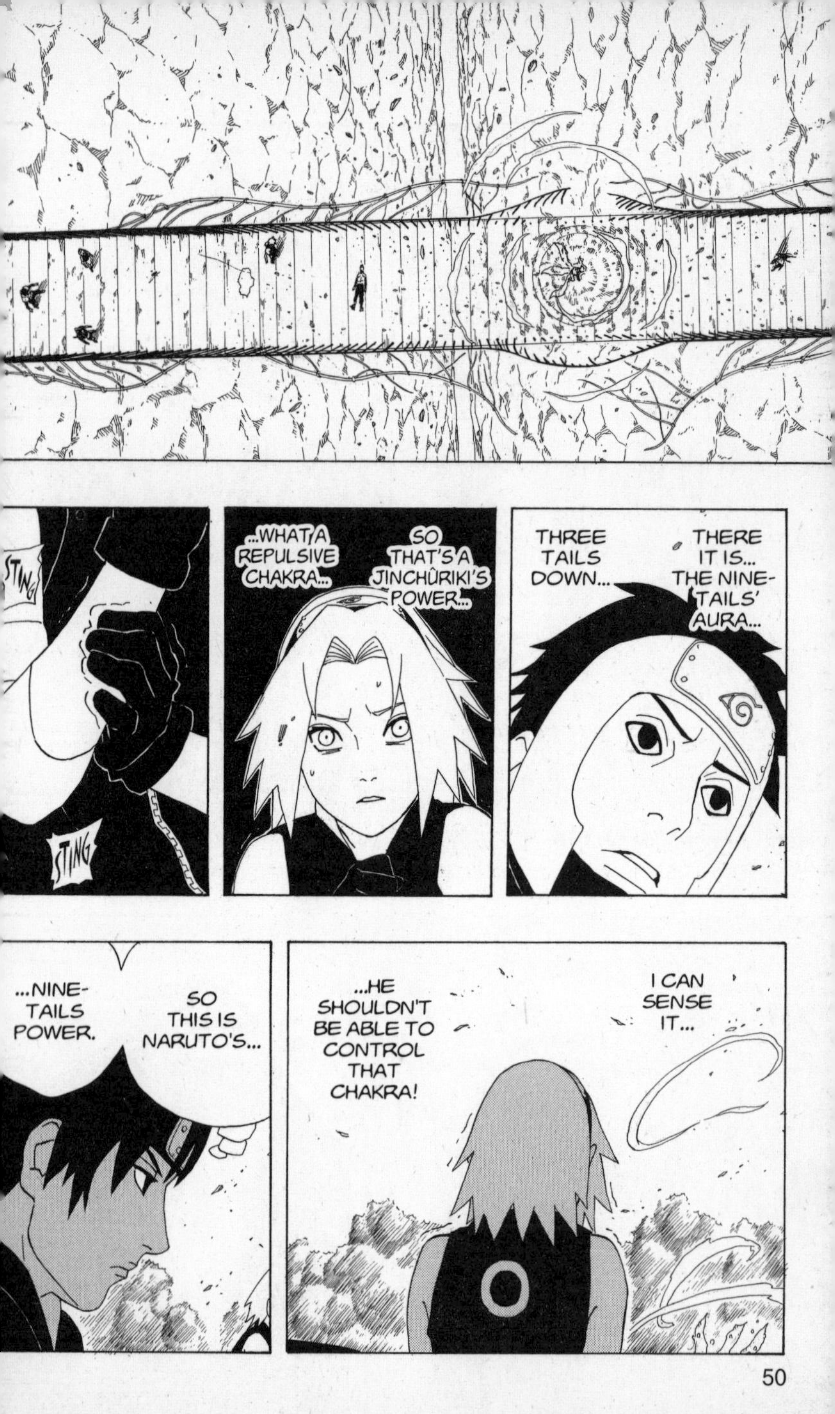
THERE IT IS... THE NINE-TAILS' AURA...
THREE TAILS DOWN...
SO THAT'S A JINCHÛRIKI'S POWER...
...WHAT A REPULSIVE CHAKRA...
STING
STING
I CAN SENSE IT...
...HE SHOULDN'T BE ABLE TO CONTROL THAT CHAKRA!
SO THIS IS NARUTO'S...
...NINE-TAILS POWER.

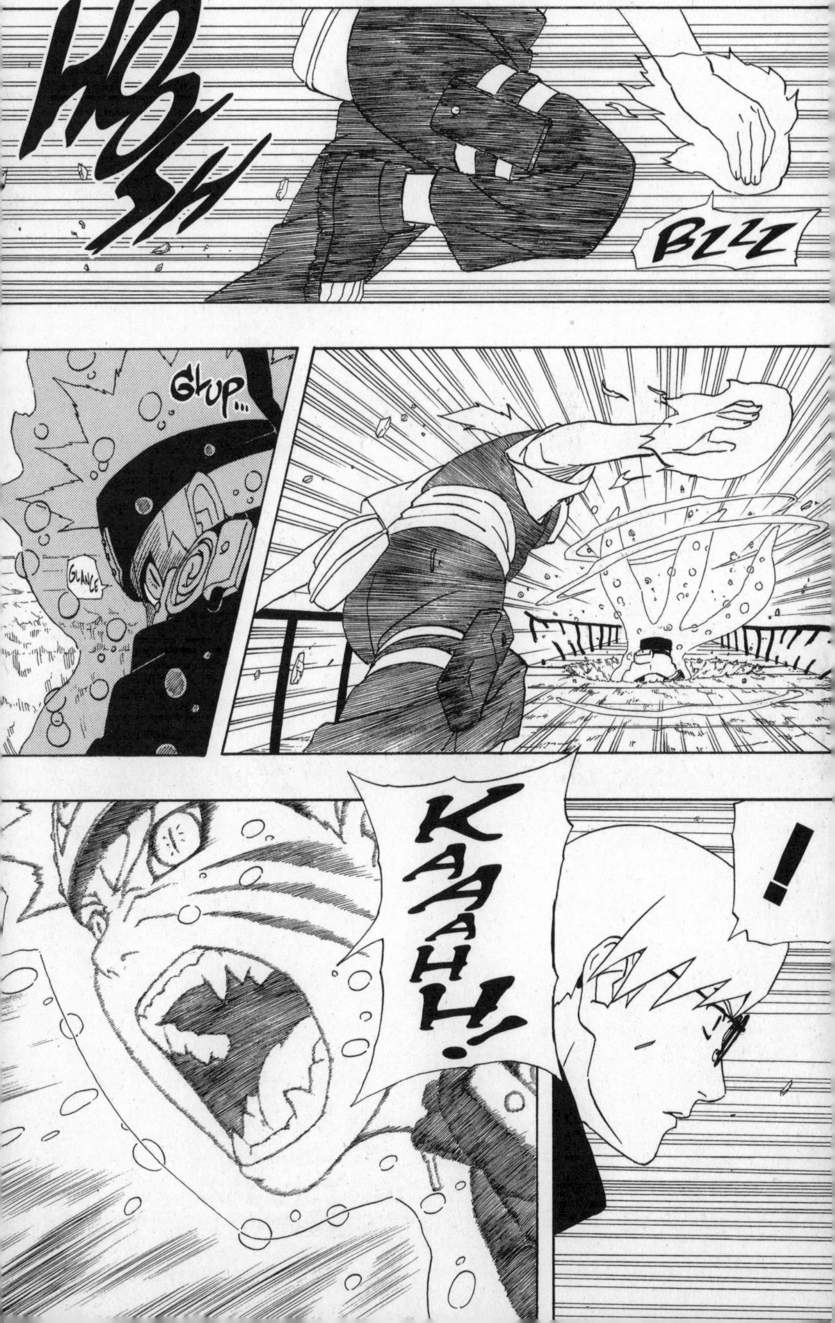
WHOOSH
BZZZ
GLUP...
GLANCE
!
KAAAAH!

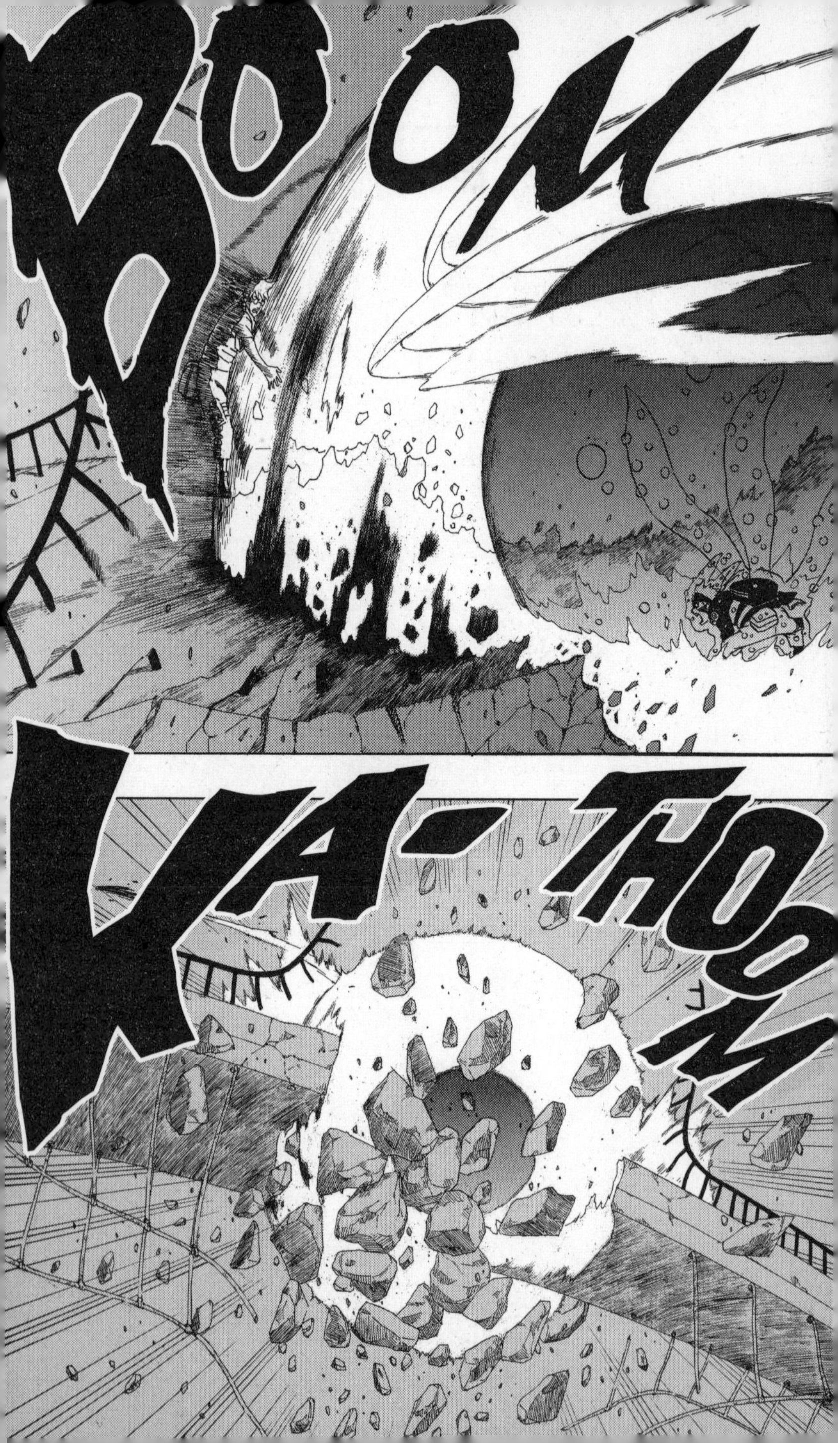
BOOM
KA-THOOM

READ THIS WAY

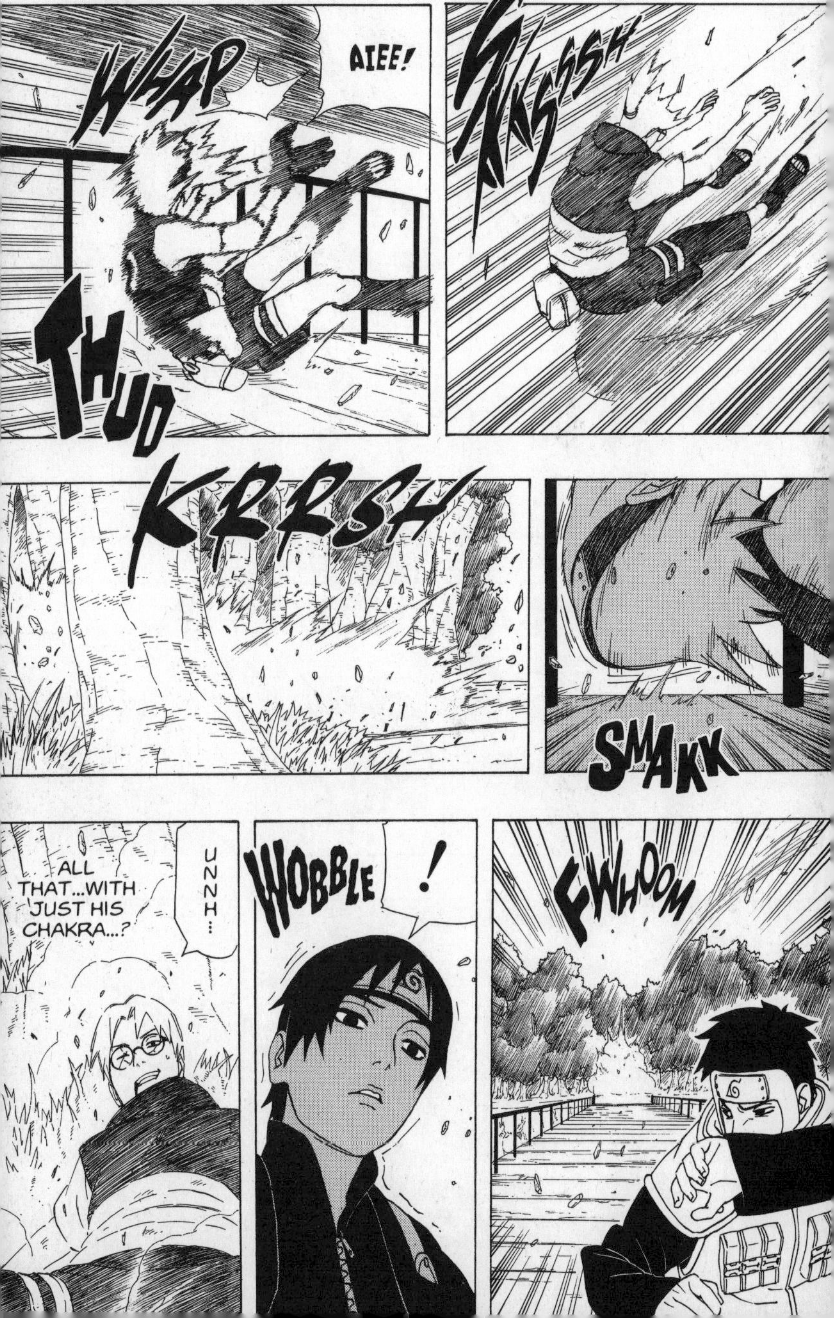
SKKSSSH
AIEE!
WHAP
THUD
SMAKK
KRRSH
FWHOOM
!
WOBBLE
UNNH...
ALL THAT...WITH JUST HIS CHAKRA...?

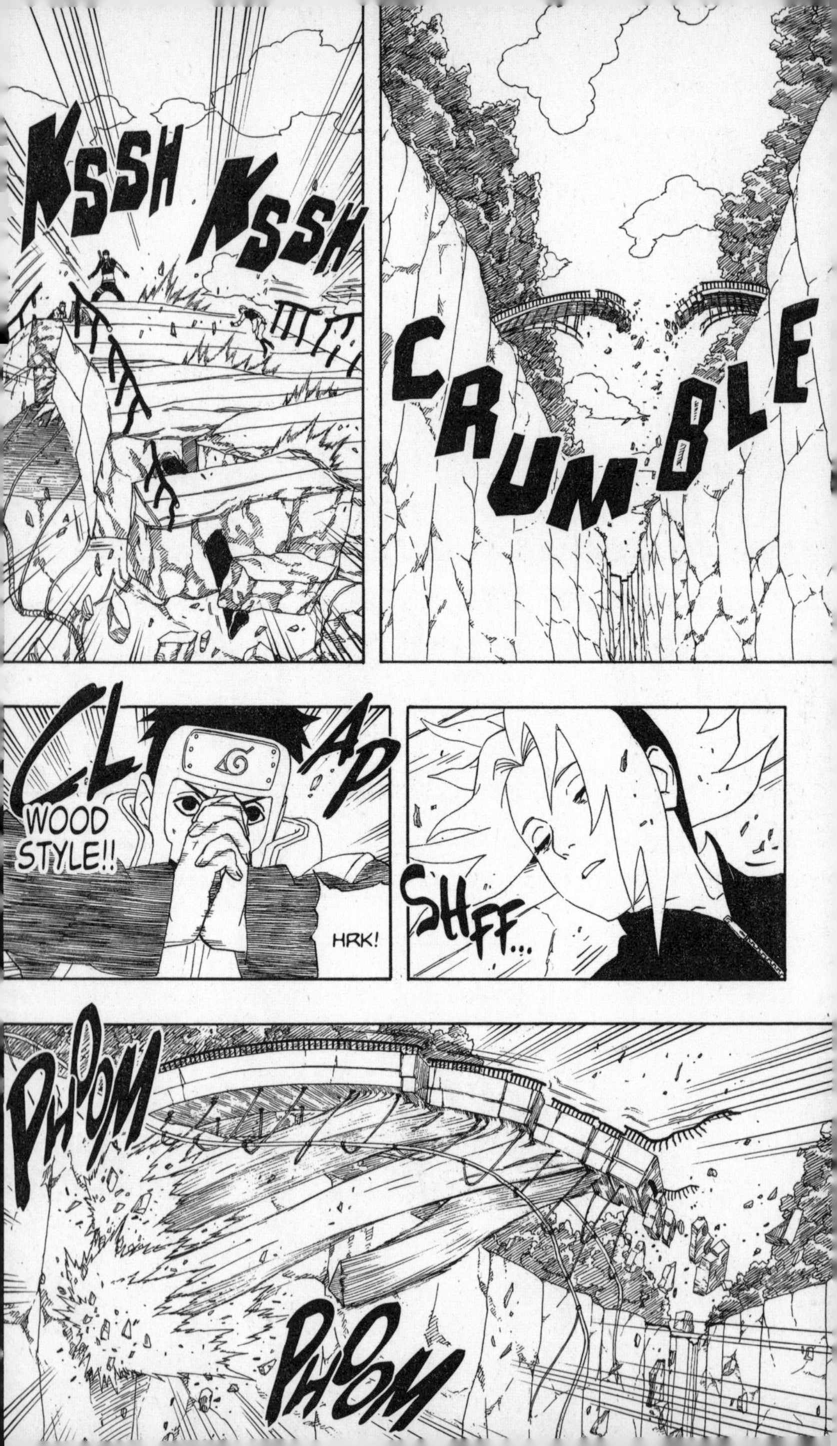
CRUMBLE
KSSH KSSH
SHFF...
CLAP
WOOD STYLE!!
HRK!
PHOOM
PHOOM

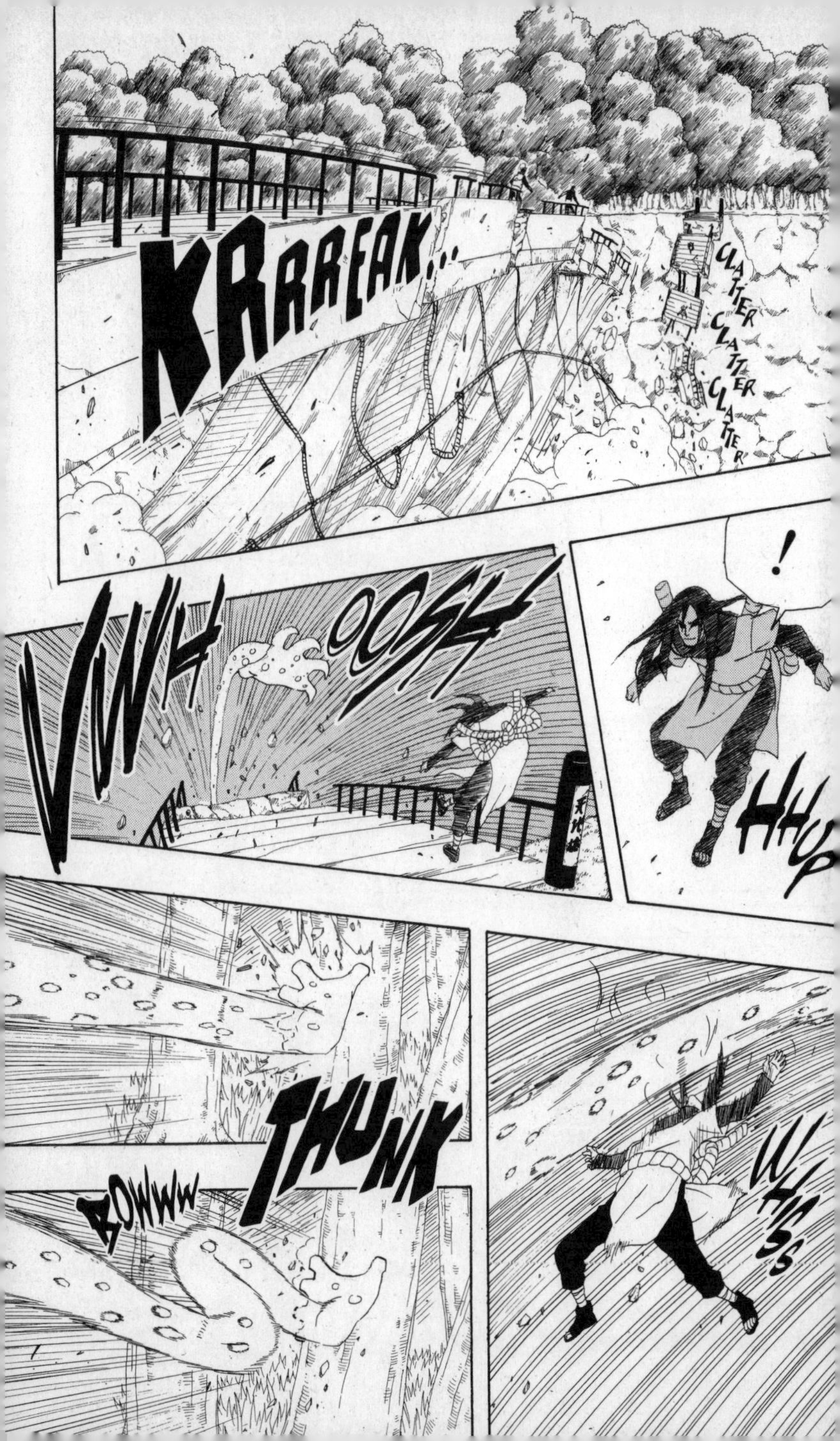
CLATTER
CLATTER
CLATTER
CLATTER
KRRREAK...
!
HHUP
VWHOOOSH
WHISS
THUNK
ROWWW

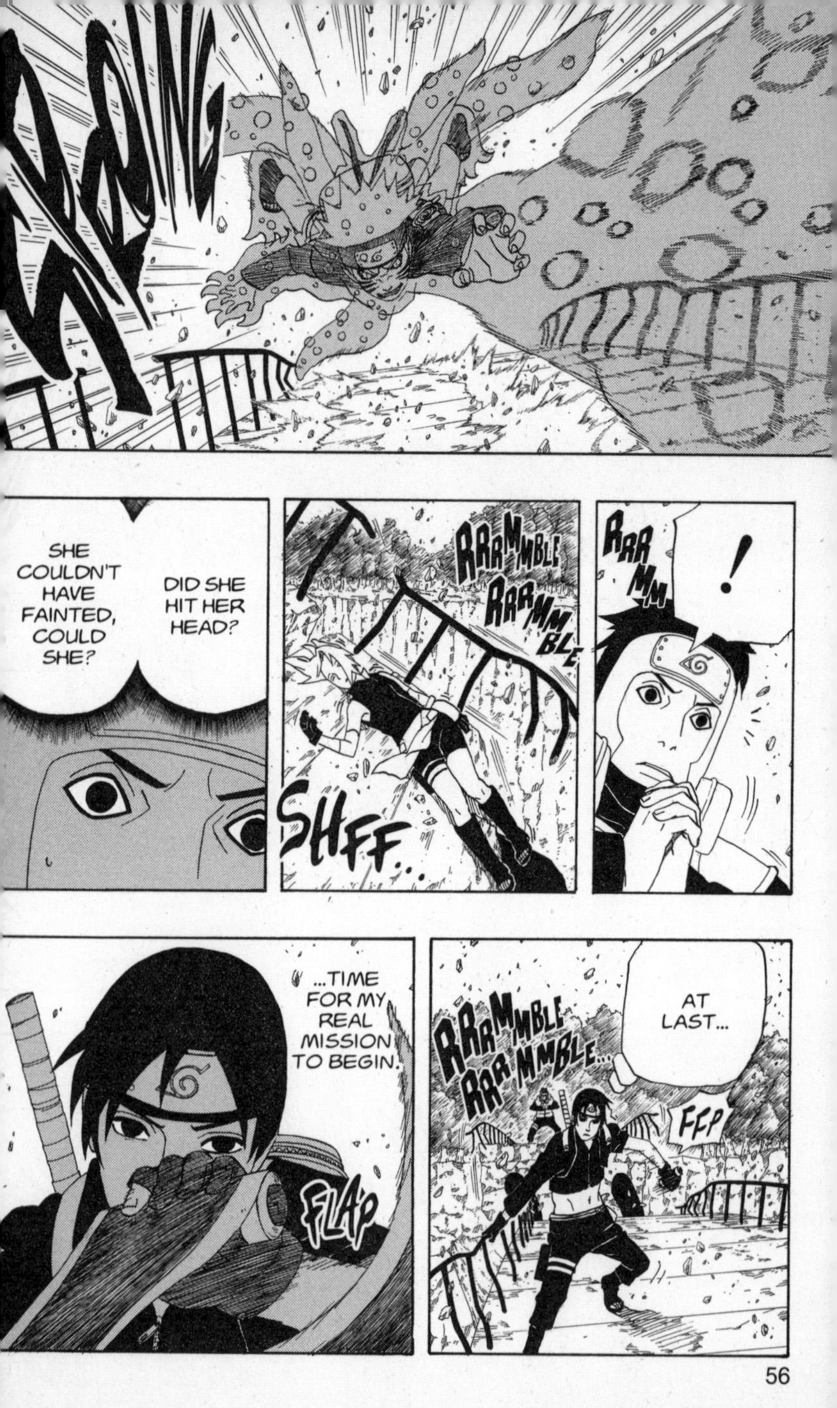
RRR MM
!
RRRMMBLE RRRMMBLE
SHFF...
DID SHE HIT HER HEAD?
SHE COULDN'T HAVE FAINTED, COULD SHE?
AT LAST...
RRAMMBLE RRRMMBLE...
FFP
...TIME FOR MY REAL MISSION TO BEGIN.
FLAP

READ THIS WAY

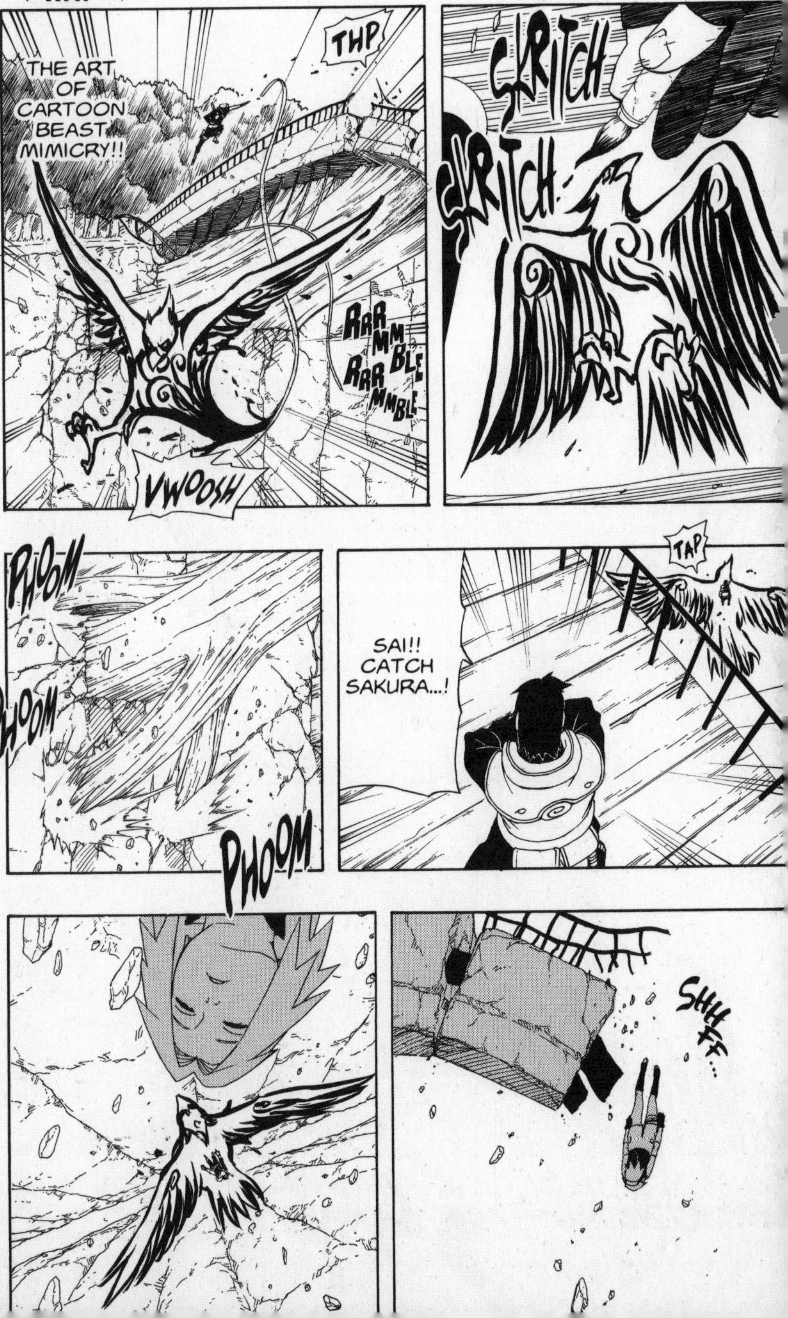
SKRITCH
SKRITCH
THE ART OF CARTOON BEAST MIMICRY!!
THP
RRRMMBLE
RRRMMBLE
VWOOSH
TAP
SAI!! CATCH SAKURA...!
PHOOM
PHOOM
PHOOM
SHHFF...

FLAP

!

SUNISH

WHISsss

WHoooosh

SLAP

SAKURA!

READ THIS WAY

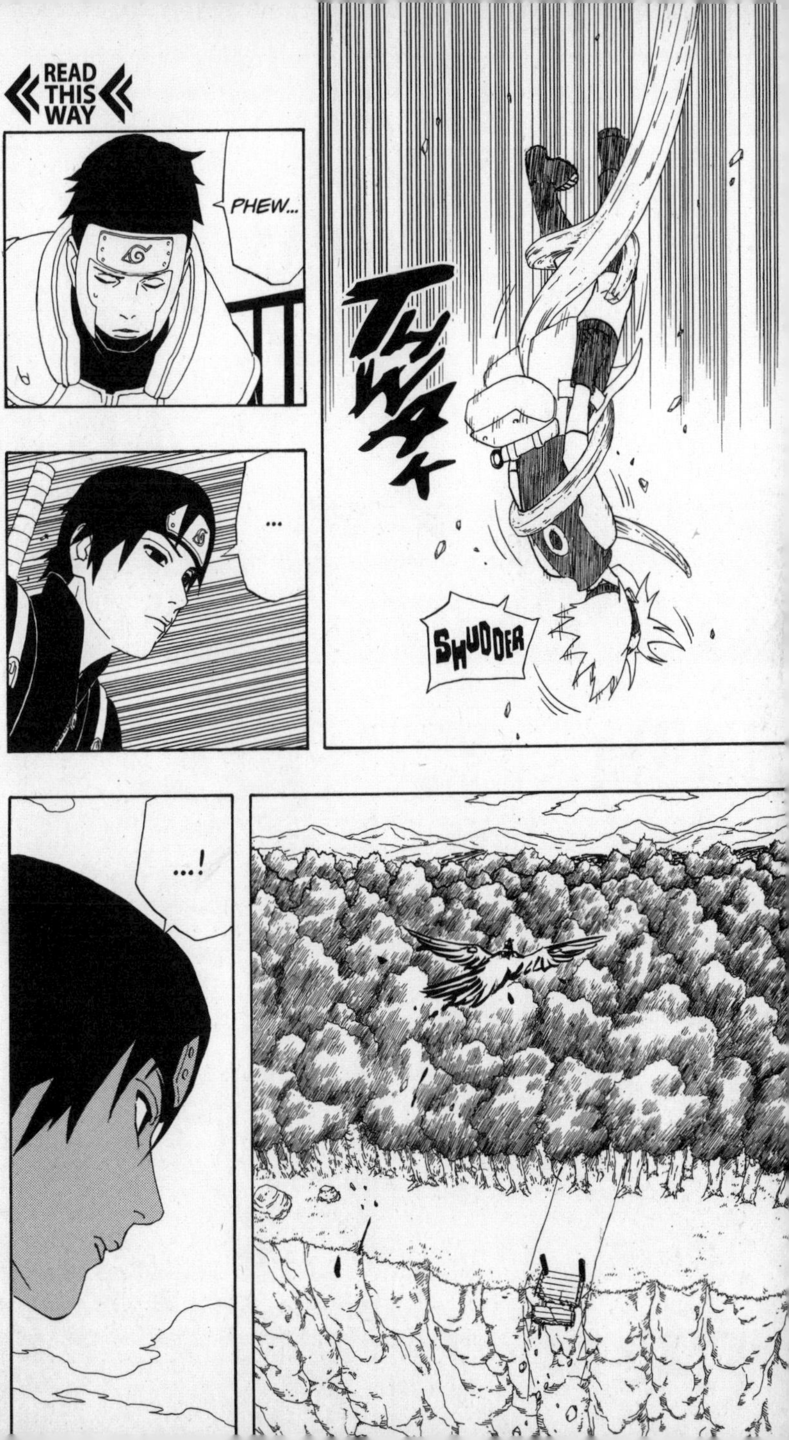
THWAK
SHUDDER
PHEW...
...
...!

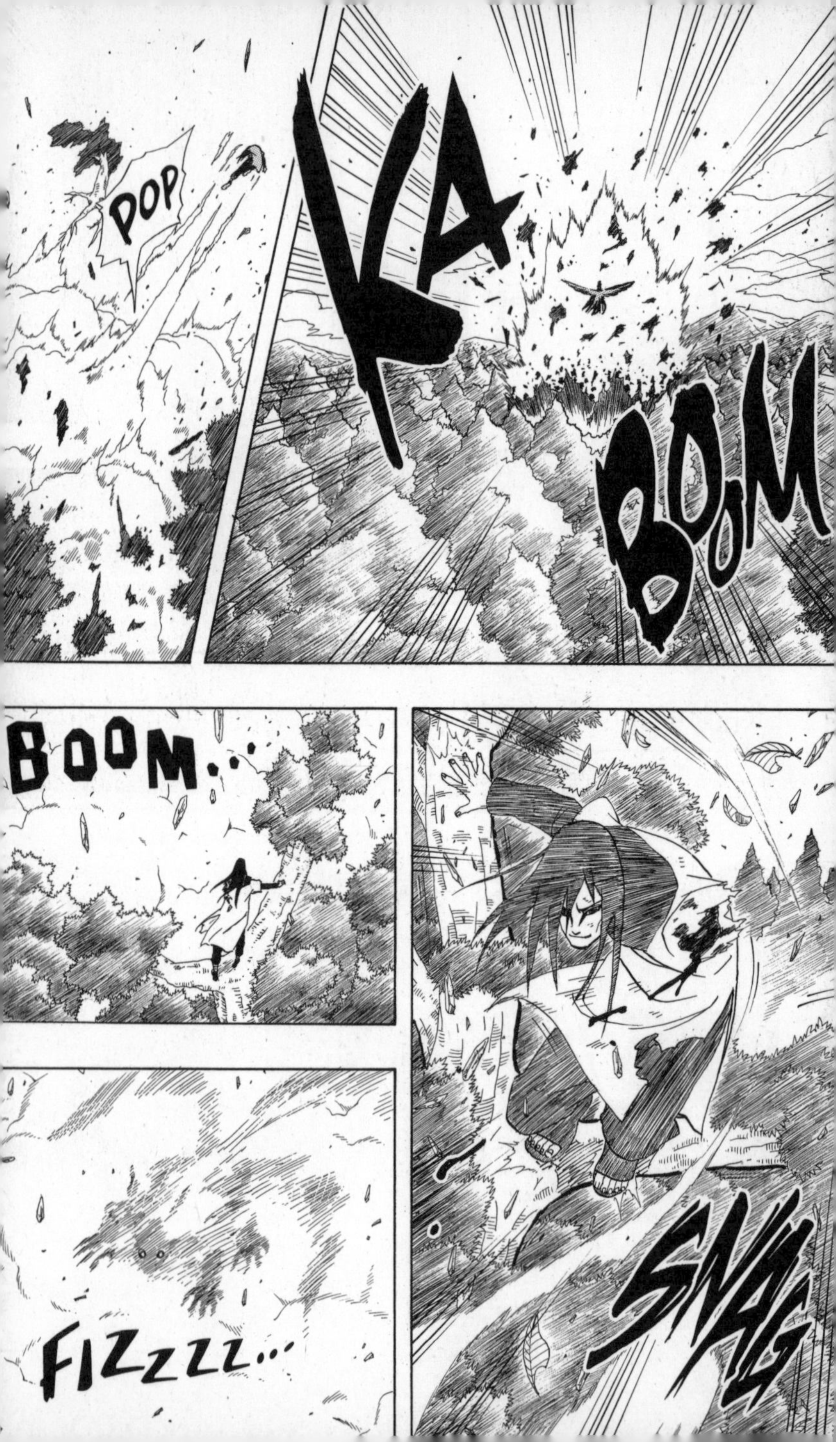
KA BOOM
POP
SNAG
BOOM...
FIZzzz...

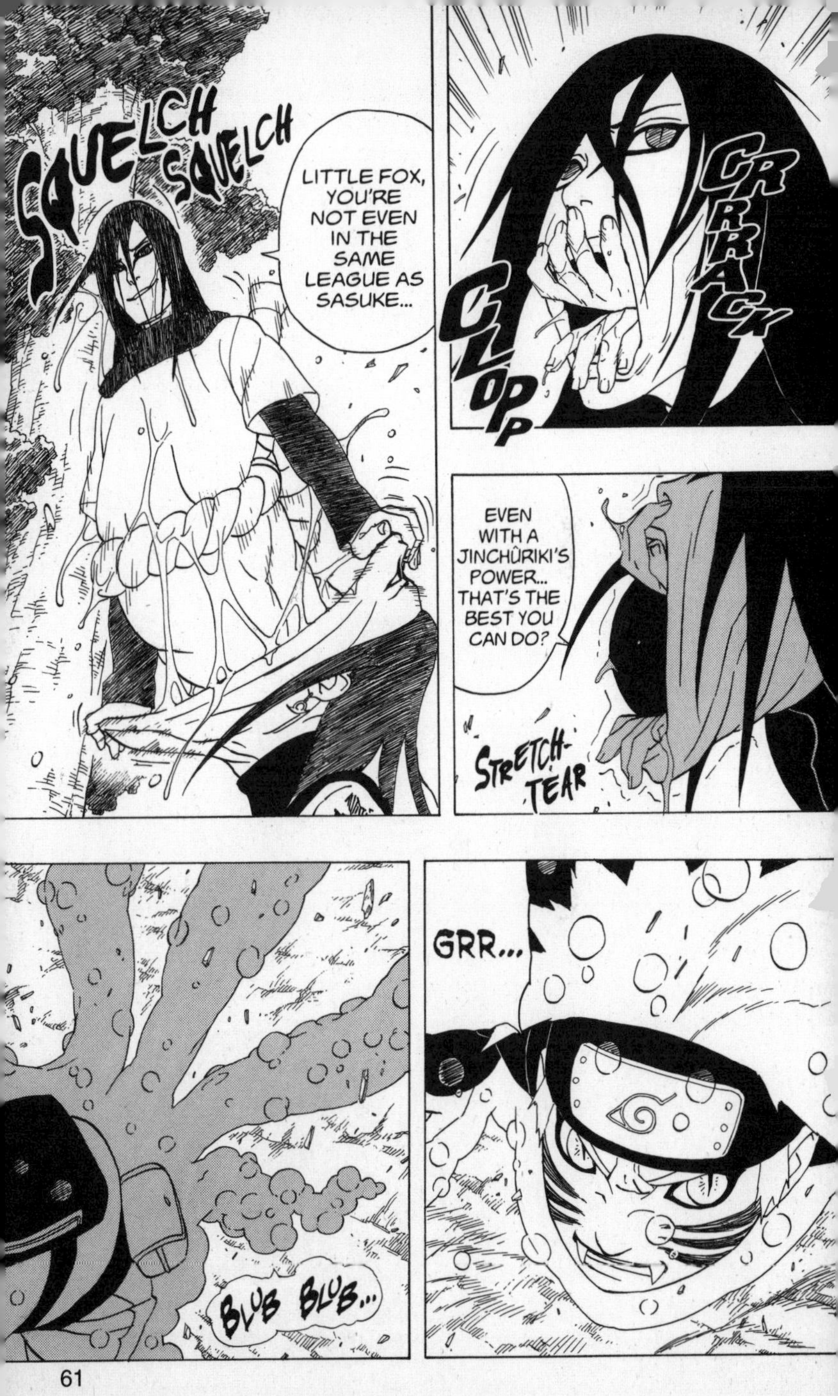
CRRRACK
CLOPP
EVEN WITH A JINCHÛRIKI'S POWER... THAT'S THE BEST YOU CAN DO?
STRETCH-TEAR
SQUELCH SQUELCH
LITTLE FOX, YOU'RE NOT EVEN IN THE SAME LEAGUE AS SASUKE...
GRR...
BLUB BLUB...

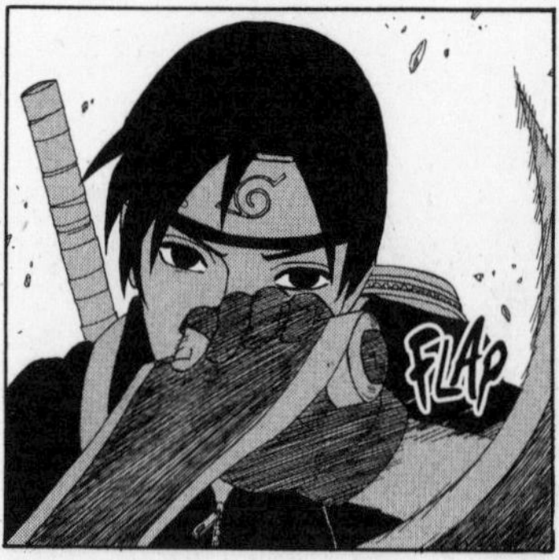
FLAP

Number 293: Rampage...!!

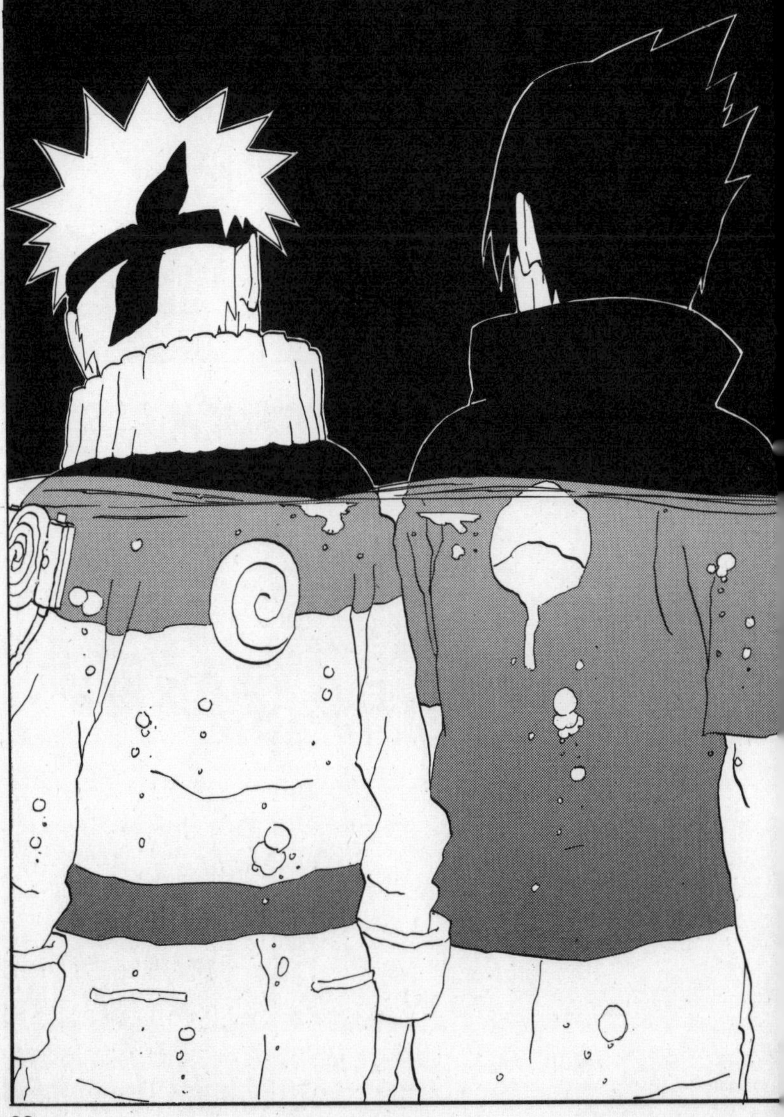

BRBBLE
BRBBLE

!

BRBBLE
BRBBLE
BRBBLE

HRK...

FRRTH
FRRTH
FRRTH

BRBBLE BRBBLE BRBBLE

JUST
YOU
WAIT...

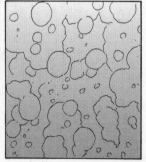

64

READ THIS WAY

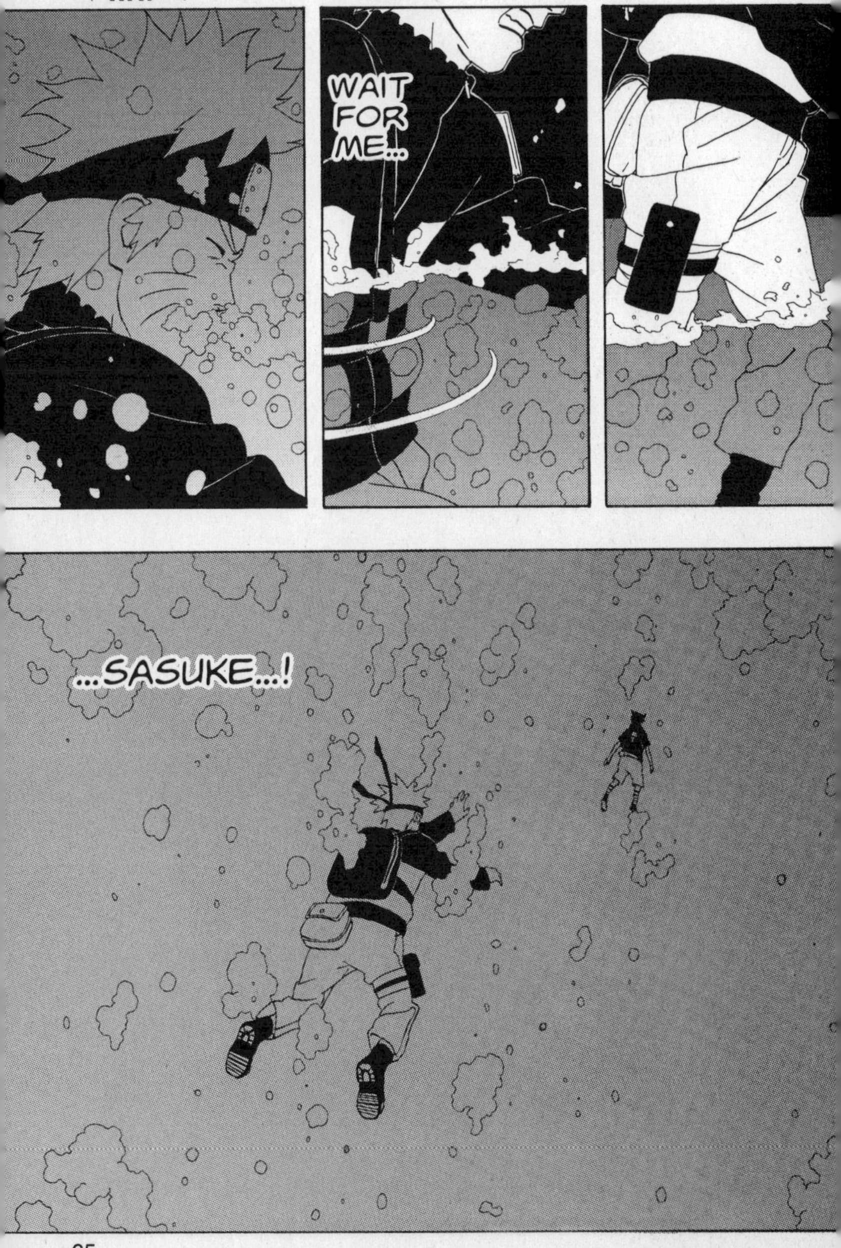

WAIT FOR ME...
...SASUKE...!

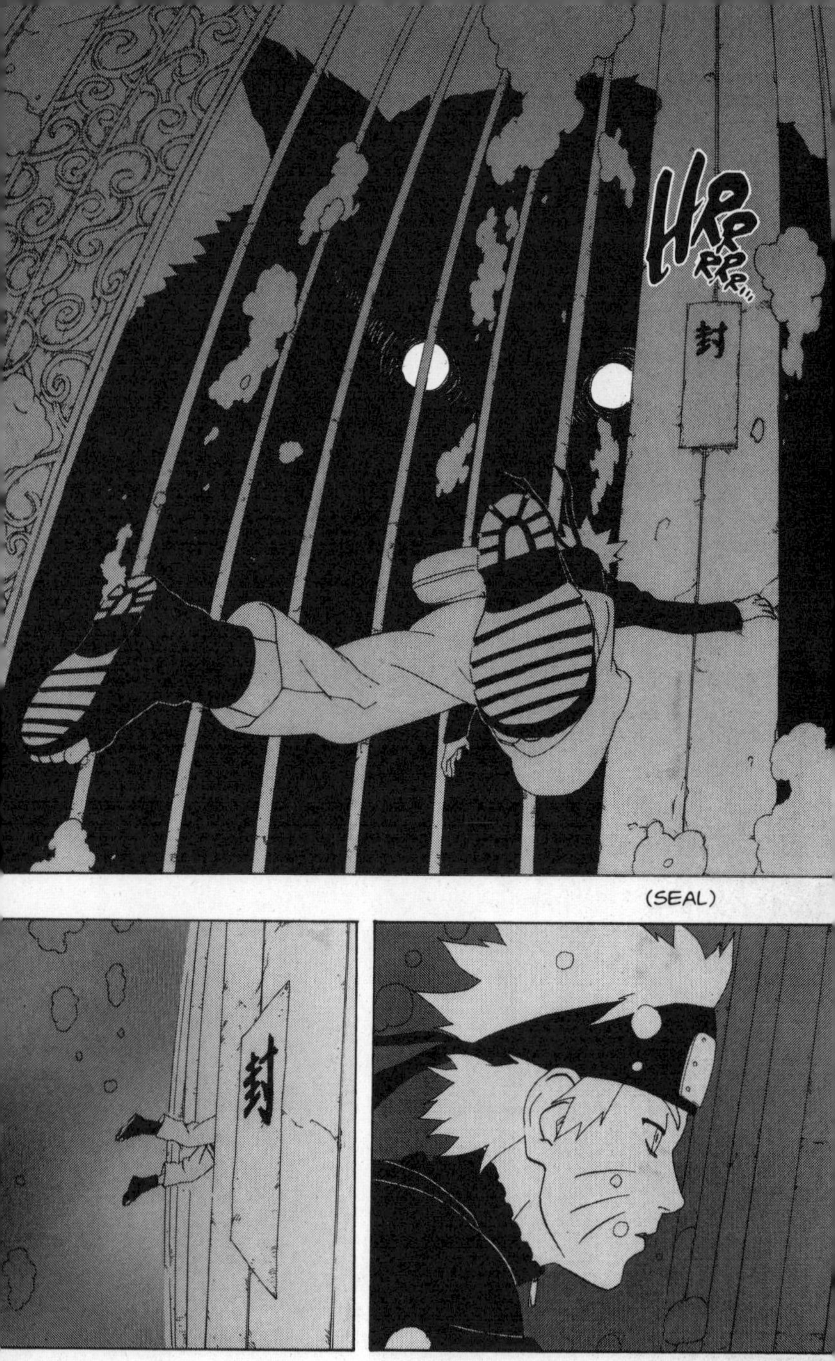
HRRRRR...
封
(SEAL)
封

READ THIS WAY

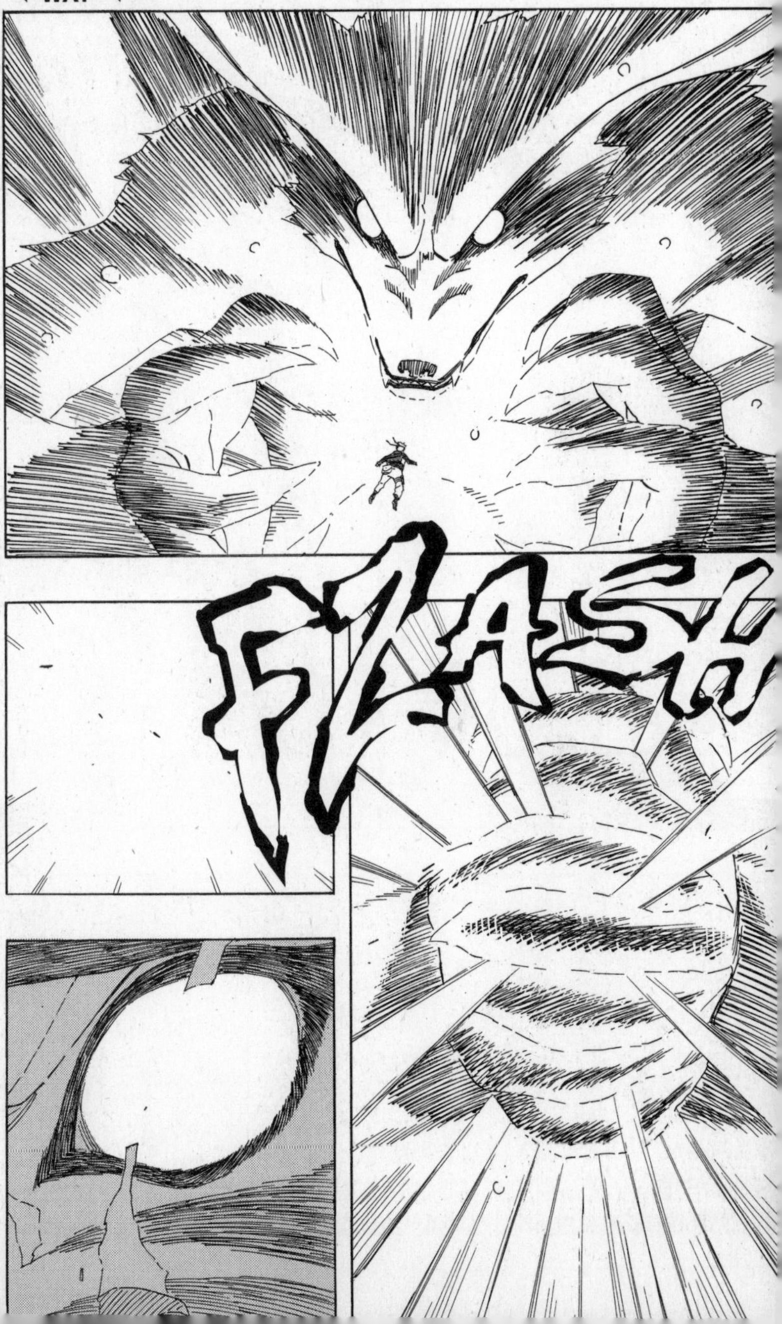
FLASH

SHRRP
SHRRP
SHRRP
SHRRP
SHRRP
SHRRP
SHRRP
SHRRP
SKKrrKK
BLOP
TSSSSS

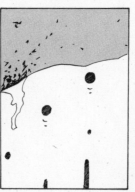

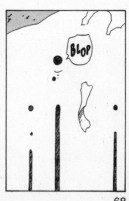

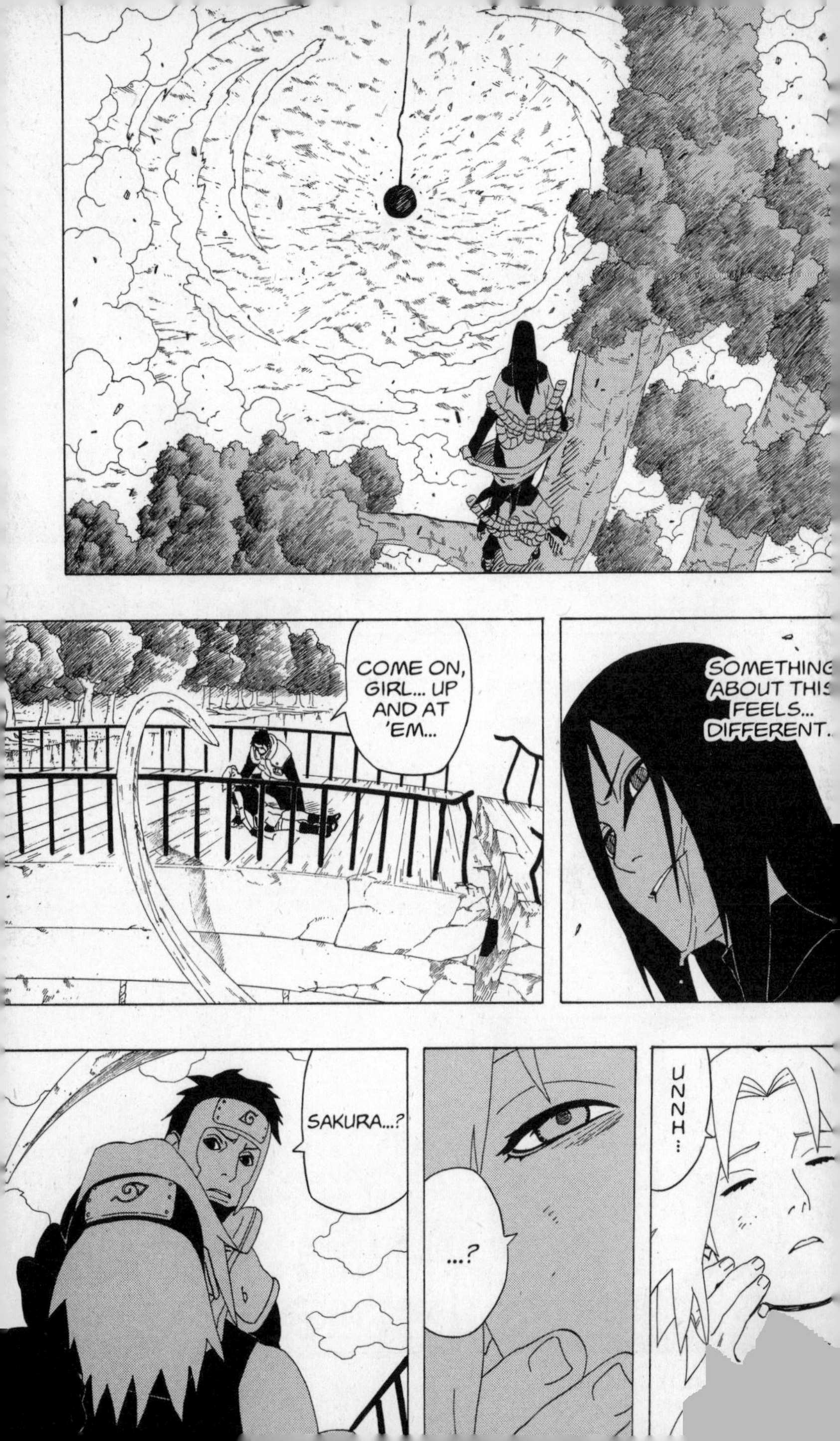
SOMETHING ABOUT THIS FEELS... DIFFERENT...
COME ON, GIRL... UP AND AT 'EM...
UNNH...
...?
SAKURA...?

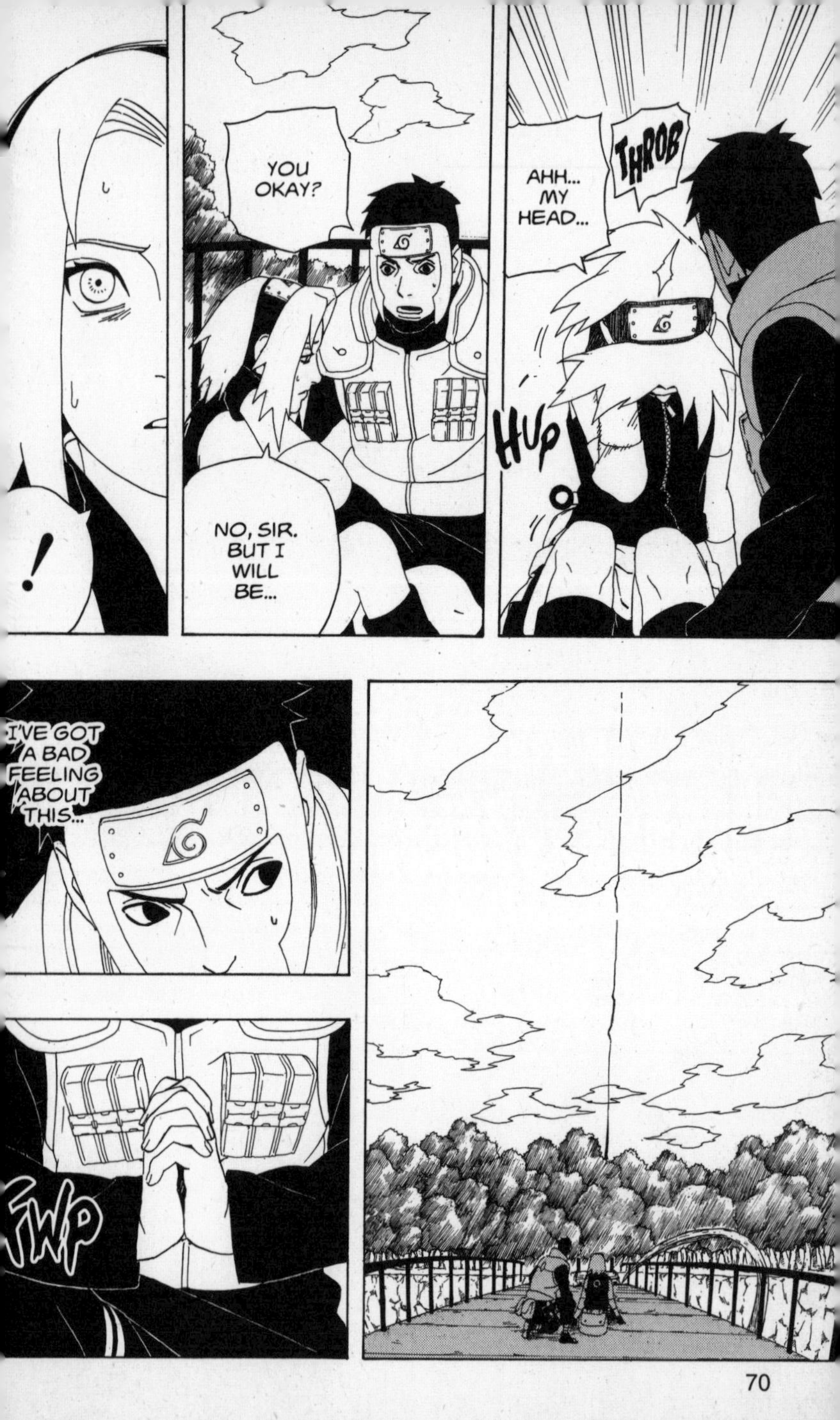
AHH... MY HEAD...
THROB
HUP
YOU OKAY?
NO, SIR. BUT I WILL BE...
!
I'VE GOT A BAD FEELING ABOUT THIS...
FWP

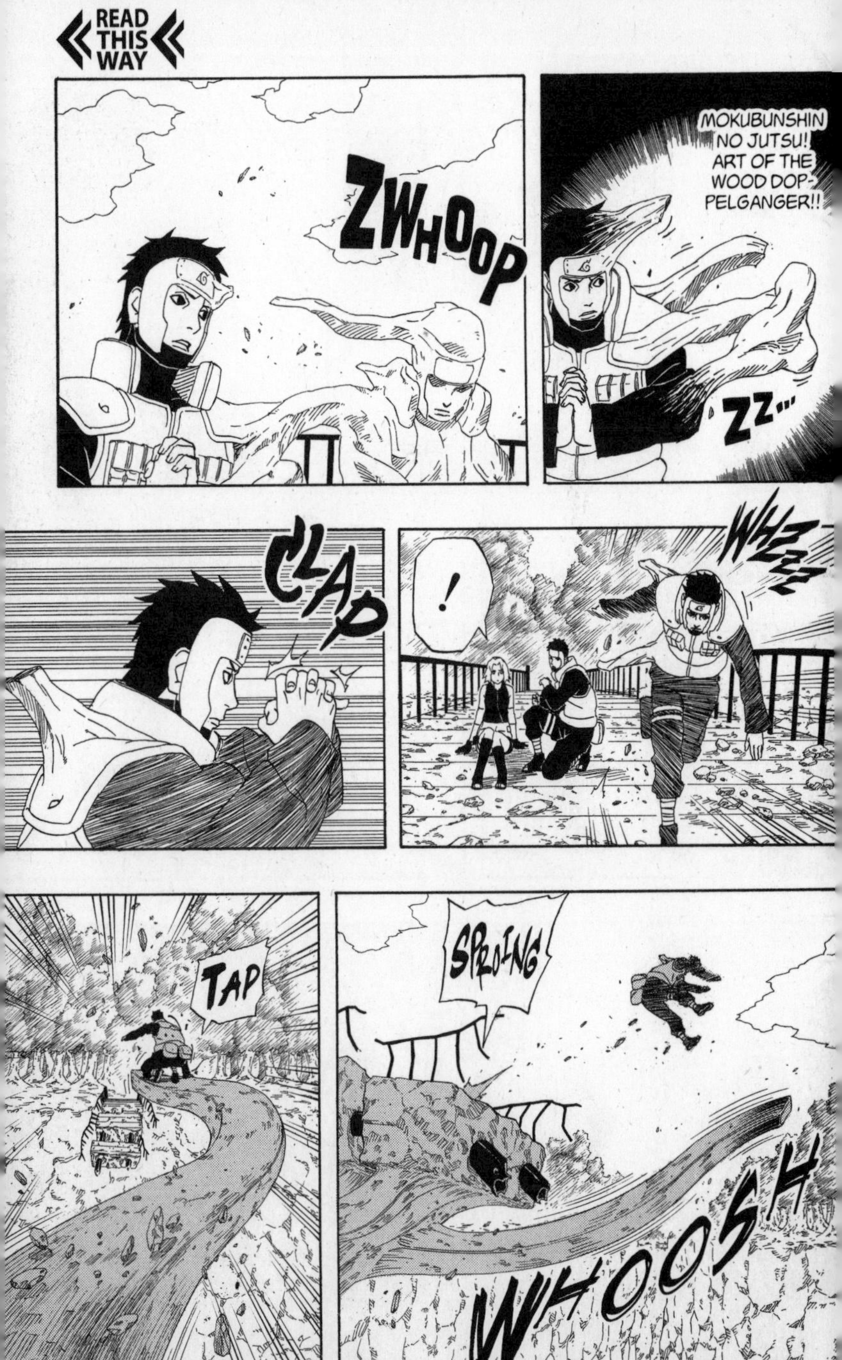
READ THIS WAY
MOKUBUNSHIN NO JUTSU! ART OF THE WOOD DOP-PELGANGER!!
ZZ...
ZWHOOP
WHZZZ
!
CLAP
SPROING
WHOOSH
TAP

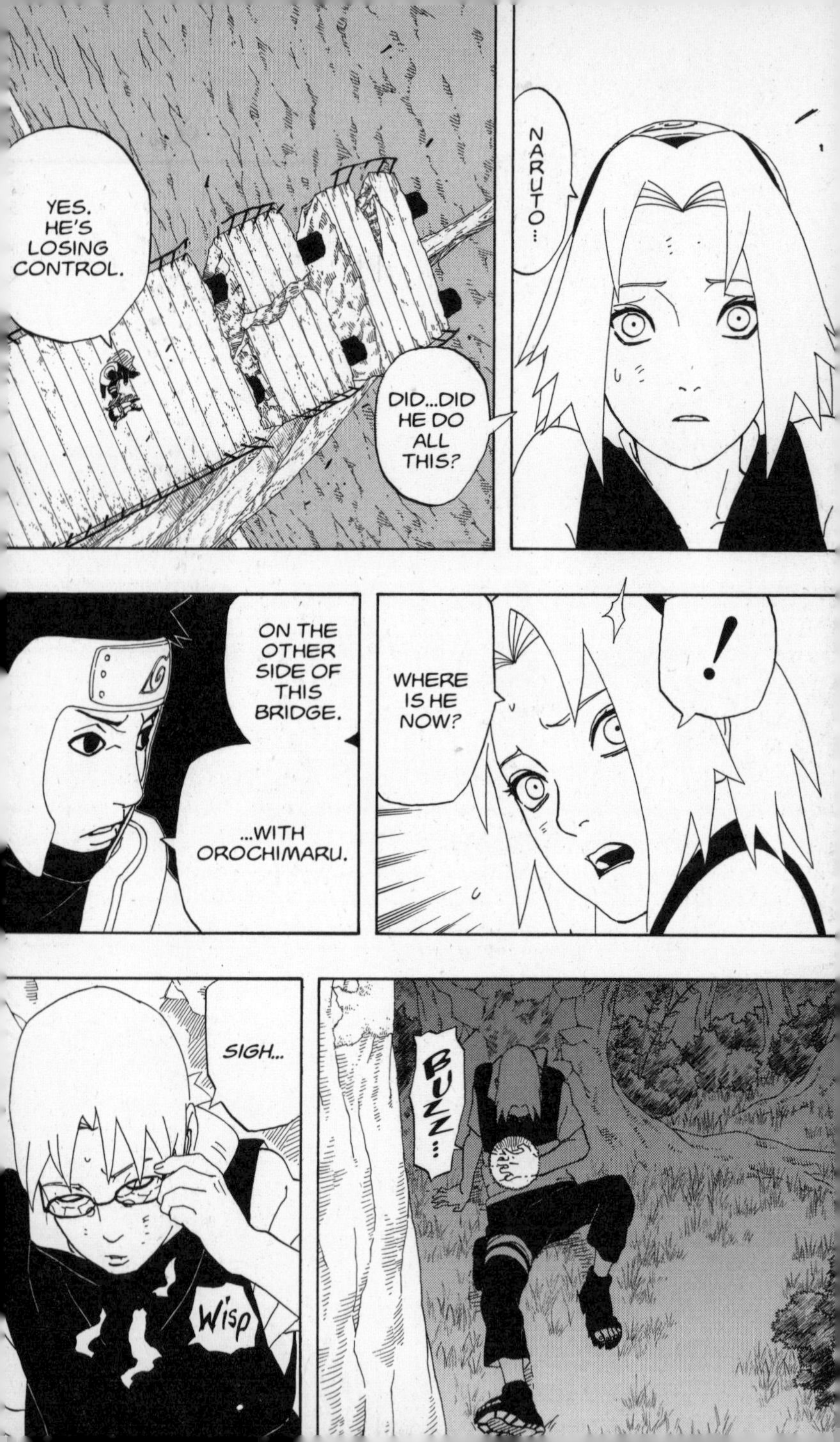
NARUTO...
DID...DID HE DO ALL THIS?
YES. HE'S LOSING CONTROL.
!
WHERE IS HE NOW?
ON THE OTHER SIDE OF THIS BRIDGE.
...WITH OROCHIMARU.
BUZZ...
SIGH...
Wisp

READ THIS WAY

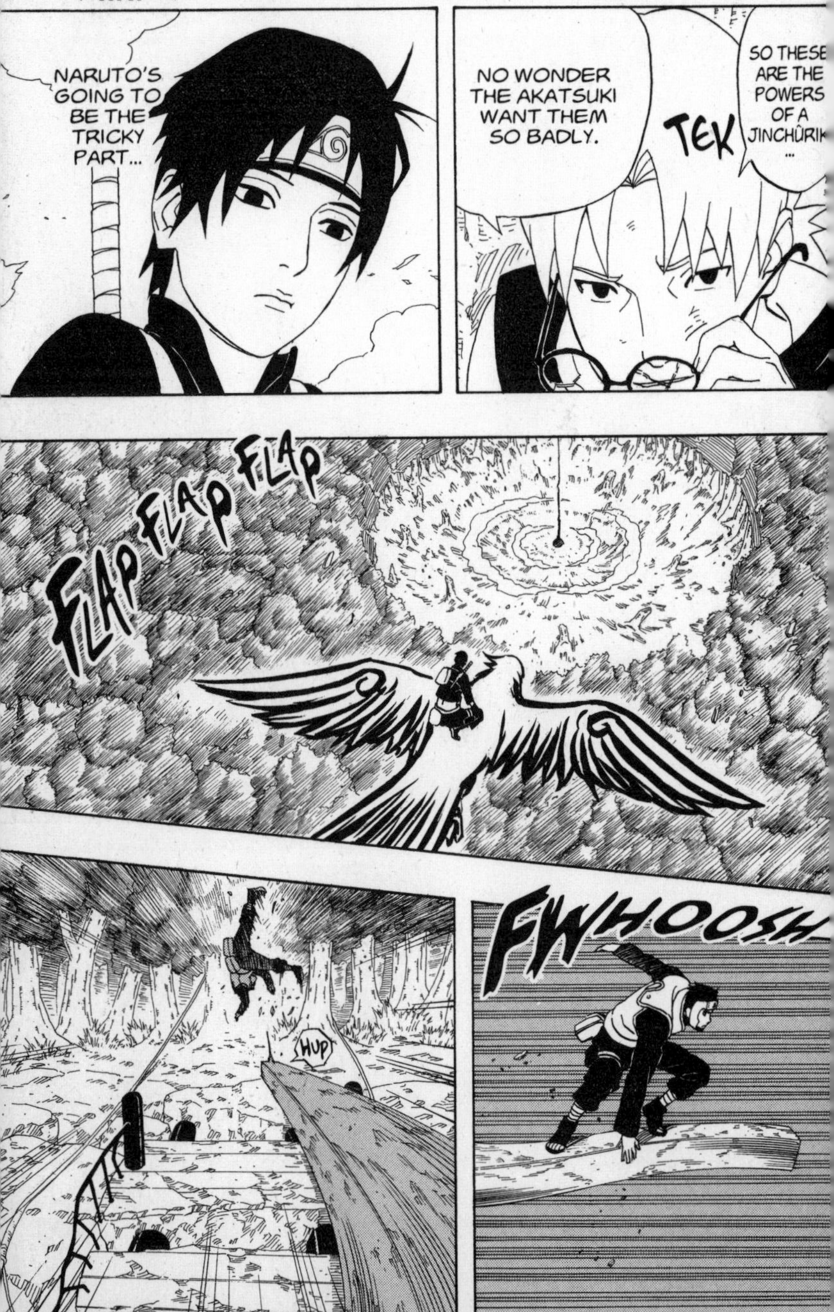
SO THESE ARE THE POWERS OF A JINCHÛRIK ...
TEK
NO WONDER THE AKATSUKI WANT THEM SO BADLY.
NARUTO'S GOING TO BE THE TRICKY PART...
FLAP FLAP FLAP
FWHOOSH
HUP

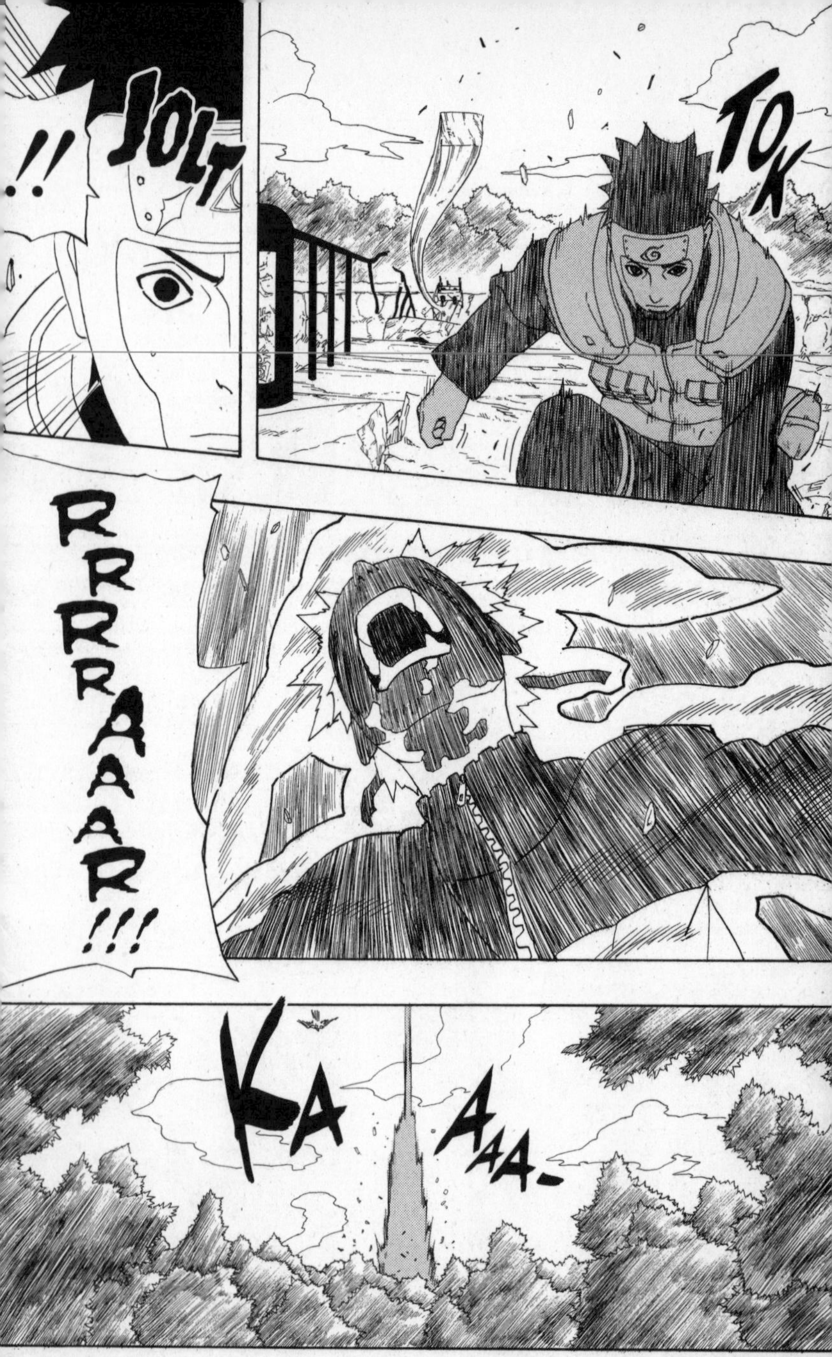
TOK
JOLT
!!
RRRRAAAR!!!
KA AAA-

READ THIS WAY

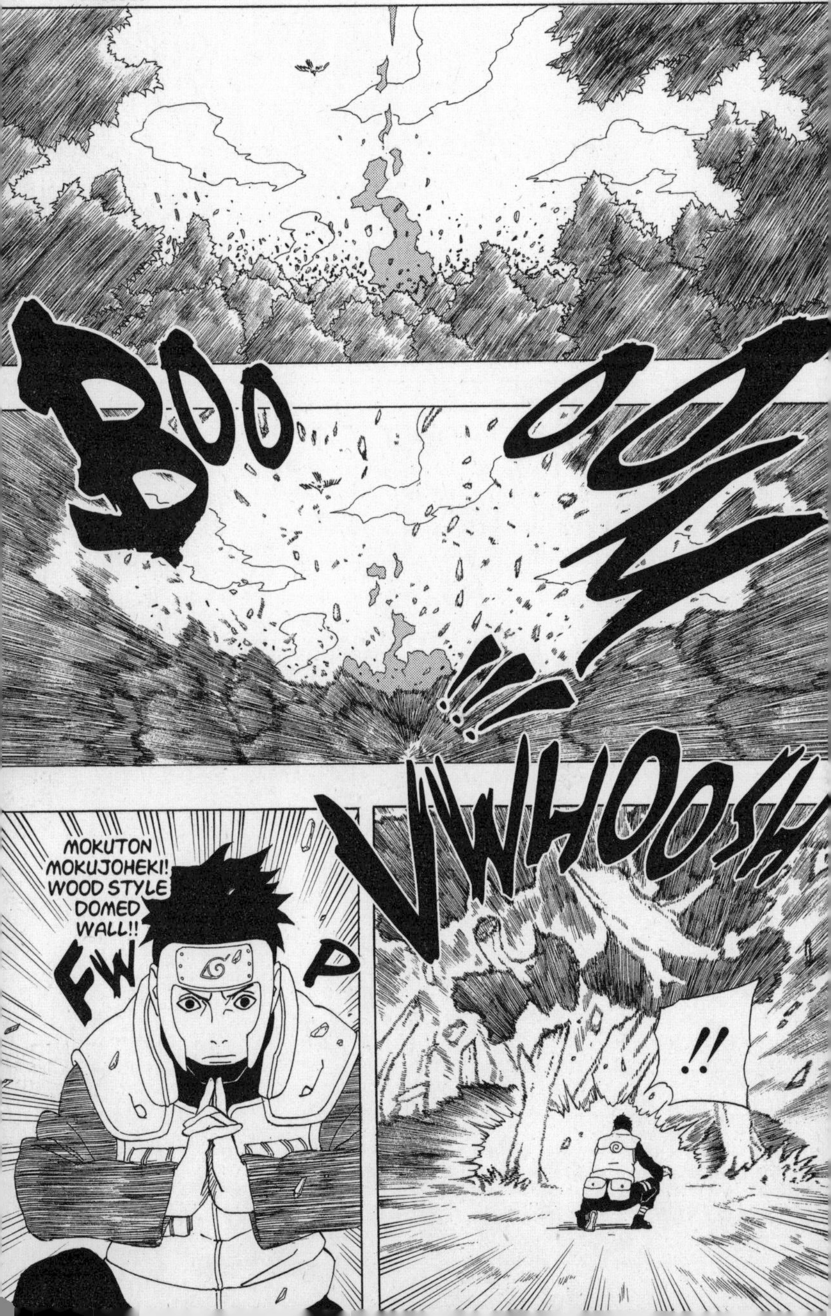
BOOOOM!!!
VWHOOSH
!!
MOKUTON MOKUJOHEKI! WOOD STYLE DOMED WALL!!
FWP

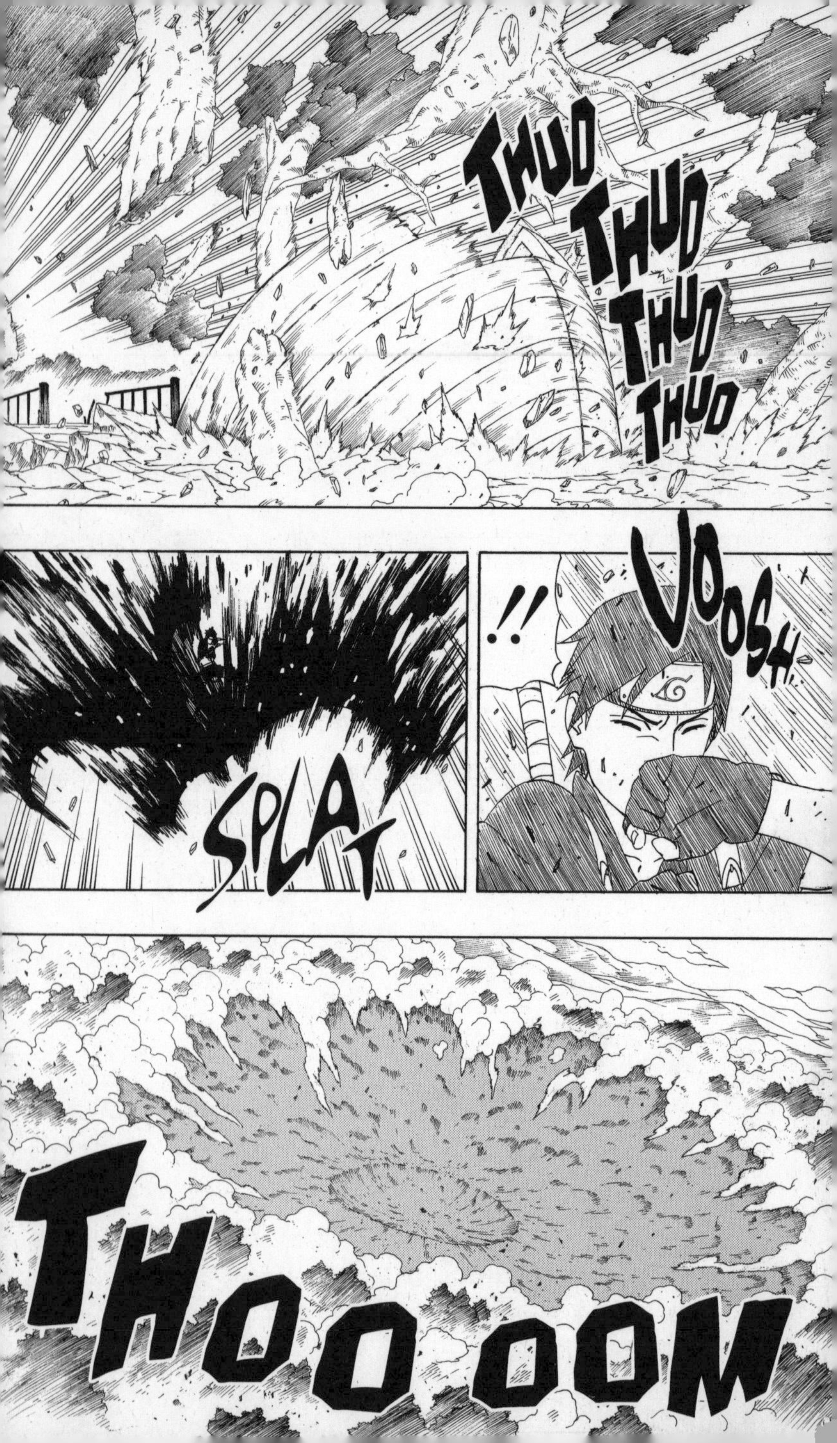
THUD THUD THUD THUD
!!
VOOSH
SPLAT
THOOOOM

READ THIS WAY

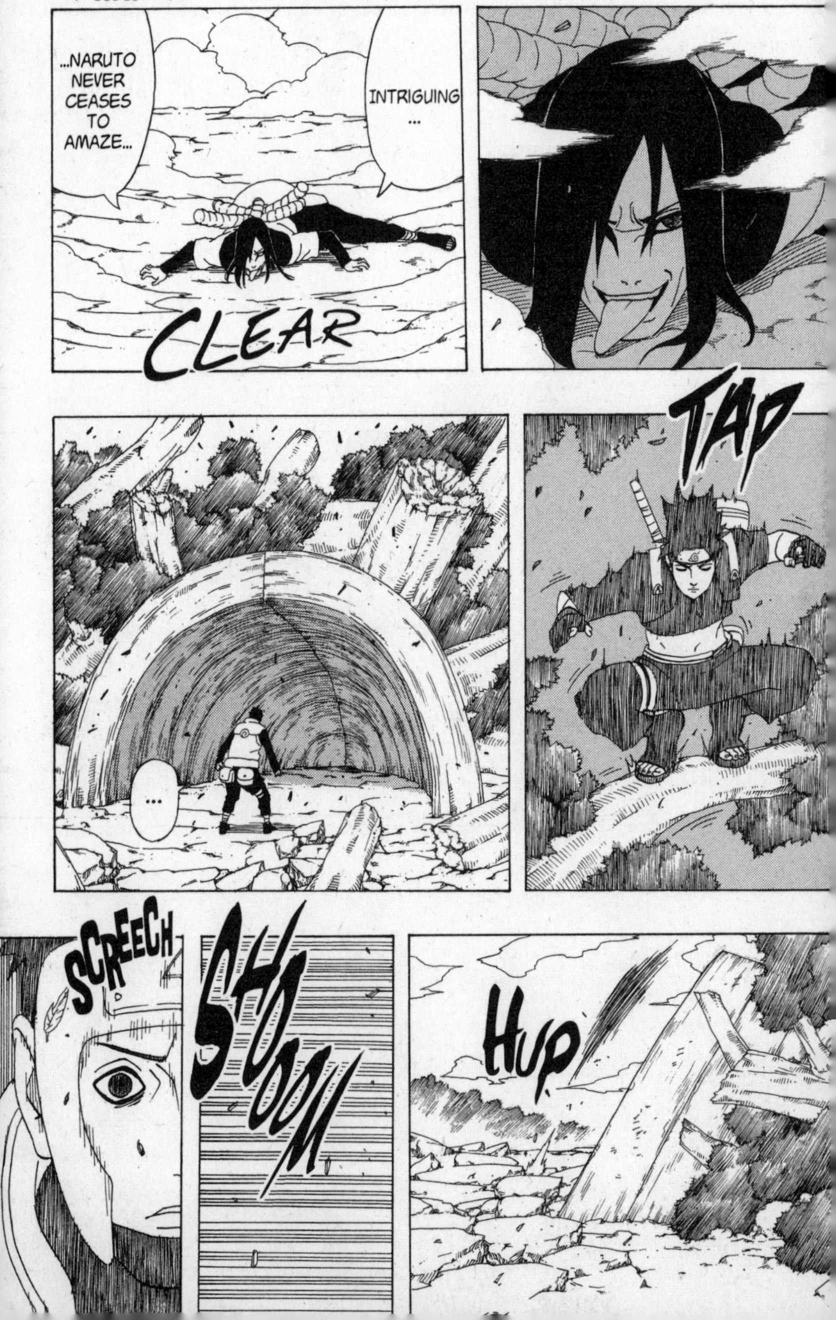
INTRIGUING...
...NARUTO NEVER CEASES TO AMAZE...
CLEAR
TAP
...
HUP
SHOOM
SCREECH

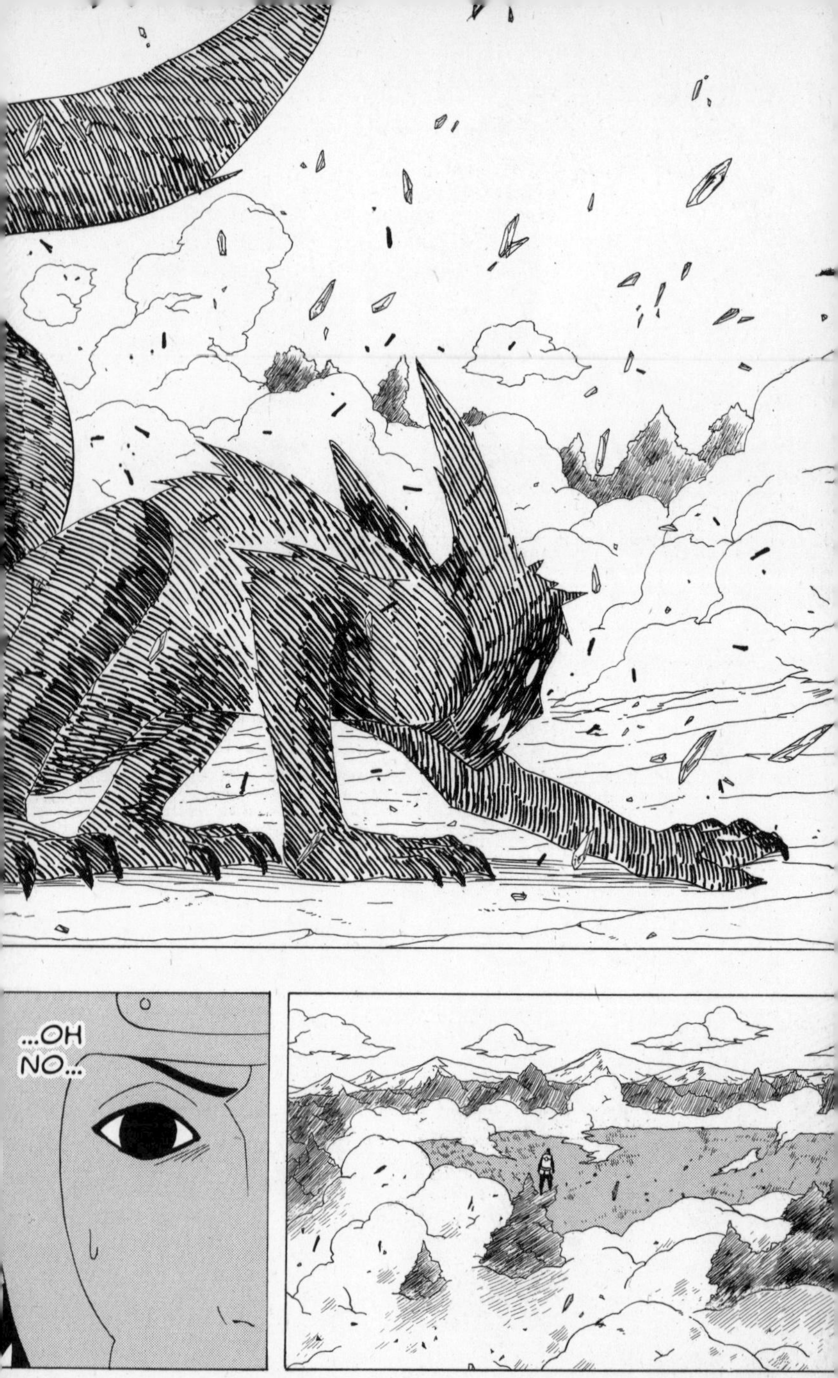
...OH NO...

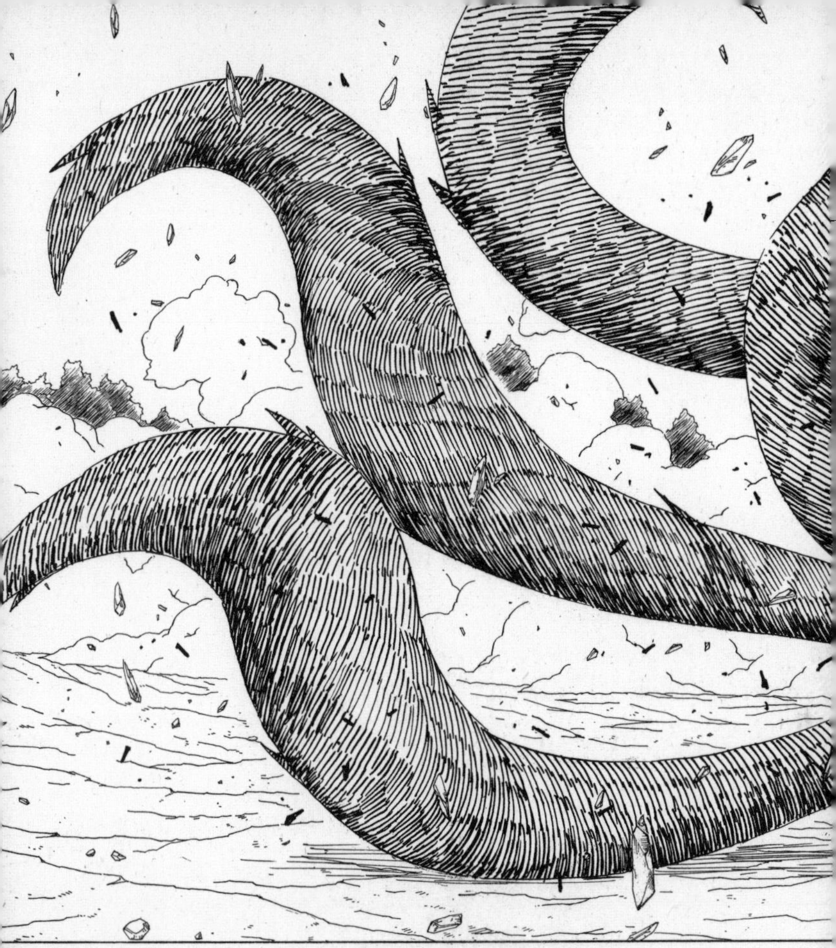

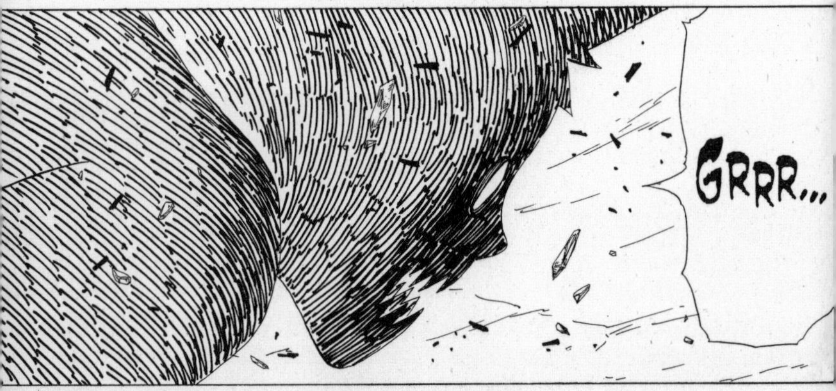
GRRR...

Number 294: The Fourth Tail...!!

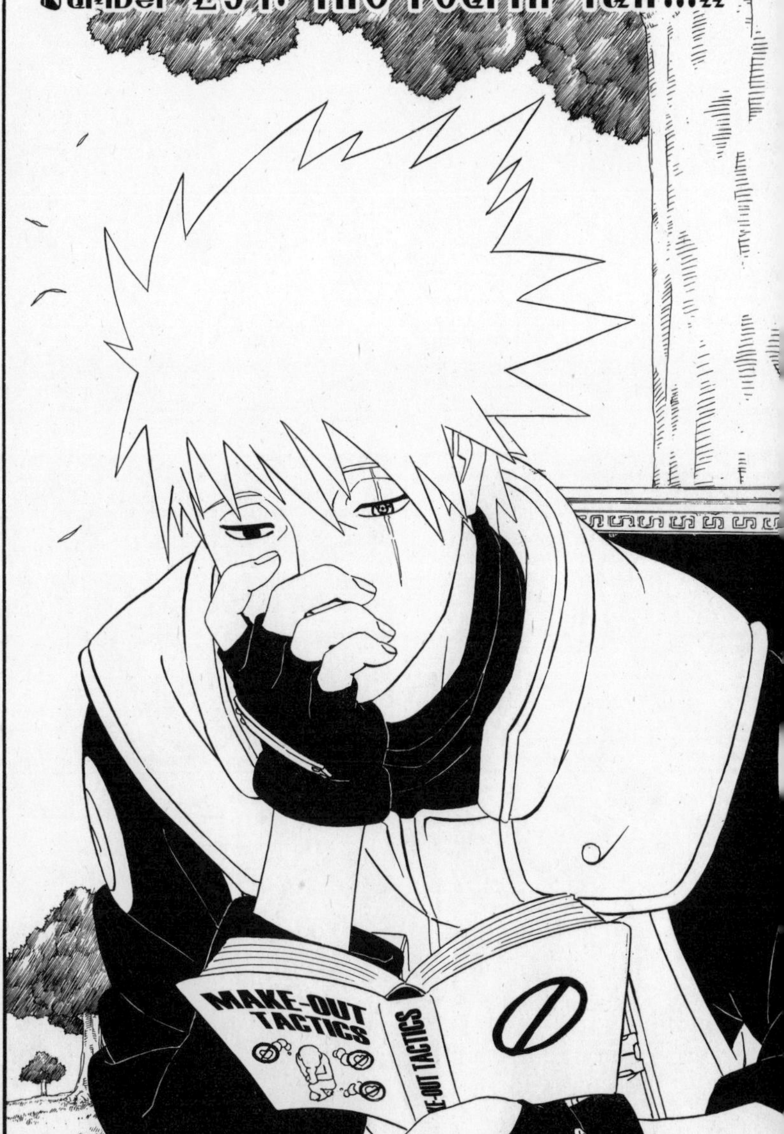
MAKE-OUT TACTICS

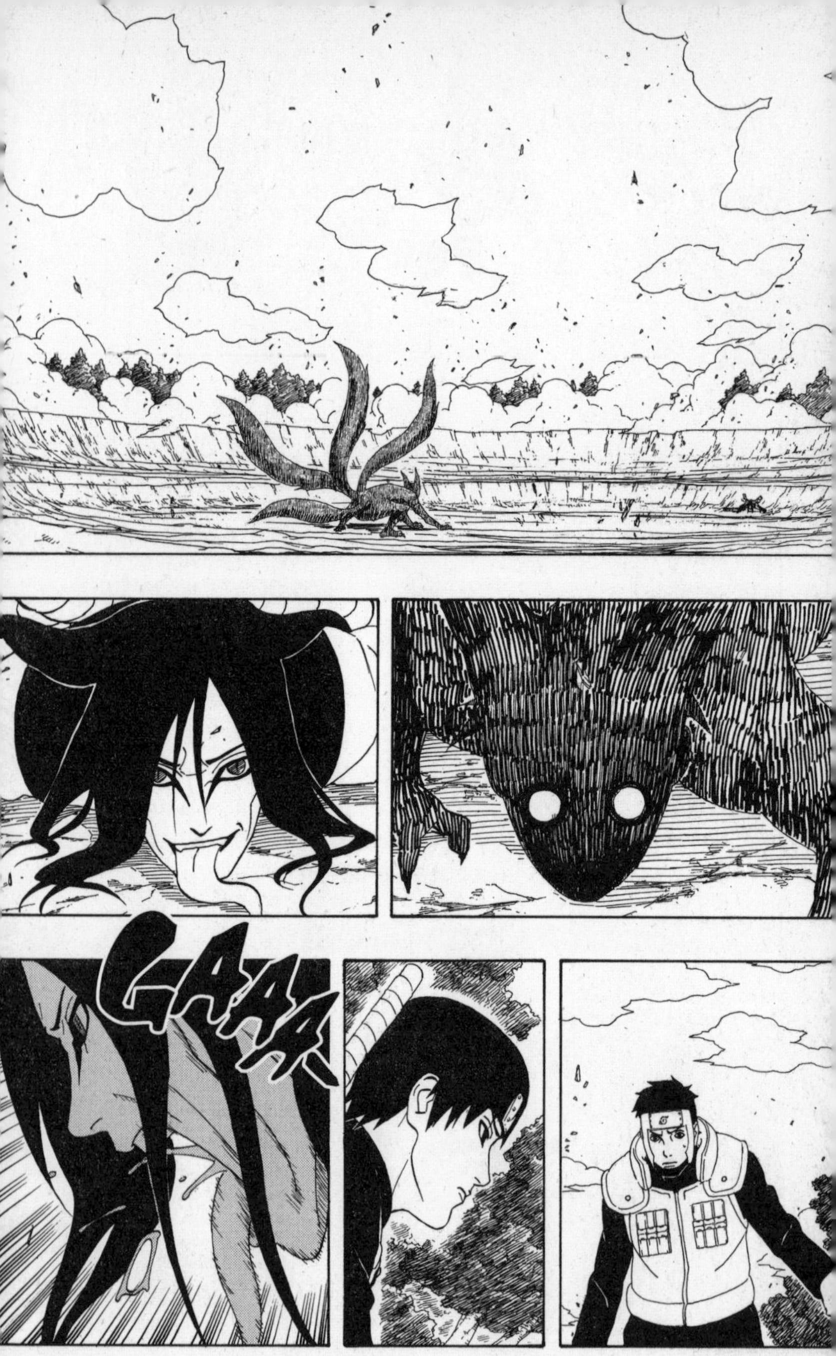
GAAA

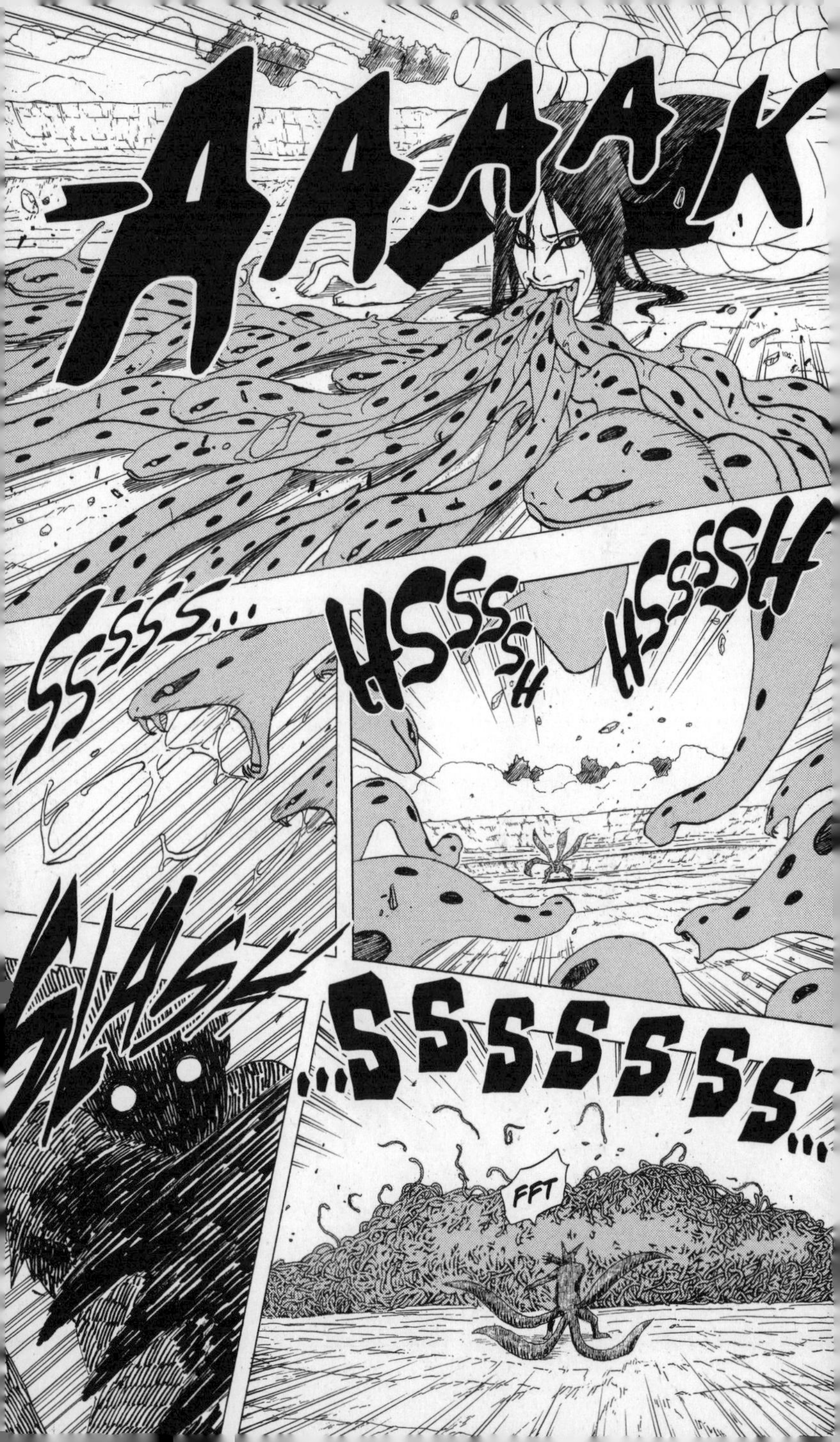
AAAAK
HSSSSH!
HSSSSSH
SSSSS...
...SSSSSSSS...
FFT

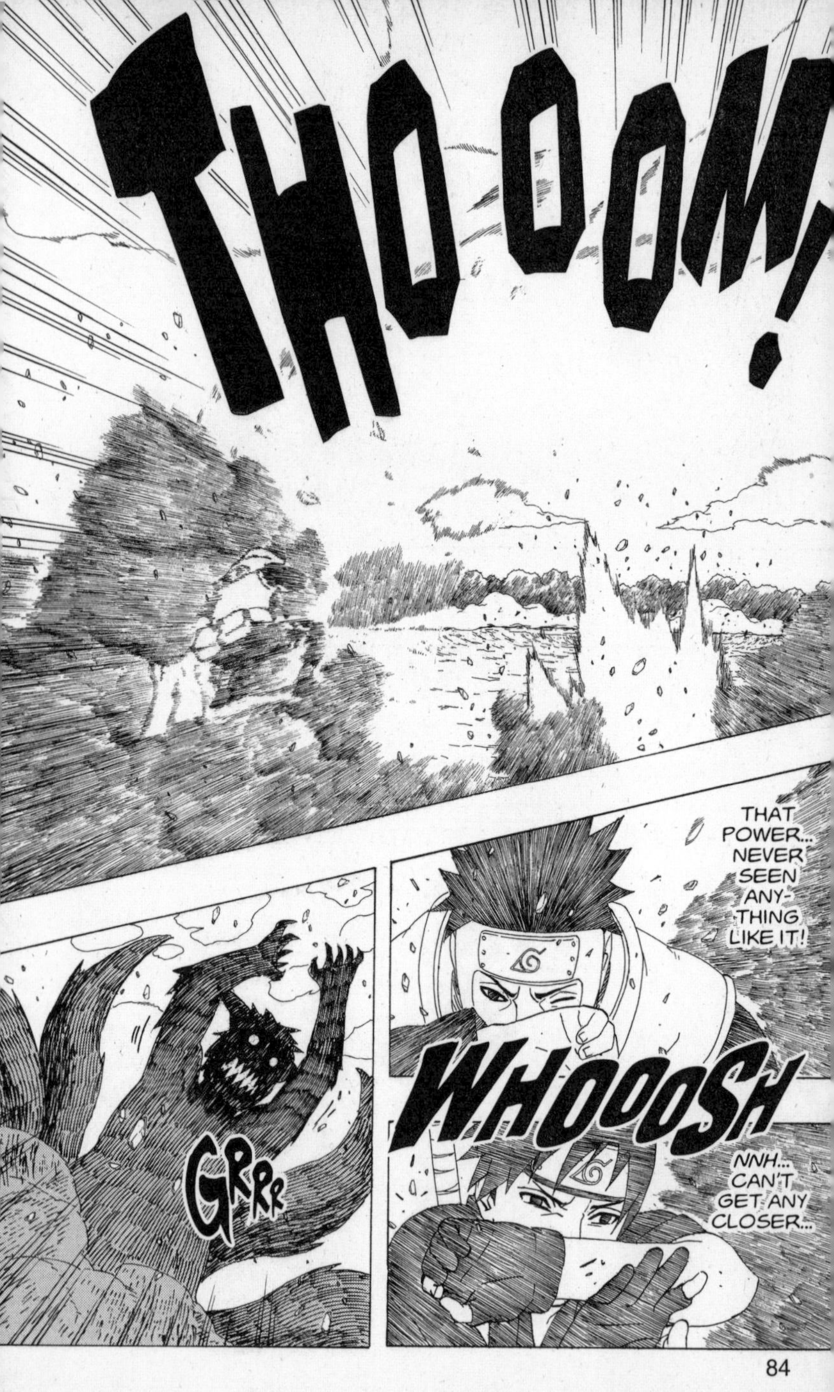
THOOOM!
THAT POWER... NEVER SEEN ANYTHING LIKE IT!
WHOOOSH
NNH... CAN'T GET ANY CLOSER...
GRRR

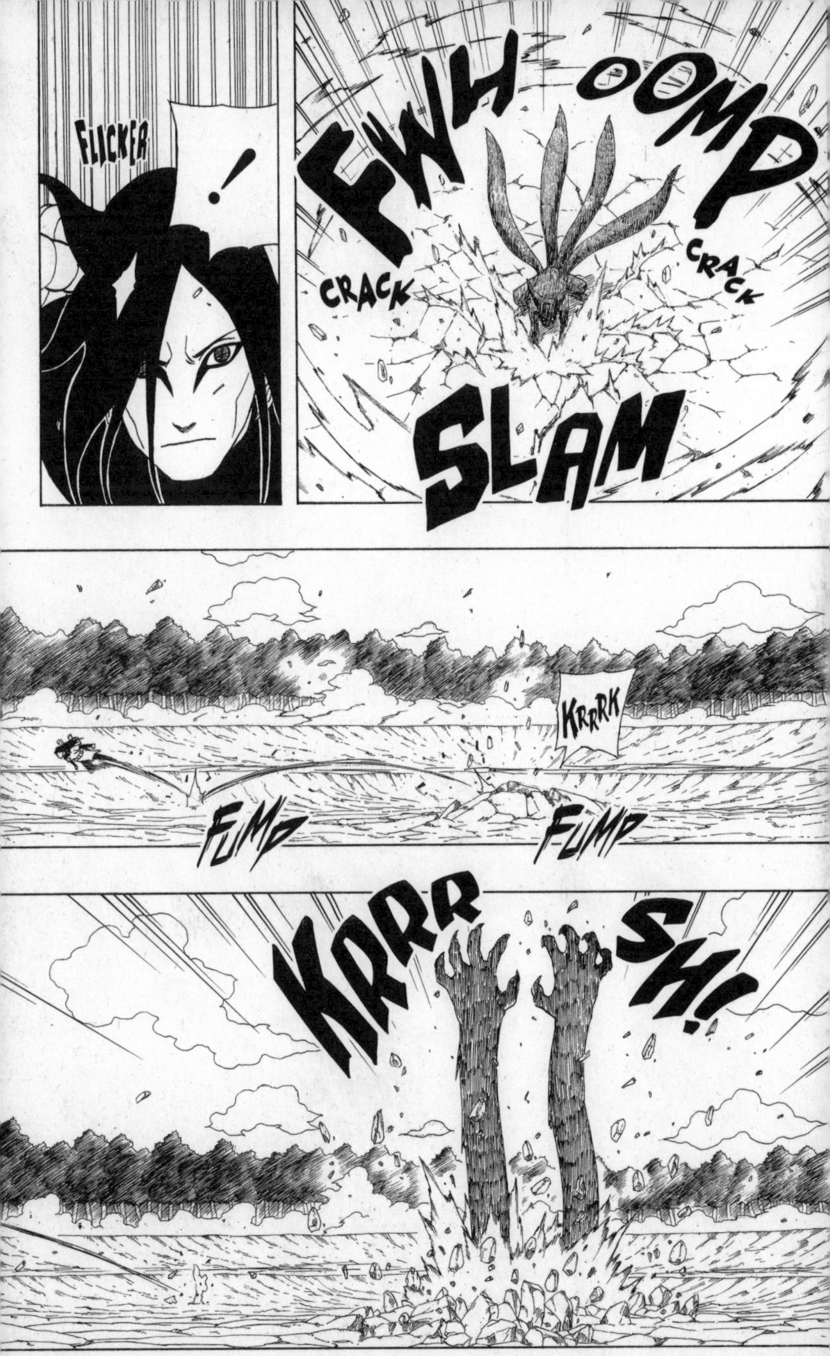
FWHOOMP
CRACK
CRACK
SLAM
FLICKER
!
KRRRK
FUMP
FUMP
KRRRSH!

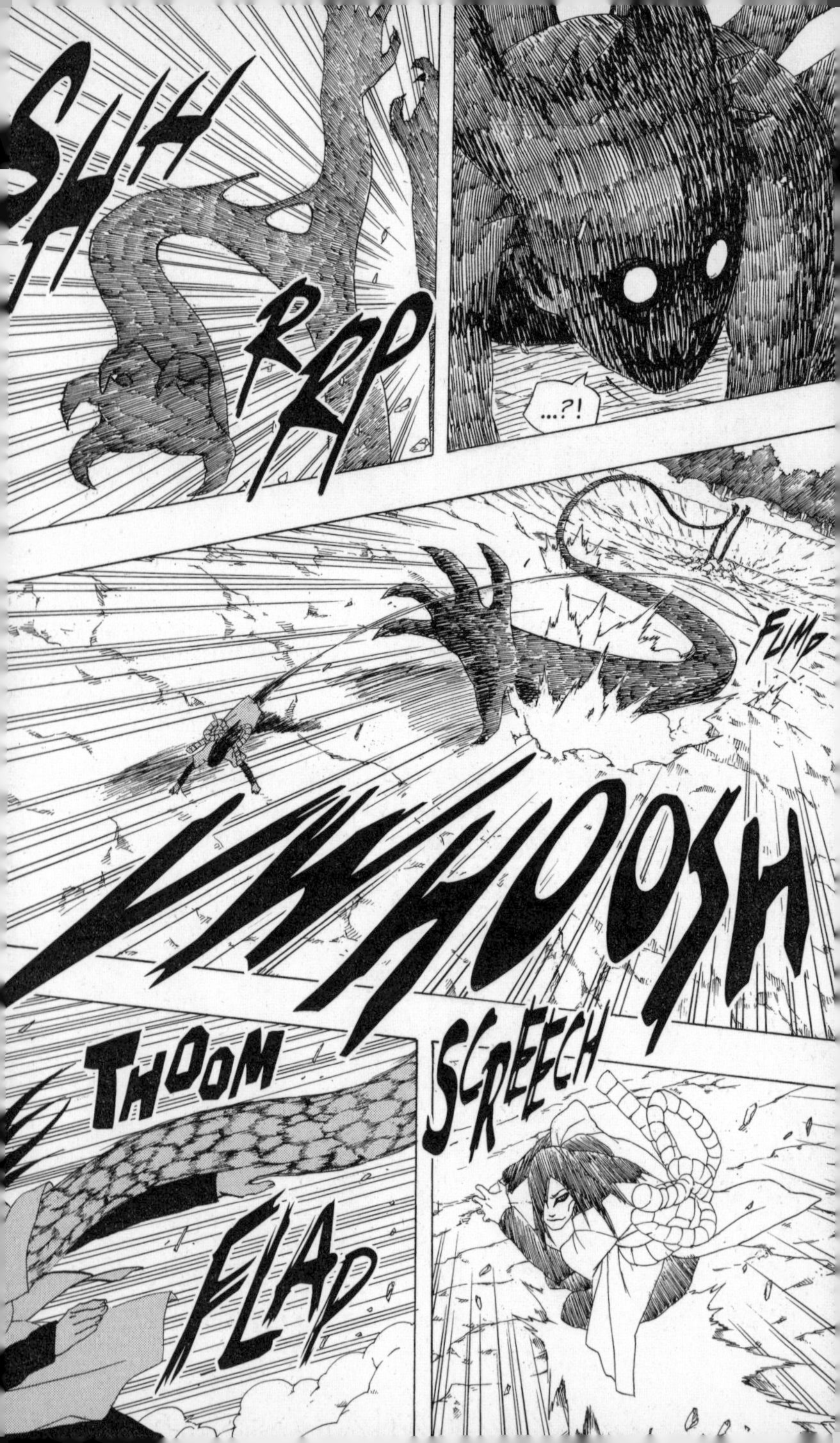
...?!
SHH
RAP
FUMP
WHOOSH
SCREECH
THOOM
FLAP

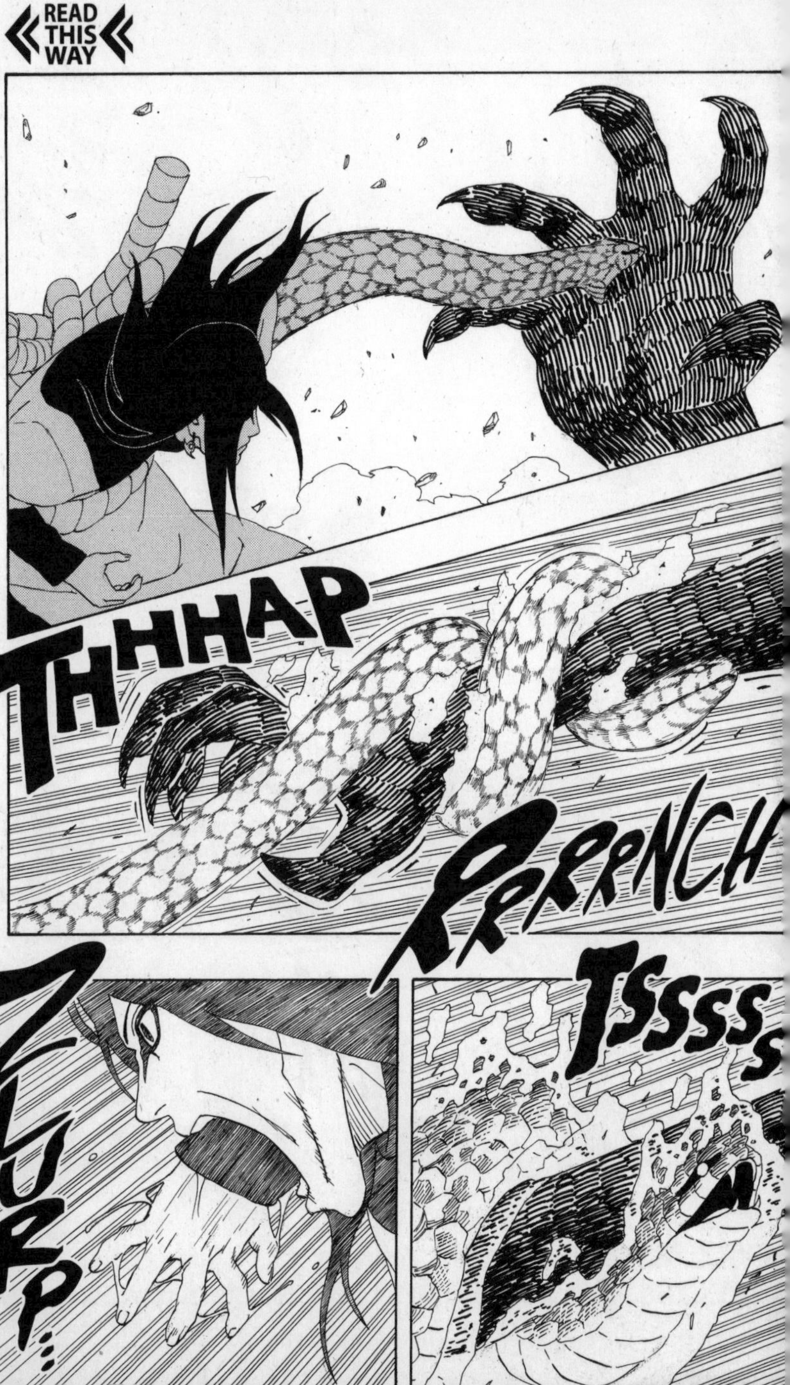
READ THIS WAY
THHHAP
RRRRRNCH
TSSSSS
SLLURP...

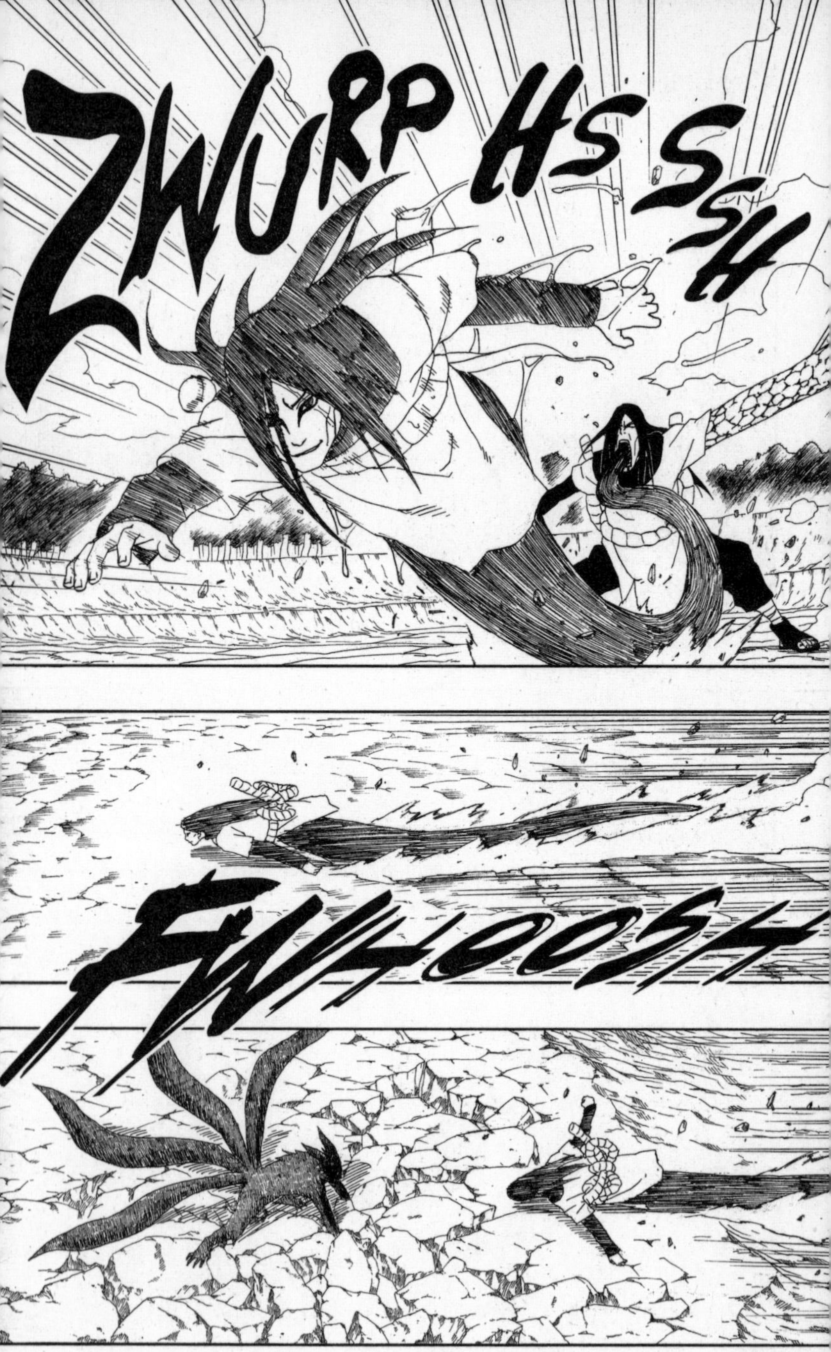
ZWURP
HSSSH
FWHOOSH

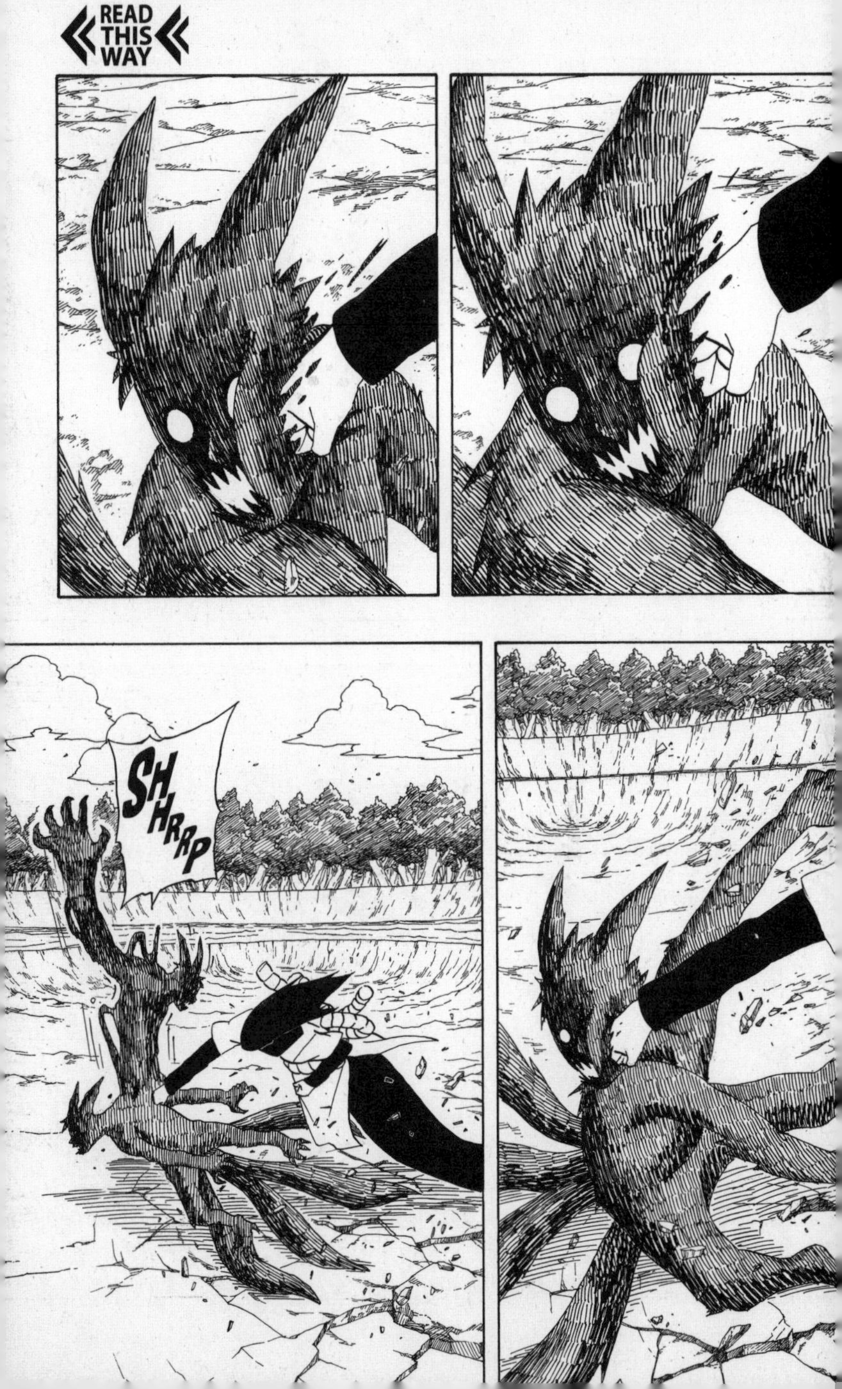
READ THIS WAY
SHHRRP

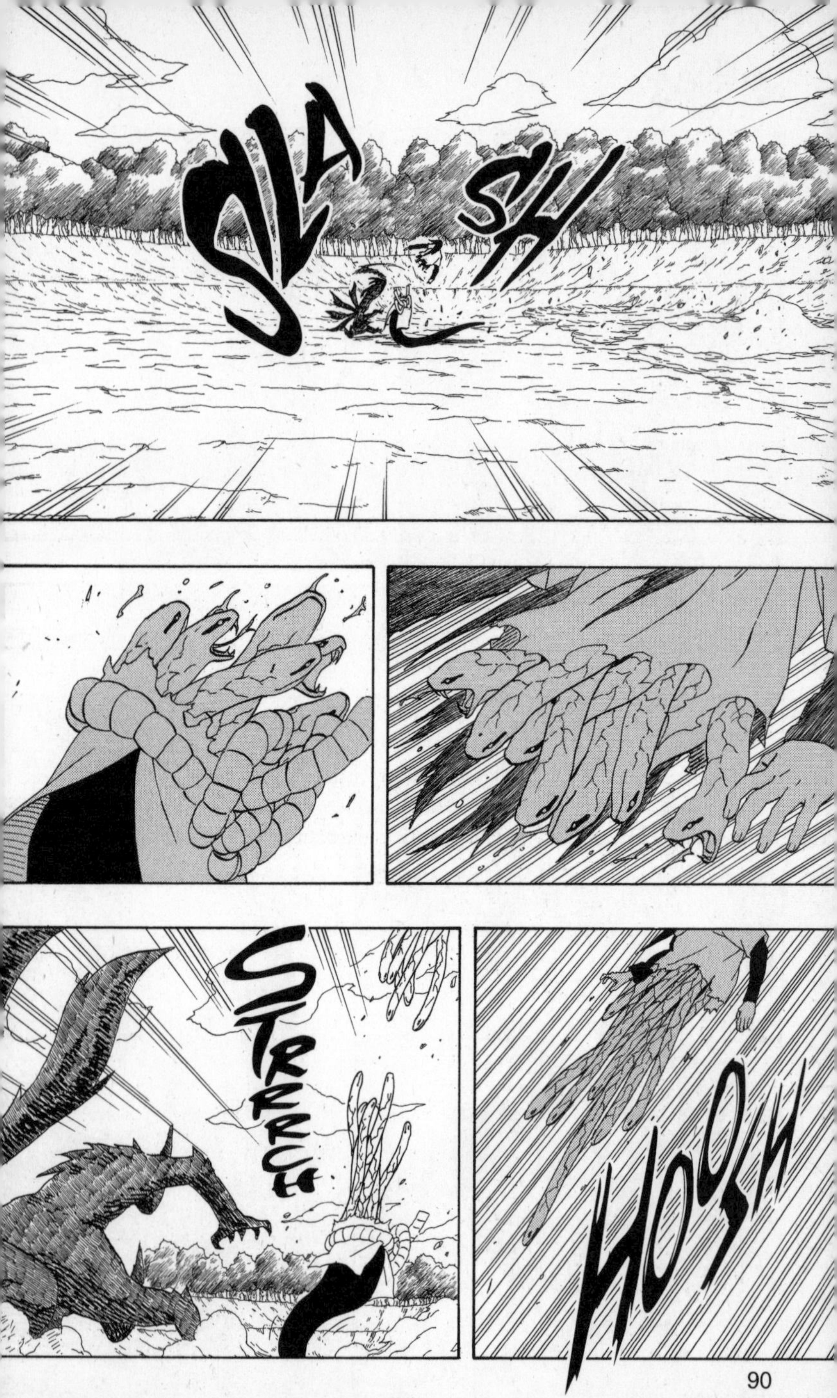
SLASH
HOOSH
STRRRCH

READ THIS WAY

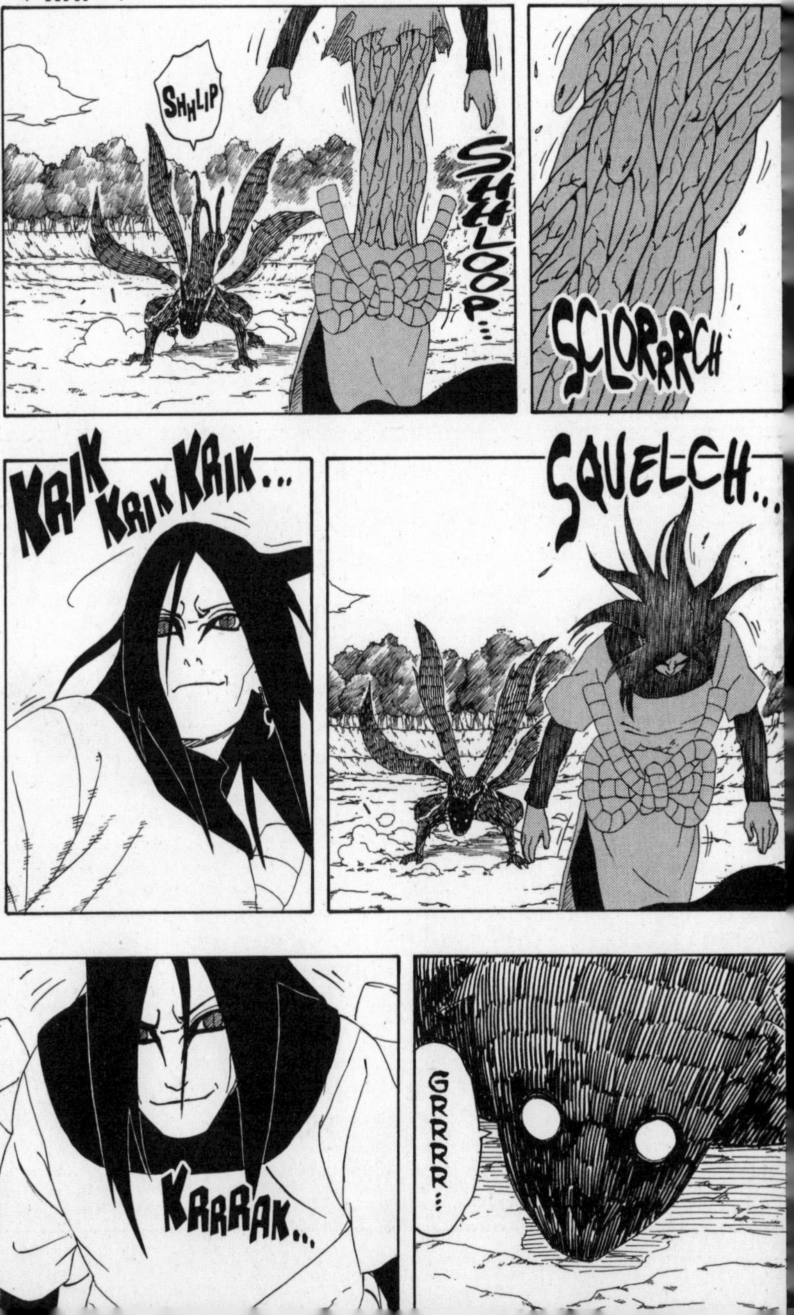
SCLORRRCH
SHHLIP
SHHHLOOP...
SQUELCH...
KRIK KRIK KRIK...
GRRRRR...
KRRRAK...

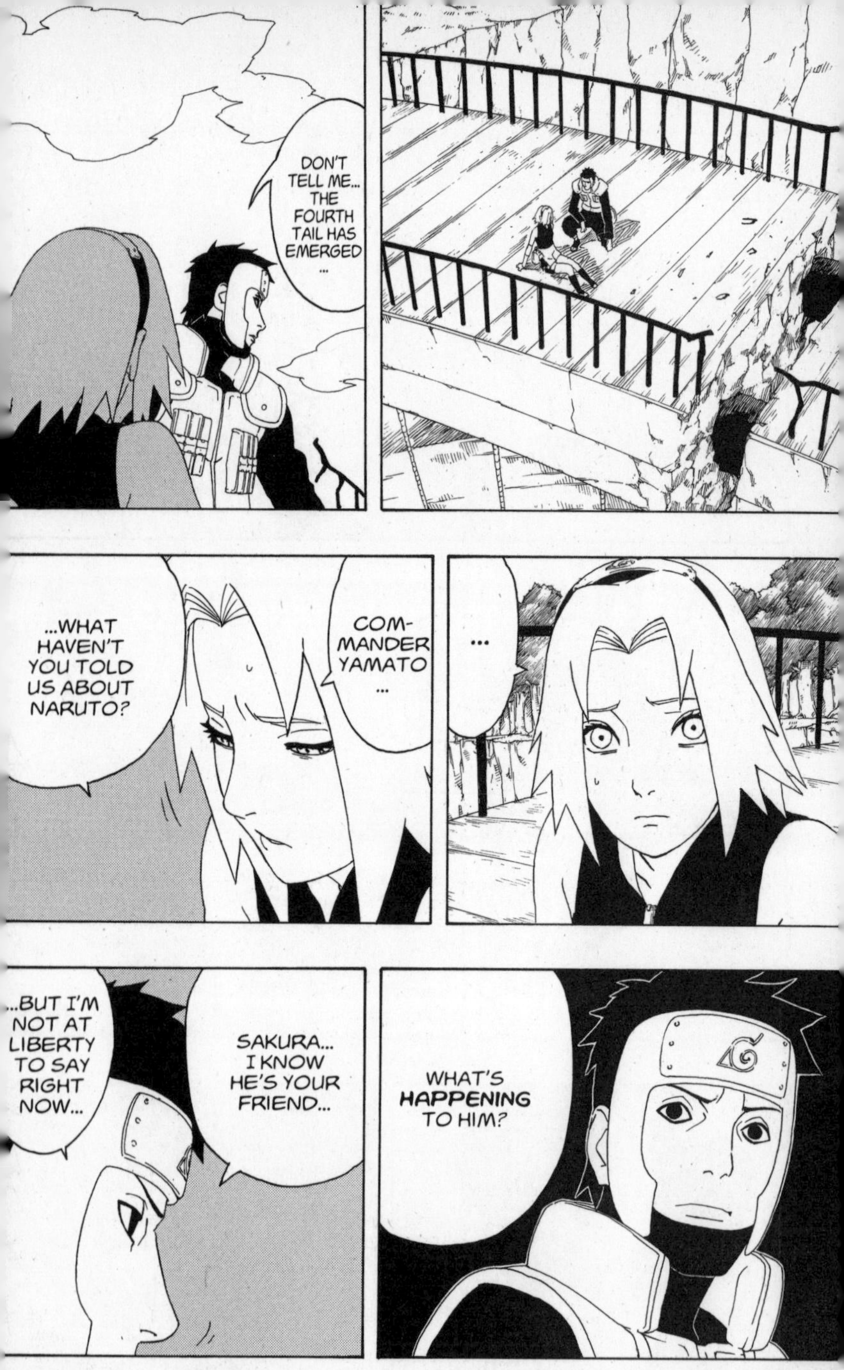
DON'T TELL ME... THE FOURTH TAIL HAS EMERGED ...
...
COM-MANDER YAMATO ...
...WHAT HAVEN'T YOU TOLD US ABOUT NARUTO?
WHAT'S **HAPPENING** TO HIM?
SAKURA... I KNOW HE'S YOUR FRIEND...
...BUT I'M NOT AT LIBERTY TO SAY RIGHT NOW...

READ THIS WAY

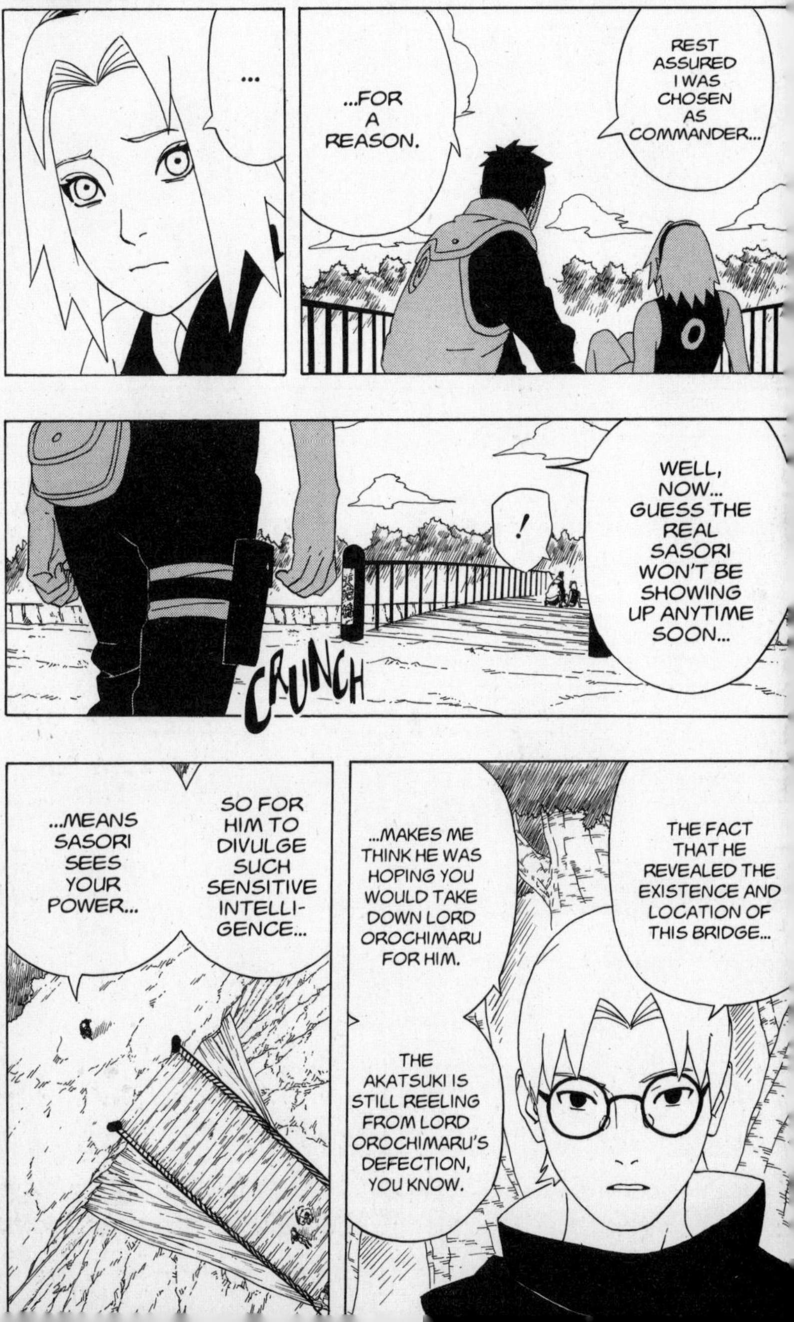
REST ASSURED I WAS CHOSEN AS COMMANDER...
...FOR A REASON.
...
WELL, NOW... GUESS THE REAL SASORI WON'T BE SHOWING UP ANYTIME SOON...
!
CRUNCH
THE FACT THAT HE REVEALED THE EXISTENCE AND LOCATION OF THIS BRIDGE...
...MAKES ME THINK HE WAS HOPING YOU WOULD TAKE DOWN LORD OROCHIMARU FOR HIM.
THE AKATSUKI IS STILL REELING FROM LORD OROCHIMARU'S DEFECTION, YOU KNOW.
SO FOR HIM TO DIVULGE SUCH SENSITIVE INTELLIGENCE...
...MEANS SASORI SEES YOUR POWER...

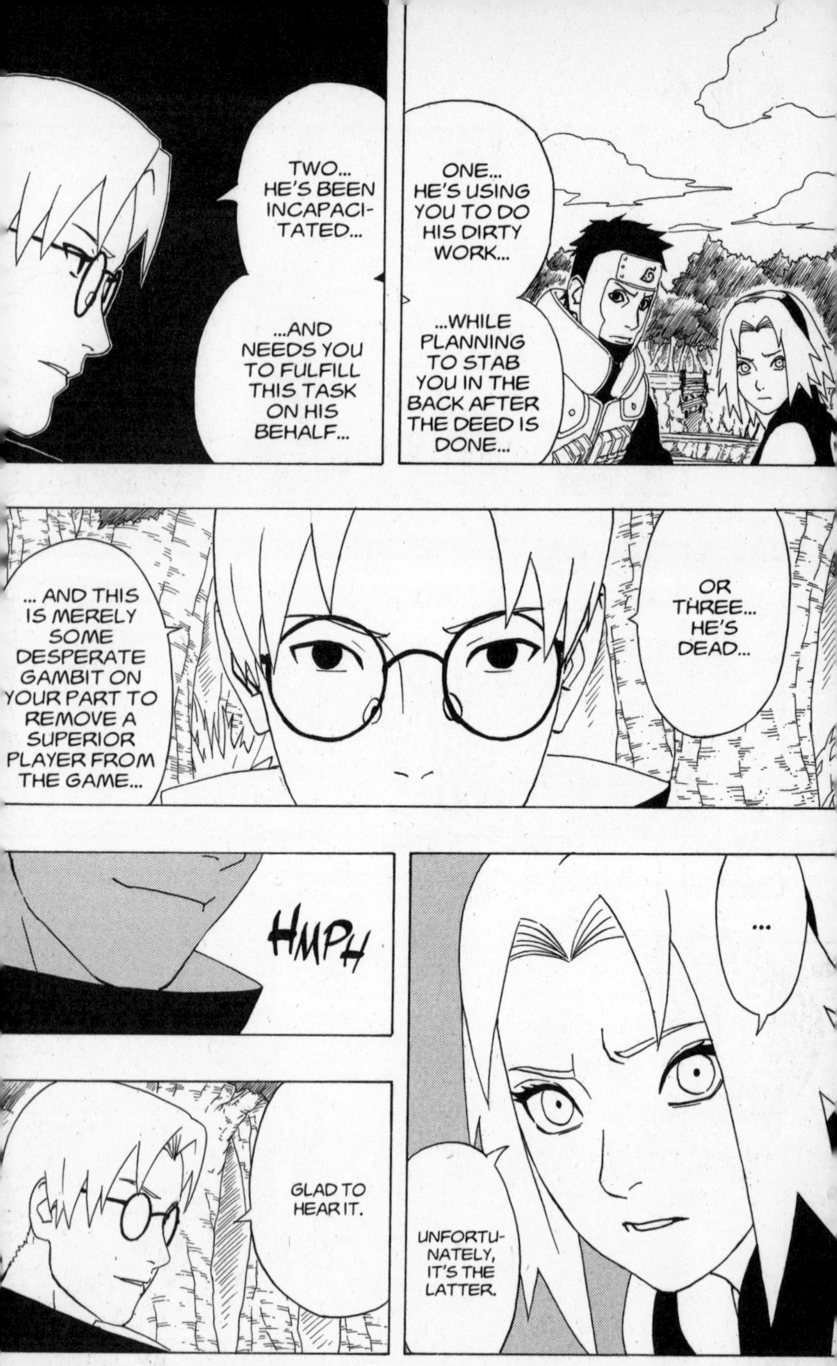
ONE... HE'S USING YOU TO DO HIS DIRTY WORK...
...WHILE PLANNING TO STAB YOU IN THE BACK AFTER THE DEED IS DONE...
TWO... HE'S BEEN INCAPACI-TATED...
...AND NEEDS YOU TO FULFILL THIS TASK ON HIS BEHALF...
OR THREE... HE'S DEAD...
... AND THIS IS MERELY SOME DESPERATE GAMBIT ON YOUR PART TO REMOVE A SUPERIOR PLAYER FROM THE GAME...
...
UNFORTU-NATELY, IT'S THE LATTER.
HMPH
GLAD TO HEAR IT.

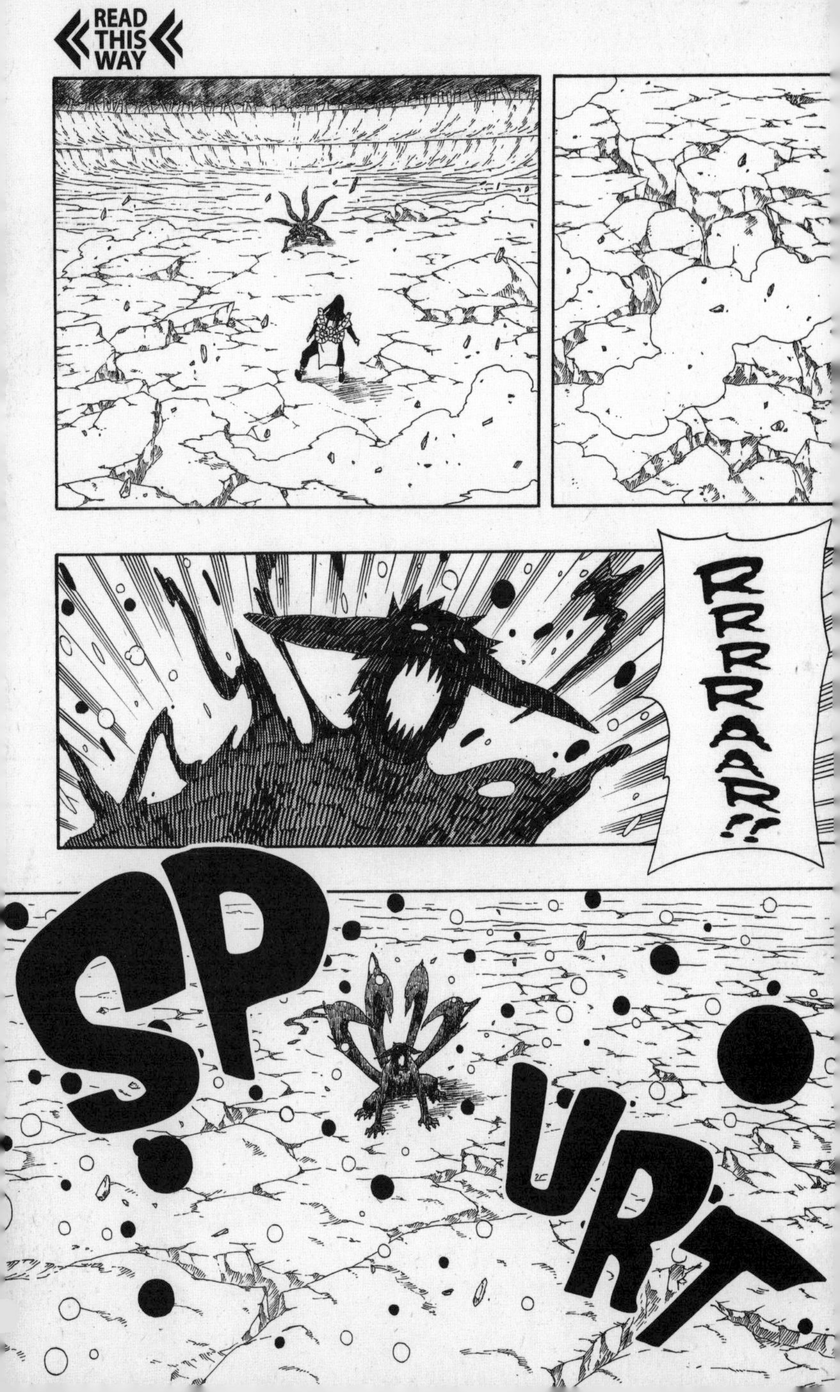

READ THIS WAY
RRRRAAR!?
SPURT

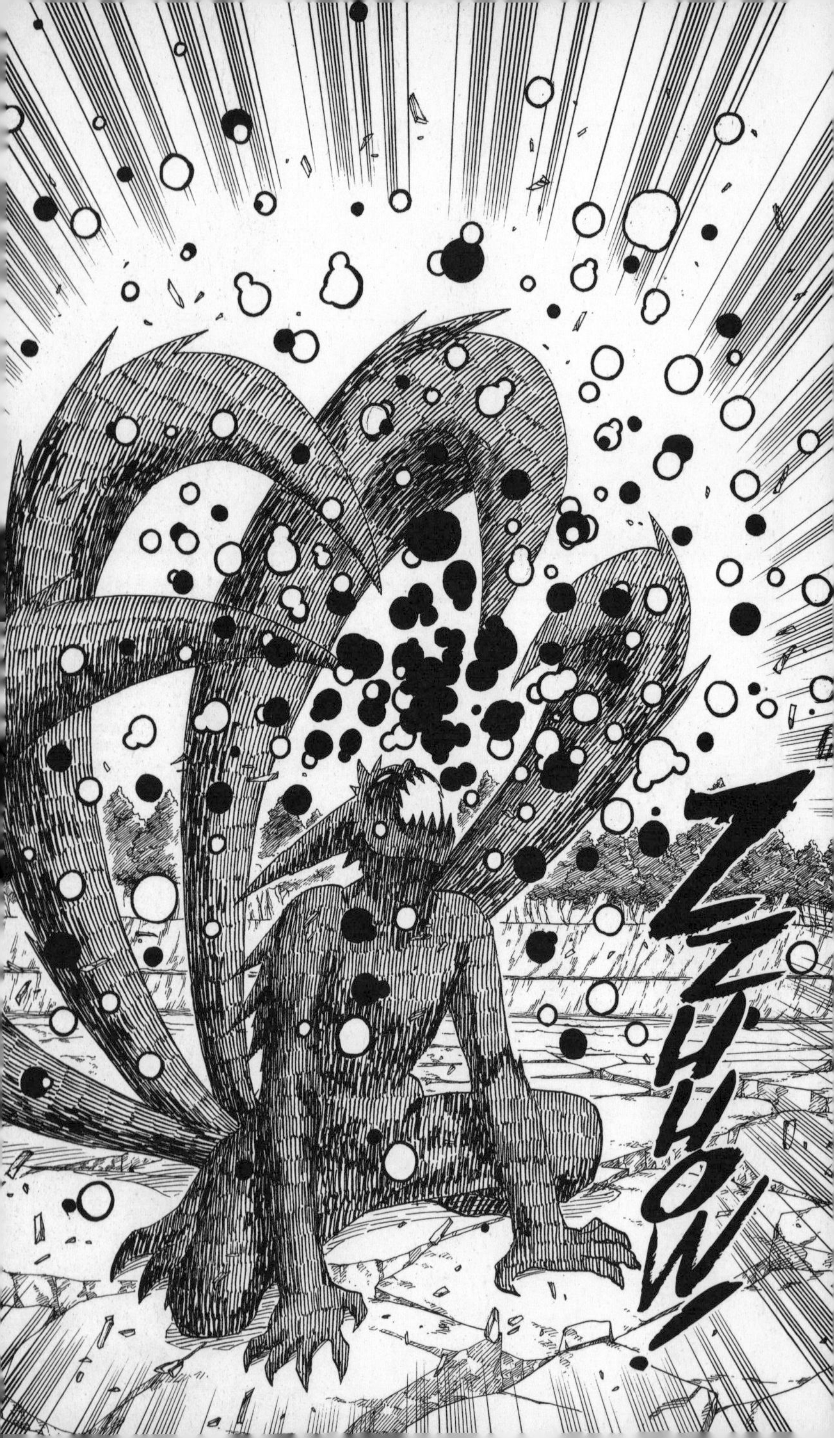
ZZHHOOM!

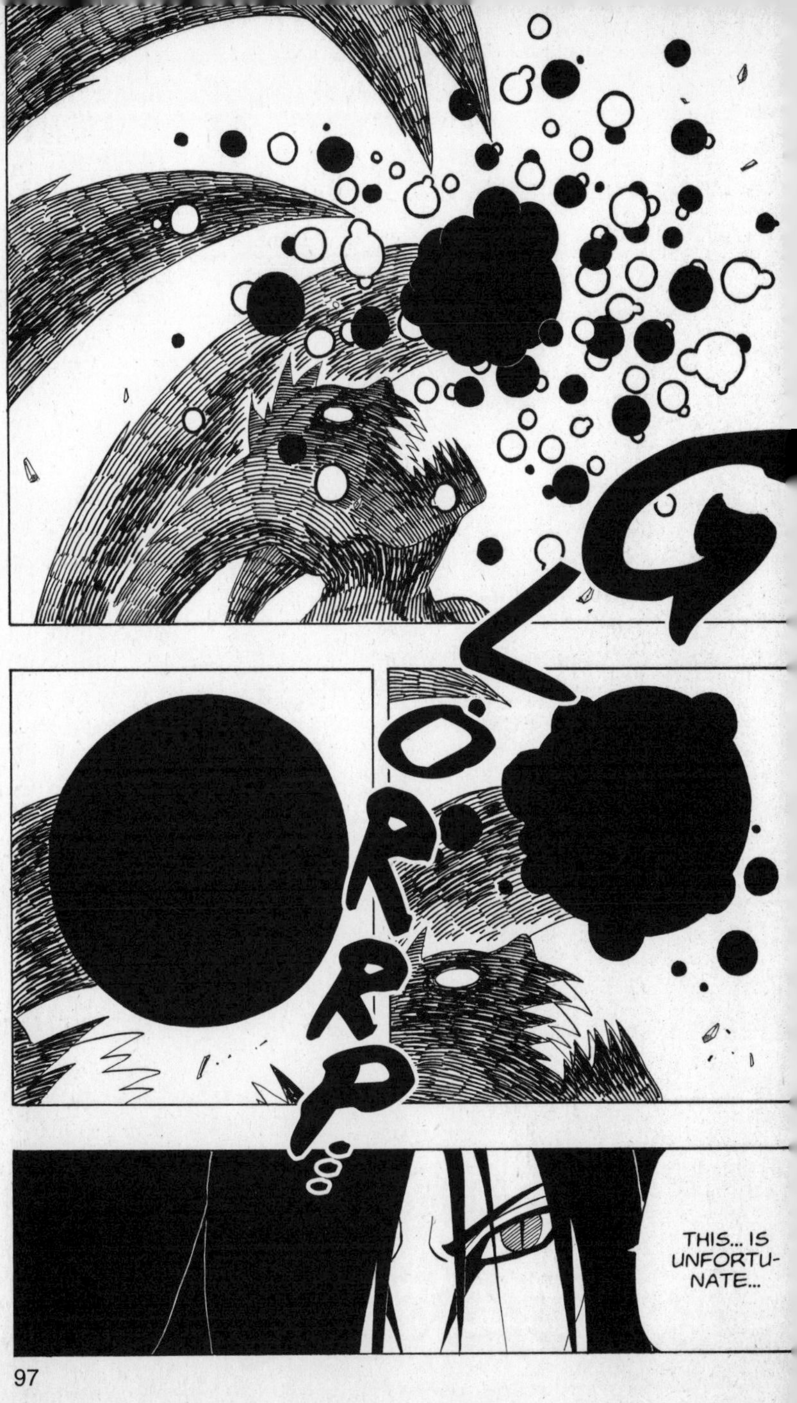
THIS... IS UNFORTU-NATE...

NARUTO

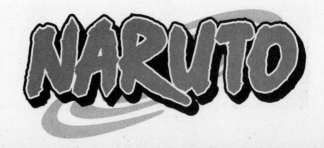

Number 295: Toward Nine Tails...!!

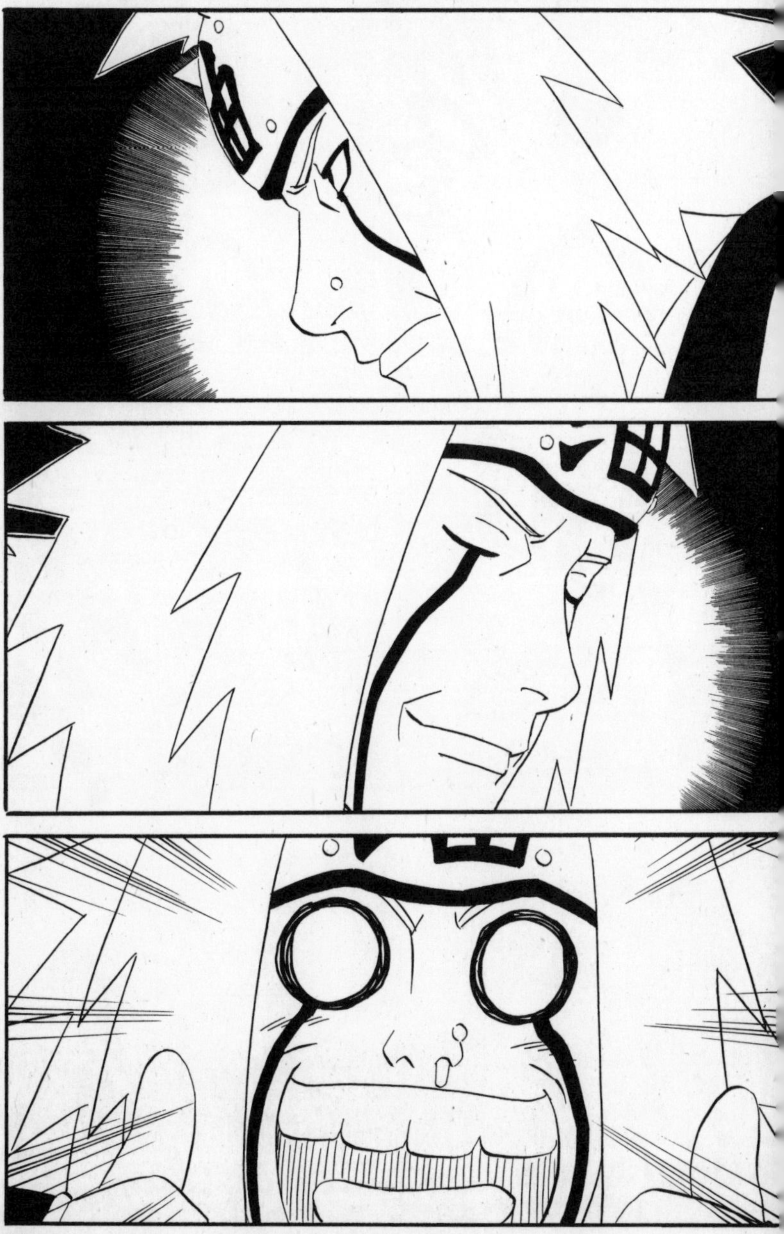

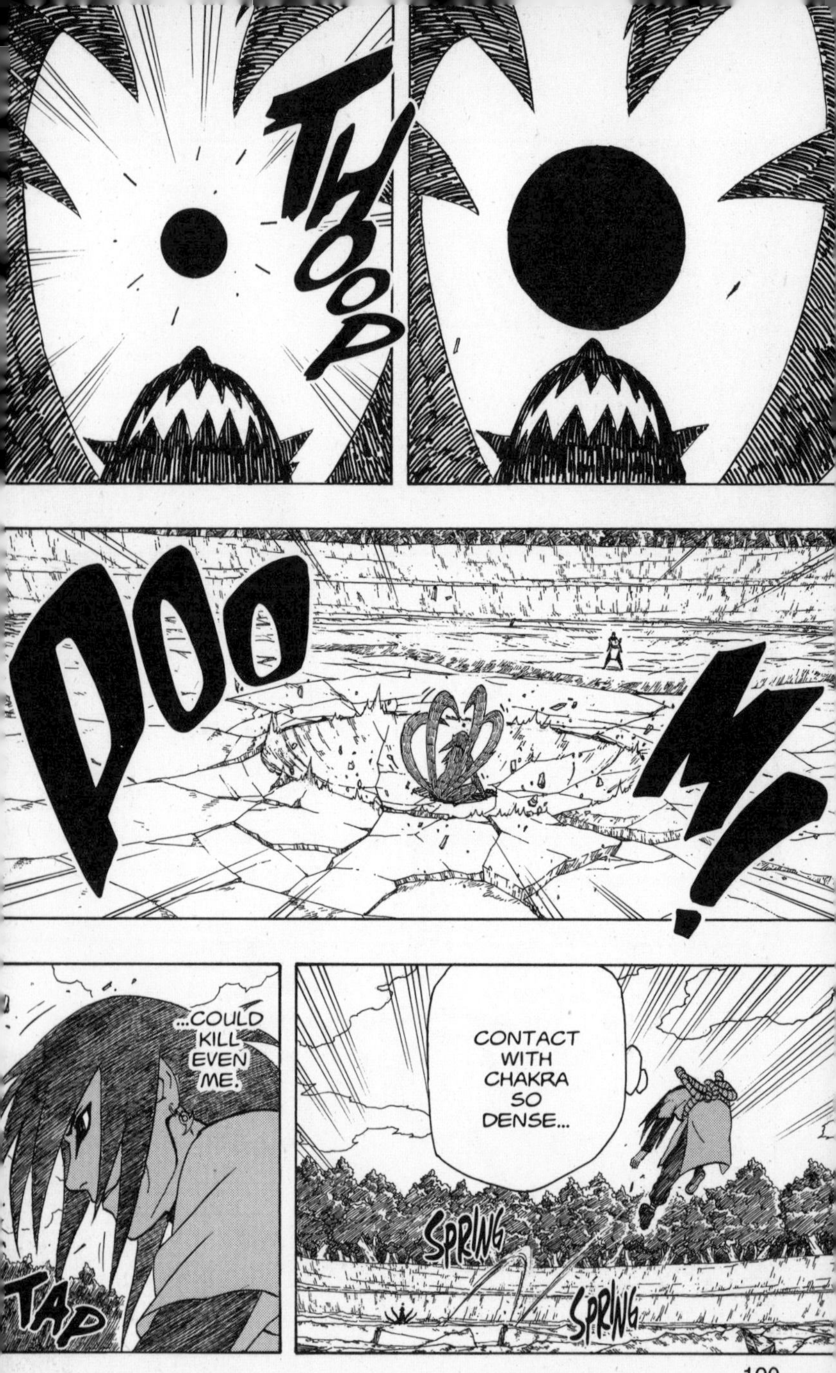
THOOOP
DOOOM!
CONTACT WITH CHAKRA SO DENSE...
SPRING
SPRING
...COULD KILL EVEN ME.
TAP

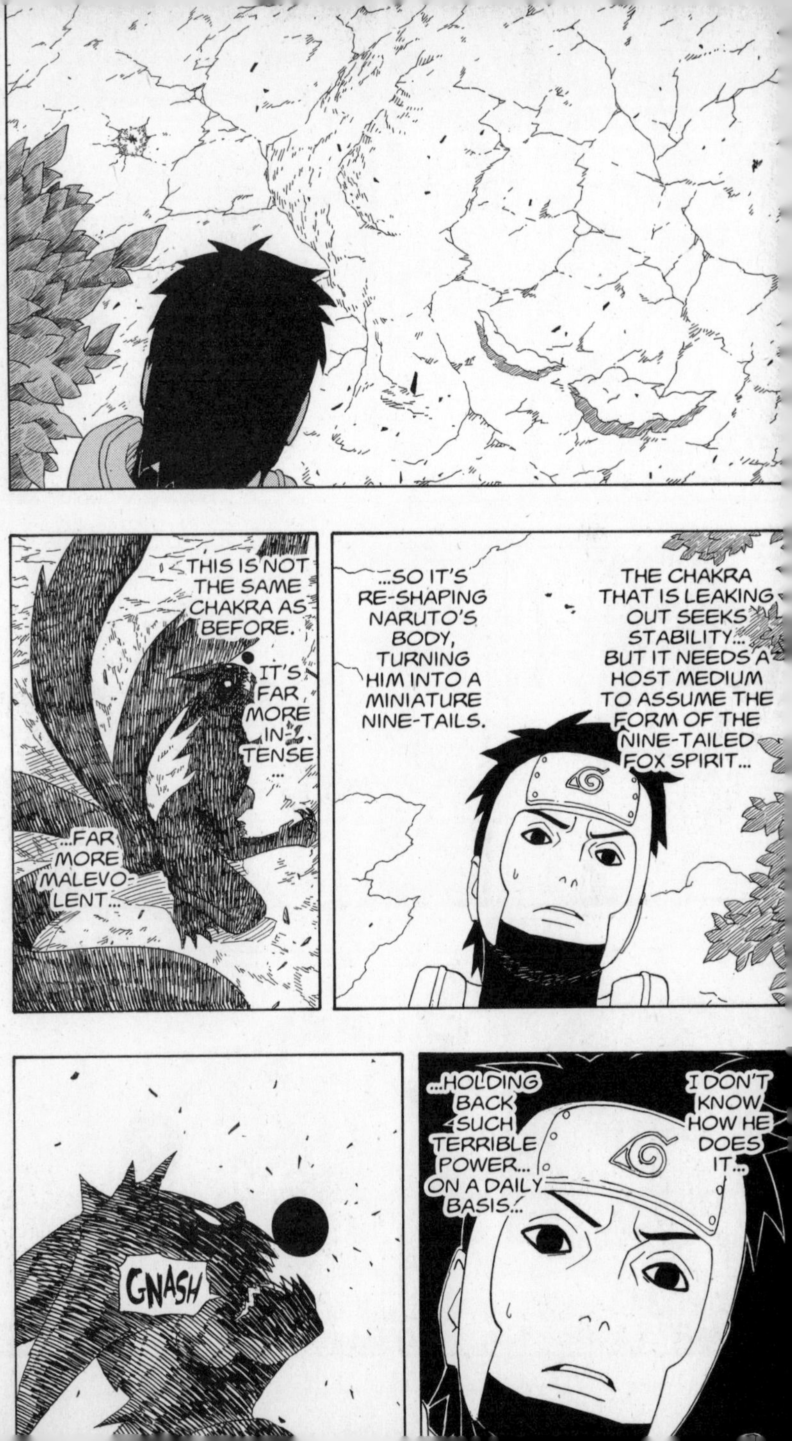
THE CHAKRA THAT IS LEAKING OUT SEEKS STABILITY... BUT IT NEEDS A HOST MEDIUM TO ASSUME THE FORM OF THE NINE-TAILED FOX SPIRIT...
...SO IT'S RE-SHAPING NARUTO'S BODY, TURNING HIM INTO A MINIATURE NINE-TAILS.
THIS IS NOT THE SAME CHAKRA AS BEFORE.
IT'S FAR MORE IN-TENSE...
...FAR MORE MALEVO-LENT...
I DON'T KNOW HOW HE DOES IT...
...HOLDING BACK SUCH TERRIBLE POWER... ON A DAILY BASIS...
GNASH

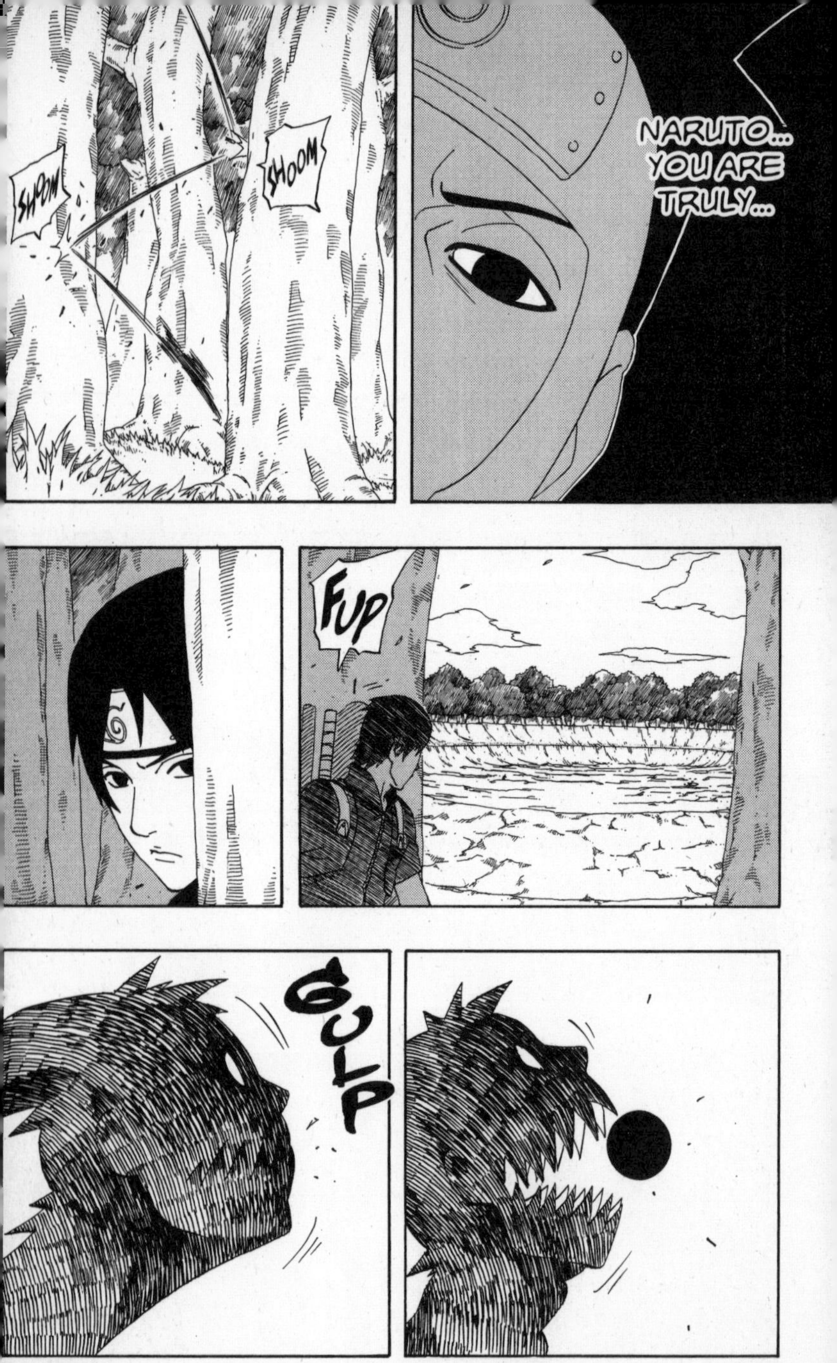
NARUTO... YOU ARE TRULY...
SHOOM
SHOOM
FUP
GULP

READ THIS WAY

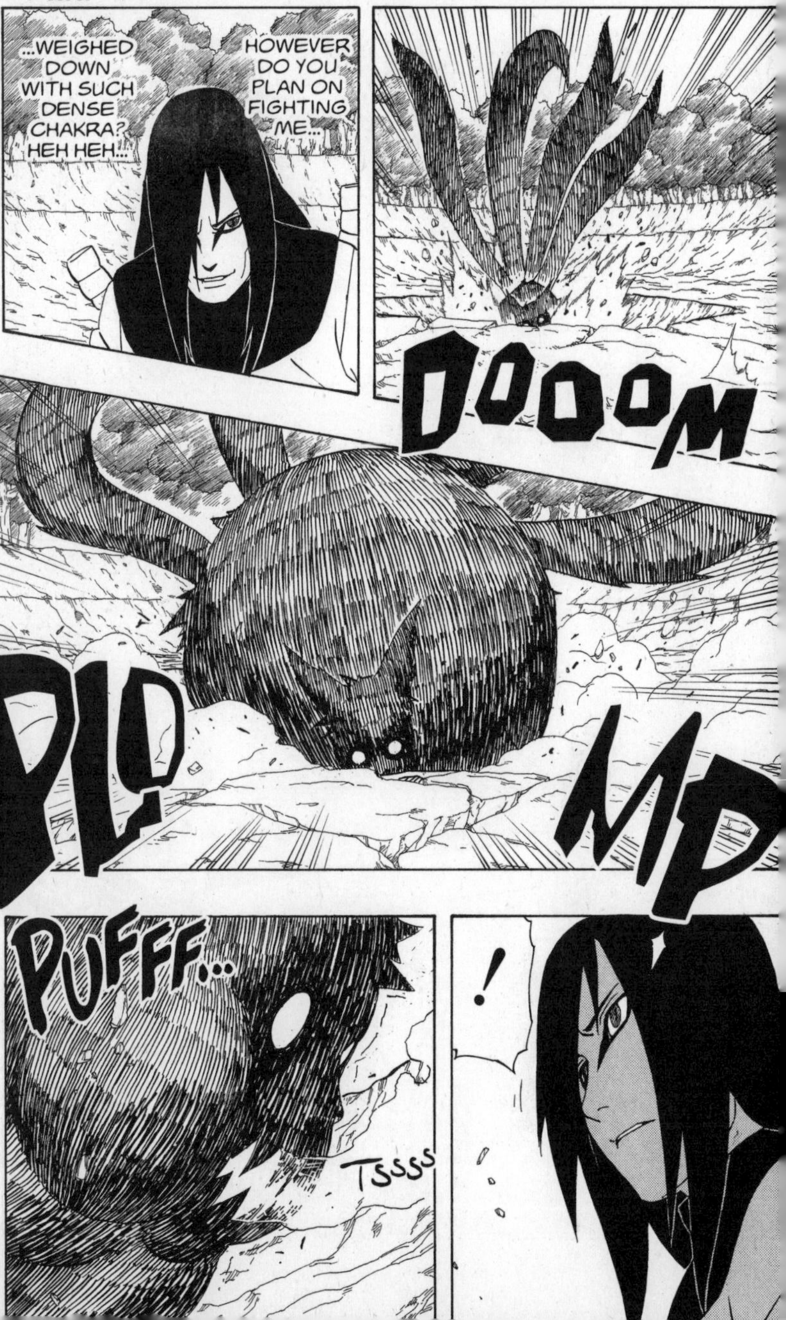

DOOOM
HOWEVER DO YOU PLAN ON FIGHTING ME...
...WEIGHED DOWN WITH SUCH DENSE CHAKRA? HEH HEH...
PLOMP
!
PUFFF...
Tssss

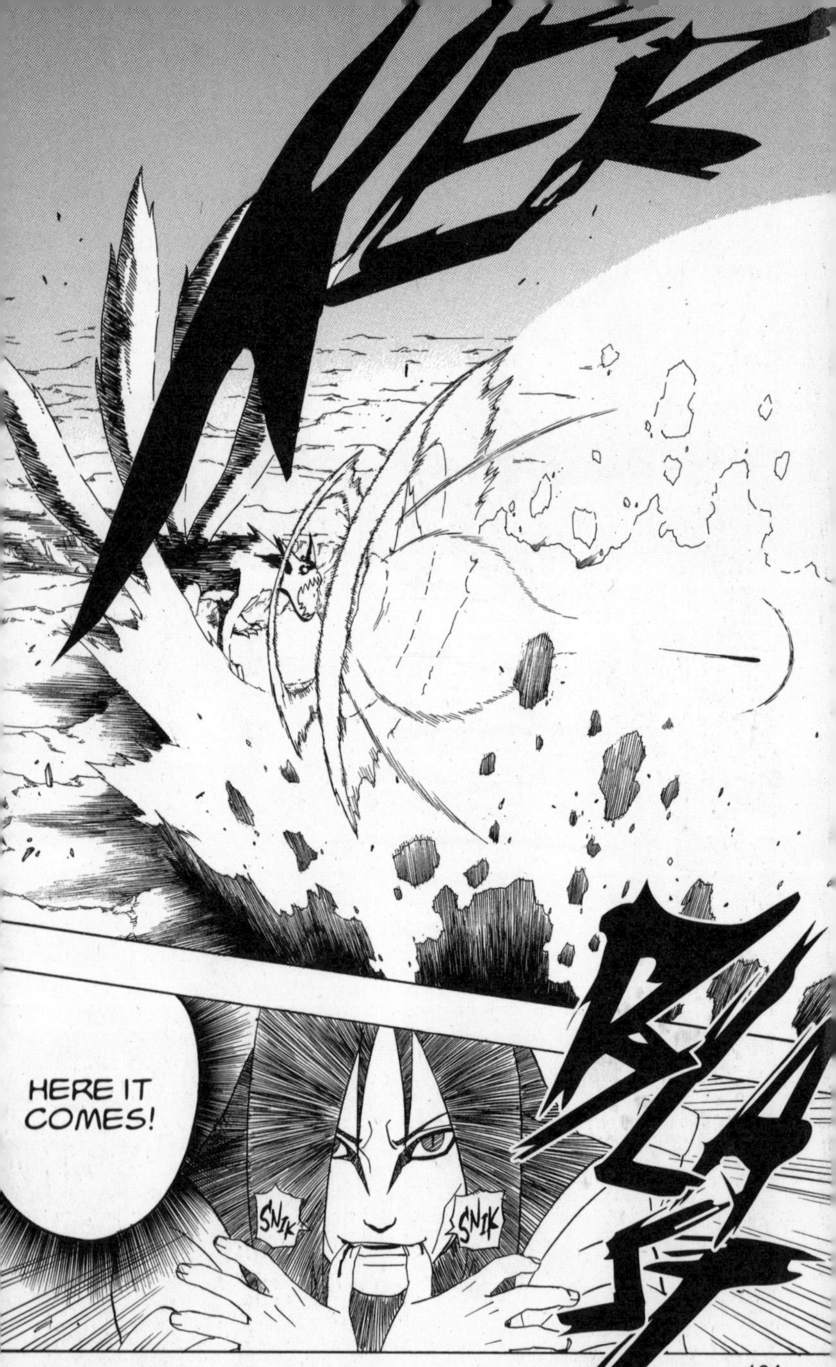
HERE IT COMES!
SNIK
SNIK

READ THIS WAY

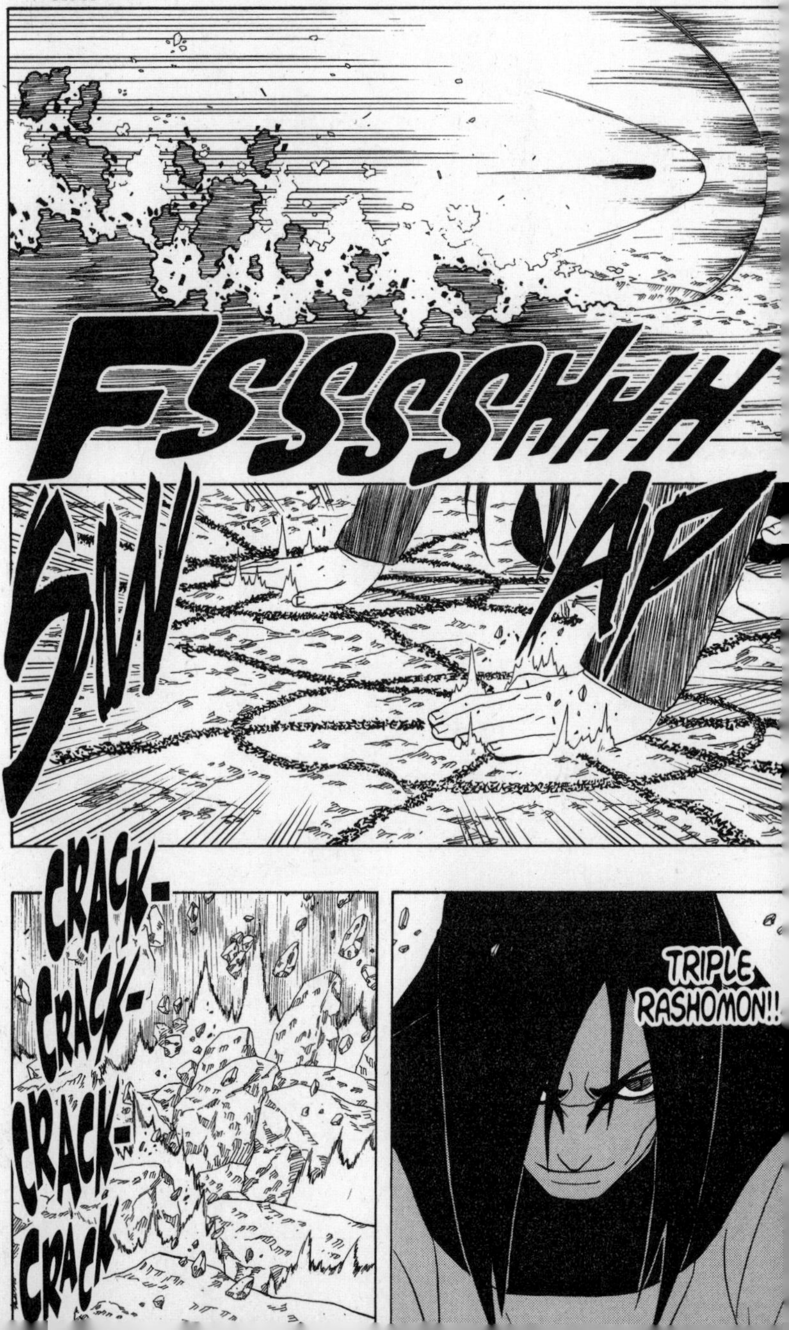
FSSSSHHH
TRIPLE RASHOMON!!
CRACK-CRACK-CRACK-CRACK

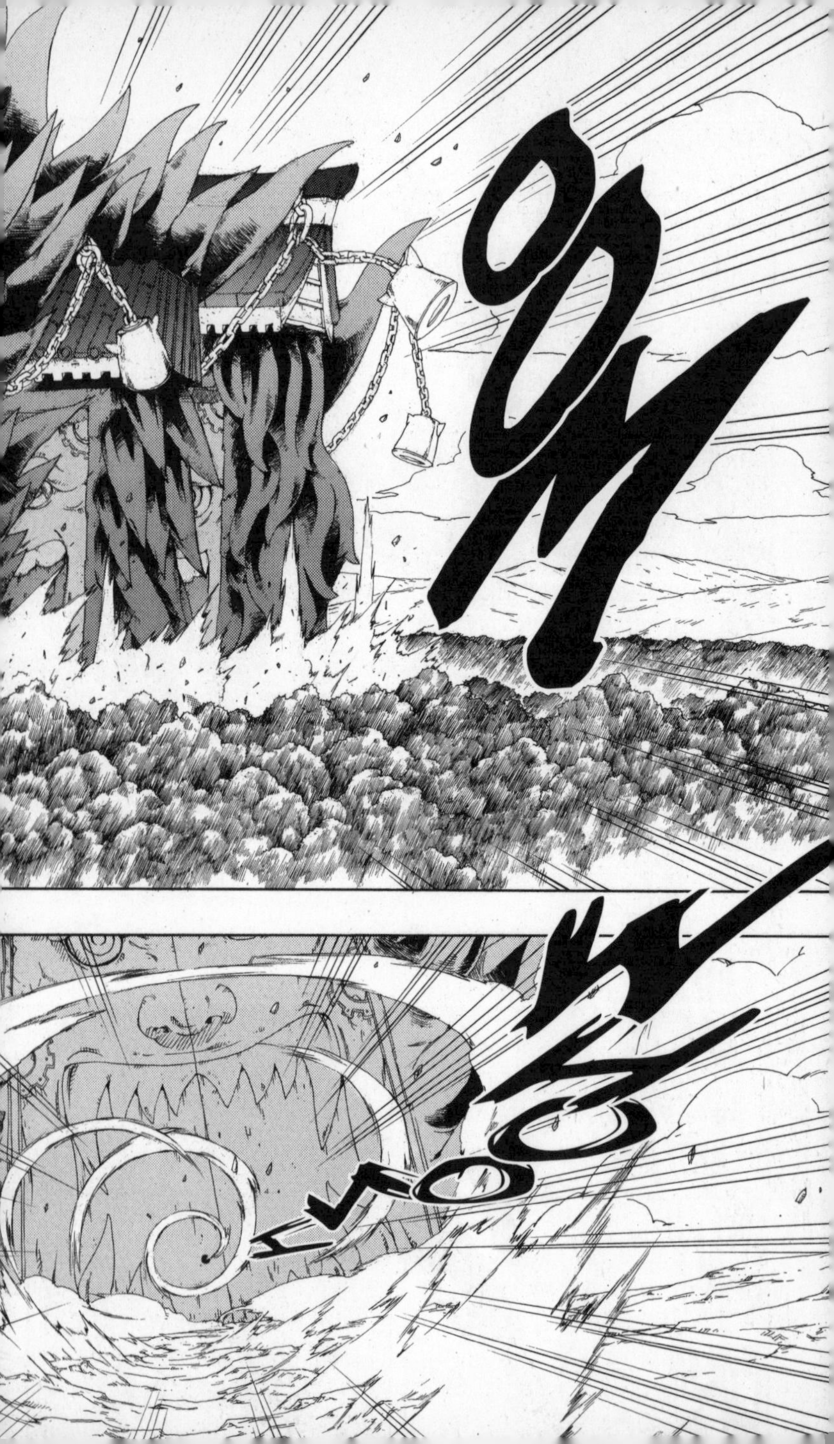

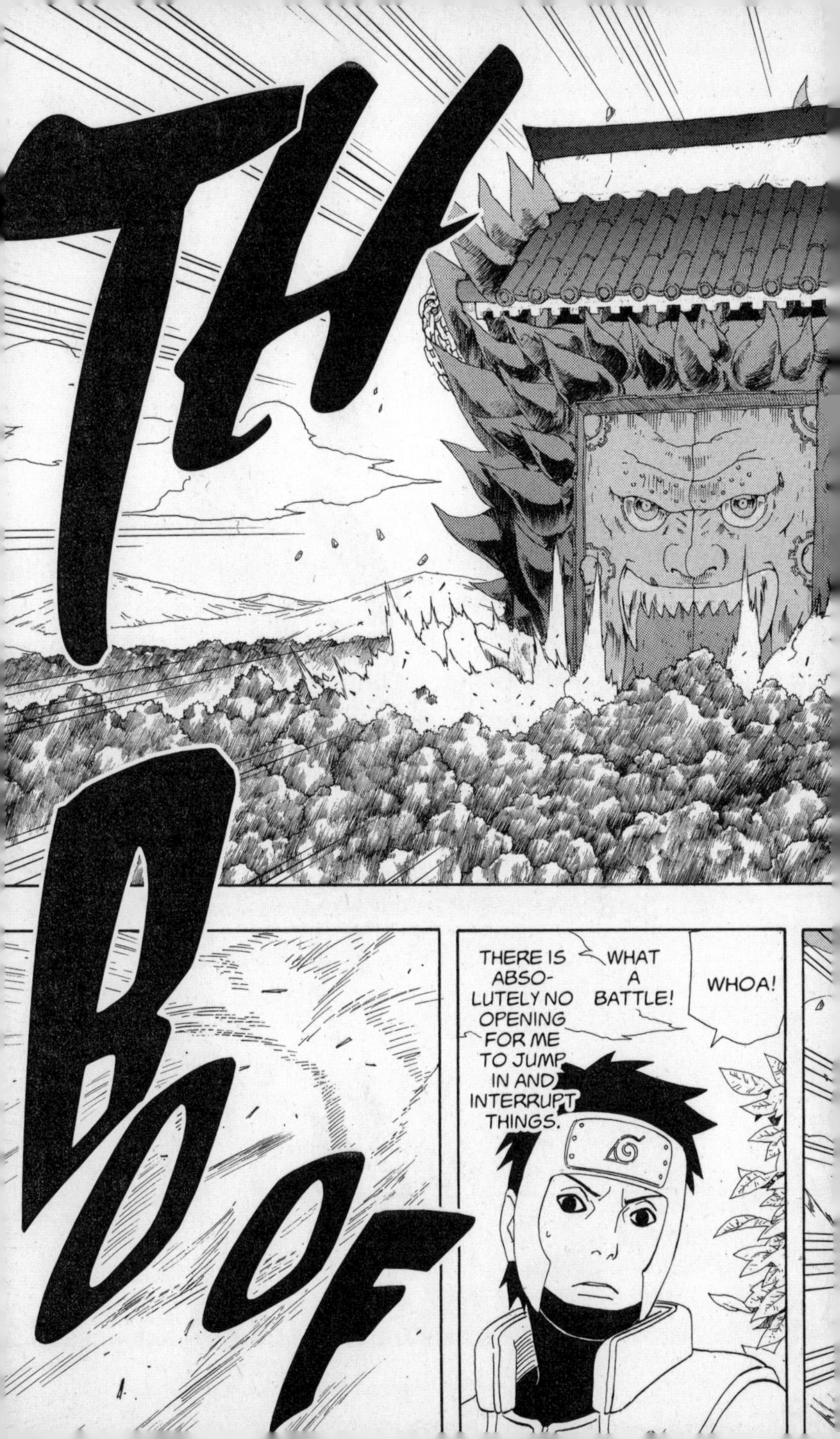
THBOOF
WHOA!
WHAT A BATTLE!
THERE IS ABSOLUTELY NO OPENING FOR ME TO JUMP IN AND INTERRUPT THINGS.

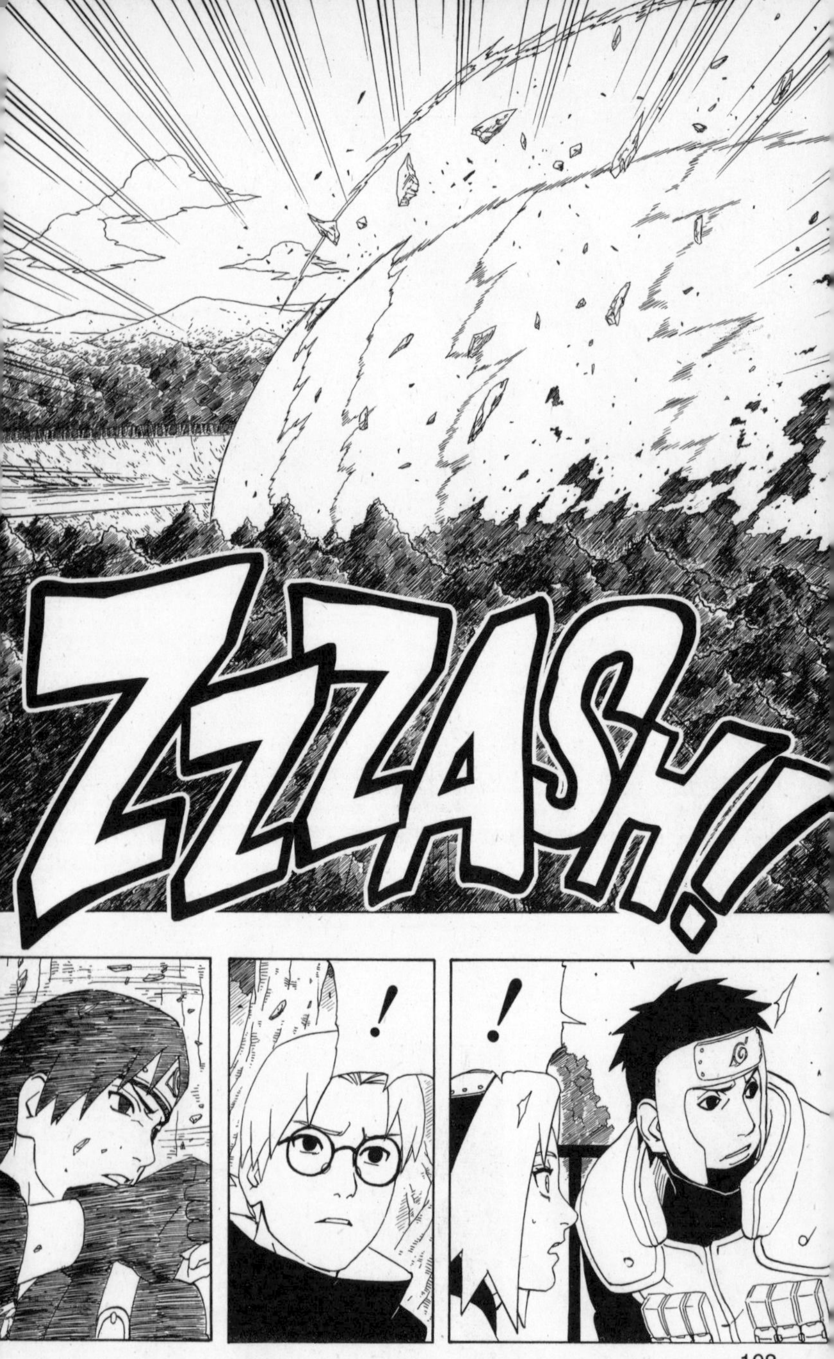
ZZASH!!
!
!

READ THIS WAY

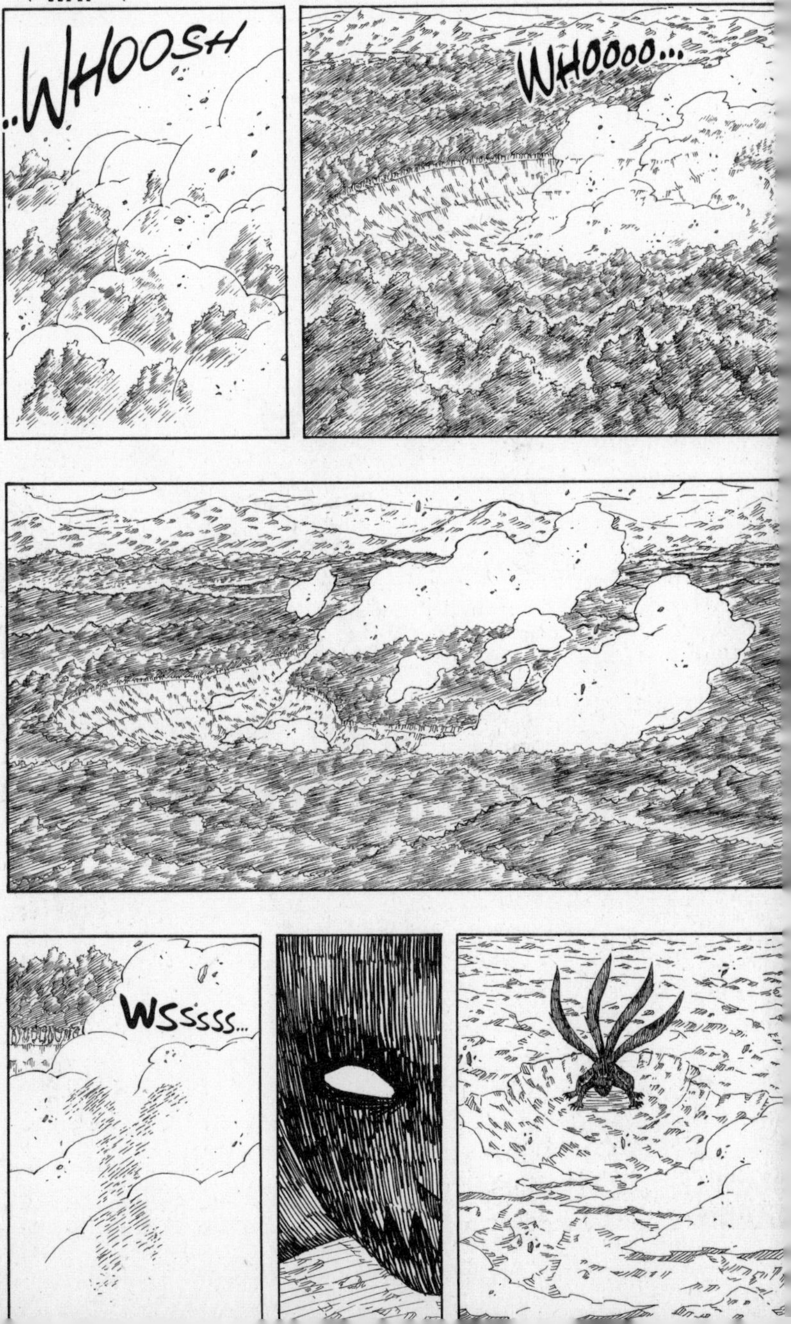
WHOOOO...
...WHOOSH
WSSSSS...

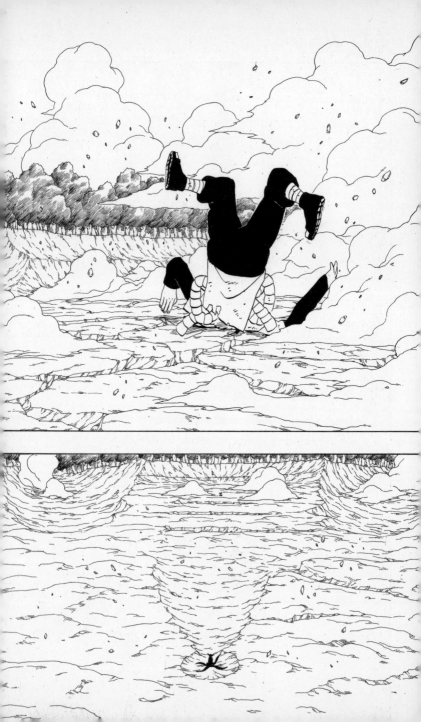

READ THIS WAY

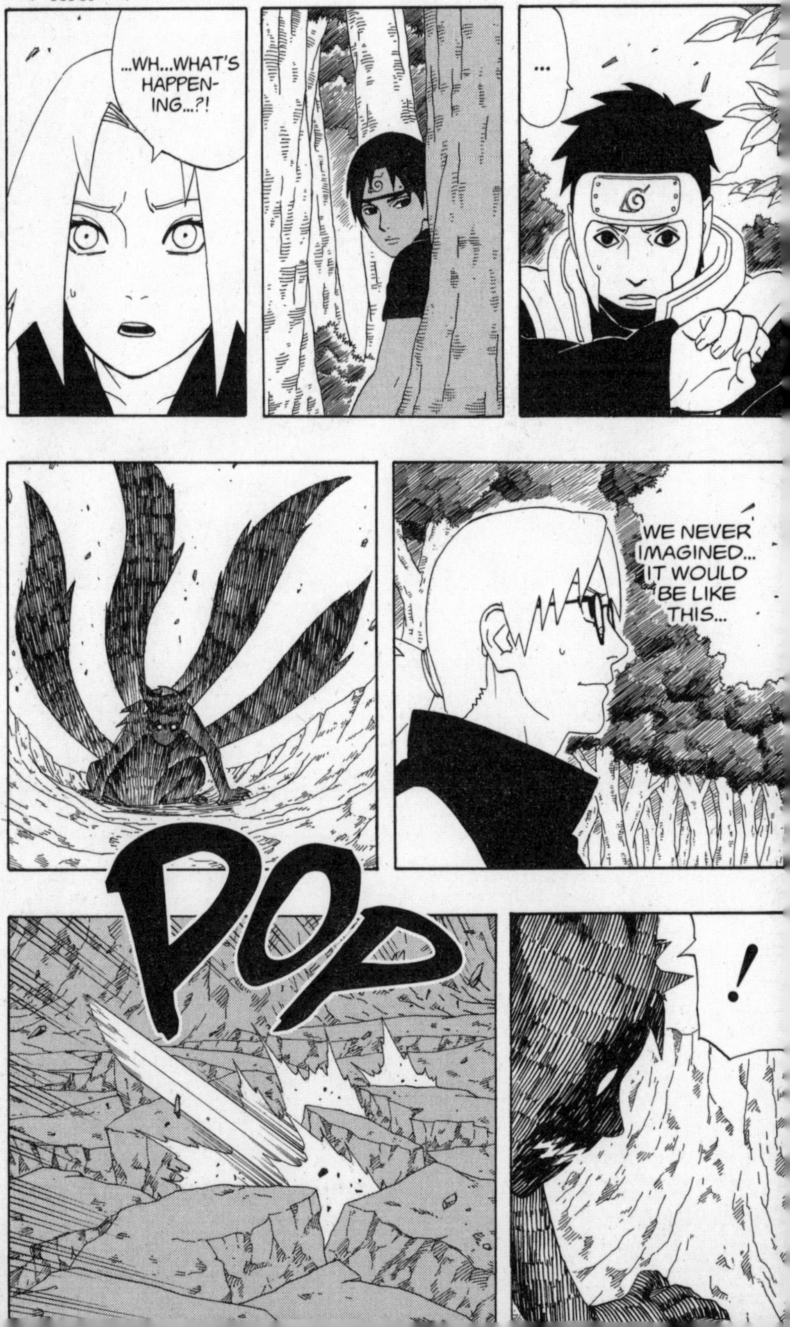

...
...WH...WHAT'S HAPPENING...?!
WE NEVER IMAGINED... IT WOULD BE LIKE THIS...
POP
!

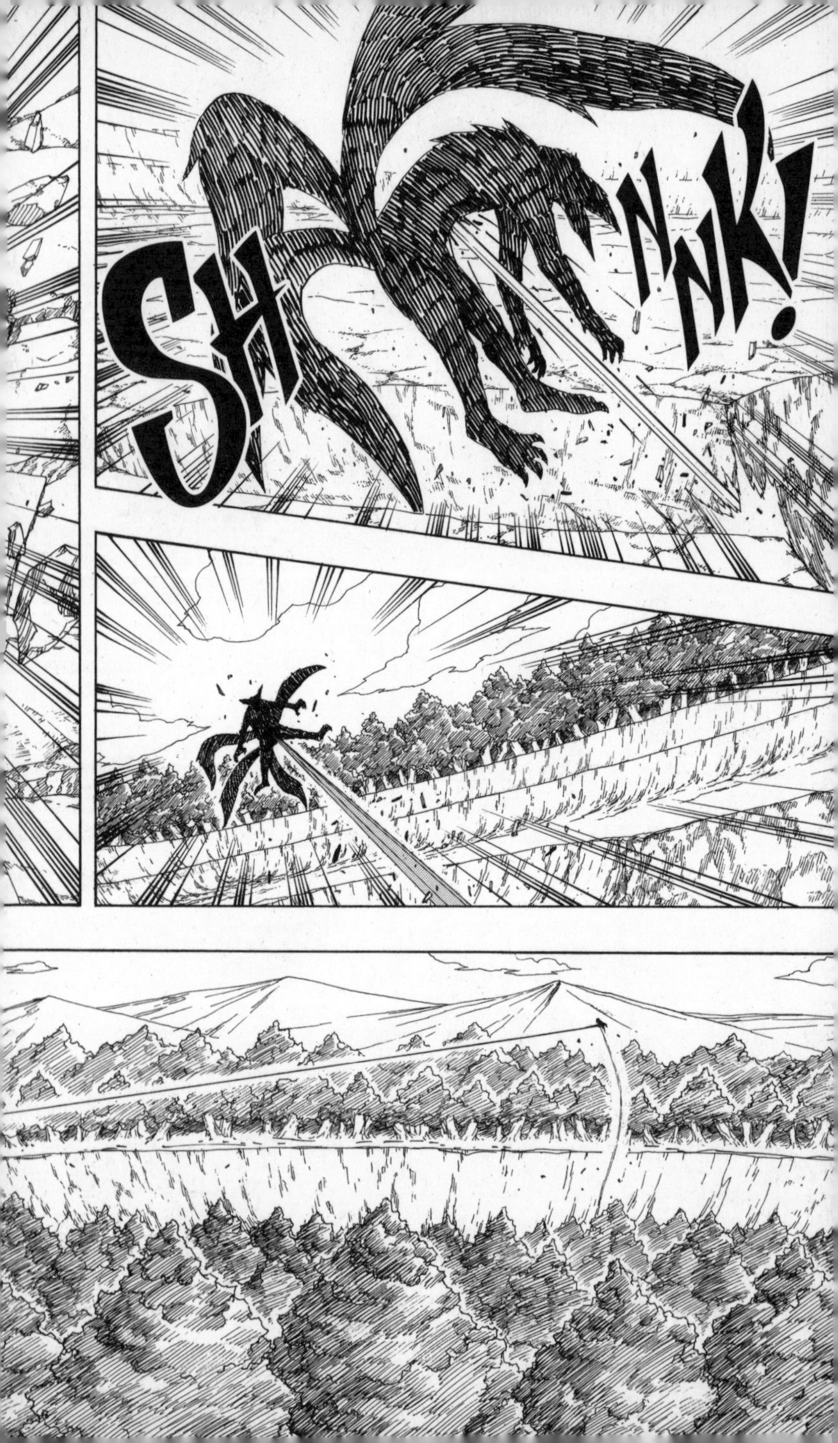
SHHNNK!

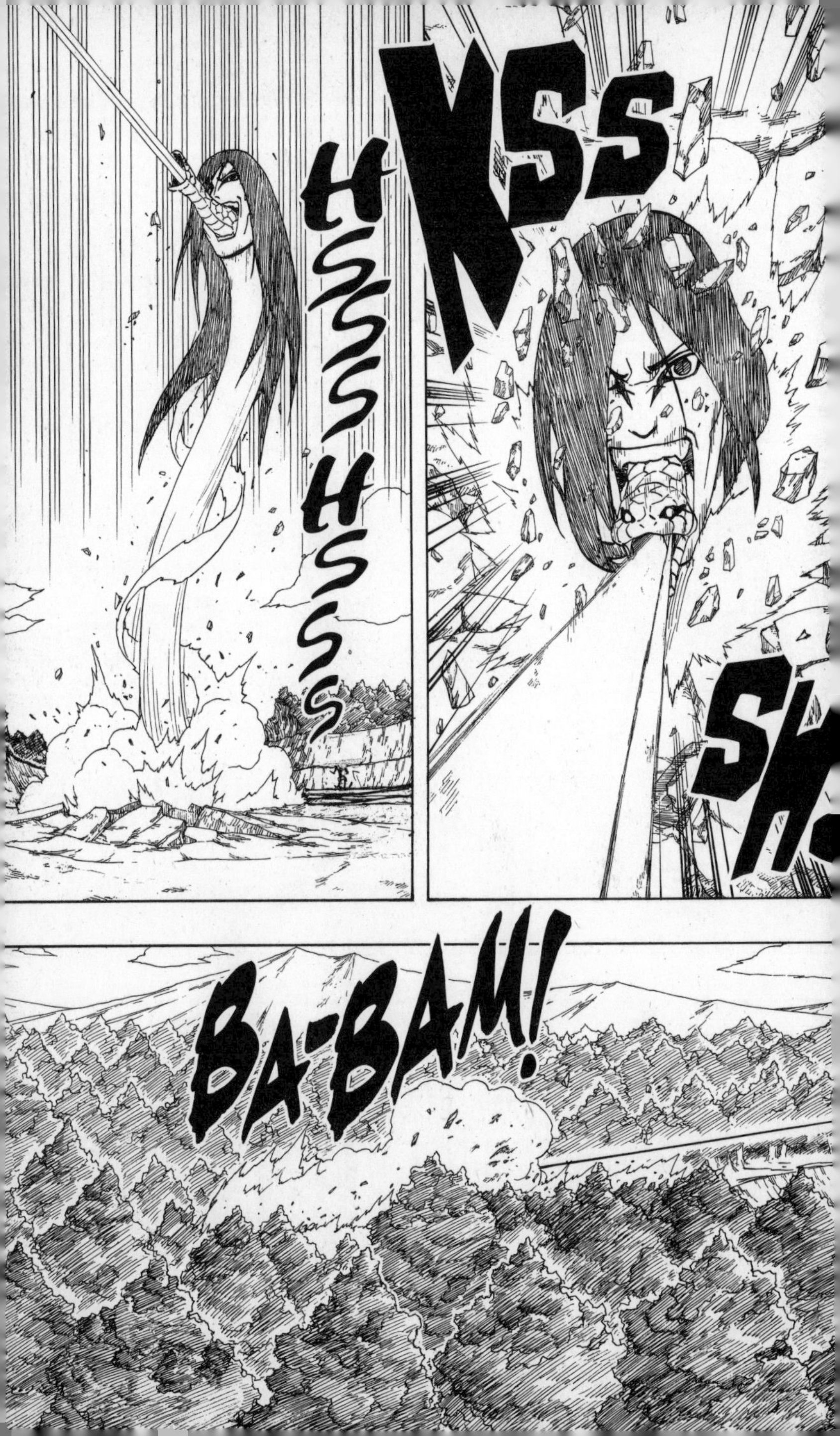
KSS
SH
HSSSHSSS
BA-BAM!

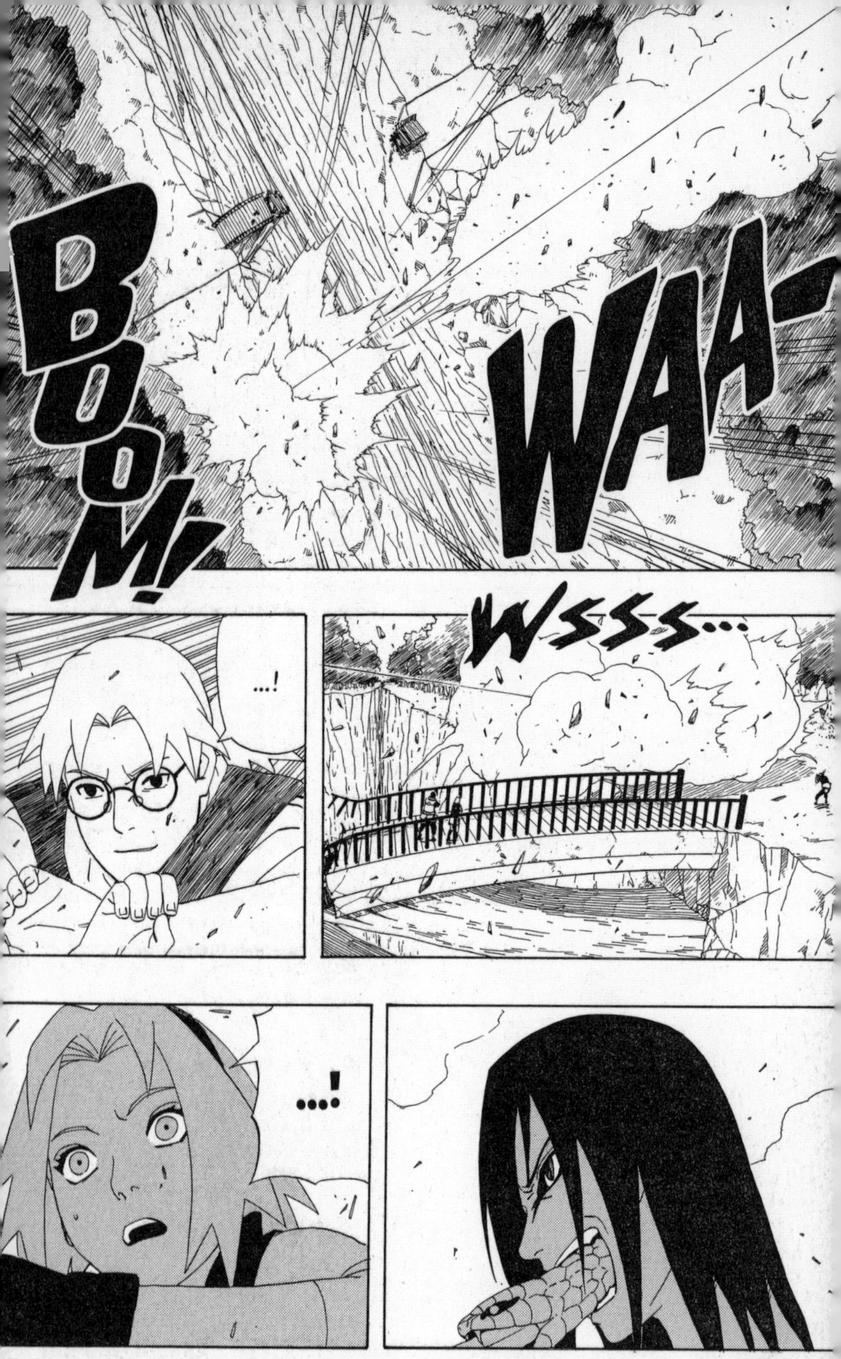

WAA-
BOOM!
WSSS...
...!
...!

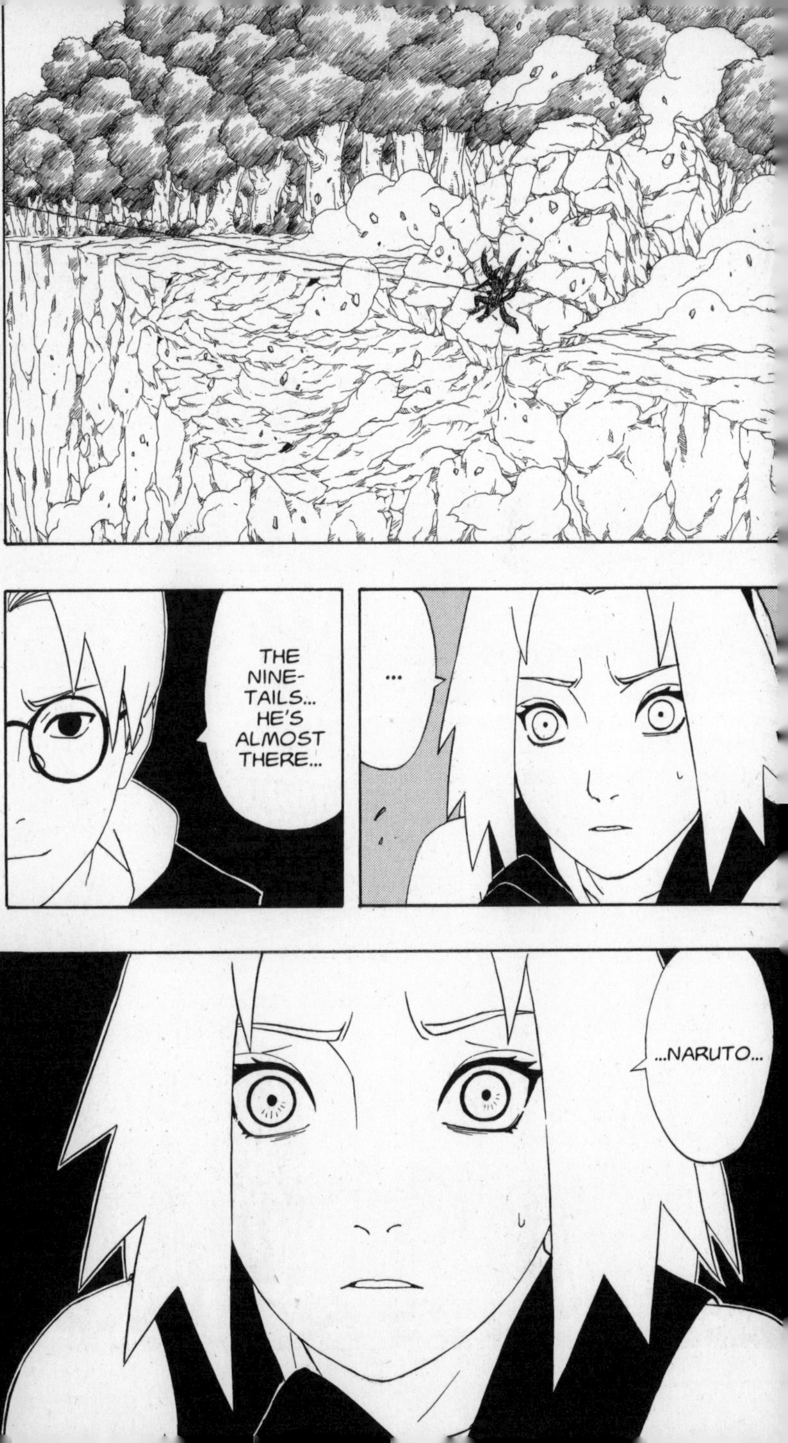
...
THE NINE-TAILS... HE'S ALMOST THERE...
...NARUTO...

NARUTO

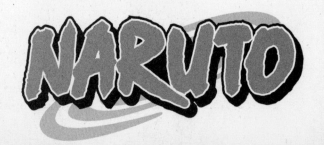

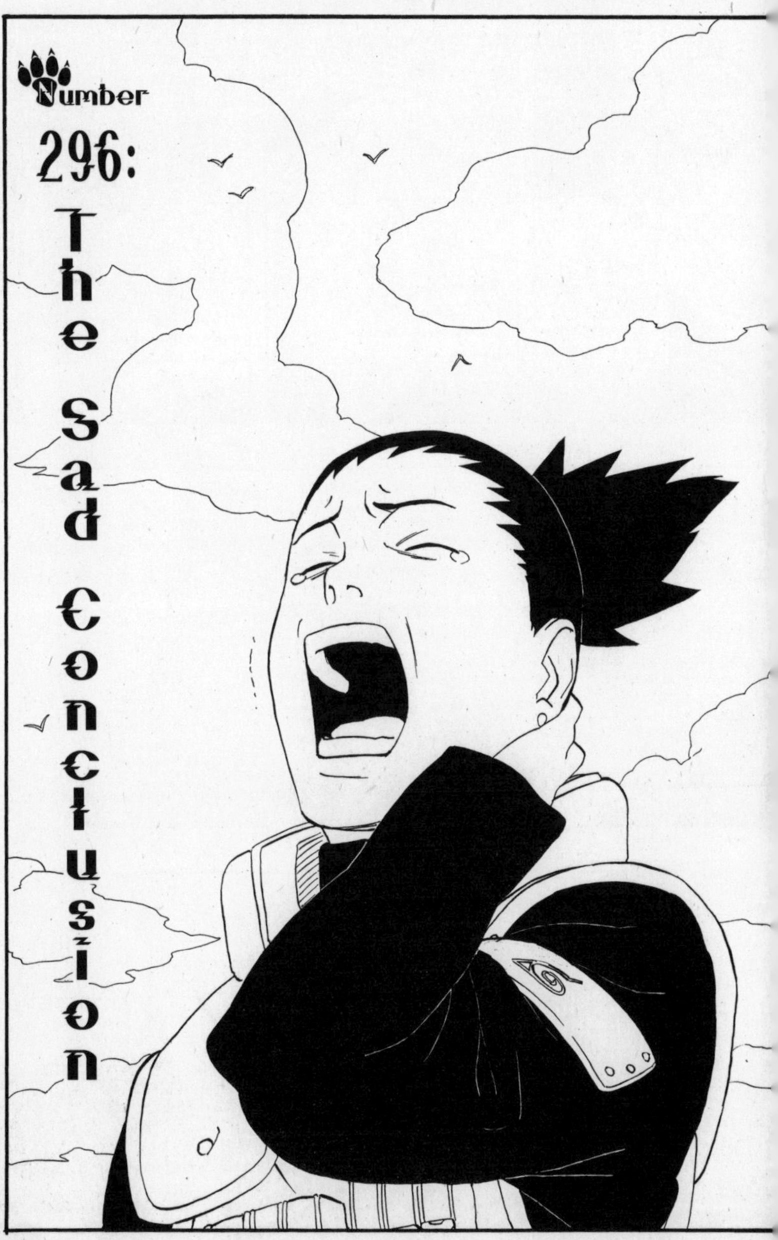
Number
296:
The Sad Conclusion

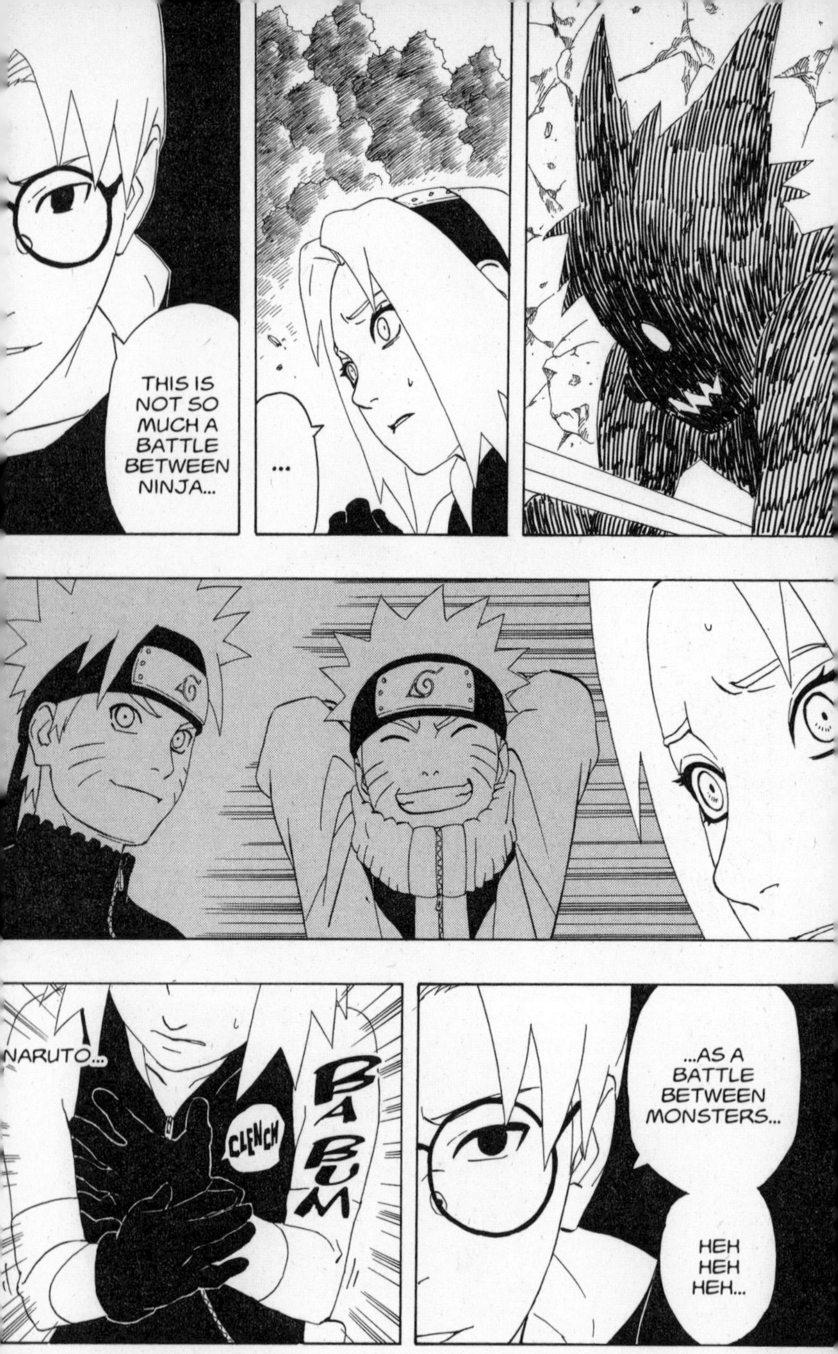
...
THIS IS NOT SO MUCH A BATTLE BETWEEN NINJA...
...AS A BATTLE BETWEEN MONSTERS...
HEH HEH HEH...
BABUM
NARUTO...
CLENCH

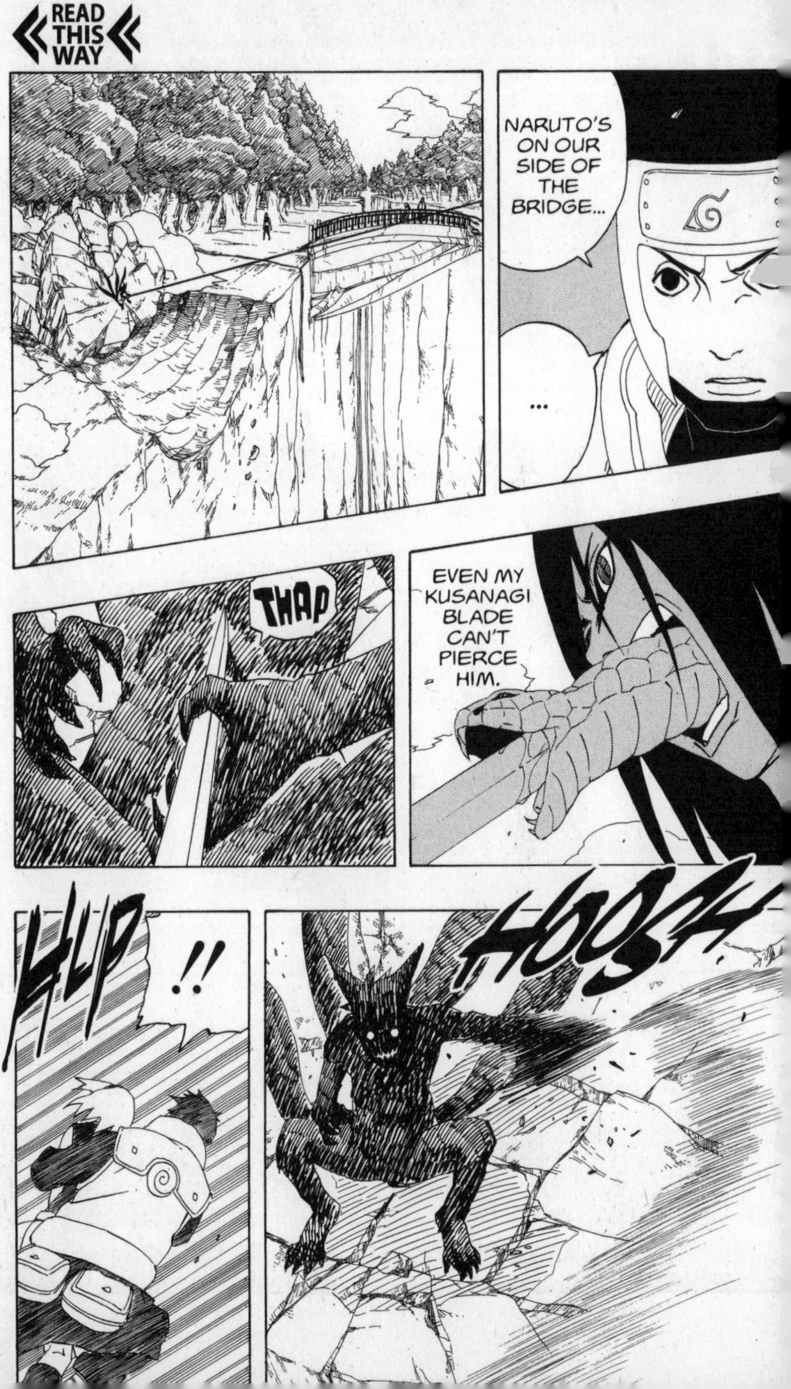
READ THIS WAY
NARUTO'S ON OUR SIDE OF THE BRIDGE...
...
EVEN MY KUSANAGI BLADE CAN'T PIERCE HIM.
THAP
HOOSH
HUP
!!

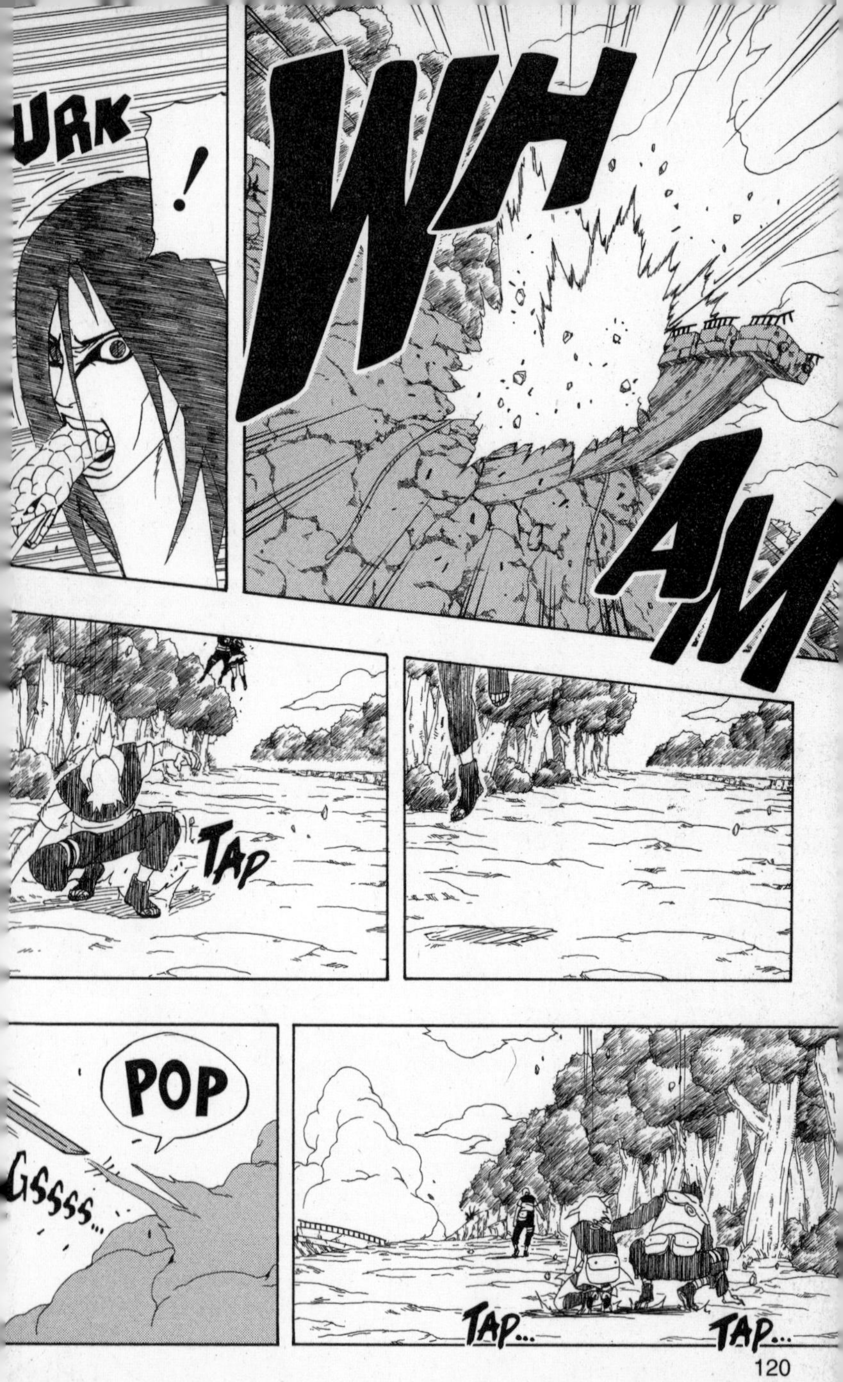
WHAM
URK
!
TAP
TAP...
TAP...
POP
GSSSS...

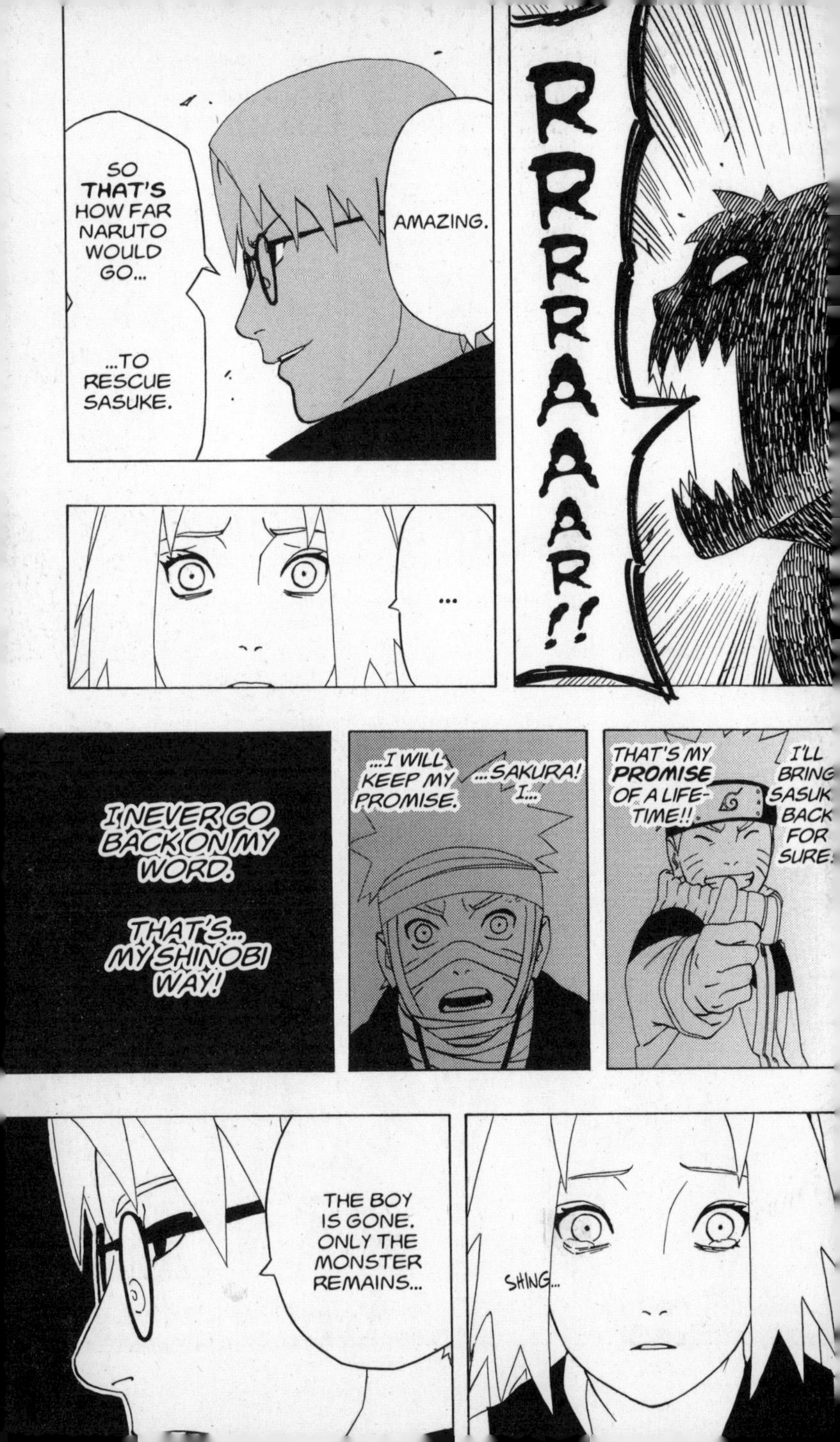
RRRRAAAAR!!
AMAZING.
SO THAT'S HOW FAR NARUTO WOULD GO...
...TO RESCUE SASUKE.
...
I'LL BRING SASUK BACK FOR SURE!
THAT'S MY PROMISE OF A LIFE-TIME!!
...SAKURA! I...
...I WILL KEEP MY PROMISE.
I NEVER GO BACK ON MY WORD.
THAT'S... MY SHINOBI WAY!
SHING...
THE BOY IS GONE. ONLY THE MONSTER REMAINS...

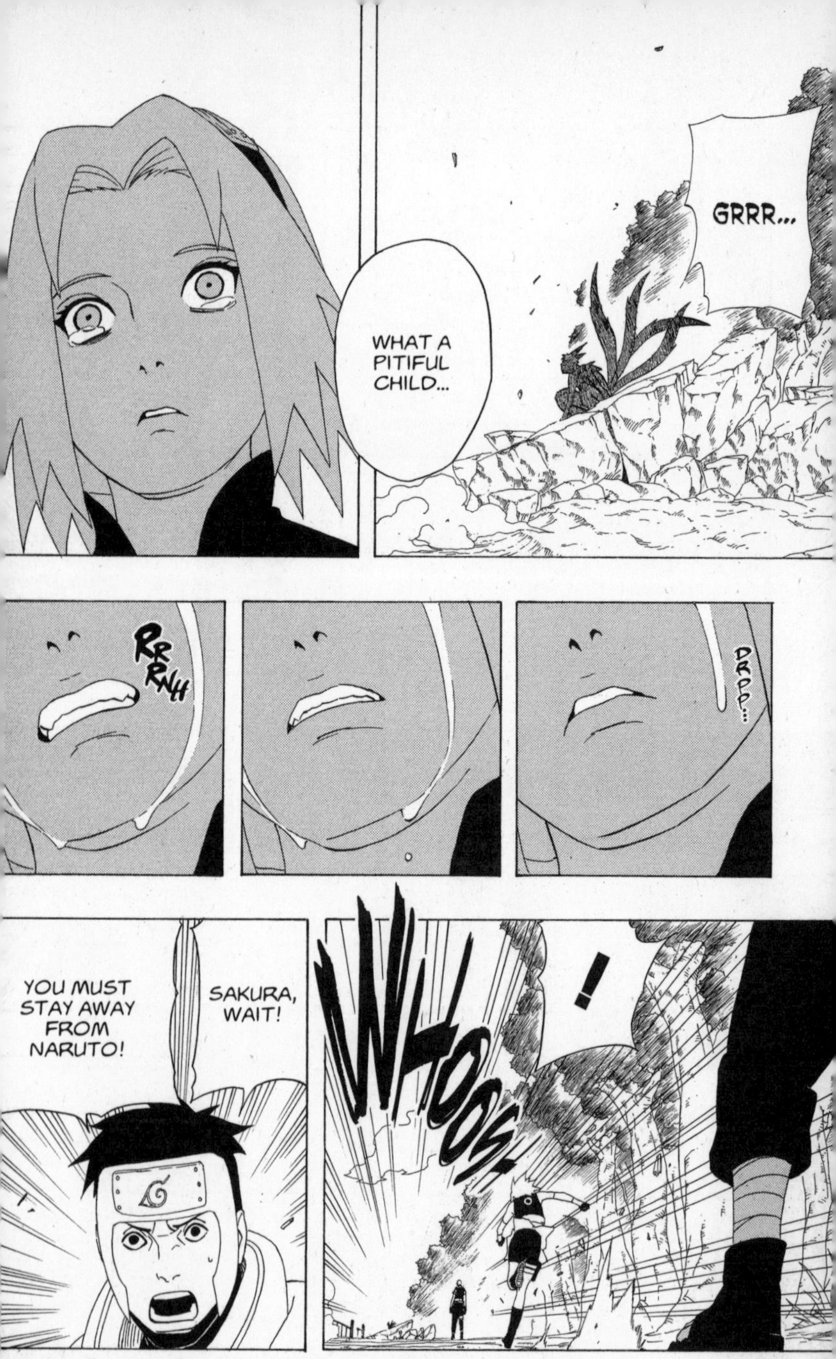
GRRR...
WHAT A PITIFUL CHILD...
DRPP...
RRRNH
!
WHOOSH
SAKURA, WAIT!
YOU MUST STAY AWAY FROM NARUTO!

READ THIS WAY

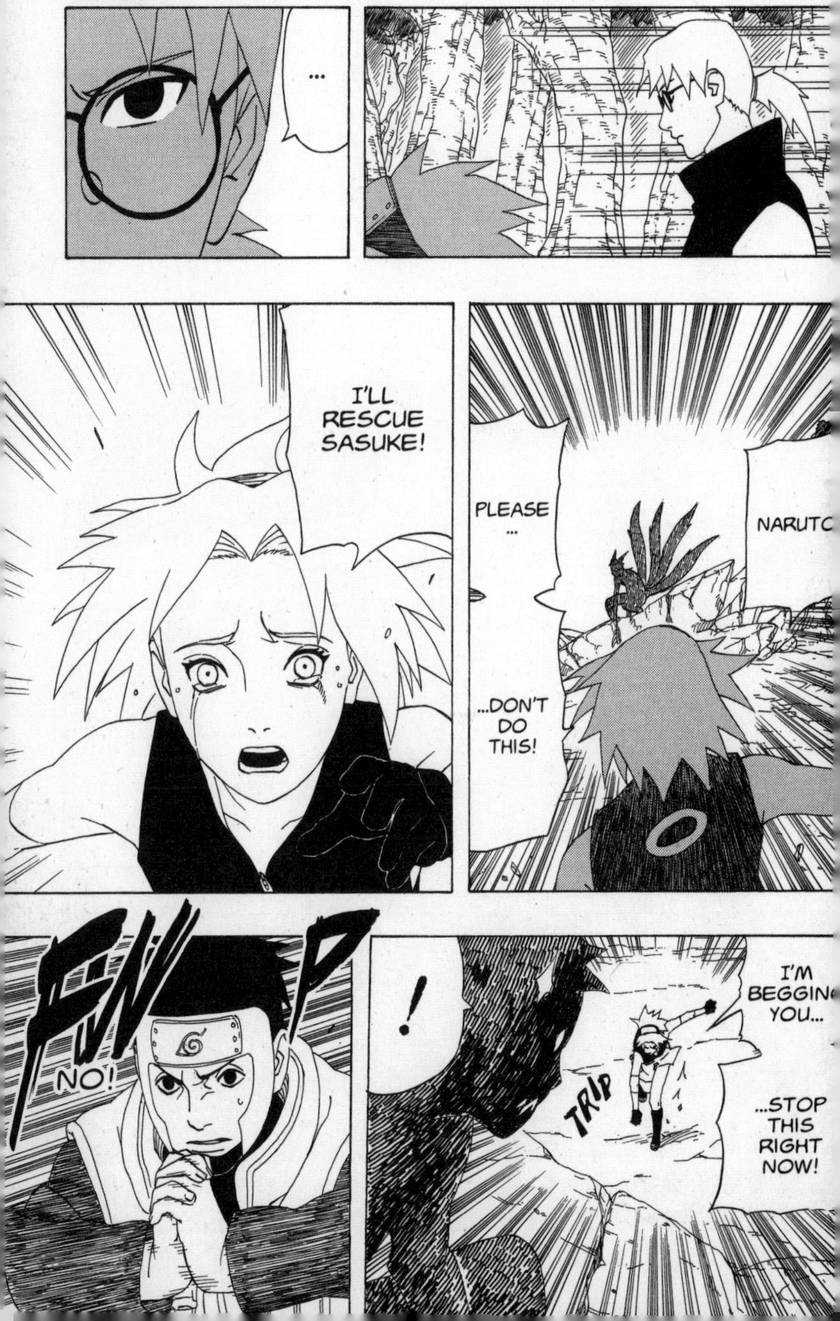
...
NARUT
PLEASE ...
...DON'T DO THIS!
I'LL RESCUE SASUKE!
I'M BEGGIN YOU...
...STOP THIS RIGHT NOW!
!
TRIP
NO!

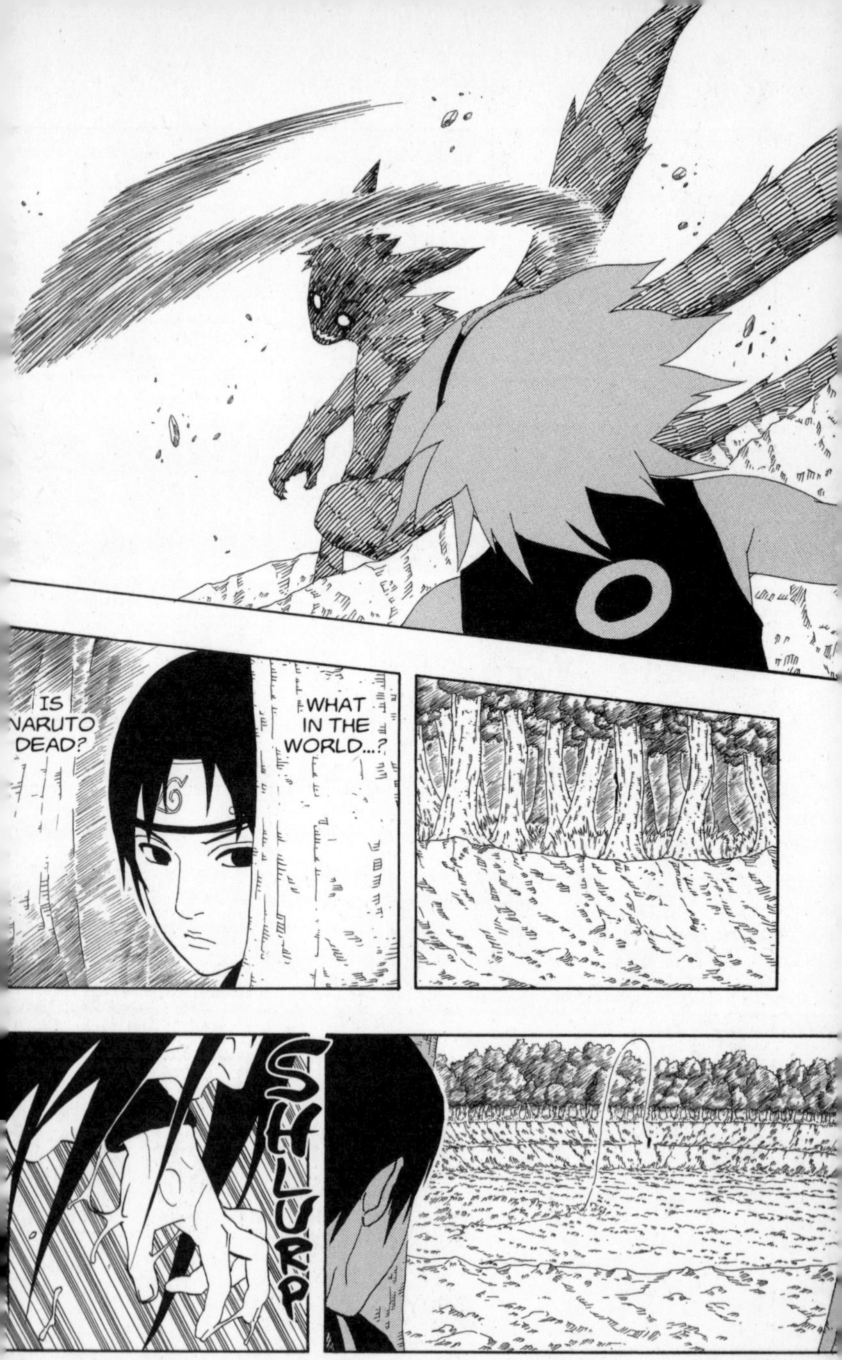
WHAT IN THE WORLD...?
IS NARUTO DEAD?
SHLURP

READ THIS WAY

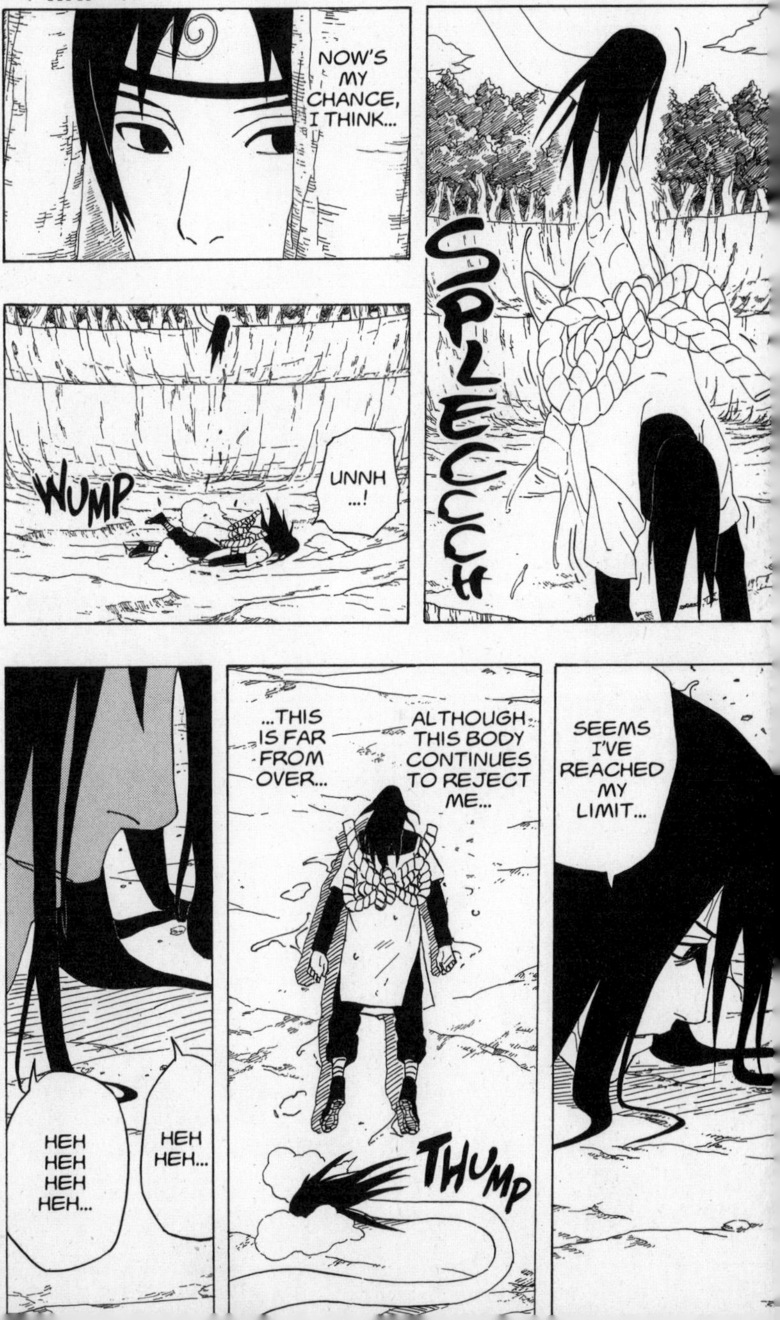
SPLECCCH
NOW'S MY CHANCE, I THINK...
WUMP
UNNH ...!
SEEMS I'VE REACHED MY LIMIT...
ALTHOUGH THIS BODY CONTINUES TO REJECT ME...
...THIS IS FAR FROM OVER...
THUMP
HEH HEH...
HEH HEH HEH HEH...

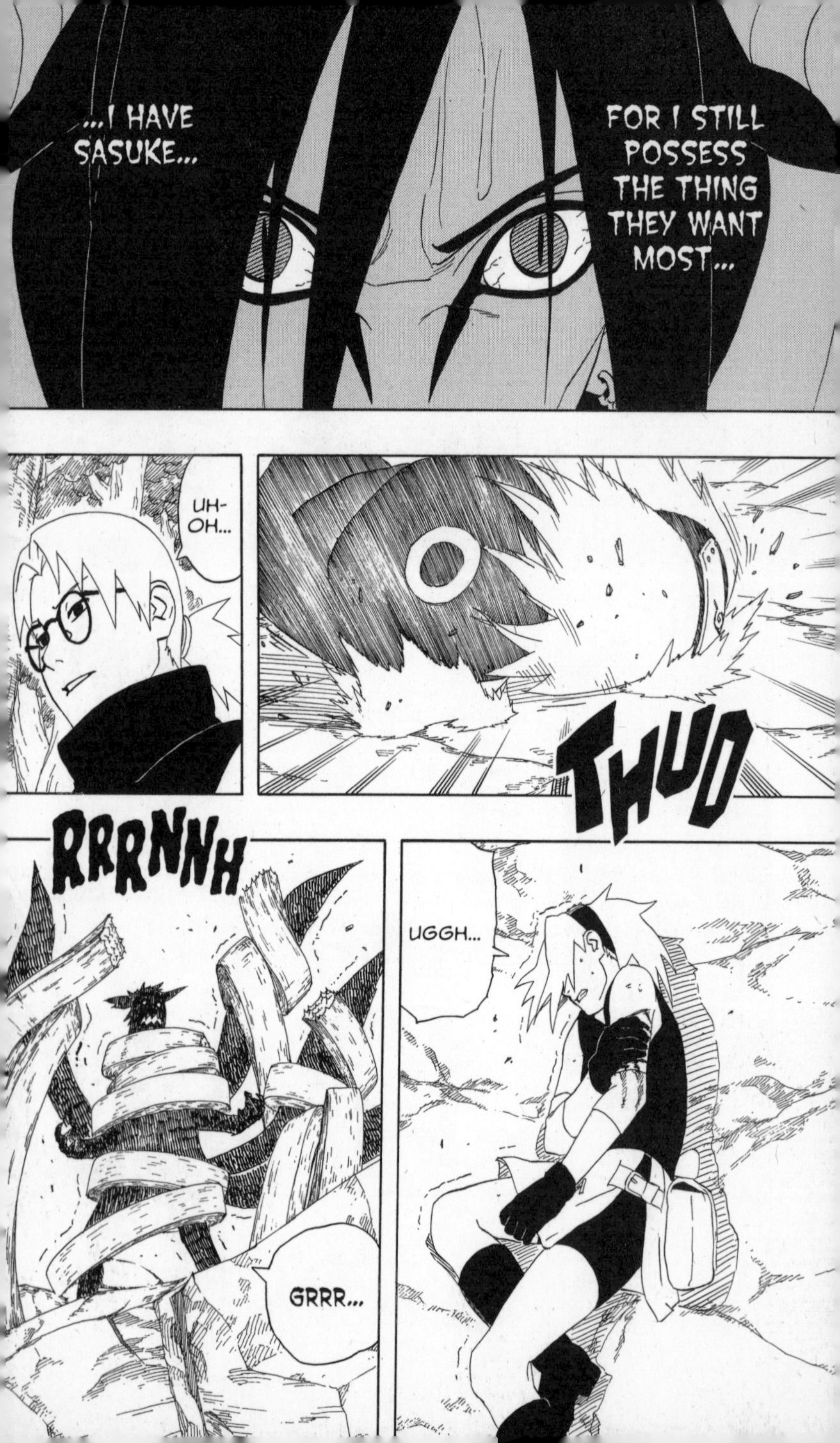
FOR I STILL POSSESS THE THING THEY WANT MOST...
...I HAVE SASUKE...
THUD
UH-OH...
UGGH...
RRRNNH
GRRR...

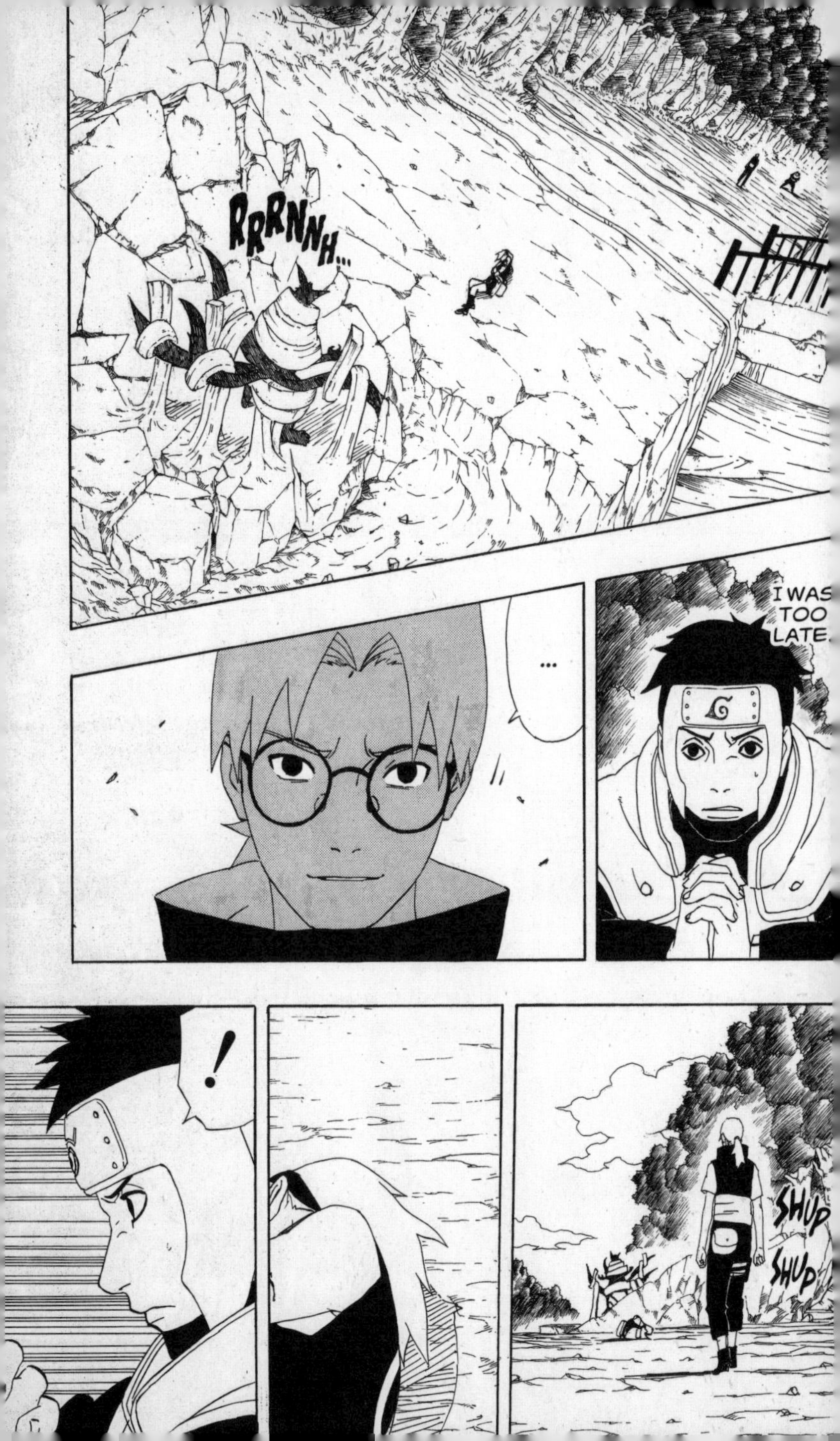
RRRNNH...
I WAS TOO LATE...
...
SHUP
SHUP
!

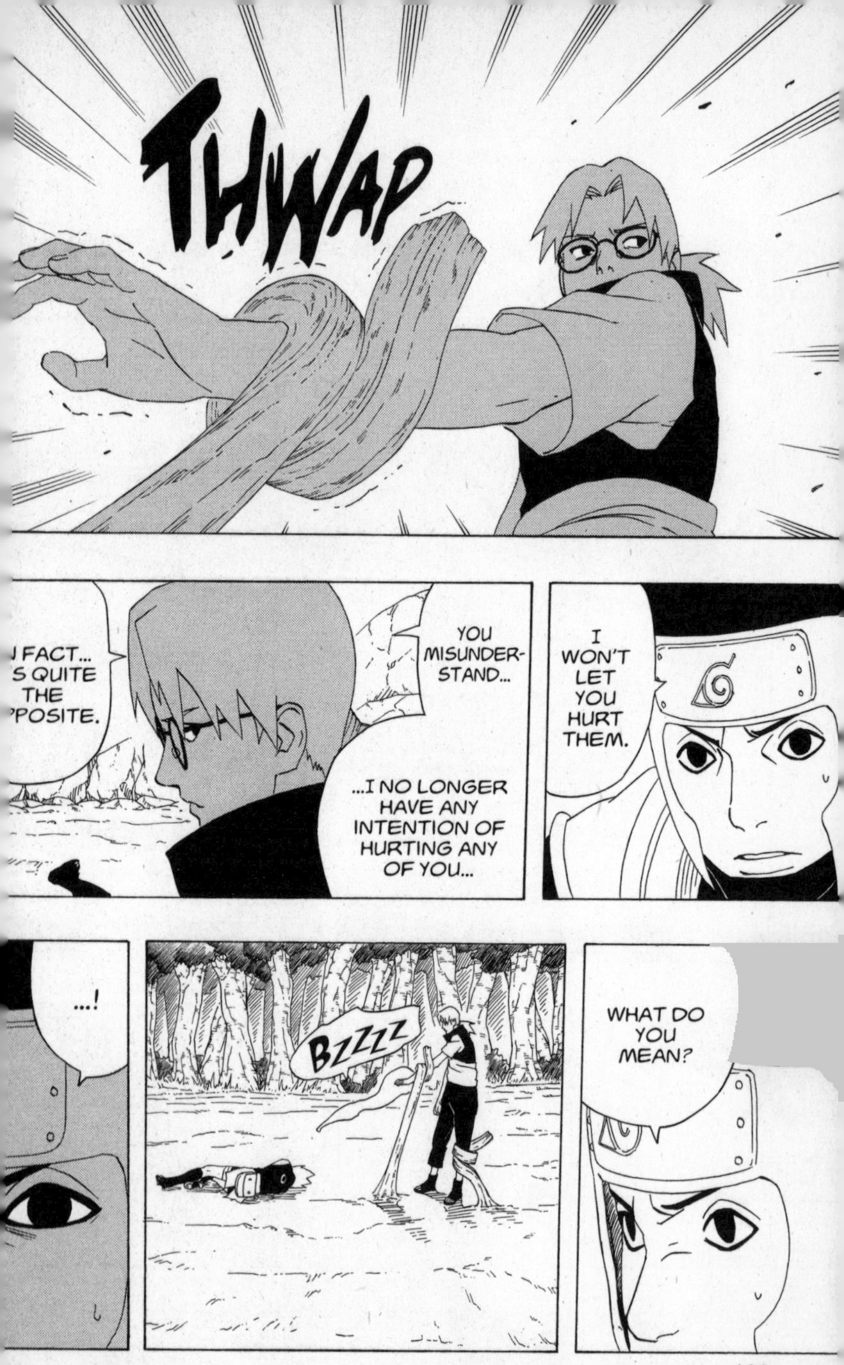
THWAP
I WON'T LET YOU HURT THEM.
YOU MISUNDER-STAND...
...I NO LONGER HAVE ANY INTENTION OF HURTING ANY OF YOU...
N FACT... S QUITE THE PPOSITE.
WHAT DO YOU MEAN?
BZZZZ
...!

READ THIS WAY

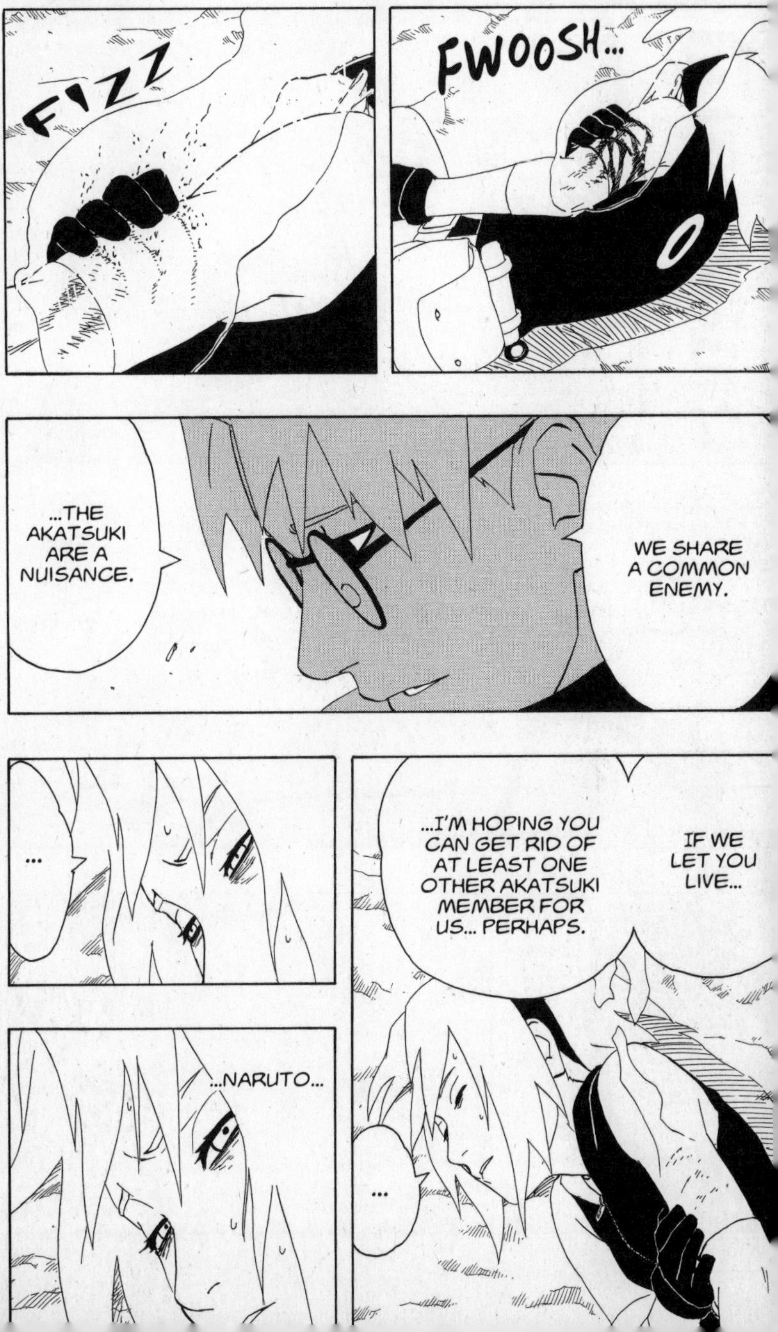
FWOOSH...
FIZZ
WE SHARE A COMMON ENEMY.
...THE AKATSUKI ARE A NUISANCE.
IF WE LET YOU LIVE...
...I'M HOPING YOU CAN GET RID OF AT LEAST ONE OTHER AKATSUKI MEMBER FOR US... PERHAPS.
...
...
...NARUTO...

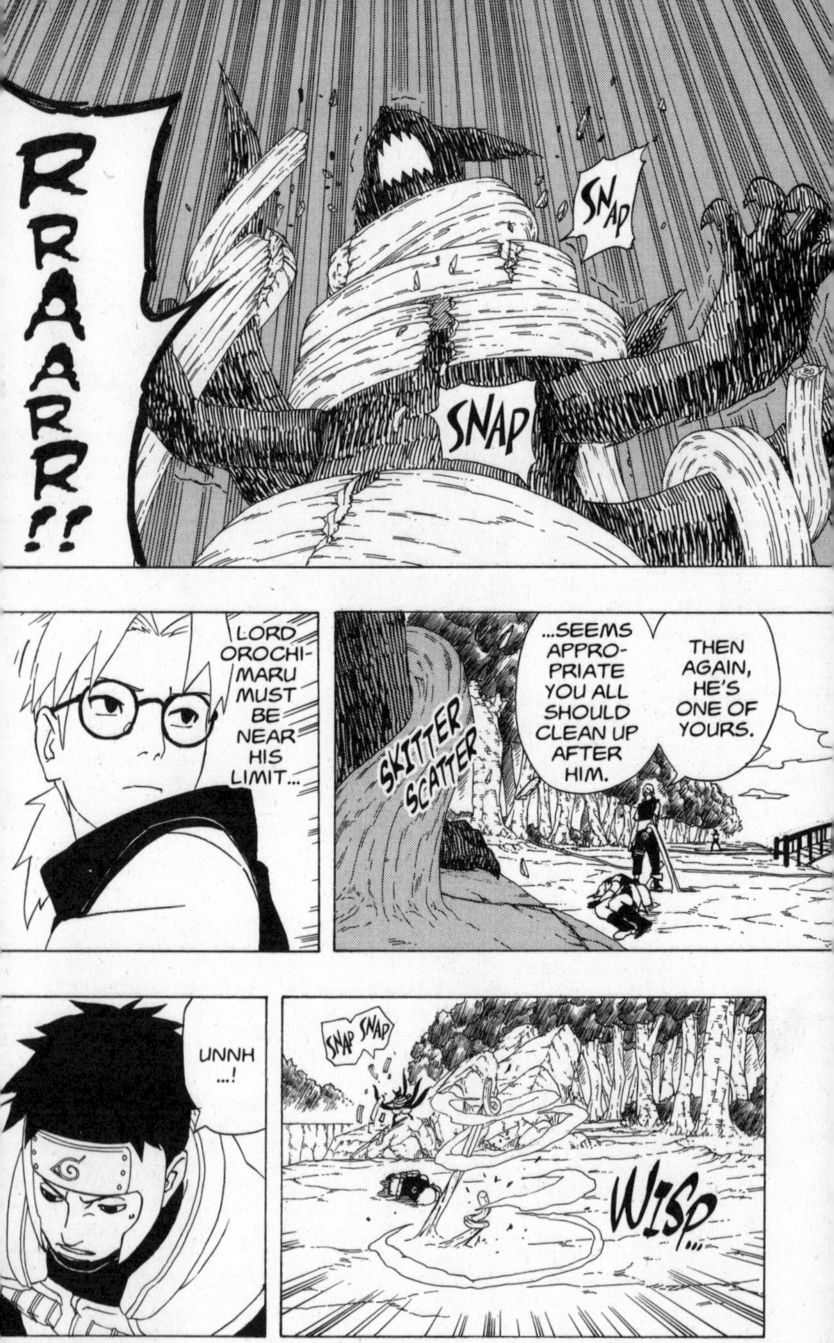
RRAARRR!!
SNAP
SNAP
THEN AGAIN, HE'S ONE OF YOURS.
...SEEMS APPROPRIATE YOU ALL SHOULD CLEAN UP AFTER HIM.
SKITTER SCATTER
LORD OROCHIMARU MUST BE NEAR HIS LIMIT...
SNAP SNAP
WISP...
UNNH...!

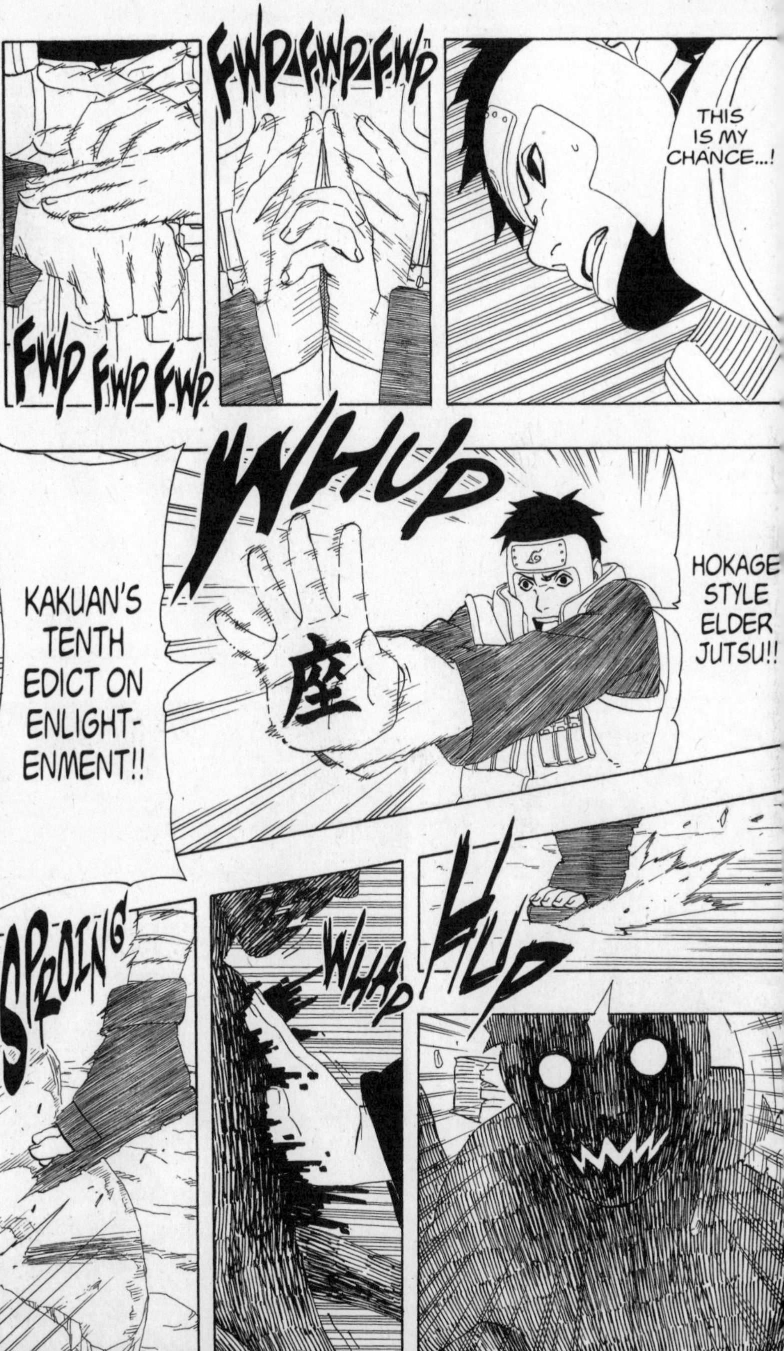
THIS IS MY CHANCE...!
FWP FWP FWP
FWP FWP FWP
WHUP
HOKAGE STYLE ELDER JUTSU!!
KAKUAN'S TENTH EDICT ON ENLIGHT-ENMENT!!
HUP
WHAP
SPROING

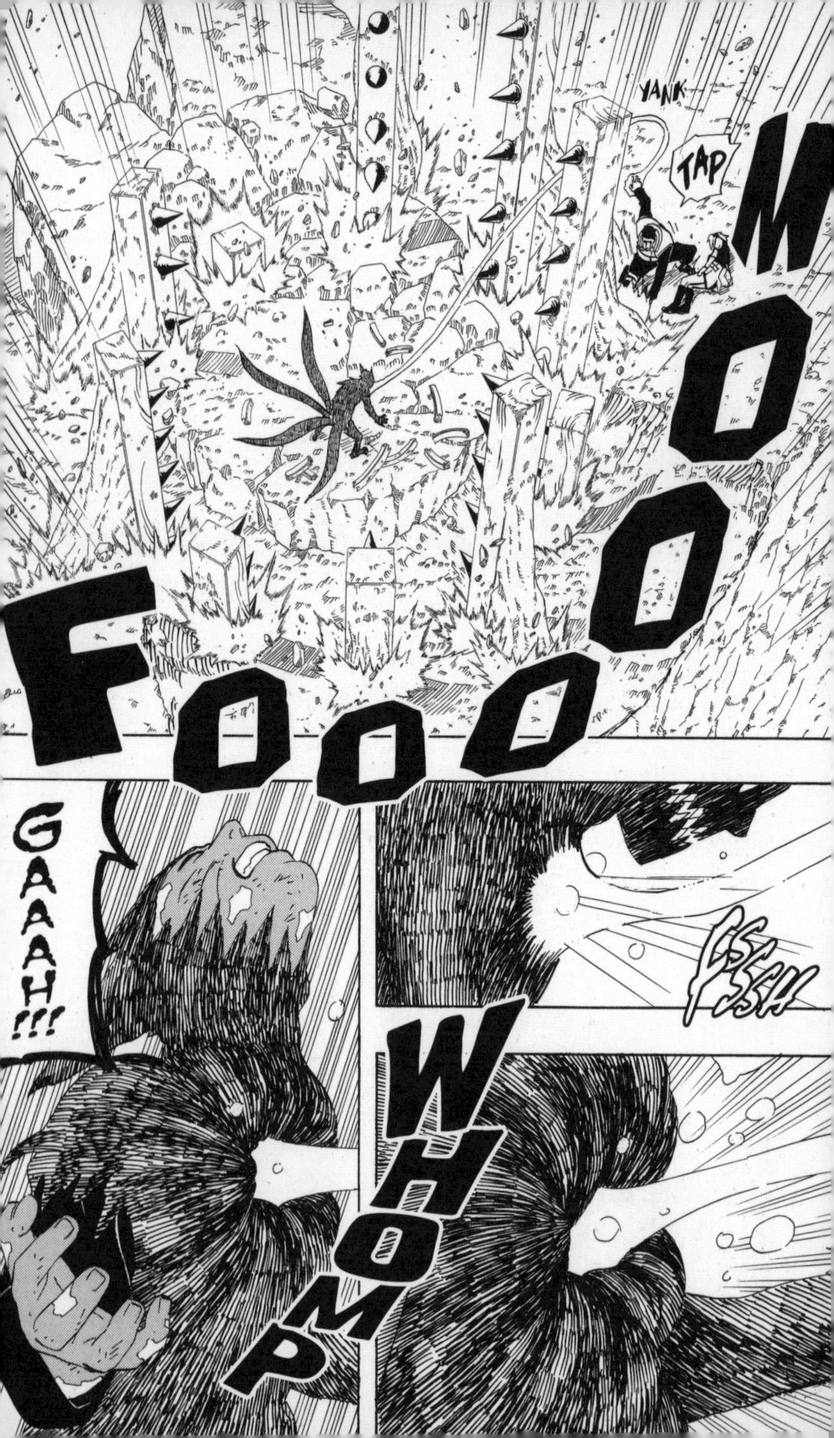

YANK
TAP
FOOOOOM
FSSH
WHOMP
GAAAH!!!

READ THIS WAY

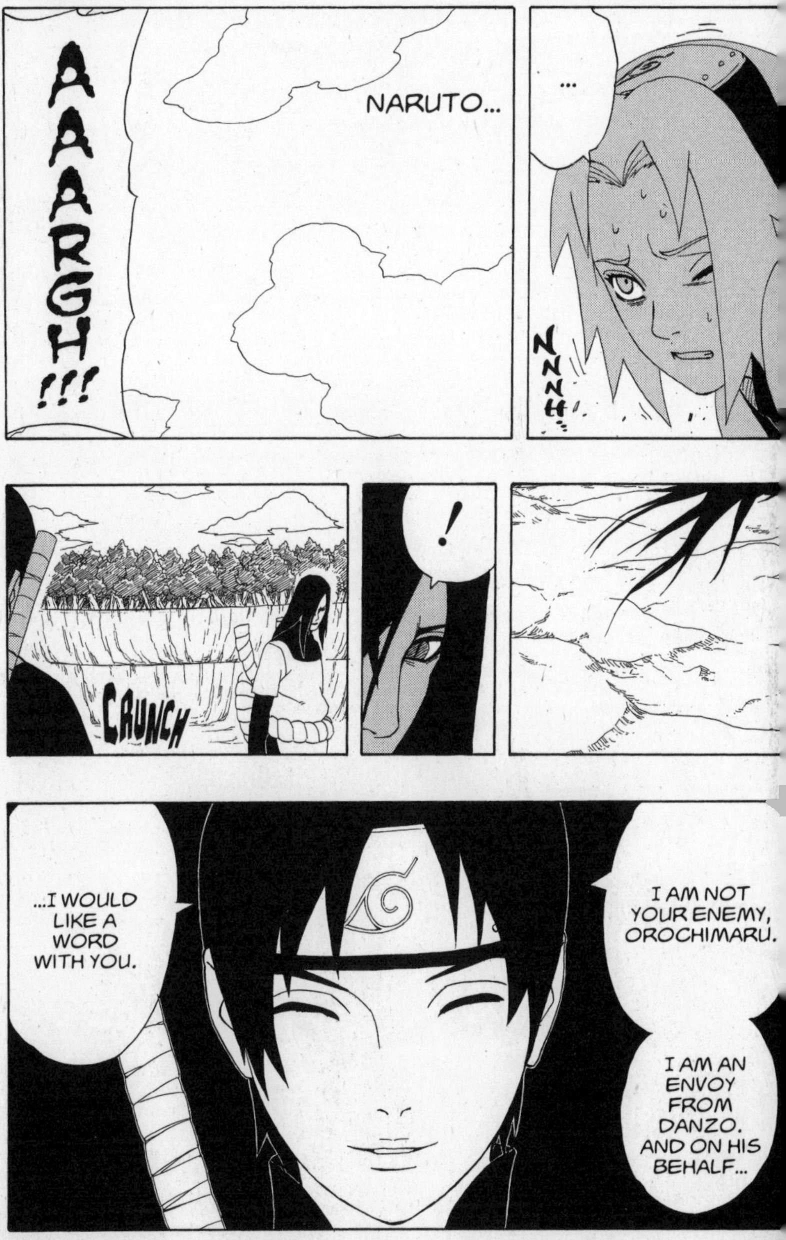
...
NNNH...
NARUTO...
AAAARGH!!!
!
CRUNCH
I AM NOT YOUR ENEMY, OROCHIMARU.
I AM AN ENVOY FROM DANZO. AND ON HIS BEHALF...
...I WOULD LIKE A WORD WITH YOU.

NARUTO

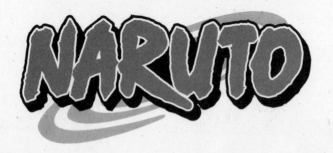

Number 297: Sai's Mission!!

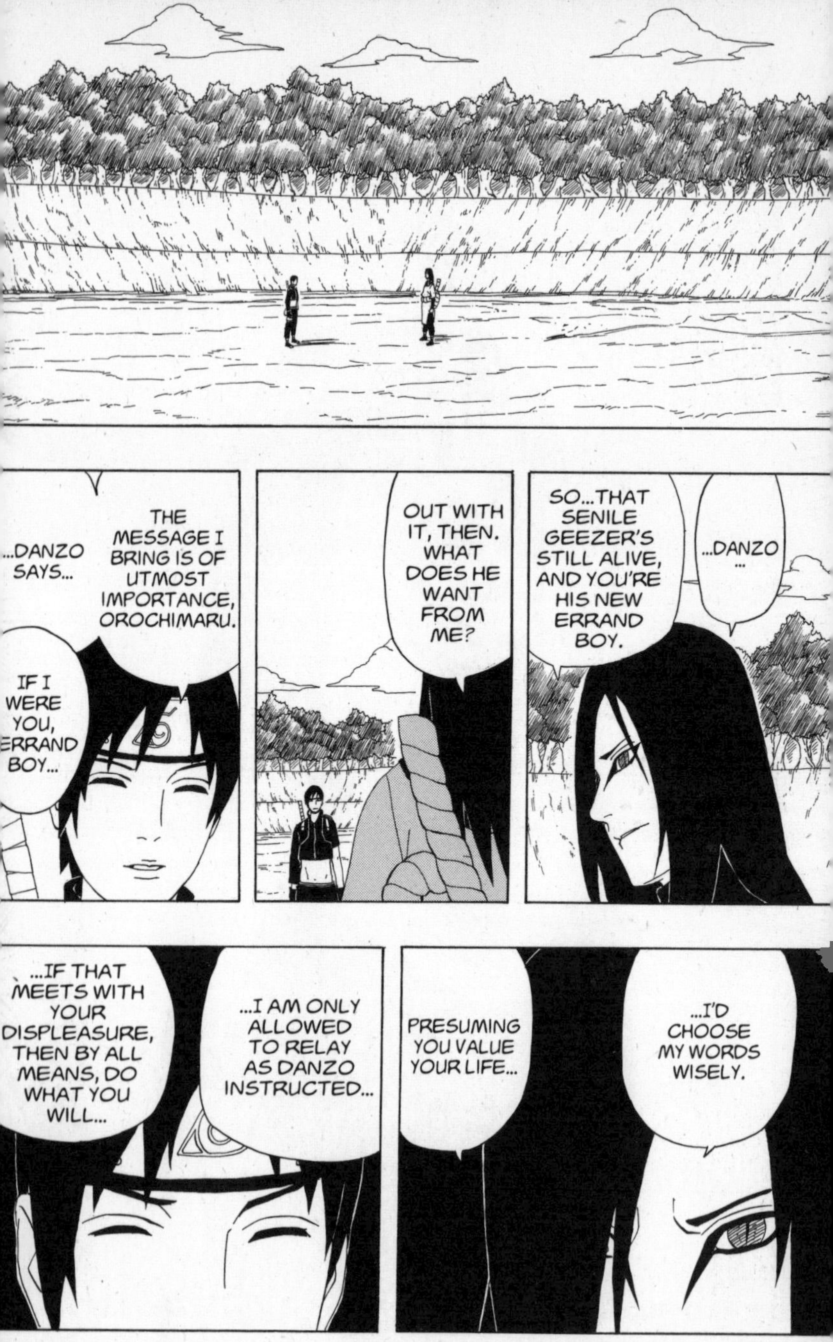
...DANZO ...
SO...THAT SENILE GEEZER'S STILL ALIVE, AND YOU'RE HIS NEW ERRAND BOY.
OUT WITH IT, THEN. WHAT DOES HE WANT FROM ME?
THE MESSAGE I BRING IS OF UTMOST IMPORTANCE, OROCHIMARU.
...DANZO SAYS...
IF I WERE YOU, ERRAND BOY...
...I'D CHOOSE MY WORDS WISELY.
PRESUMING YOU VALUE YOUR LIFE...
...I AM ONLY ALLOWED TO RELAY AS DANZO INSTRUCTED...
...IF THAT MEETS WITH YOUR DISPLEASURE, THEN BY ALL MEANS, DO WHAT YOU WILL...

READ THIS WAY

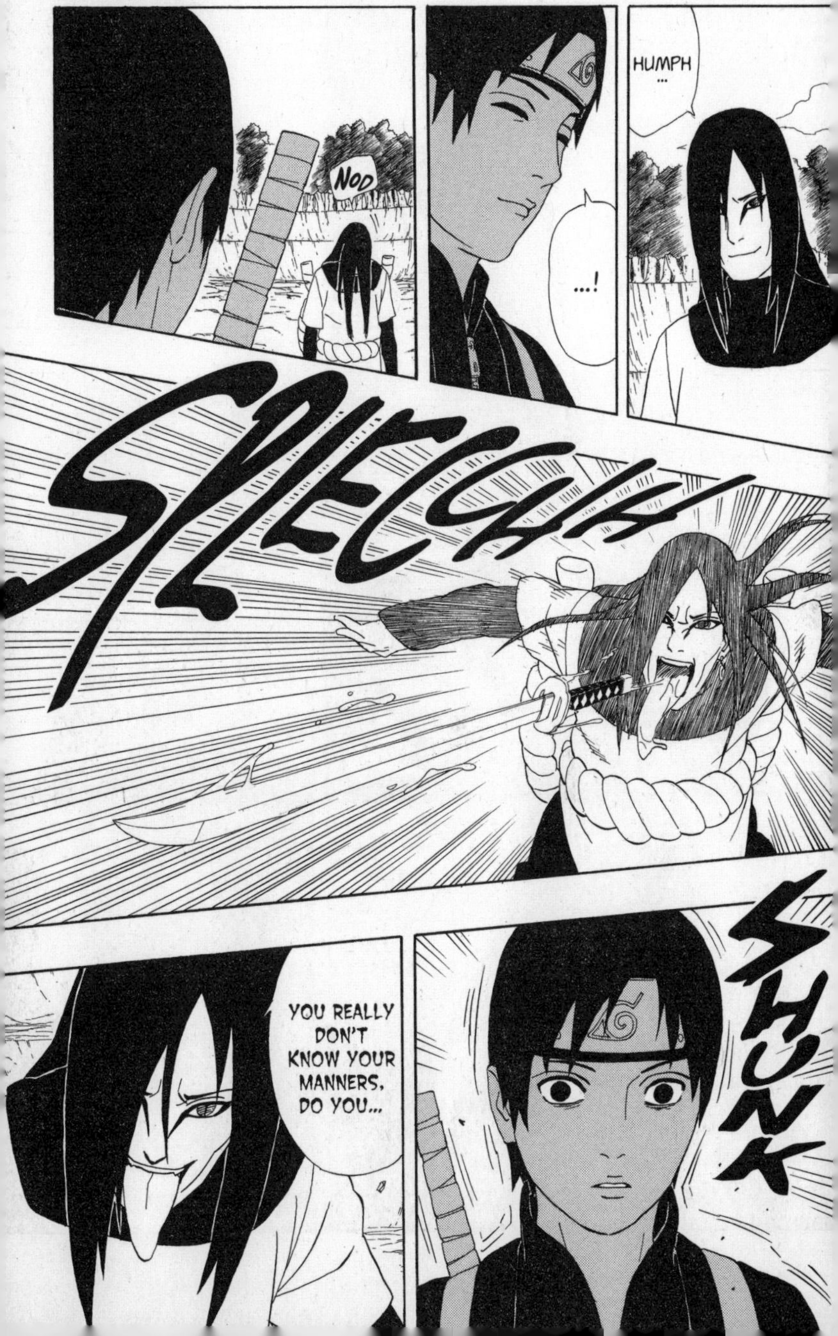
HUMPH …
…!
NOD
SPLECHH
SHUNK
YOU REALLY DON'T KNOW YOUR MANNERS, DO YOU...

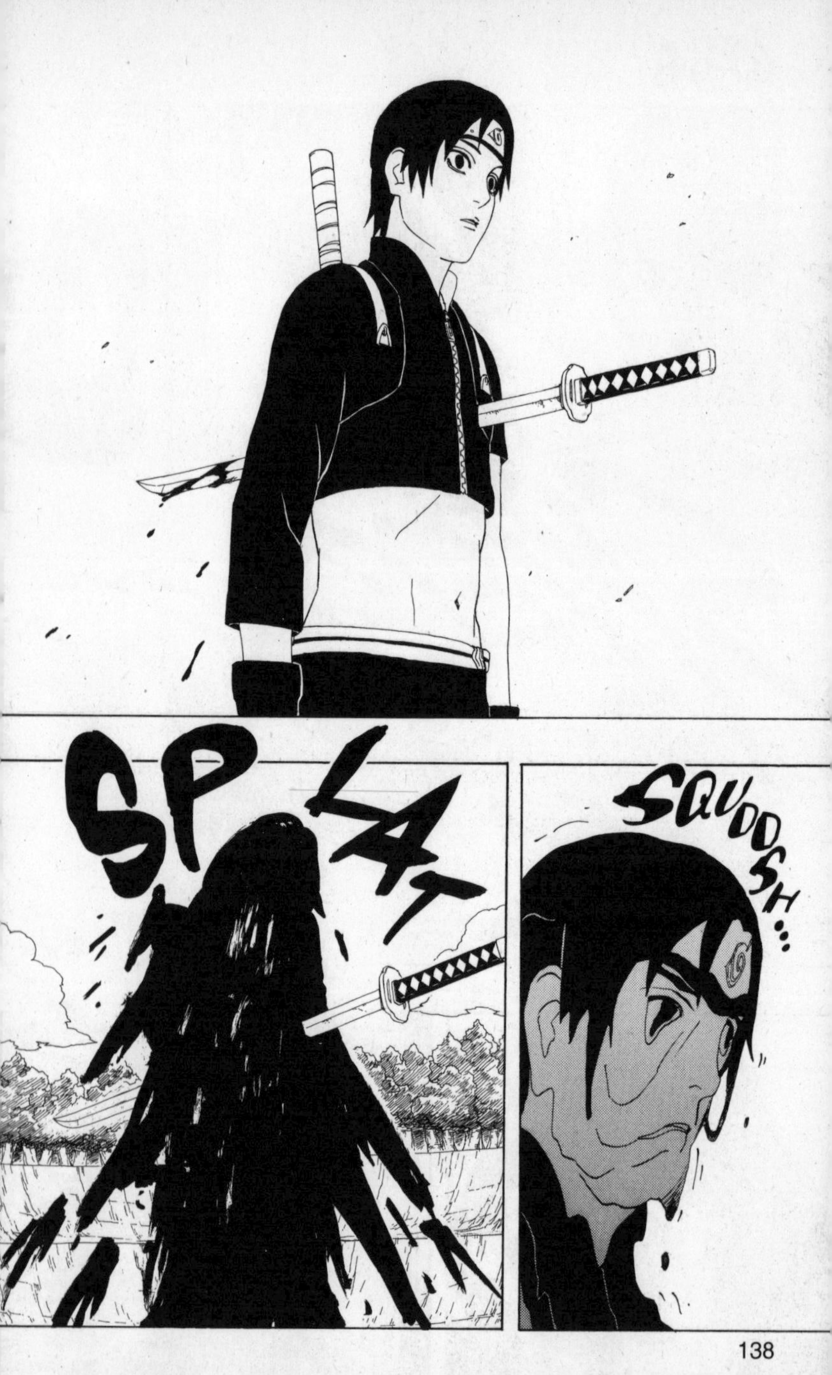
SPLAT
SQUOOSH...

READ THIS WAY

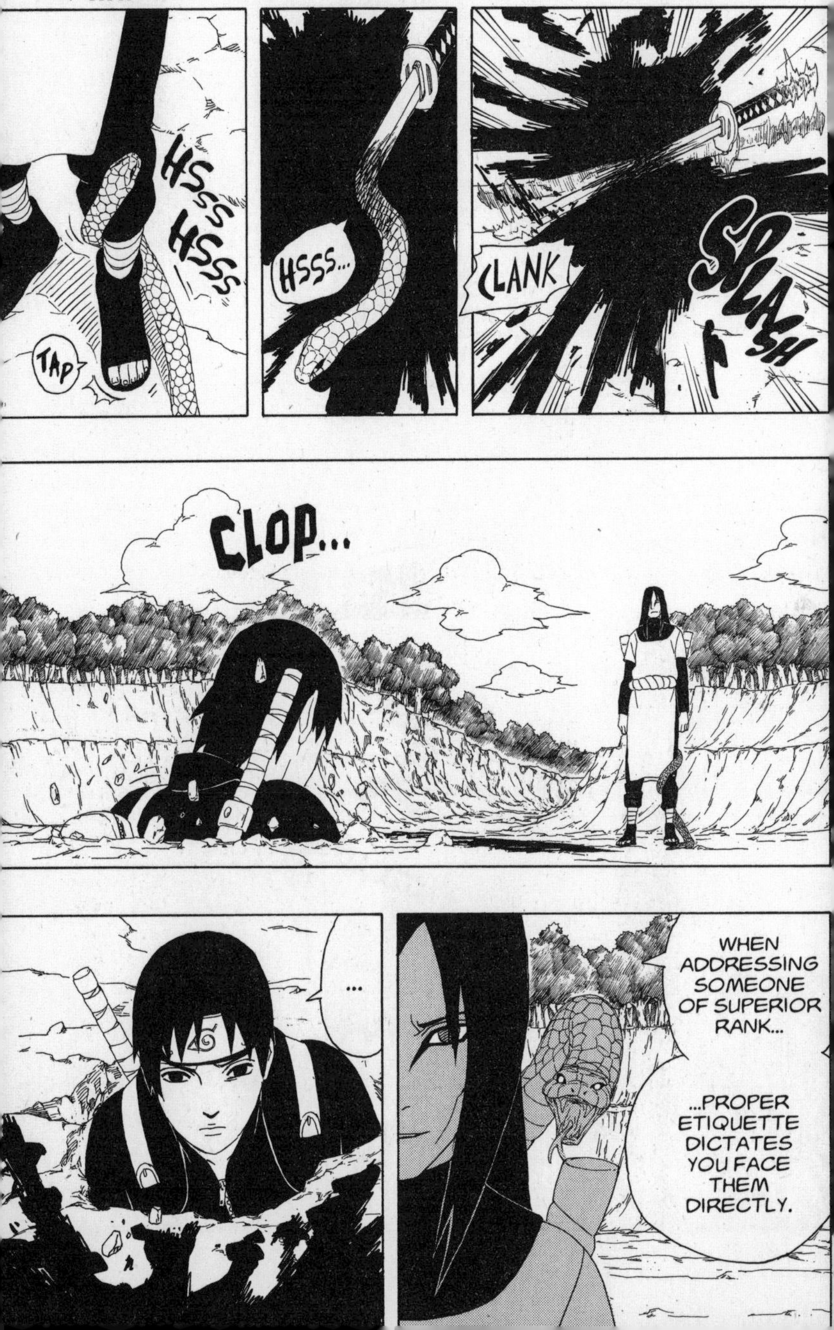

CLANK
SPLASH
HSSS...
HSSS HSSS
TAP
CLOP...
WHEN ADDRESSING SOMEONE OF SUPERIOR RANK...
...PROPER ETIQUETTE DICTATES YOU FACE THEM DIRECTLY.
...

HUF

HUF

BUZZ

FIZZ...

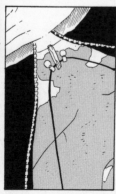

READ THIS WAY

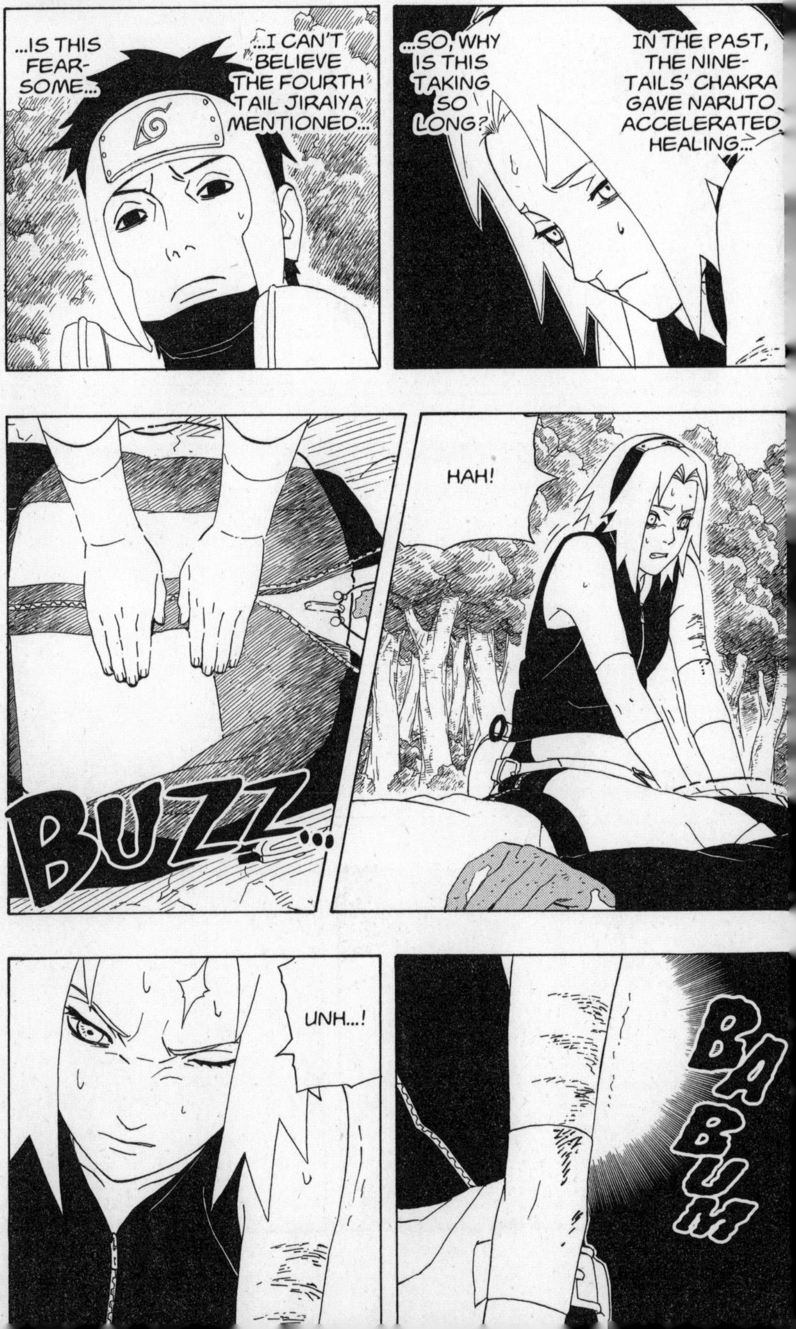
IN THE PAST, THE NINE-TAILS' CHAKRA GAVE NARUTO ACCELERATED HEALING...
...SO, WHY IS THIS TAKING SO LONG?
...I CAN'T BELIEVE THE FOURTH TAIL JIRAIYA MENTIONED...
...IS THIS FEAR-SOME...
HAH!
BUZZ...
BABUM
UNH...!

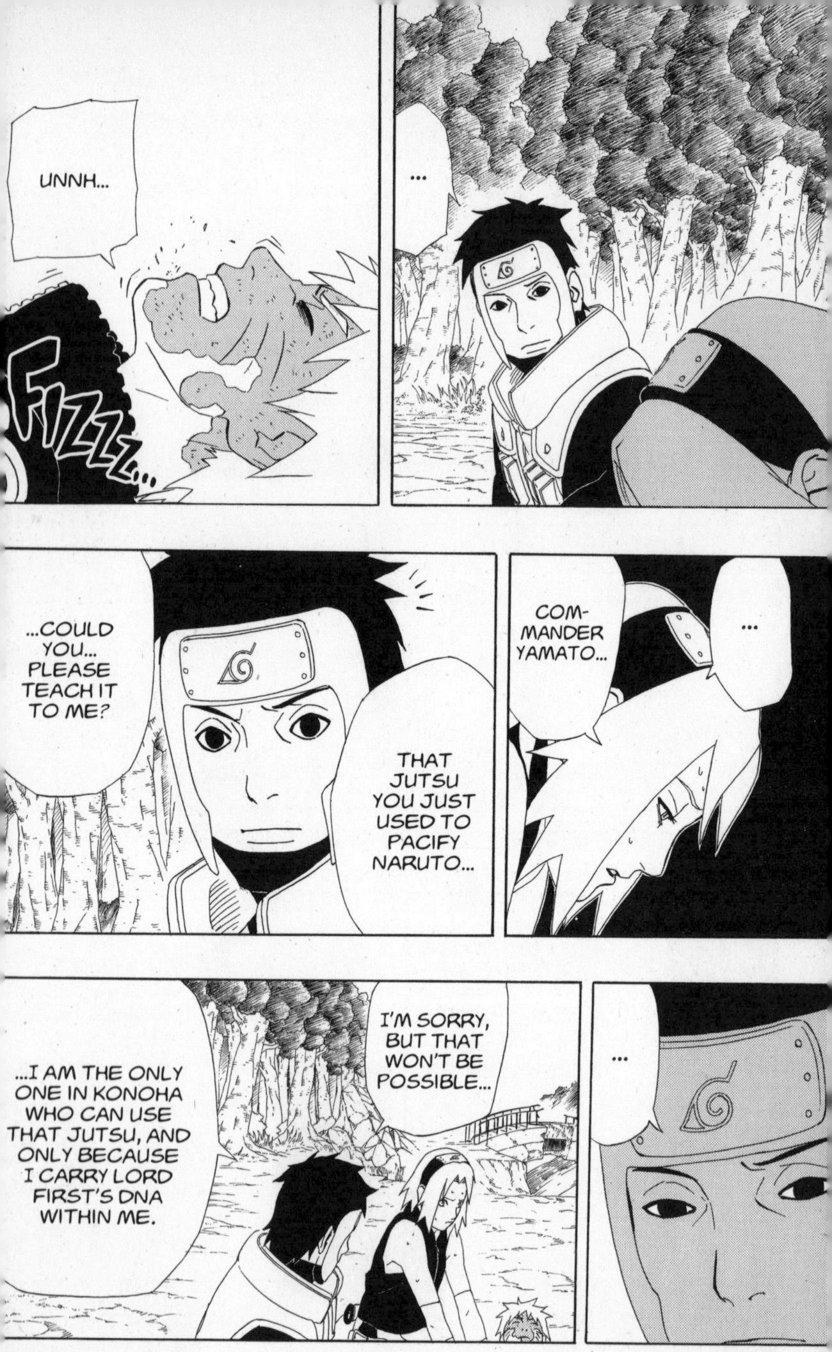
...
UNNH...
FIZZZZ...
...
COMMANDER YAMATO...
THAT JUTSU YOU JUST USED TO PACIFY NARUTO...
...COULD YOU... PLEASE TEACH IT TO ME?
...
I'M SORRY, BUT THAT WON'T BE POSSIBLE...
...I AM THE ONLY ONE IN KONOHA WHO CAN USE THAT JUTSU, AND ONLY BECAUSE I CARRY LORD FIRST'S DNA WITHIN ME.

READ THIS WAY

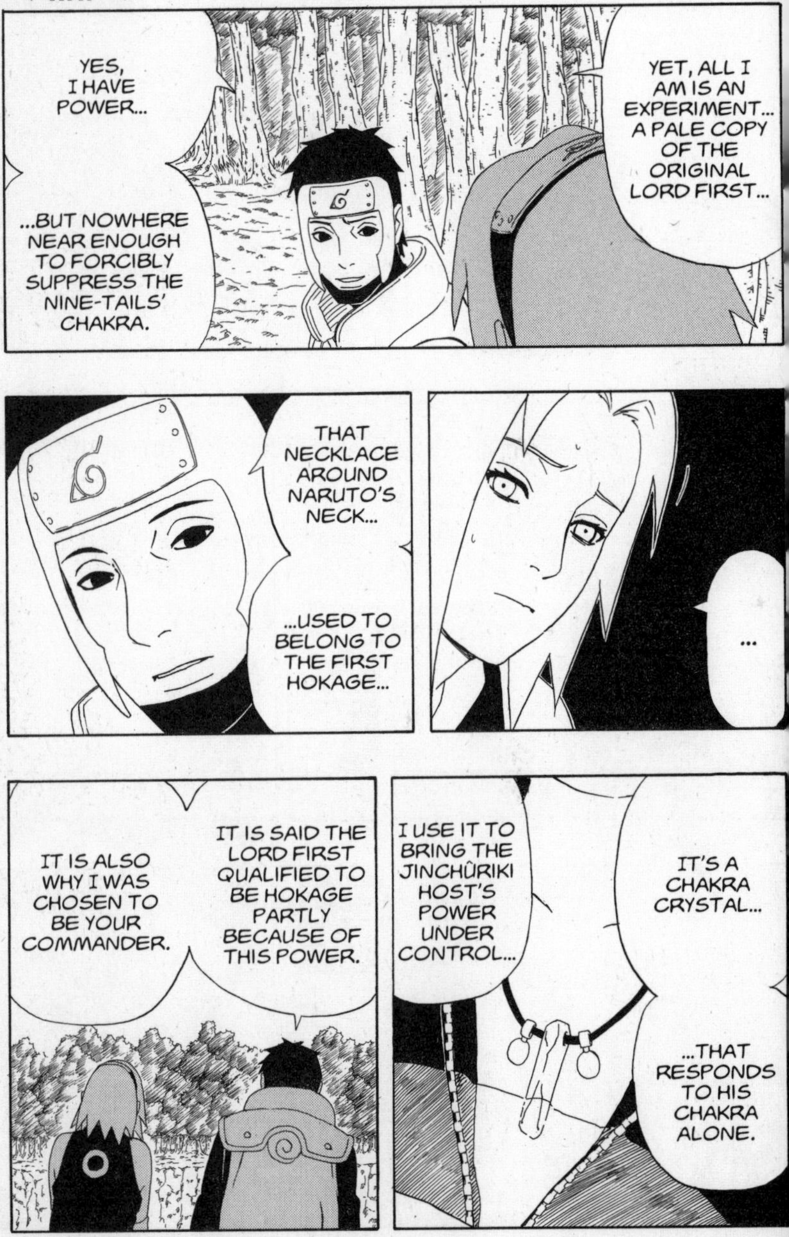
YET, ALL I AM IS AN EXPERIMENT... A PALE COPY OF THE ORIGINAL LORD FIRST...
YES, I HAVE POWER...
...BUT NOWHERE NEAR ENOUGH TO FORCIBLY SUPPRESS THE NINE-TAILS' CHAKRA.
...
THAT NECKLACE AROUND NARUTO'S NECK...
...USED TO BELONG TO THE FIRST HOKAGE...
IT'S A CHAKRA CRYSTAL...
...THAT RESPONDS TO HIS CHAKRA ALONE.
I USE IT TO BRING THE JINCHÛRIKI HOST'S POWER UNDER CONTROL...
IT IS SAID THE LORD FIRST QUALIFIED TO BE HOKAGE PARTLY BECAUSE OF THIS POWER.
IT IS ALSO WHY I WAS CHOSEN TO BE YOUR COMMANDER.

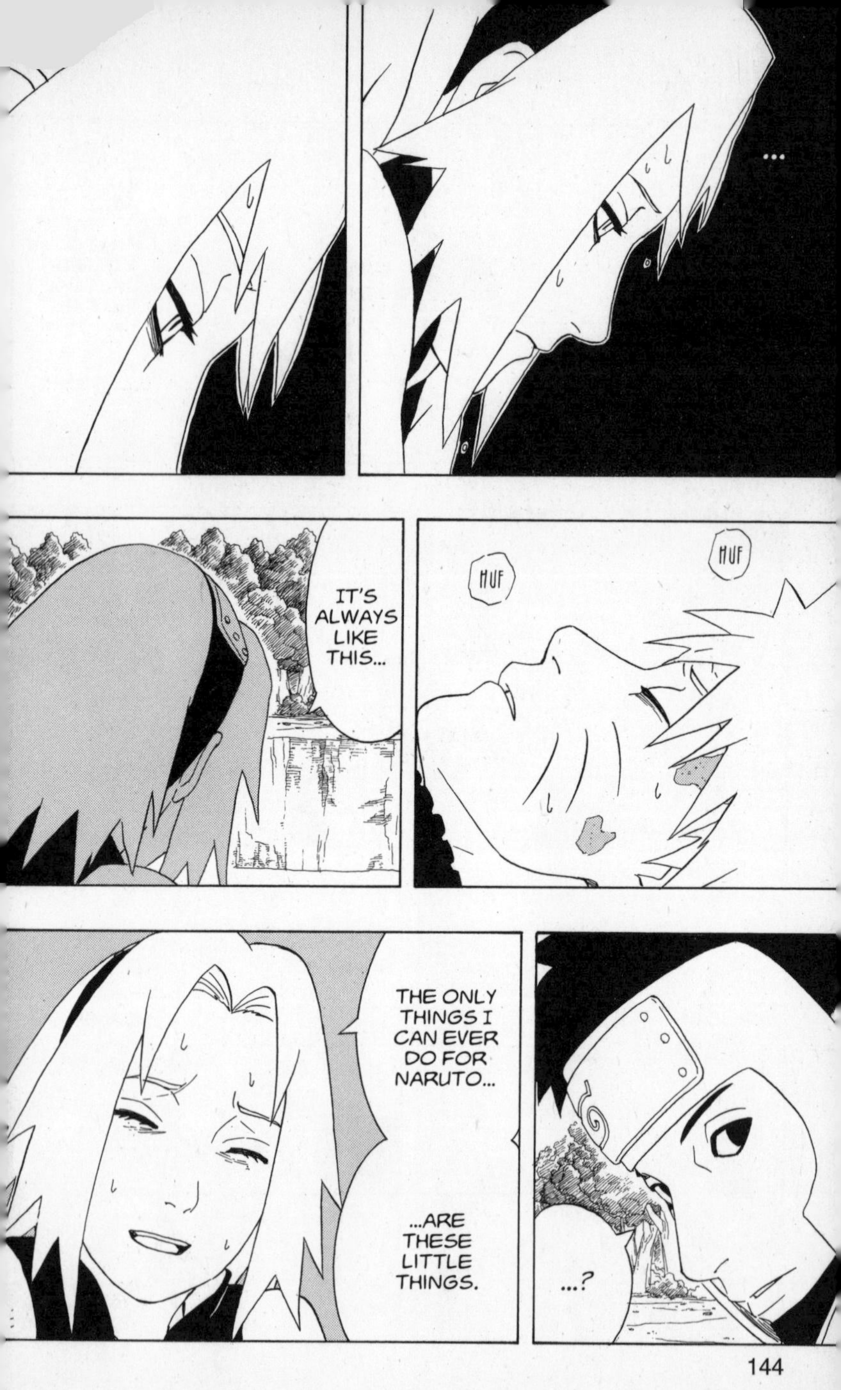
...
HUF
HUF
IT'S ALWAYS LIKE THIS...
...?
THE ONLY THINGS I CAN EVER DO FOR NARUTO...
...ARE THESE LITTLE THINGS.

READ THIS WAY

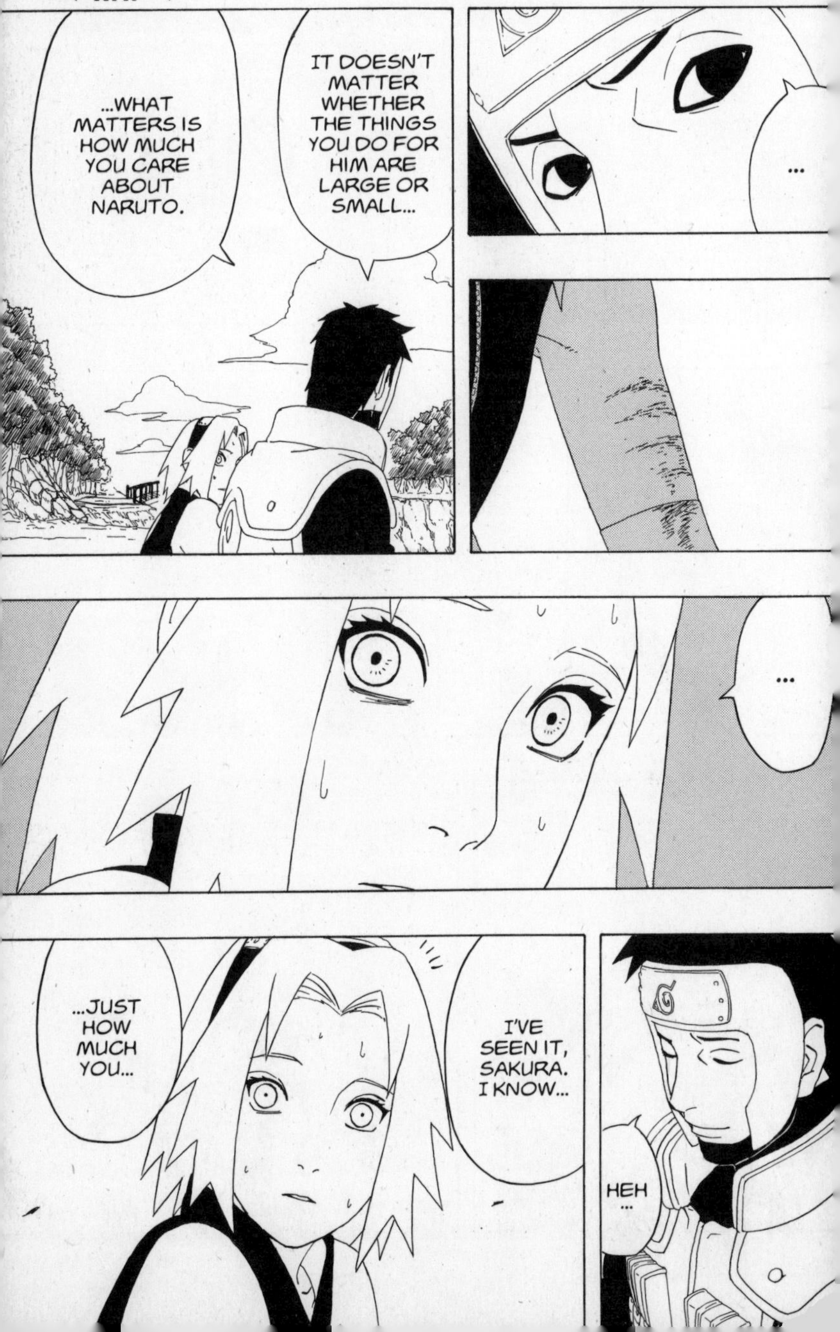
...
IT DOESN'T MATTER WHETHER THE THINGS YOU DO FOR HIM ARE LARGE OR SMALL...
...WHAT MATTERS IS HOW MUCH YOU CARE ABOUT NARUTO.
...
HEH ...
I'VE SEEN IT, SAKURA. I KNOW...
...JUST HOW MUCH YOU...

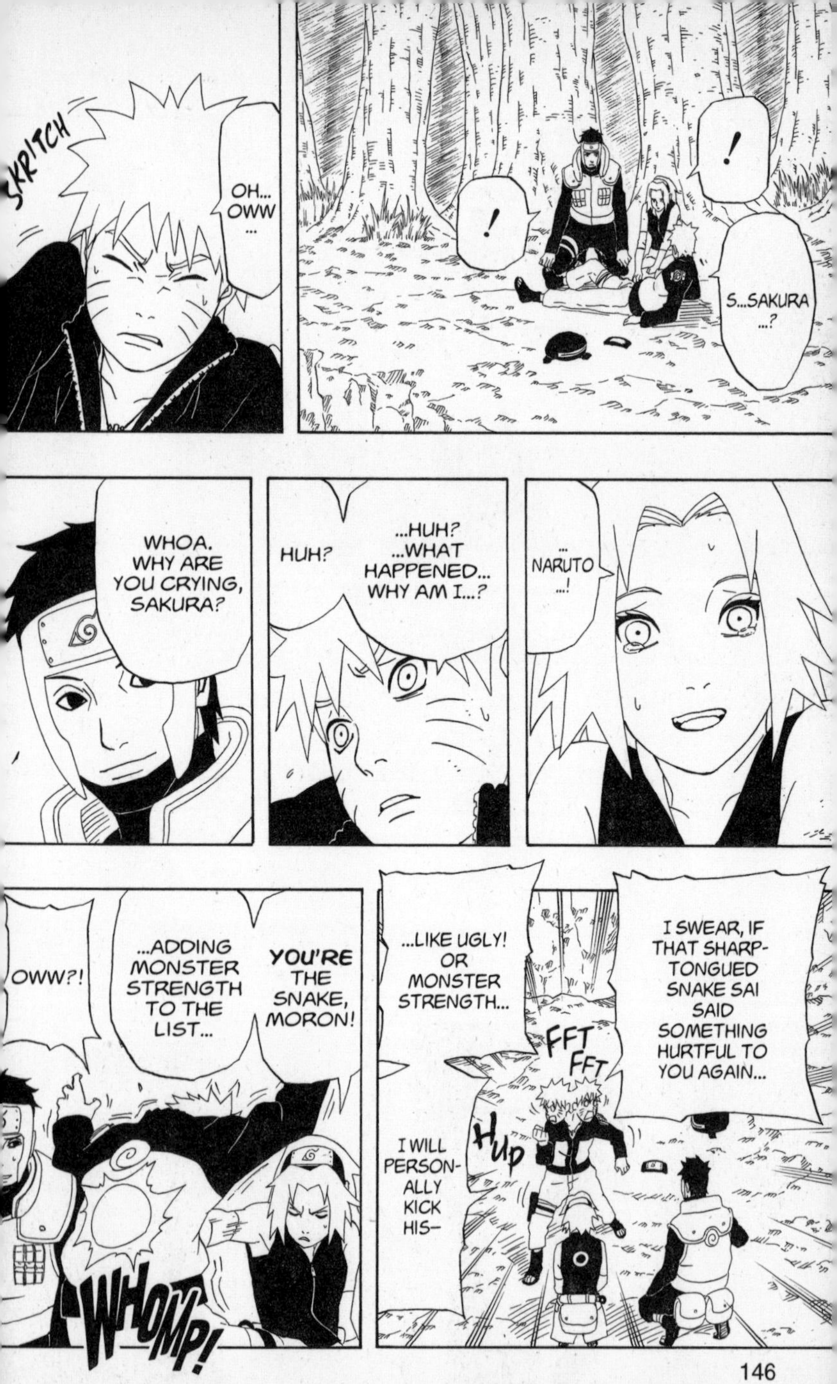
!
S...SAKURA ...?
!
SKRITCH
OH... OWW ...
... NARUTO ...!
...HUH? ...WHAT HAPPENED... WHY AM I...?
HUH?
WHOA. WHY ARE YOU CRYING, SAKURA?
I SWEAR, IF THAT SHARP-TONGUED SNAKE SAI SAID SOMETHING HURTFUL TO YOU AGAIN...
...LIKE UGLY! OR MONSTER STRENGTH...
FFT FFT
HUP
I WILL PERSON-ALLY KICK HIS–
YOU'RE THE SNAKE, MORON!
...ADDING MONSTER STRENGTH TO THE LIST...
OWW?!
WHOMP!

READ THIS WAY

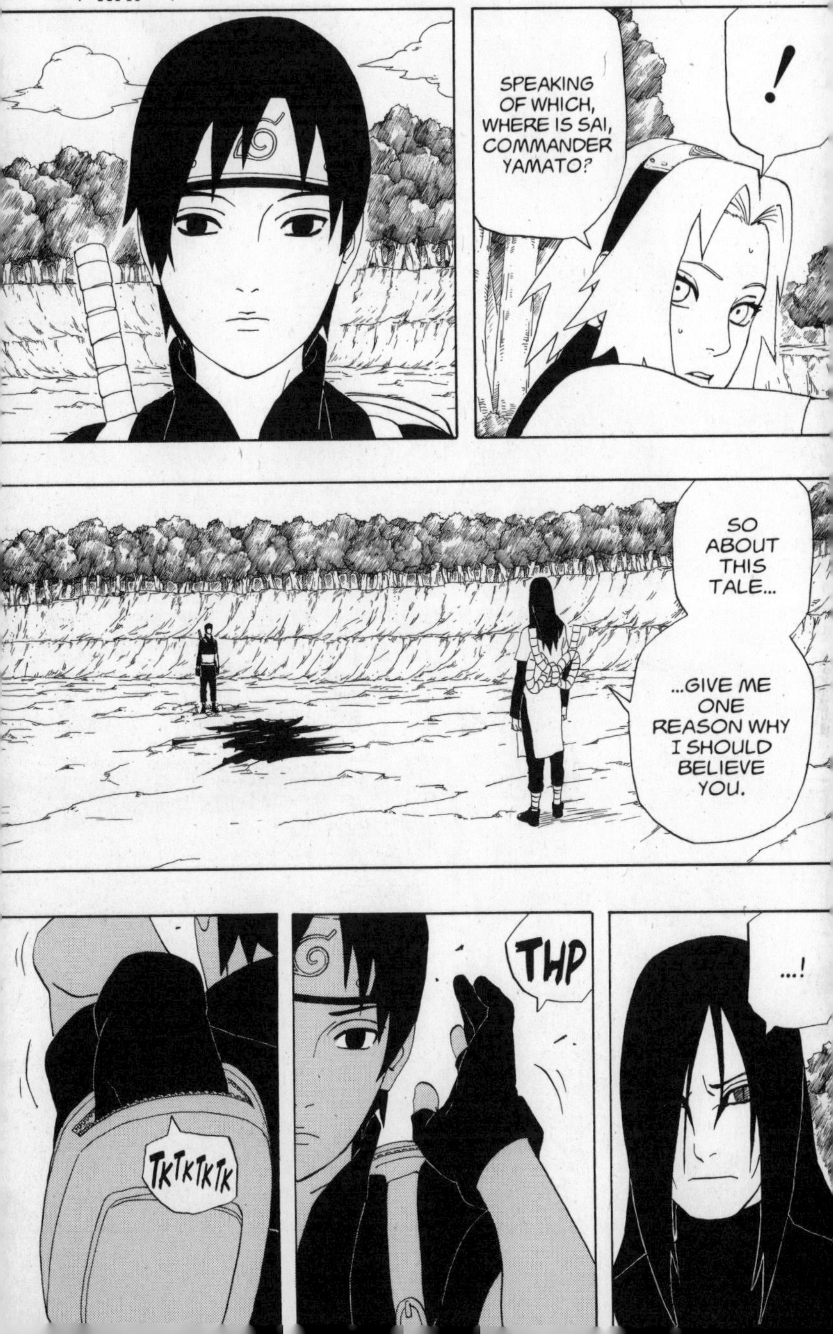
!
SPEAKING OF WHICH, WHERE IS SAI, COMMANDER YAMATO?
SO ABOUT THIS TALE...
...GIVE ME ONE REASON WHY I SHOULD BELIEVE YOU.
...!
THP
TKTKTKTK

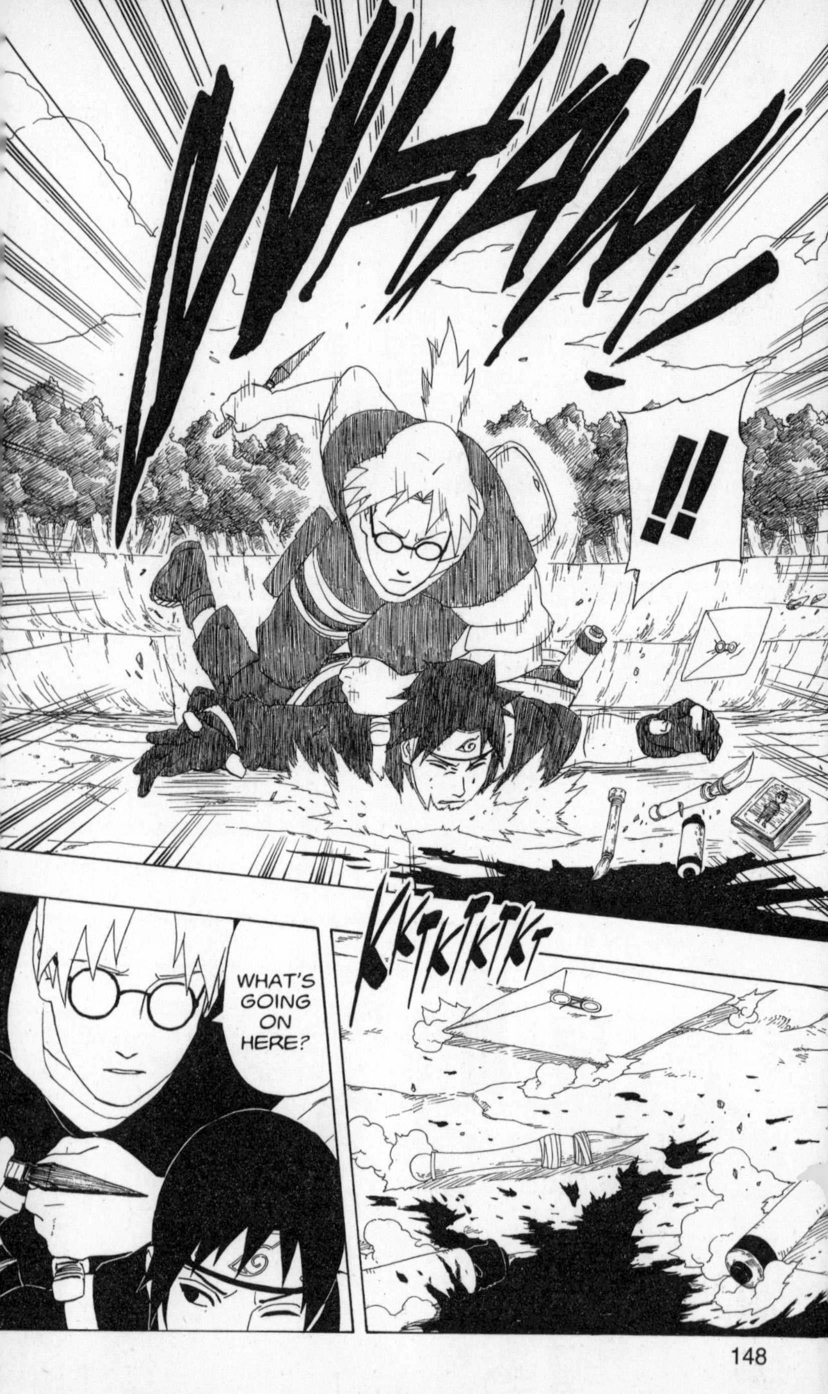
WHAM
!!
KKTKTKTKT
WHAT'S GOING ON HERE?

READ THIS WAY

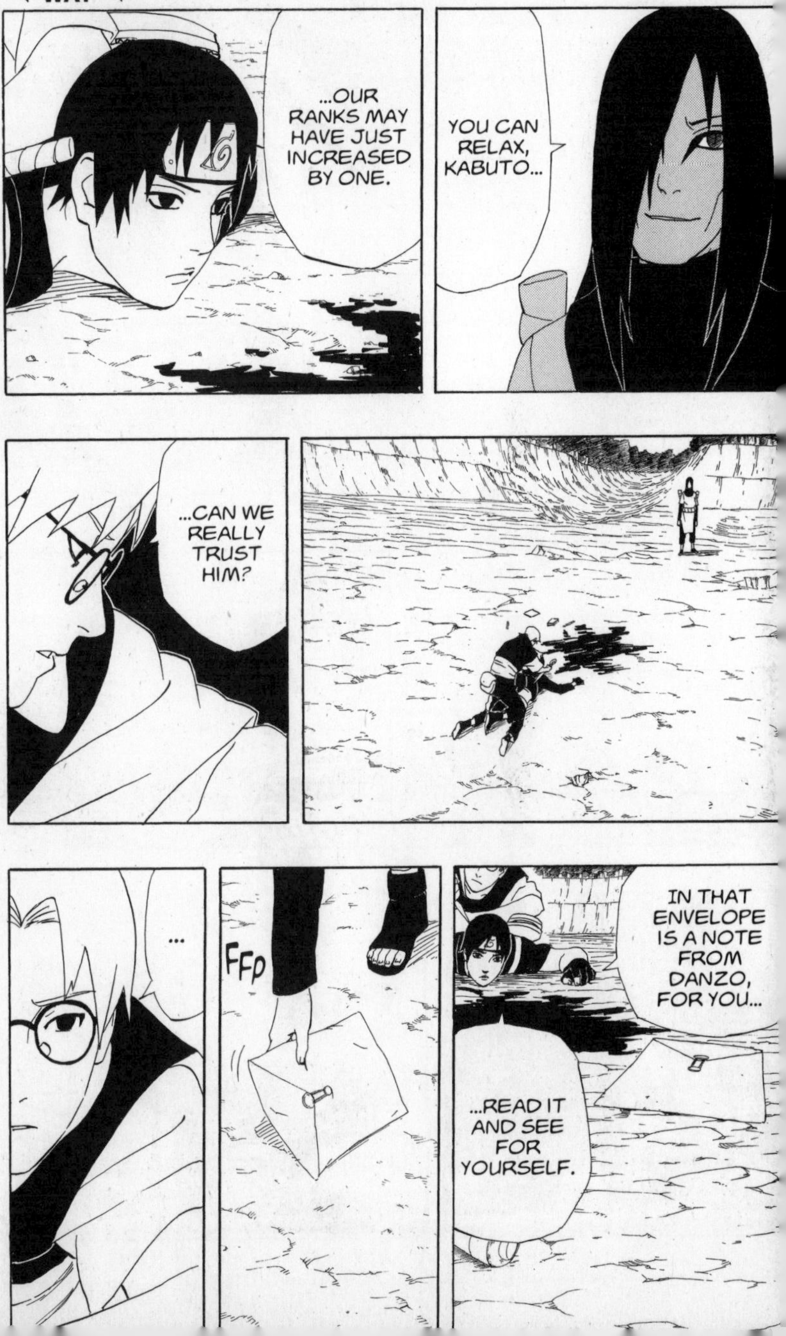
YOU CAN RELAX, KABUTO...
...OUR RANKS MAY HAVE JUST INCREASED BY ONE.
...CAN WE REALLY TRUST HIM?
IN THAT ENVELOPE IS A NOTE FROM DANZO, FOR YOU...
...READ IT AND SEE FOR YOURSELF.
FFP
...

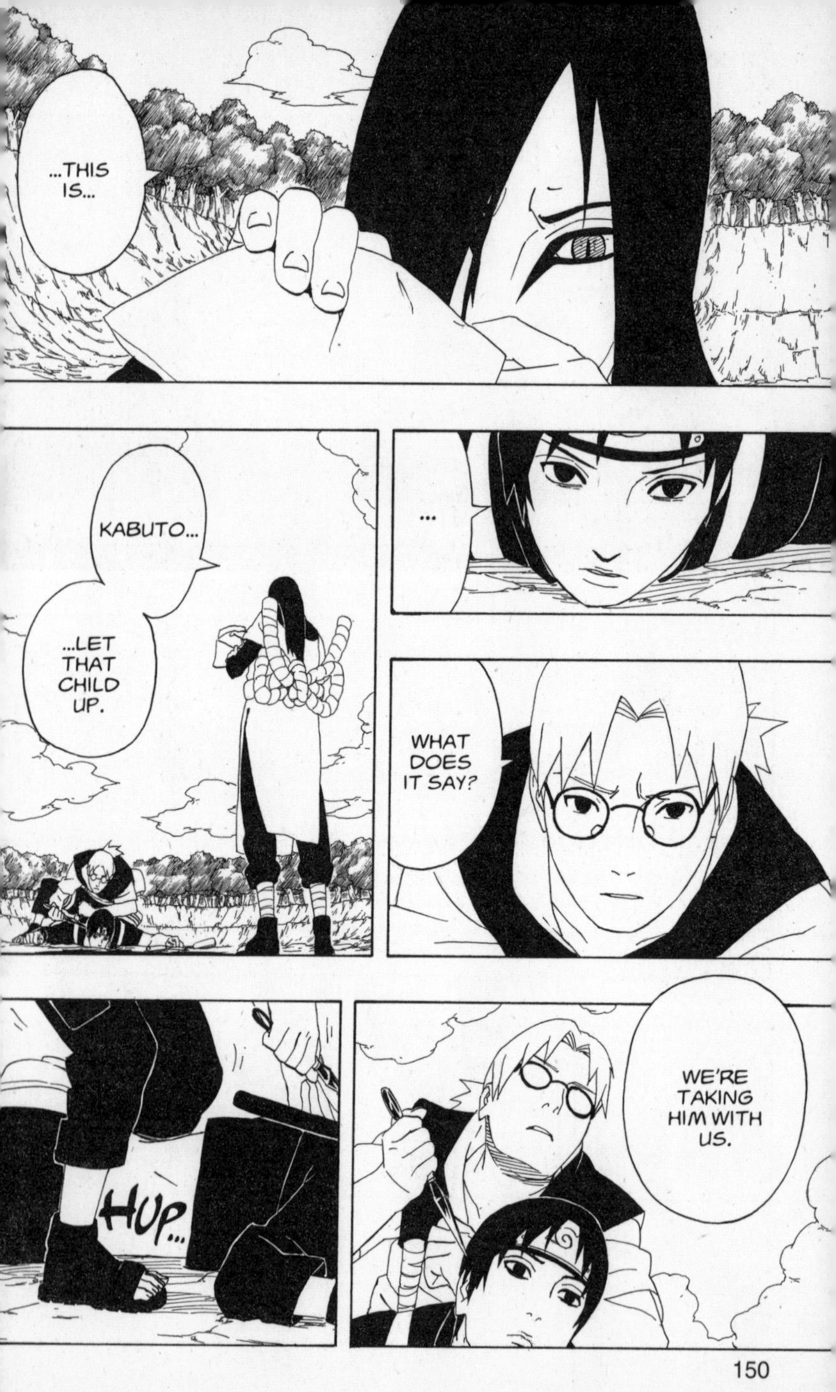
...THIS IS...
...
WHAT DOES IT SAY?
KABUTO...
...LET THAT CHILD UP.
WE'RE TAKING HIM WITH US.
HUP...

READ THIS WAY

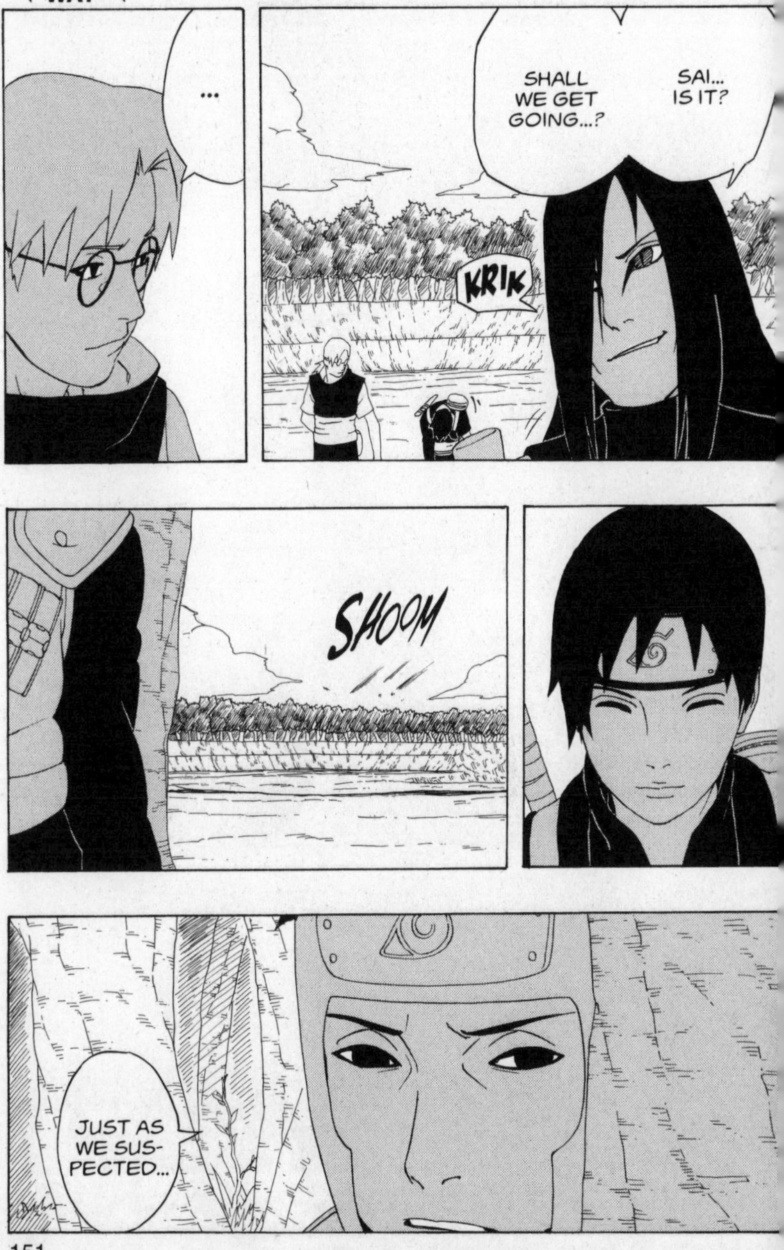

SAI... IS IT?
SHALL WE GET GOING...?
KRIK
...
SHOOM
JUST AS WE SUS-PECTED...

NARUTO

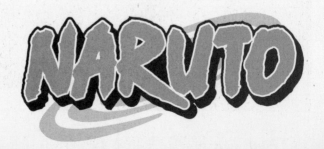

Number 298: The Secret Mission...!!

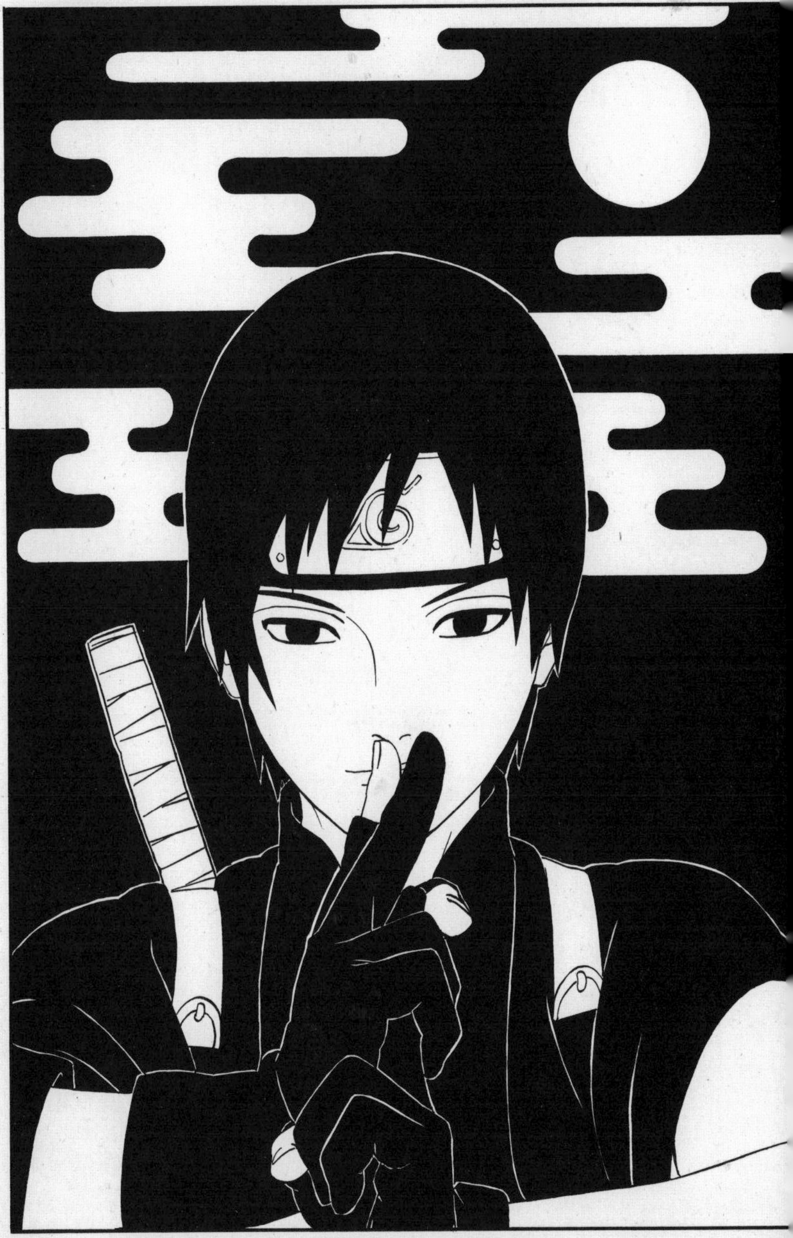

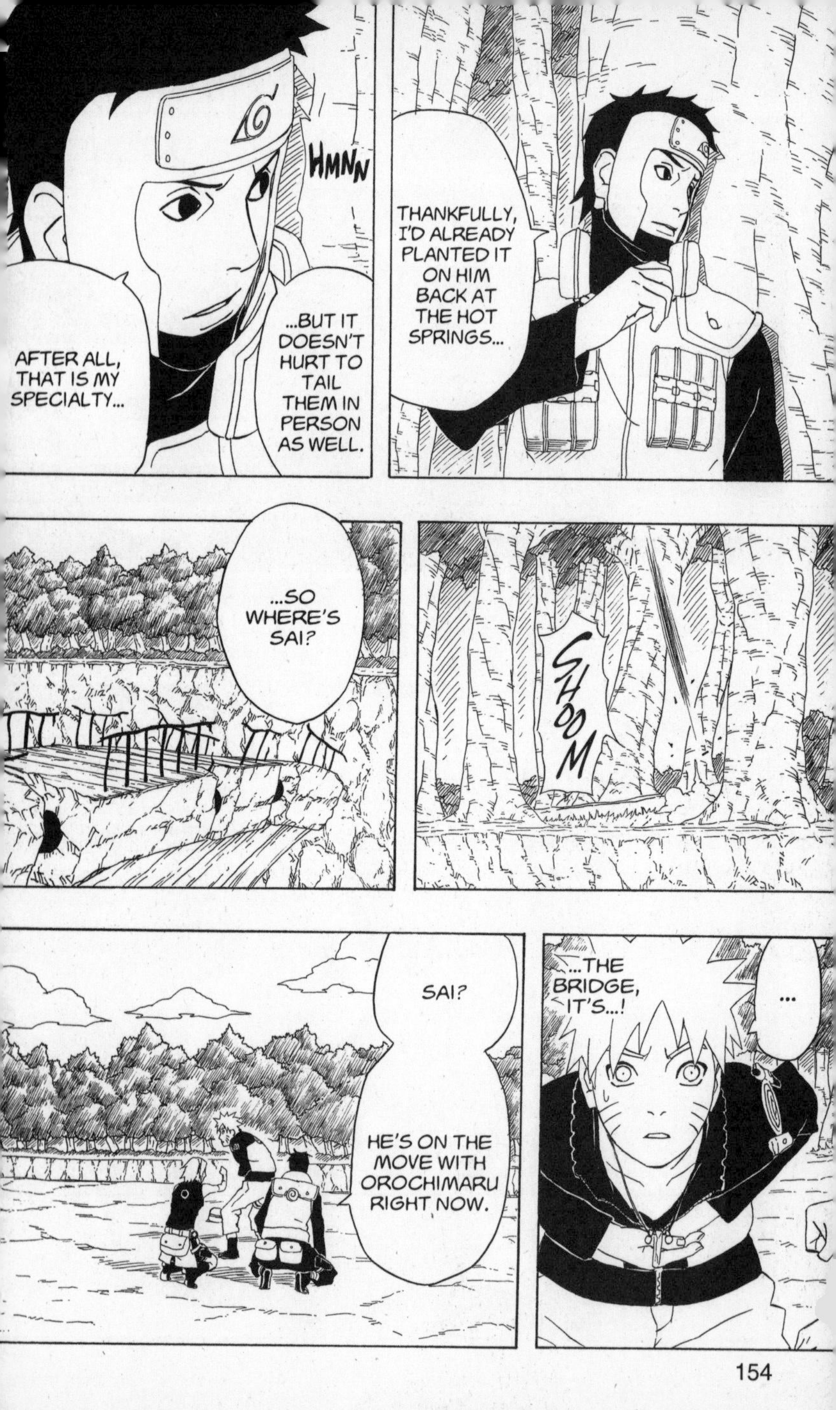
THANKFULLY, I'D ALREADY PLANTED IT ON HIM BACK AT THE HOT SPRINGS...
HMNN
...BUT IT DOESN'T HURT TO TAIL THEM IN PERSON AS WELL.
AFTER ALL, THAT IS MY SPECIALTY...
SHOOM
...SO WHERE'S SAI?
...
...THE BRIDGE, IT'S...!
SAI?
HE'S ON THE MOVE WITH OROCHIMARU RIGHT NOW.

READ THIS WAY

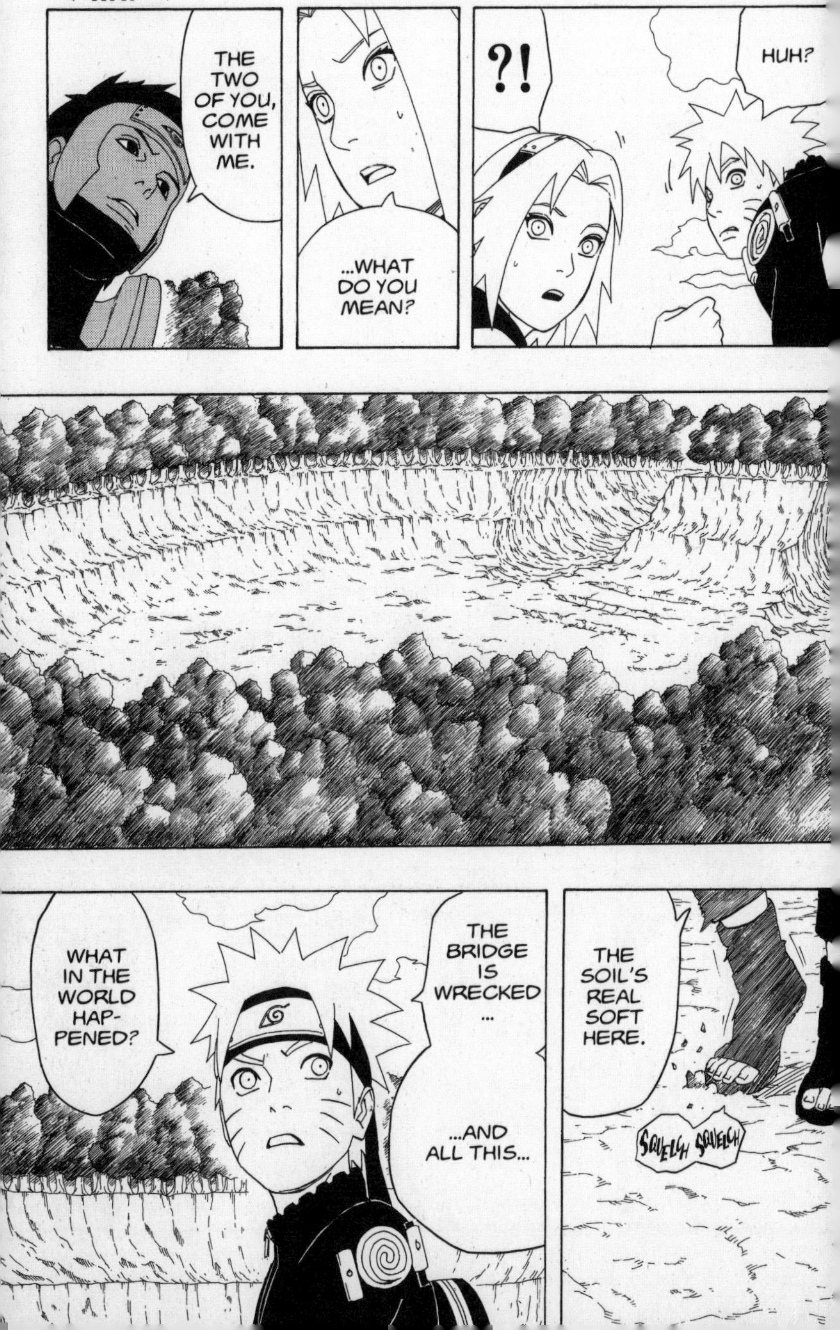
HUH?
?!
...WHAT DO YOU MEAN?
THE TWO OF YOU, COME WITH ME.
THE SOIL'S REAL SOFT HERE.
SQUELCH SQUELCH
THE BRIDGE IS WRECKED...
...AND ALL THIS...
WHAT IN THE WORLD HAP-PENED?

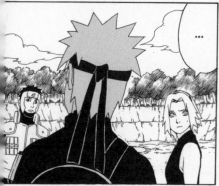

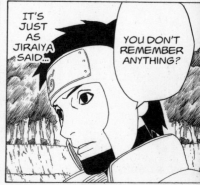

YOU DON'T REMEMBER ANYTHING?
IT'S JUST AS JIRAIYA SAID...
...
WAIT—DOES THIS HAVE SOMETHING TO DO WITH WHY I WAS UNCON-SCIOUS?
...
...
...

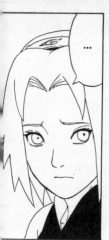

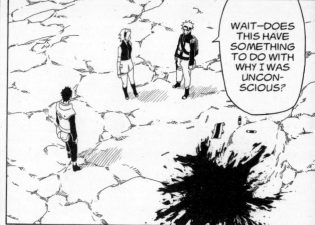

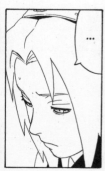

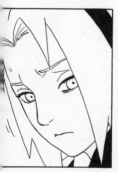

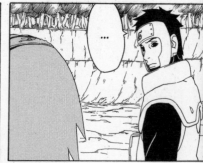

YOU GOT ATTACKED AND KNOCKED OUT BY OROCHIMARU...

...

...NO WAY... SERIOUSLY ?!

...

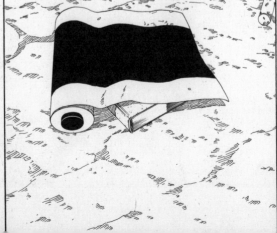

...!

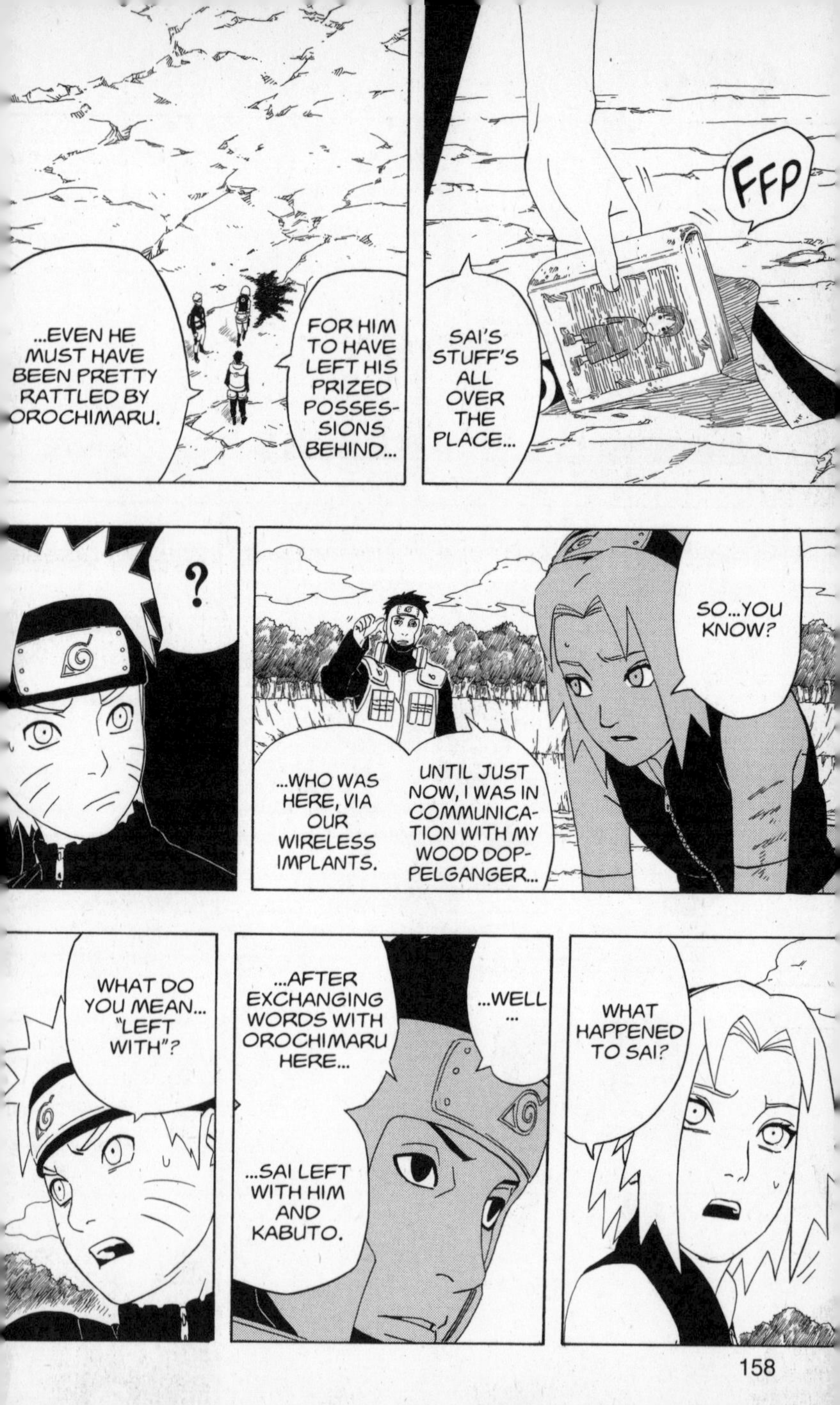
FFP
SAI'S STUFF'S ALL OVER THE PLACE...
FOR HIM TO HAVE LEFT HIS PRIZED POSSES-SIONS BEHIND...
...EVEN HE MUST HAVE BEEN PRETTY RATTLED BY OROCHIMARU.
SO...YOU KNOW?
UNTIL JUST NOW, I WAS IN COMMUNICA-TION WITH MY WOOD DOP-PELGANGER...
...WHO WAS HERE, VIA OUR WIRELESS IMPLANTS.
?
WHAT HAPPENED TO SAI?
...WELL ...
...AFTER EXCHANGING WORDS WITH OROCHIMARU HERE...
...SAI LEFT WITH HIM AND KABUTO.
WHAT DO YOU MEAN... "LEFT WITH"?

READ THIS WAY

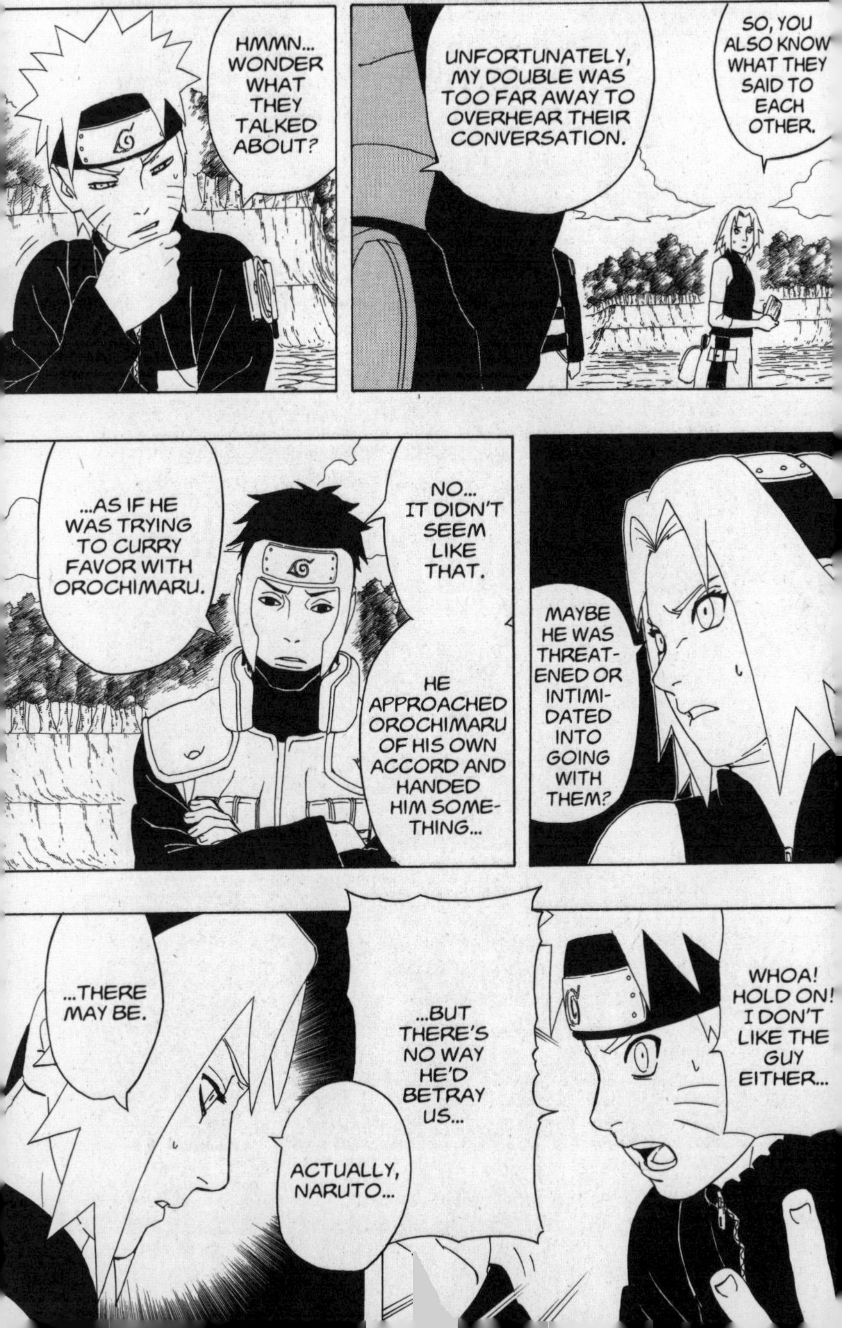
SO, YOU ALSO KNOW WHAT THEY SAID TO EACH OTHER.
UNFORTUNATELY, MY DOUBLE WAS TOO FAR AWAY TO OVERHEAR THEIR CONVERSATION.
HMMN... WONDER WHAT THEY TALKED ABOUT?
MAYBE HE WAS THREAT-ENED OR INTIMI-DATED INTO GOING WITH THEM?
NO... IT DIDN'T SEEM LIKE THAT.
HE APPROACHED OROCHIMARU OF HIS OWN ACCORD AND HANDED HIM SOME-THING...
...AS IF HE WAS TRYING TO CURRY FAVOR WITH OROCHIMARU.
WHOA! HOLD ON! I DON'T LIKE THE GUY EITHER...
...BUT THERE'S NO WAY HE'D BETRAY US...
ACTUALLY, NARUTO...
...THERE MAY BE.

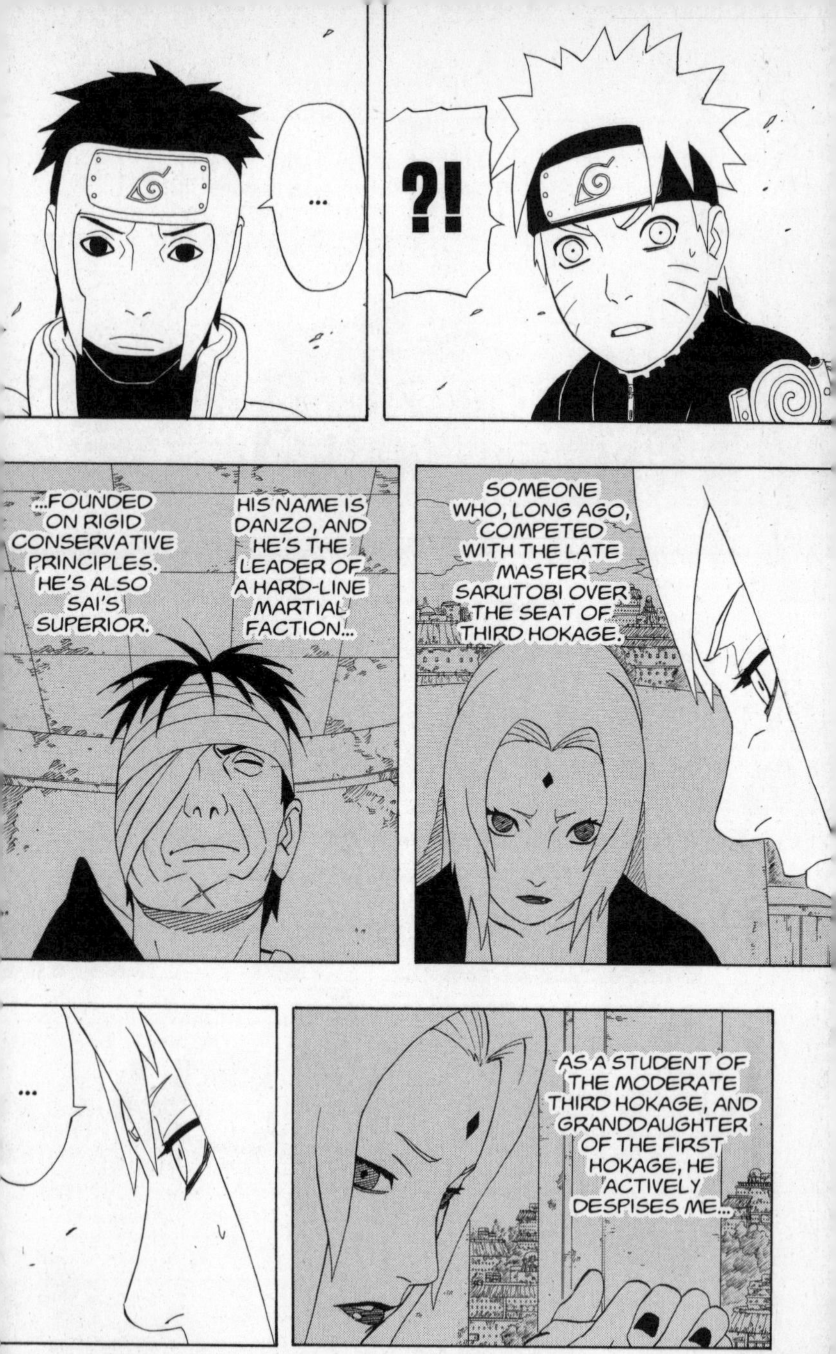
?!
...
SOMEONE WHO, LONG AGO, COMPETED WITH THE LATE MASTER SARUTOBI OVER THE SEAT OF THIRD HOKAGE.
HIS NAME IS DANZO, AND HE'S THE LEADER OF A HARD-LINE MARTIAL FACTION...
...FOUNDED ON RIGID CONSERVATIVE PRINCIPLES. HE'S ALSO SAI'S SUPERIOR.
AS A STUDENT OF THE MODERATE THIRD HOKAGE, AND GRANDDAUGHTER OF THE FIRST HOKAGE, HE ACTIVELY DESPISES ME...
...

READ THIS WAY

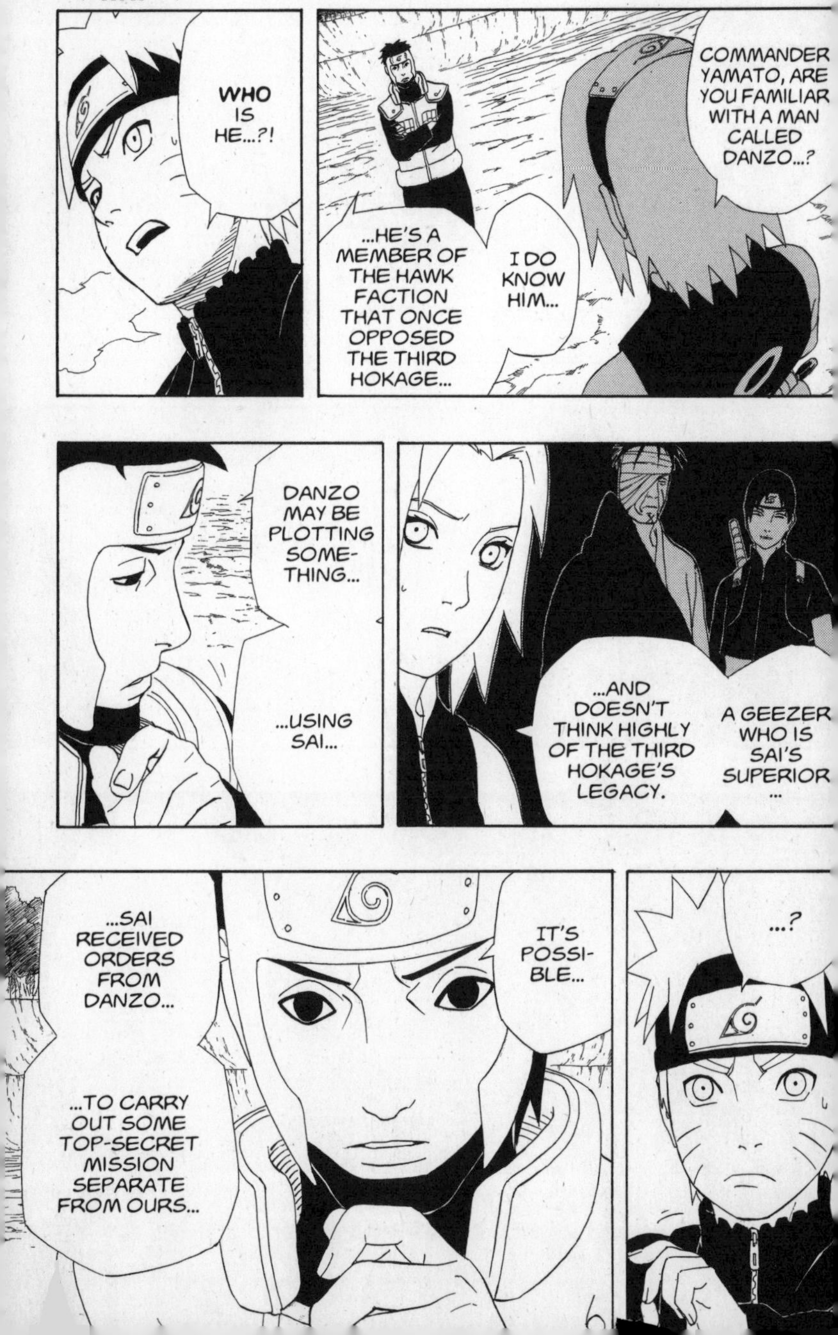
COMMANDER YAMATO, ARE YOU FAMILIAR WITH A MAN CALLED DANZO...?
I DO KNOW HIM...
...HE'S A MEMBER OF THE HAWK FACTION THAT ONCE OPPOSED THE THIRD HOKAGE...
WHO IS HE...?!
A GEEZER WHO IS SAI'S SUPERIOR...
...AND DOESN'T THINK HIGHLY OF THE THIRD HOKAGE'S LEGACY.
DANZO MAY BE PLOTTING SOME-THING...
...USING SAI...
...?
IT'S POSSI-BLE...
...SAI RECEIVED ORDERS FROM DANZO...
...TO CARRY OUT SOME TOP-SECRET MISSION SEPARATE FROM OURS...

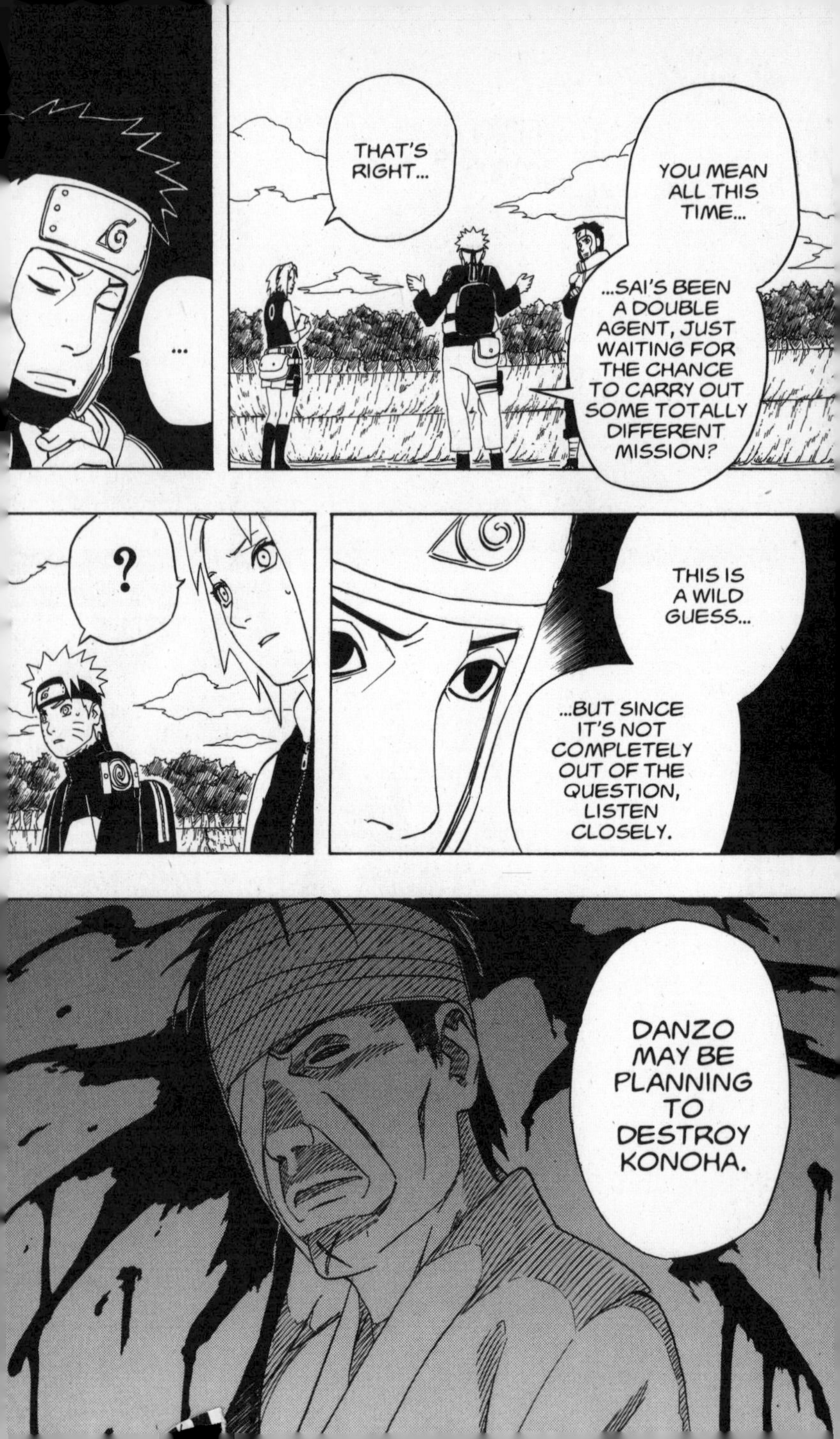
YOU MEAN ALL THIS TIME...
...SAI'S BEEN A DOUBLE AGENT, JUST WAITING FOR THE CHANCE TO CARRY OUT SOME TOTALLY DIFFERENT MISSION?
THAT'S RIGHT...
...
THIS IS A WILD GUESS...
...BUT SINCE IT'S NOT COMPLETELY OUT OF THE QUESTION, LISTEN CLOSELY.
?
DANZO MAY BE PLANNING TO DESTROY KONOHA.

READ THIS WAY

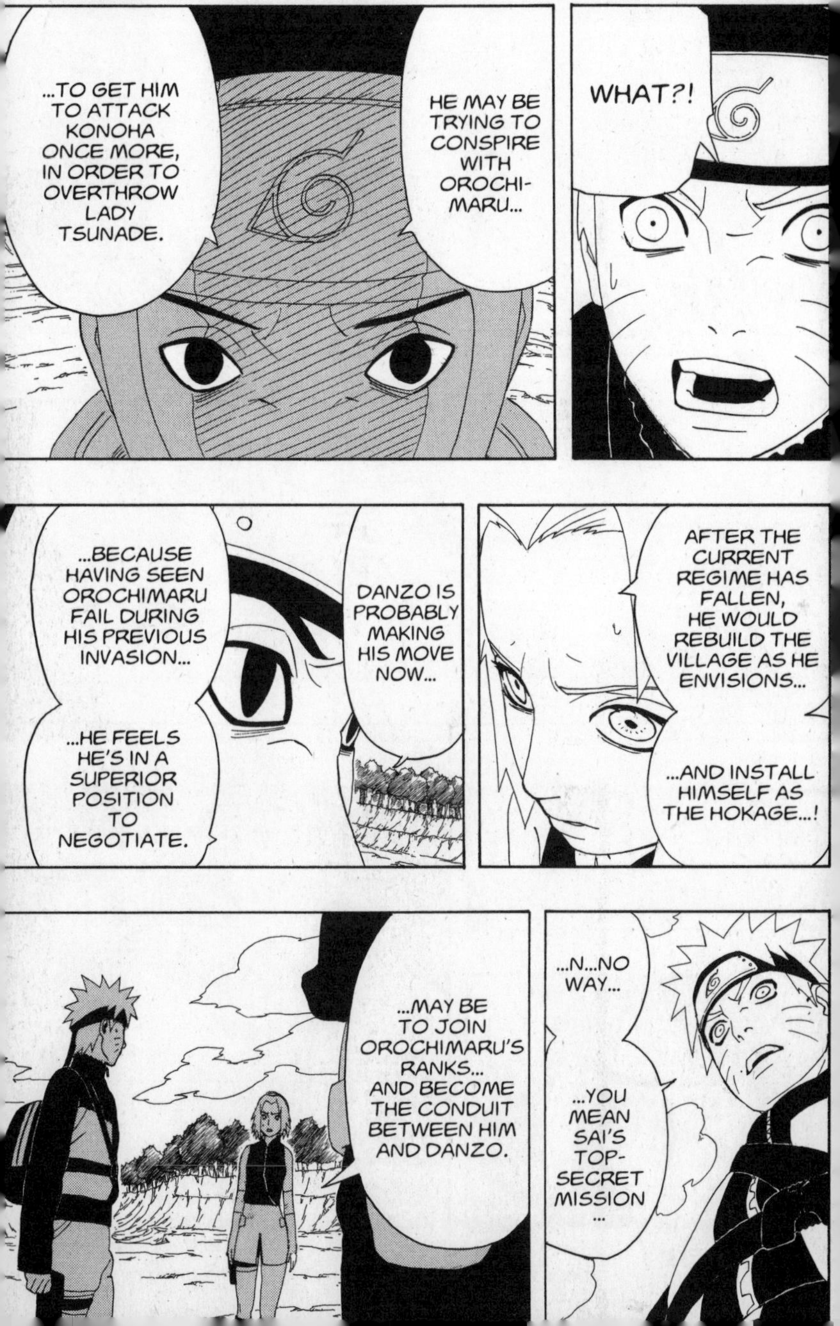
WHAT?!
HE MAY BE TRYING TO CONSPIRE WITH OROCHI-MARU...
...TO GET HIM TO ATTACK KONOHA ONCE MORE, IN ORDER TO OVERTHROW LADY TSUNADE.
AFTER THE CURRENT REGIME HAS FALLEN, HE WOULD REBUILD THE VILLAGE AS HE ENVISIONS...
...AND INSTALL HIMSELF AS THE HOKAGE...!
DANZO IS PROBABLY MAKING HIS MOVE NOW...
...BECAUSE HAVING SEEN OROCHIMARU FAIL DURING HIS PREVIOUS INVASION...
...HE FEELS HE'S IN A SUPERIOR POSITION TO NEGOTIATE.
...N...NO WAY...
...YOU MEAN SAI'S TOP-SECRET MISSION ...
...MAY BE TO JOIN OROCHIMARU'S RANKS... AND BECOME THE CONDUIT BETWEEN HIM AND DANZO.

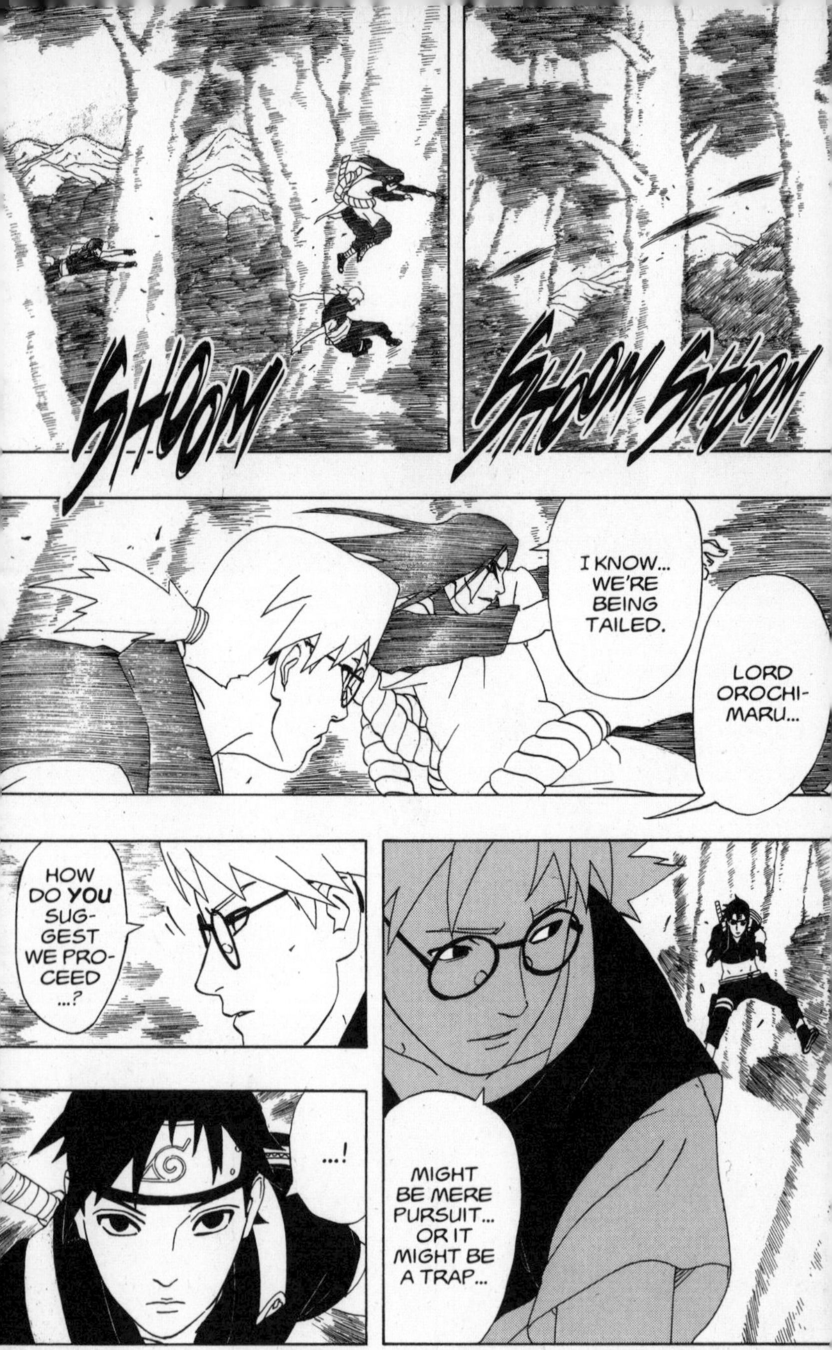
SHOOM SHOOM
SHOOM
LORD OROCHIMARU...
I KNOW... WE'RE BEING TAILED.
MIGHT BE MERE PURSUIT... OR IT MIGHT BE A TRAP...
HOW DO **YOU** SUGGEST WE PROCEED...?
...!

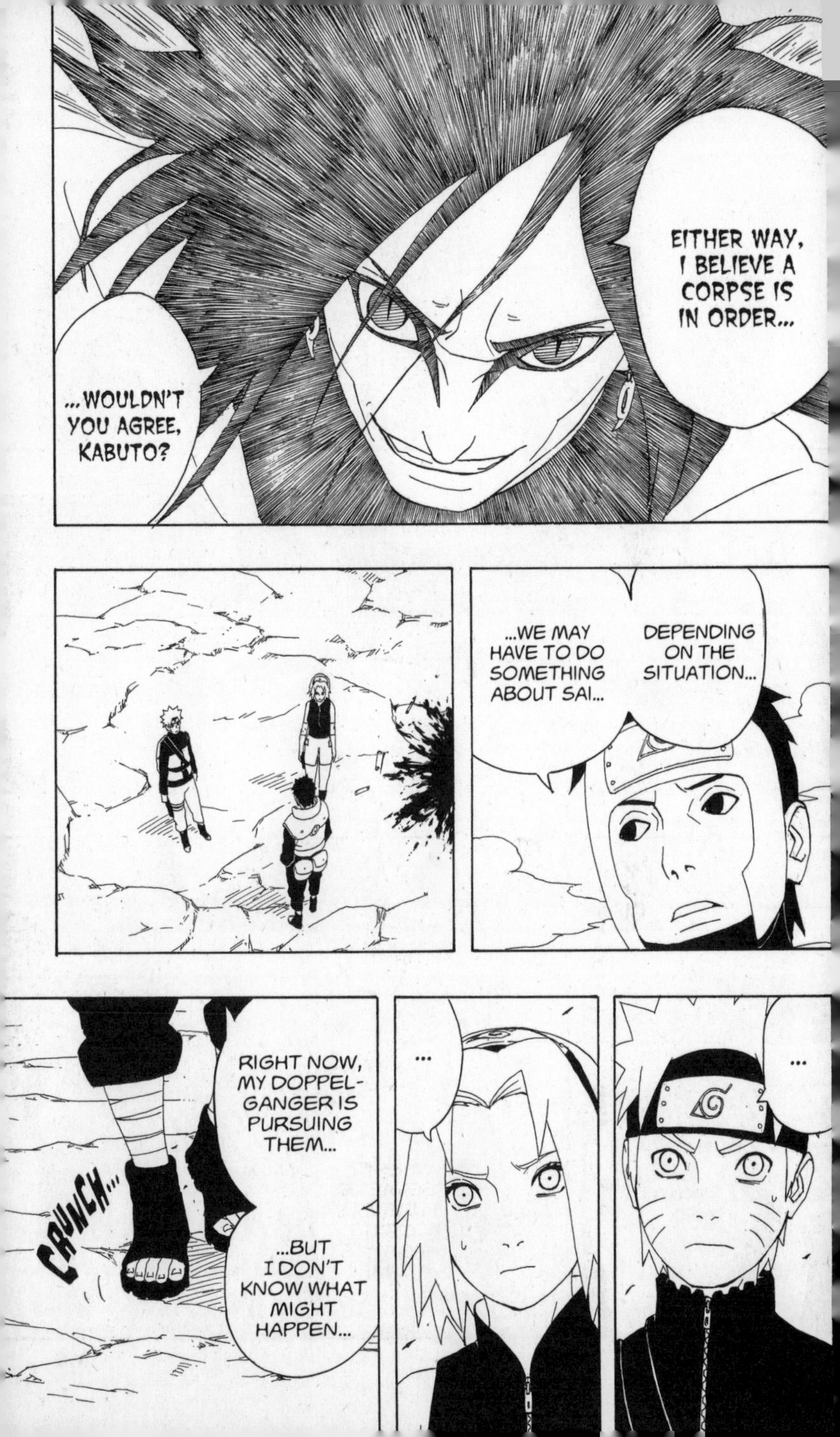
EITHER WAY, I BELIEVE A CORPSE IS IN ORDER...
...WOULDN'T YOU AGREE, KABUTO?
DEPENDING ON THE SITUATION...
...WE MAY HAVE TO DO SOMETHING ABOUT SAI...
...
...
RIGHT NOW, MY DOPPEL-GANGER IS PURSUING THEM...
...BUT I DON'T KNOW WHAT MIGHT HAPPEN...
CRUNCH...

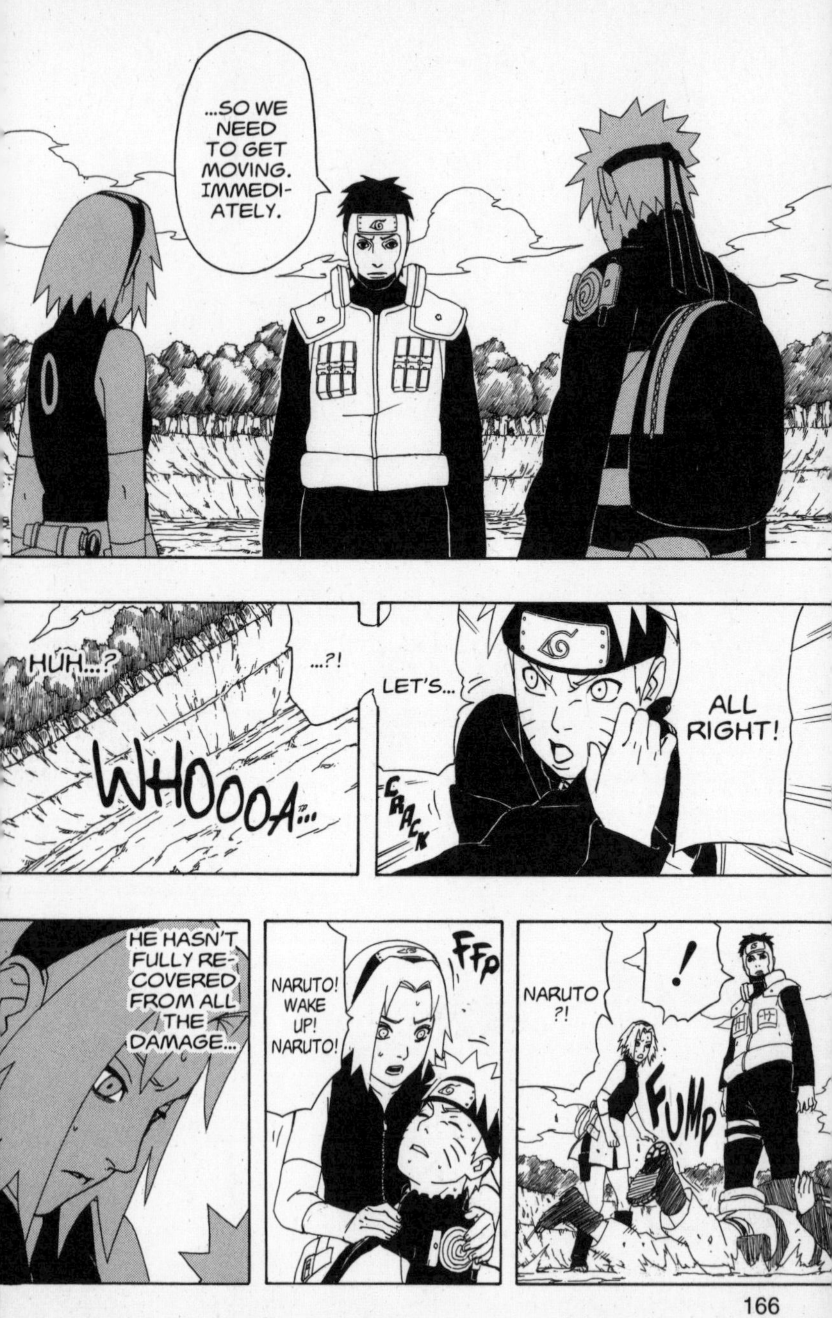
...SO WE NEED TO GET MOVING. IMMEDI- ATELY.
ALL RIGHT!
LET'S...
CRACK
...?!
HUH...?
WHOOOA...
!
NARUTO ?!
FUMP
FFP
NARUTO! WAKE UP! NARUTO!
HE HASN'T FULLY RE- COVERED FROM ALL THE DAMAGE...

READ THIS WAY

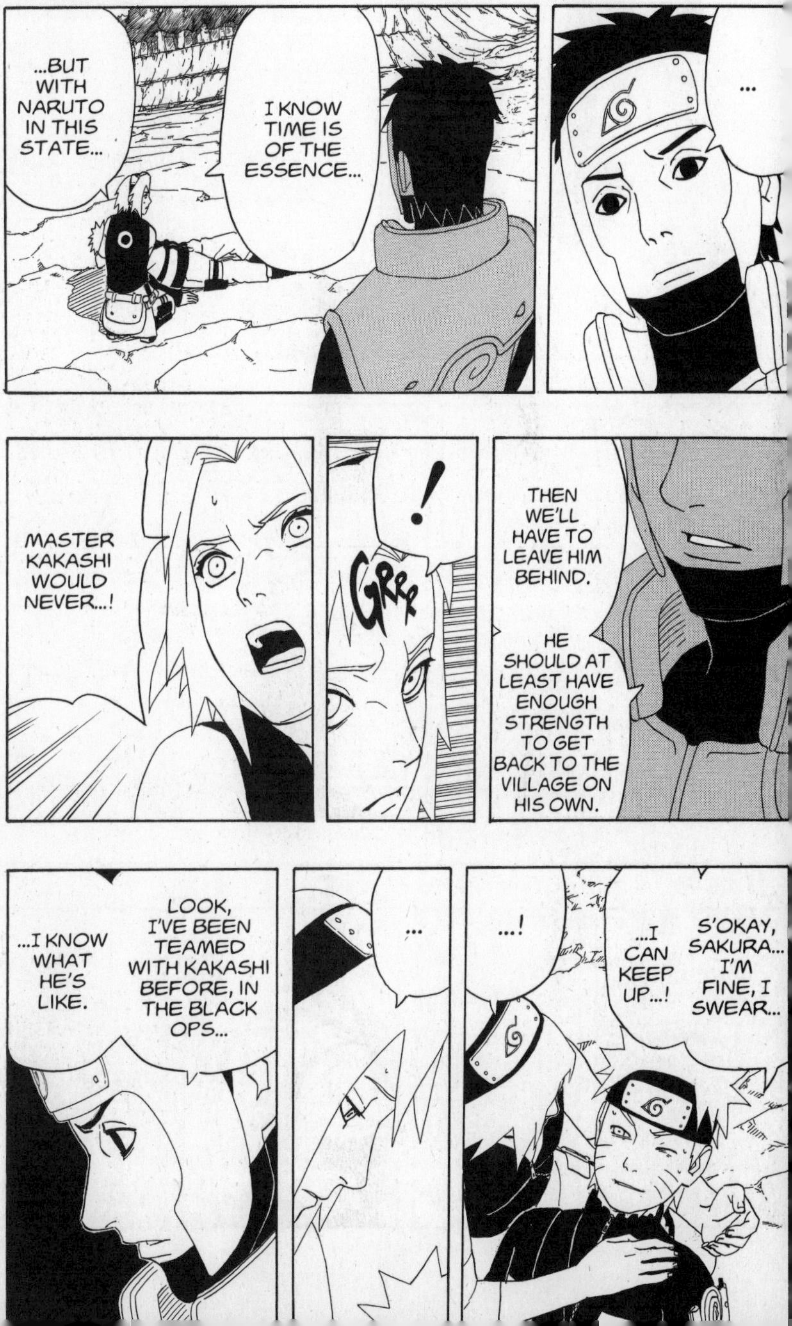
...
I KNOW TIME IS OF THE ESSENCE...
...BUT WITH NARUTO IN THIS STATE...
THEN WE'LL HAVE TO LEAVE HIM BEHIND.
HE SHOULD AT LEAST HAVE ENOUGH STRENGTH TO GET BACK TO THE VILLAGE ON HIS OWN.
!
GRRR
MASTER KAKASHI WOULD NEVER...!
S'OKAY, SAKURA... I'M FINE, I SWEAR...
...I CAN KEEP UP...!
...!
...
LOOK, I'VE BEEN TEAMED WITH KAKASHI BEFORE, IN THE BLACK OPS...
...I KNOW WHAT HE'S LIKE.

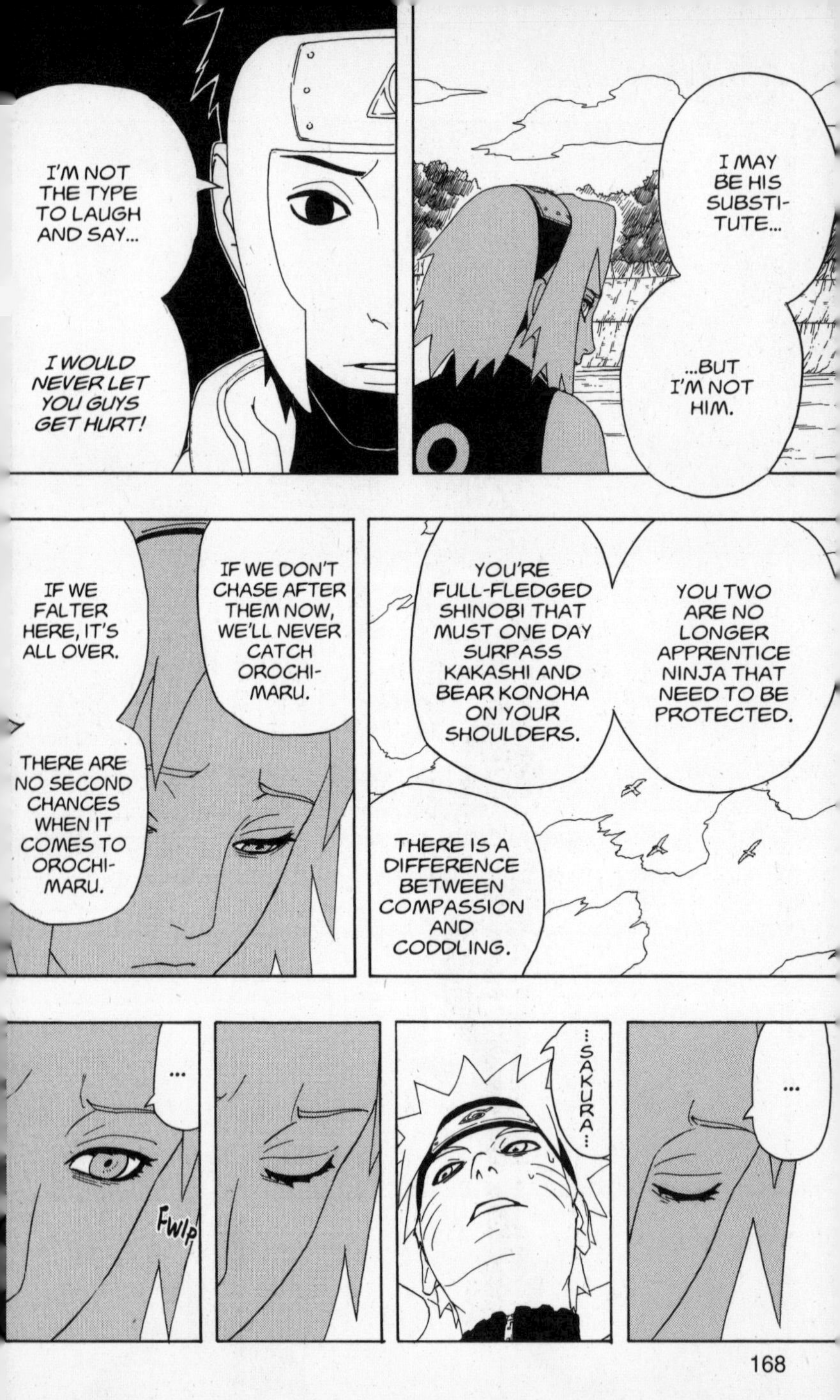
I MAY BE HIS SUBSTITUTE...
...BUT I'M NOT HIM.
I'M NOT THE TYPE TO LAUGH AND SAY...
I WOULD NEVER LET YOU GUYS GET HURT!
YOU TWO ARE NO LONGER APPRENTICE NINJA THAT NEED TO BE PROTECTED.
YOU'RE FULL-FLEDGED SHINOBI THAT MUST ONE DAY SURPASS KAKASHI AND BEAR KONOHA ON YOUR SHOULDERS.
THERE IS A DIFFERENCE BETWEEN COMPASSION AND CODDLING.
IF WE DON'T CHASE AFTER THEM NOW, WE'LL NEVER CATCH OROCHI-MARU.
IF WE FALTER HERE, IT'S ALL OVER.
THERE ARE NO SECOND CHANCES WHEN IT COMES TO OROCHI-MARU.
...
...SAKURA...
...
FWIP

READ THIS WAY

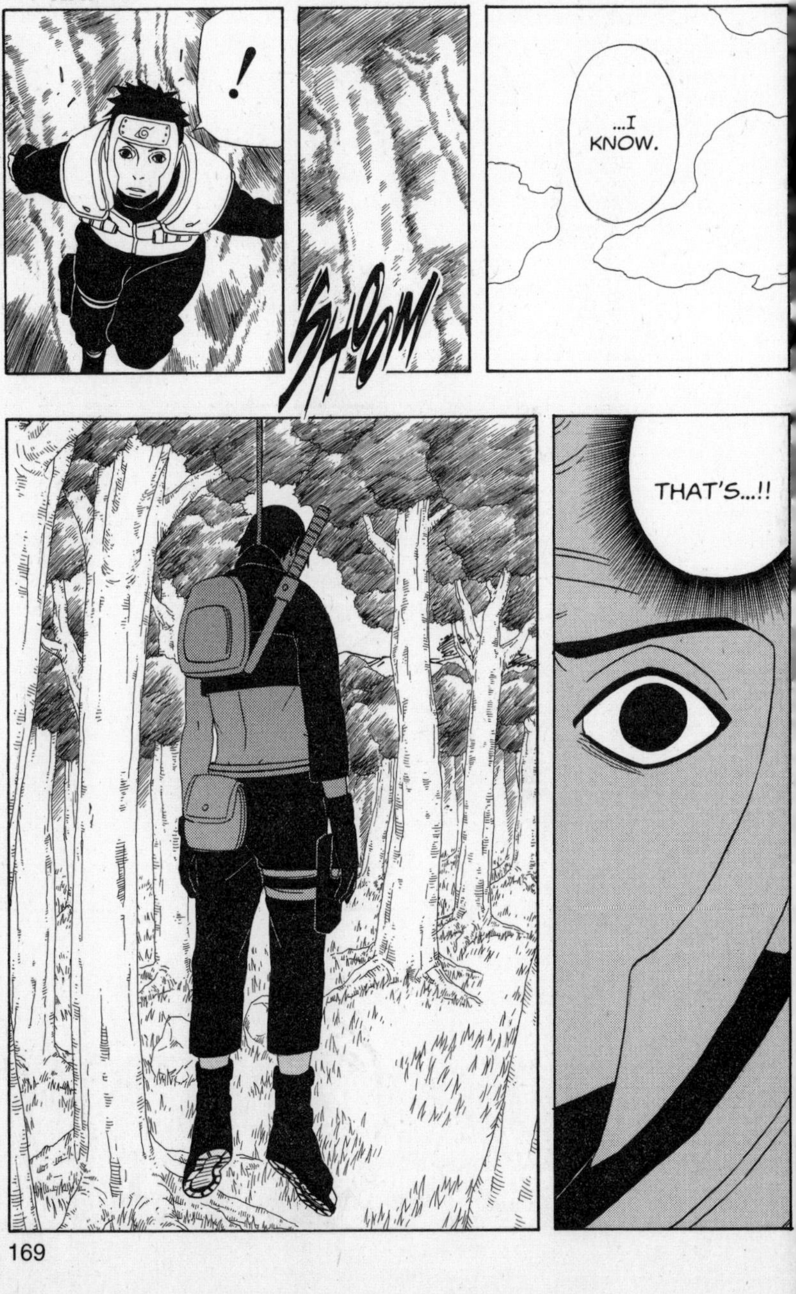

...I KNOW.
SHOOM
!
THAT'S...!!

NARUTO

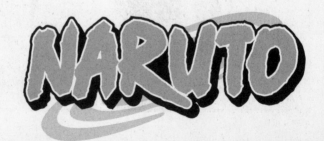

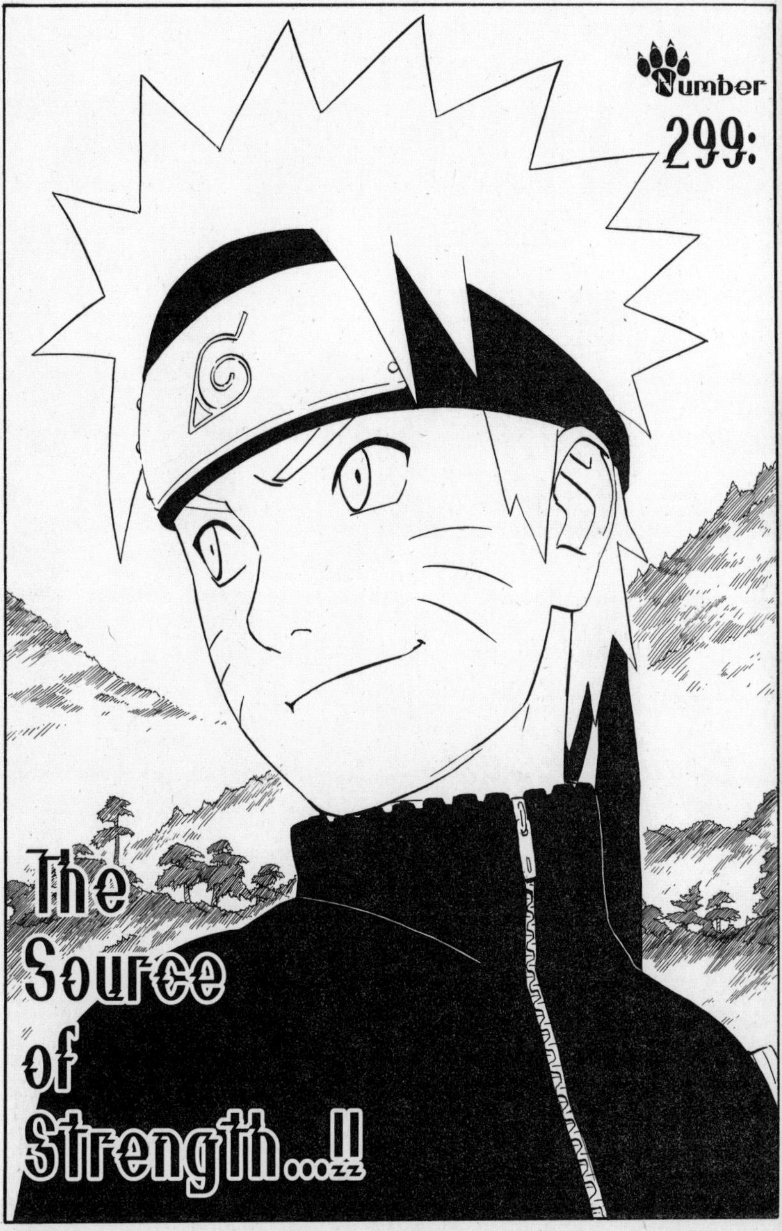
Number
299:
The Source of Strength...!!

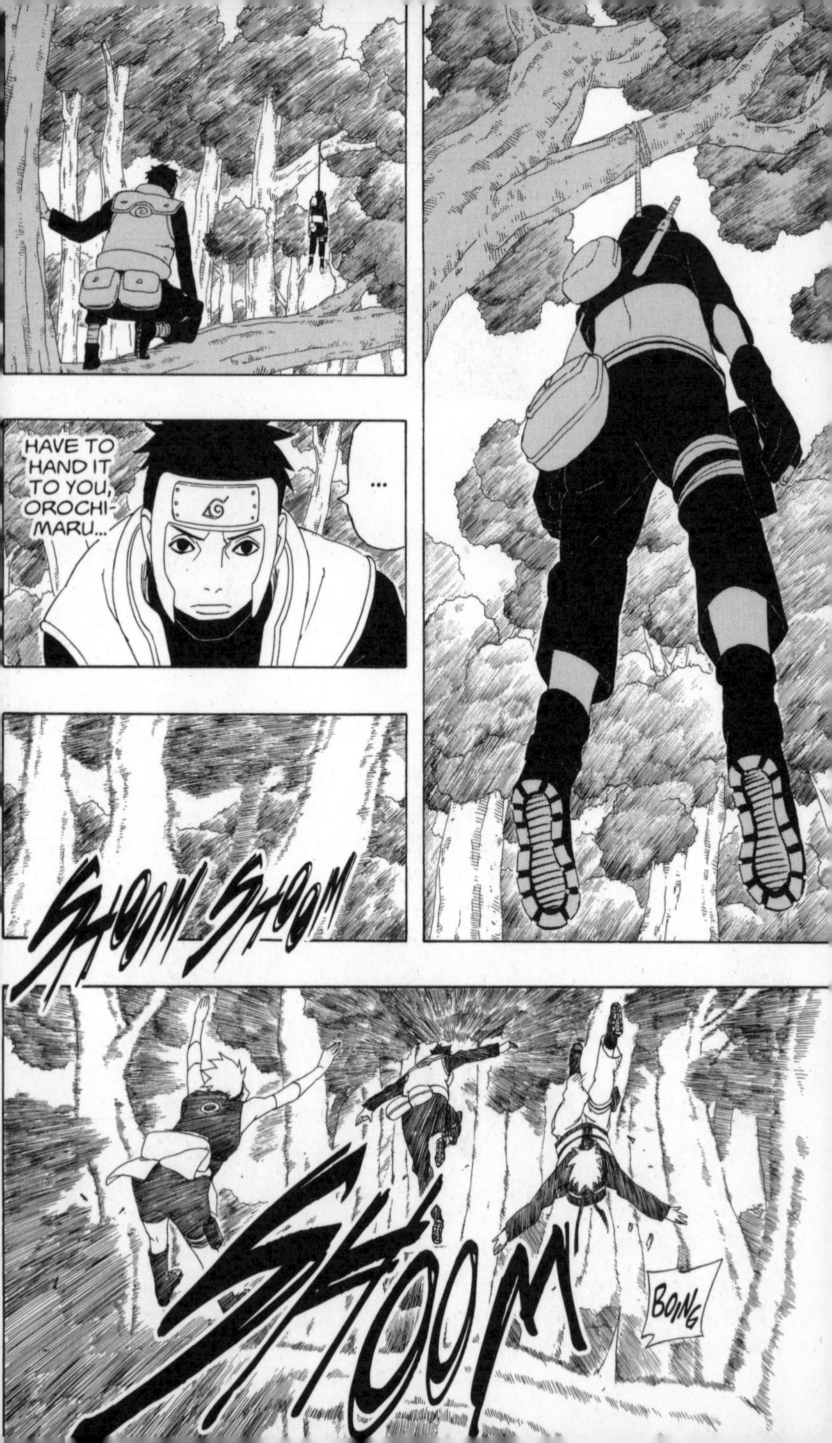
HAVE TO HAND IT TO YOU, OROCHI-MARU...
...
SHOOM SHOOM
SHOOM
BOING

READ THIS WAY

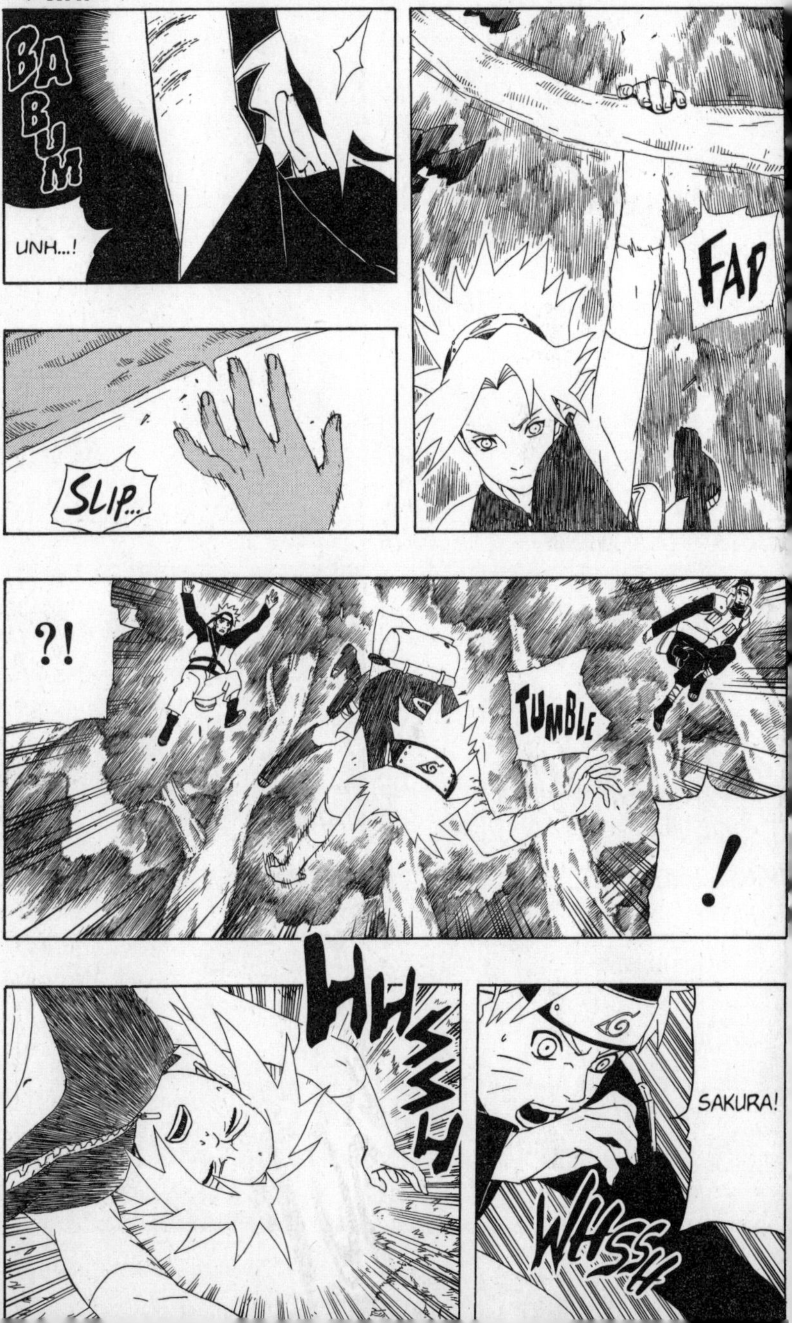
FAP
BA
BUM
UNH...!
SLIP...
TUMBLE
?!
!
SAKURA!
WHSSH
WHSSH

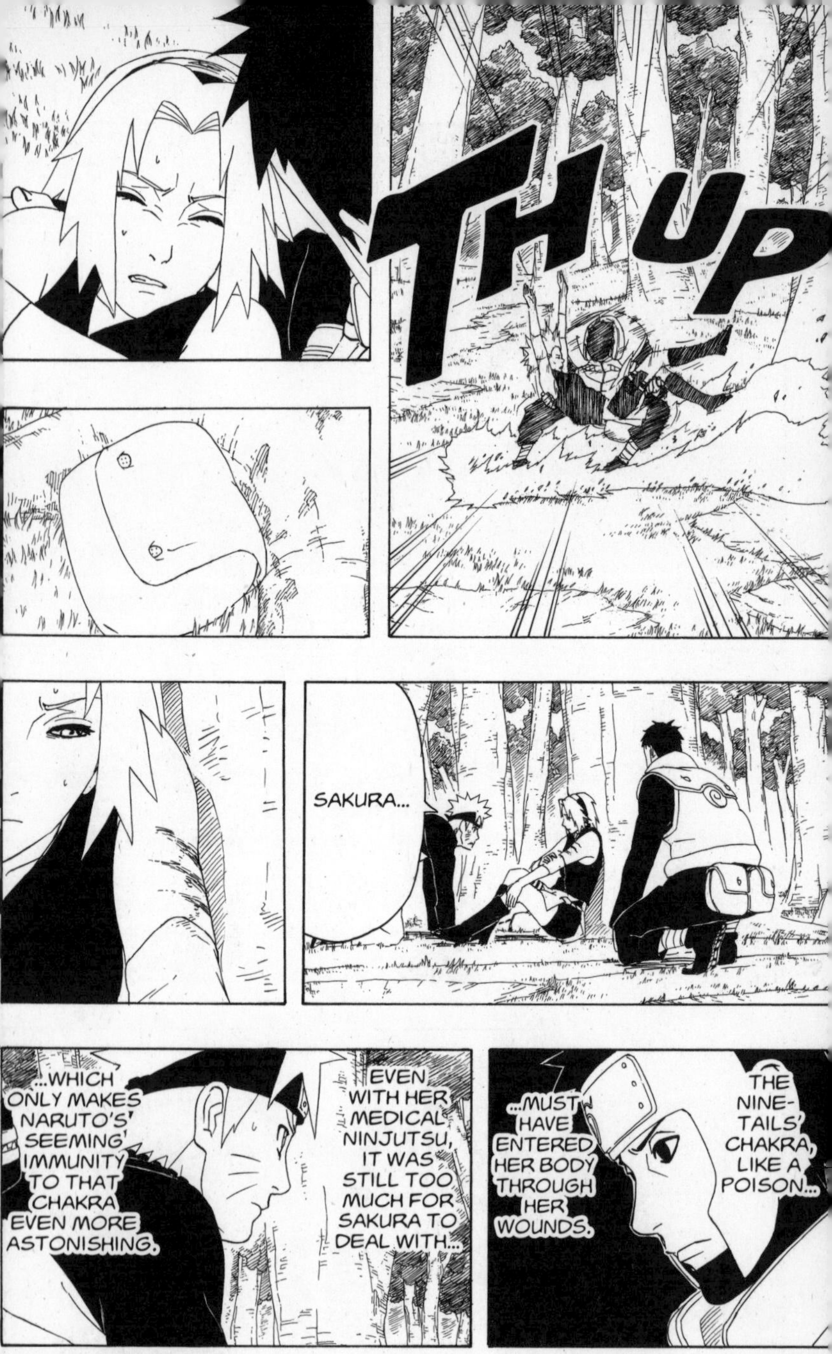
THUP
SAKURA...
THE NINE-TAILS' CHAKRA, LIKE A POISON...
...MUST HAVE ENTERED HER BODY THROUGH HER WOUNDS.
EVEN WITH HER MEDICAL NINJUTSU, IT WAS STILL TOO MUCH FOR SAKURA TO DEAL WITH...
...WHICH ONLY MAKES NARUTO'S SEEMING IMMUNITY TO THAT CHAKRA EVEN MORE ASTONISHING.

READ THIS WAY

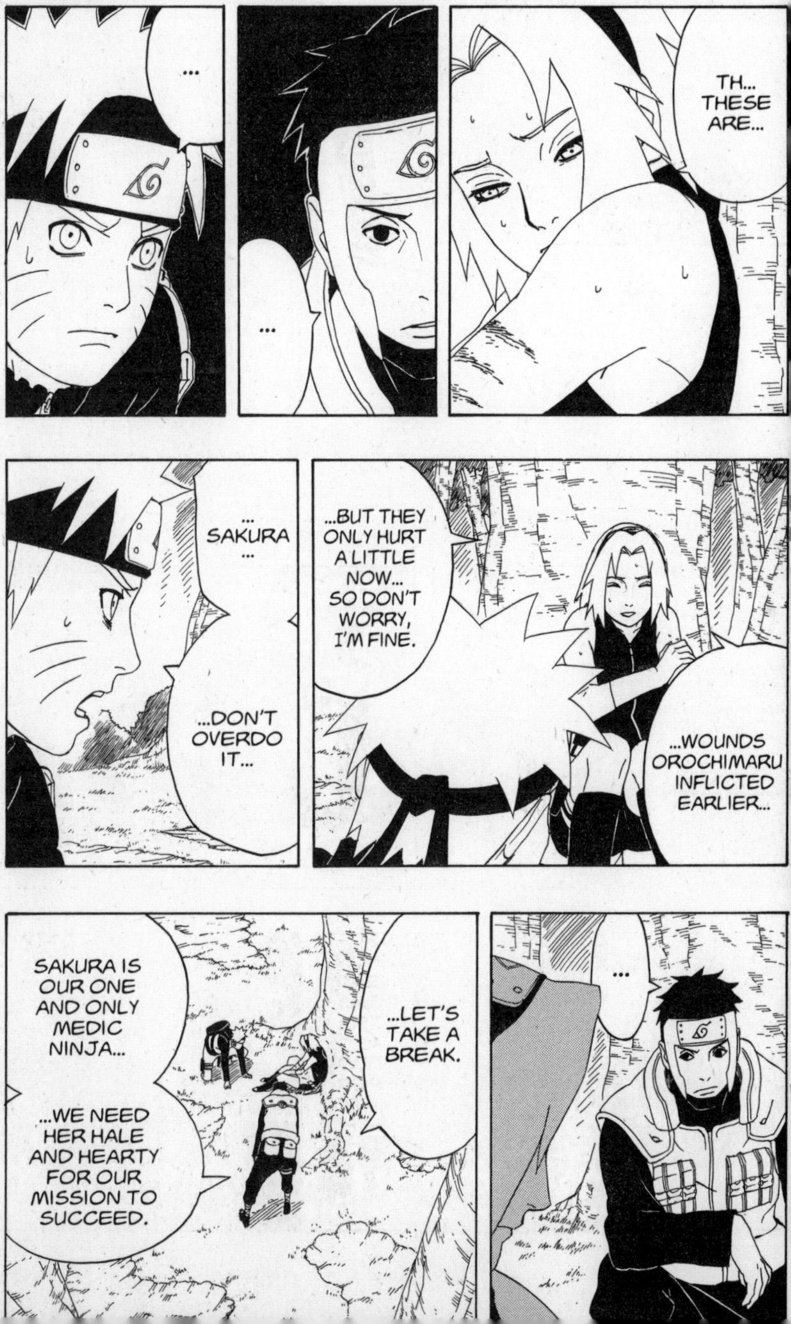

TH... THESE ARE...
...
...
...WOUNDS OROCHIMARU INFLICTED EARLIER...
...BUT THEY ONLY HURT A LITTLE NOW... SO DON'T WORRY, I'M FINE.
... SAKURA ...
...DON'T OVERDO IT...
...
...LET'S TAKE A BREAK.
SAKURA IS OUR ONE AND ONLY MEDIC NINJA...
...WE NEED HER HALE AND HEARTY FOR OUR MISSION TO SUCCEED.

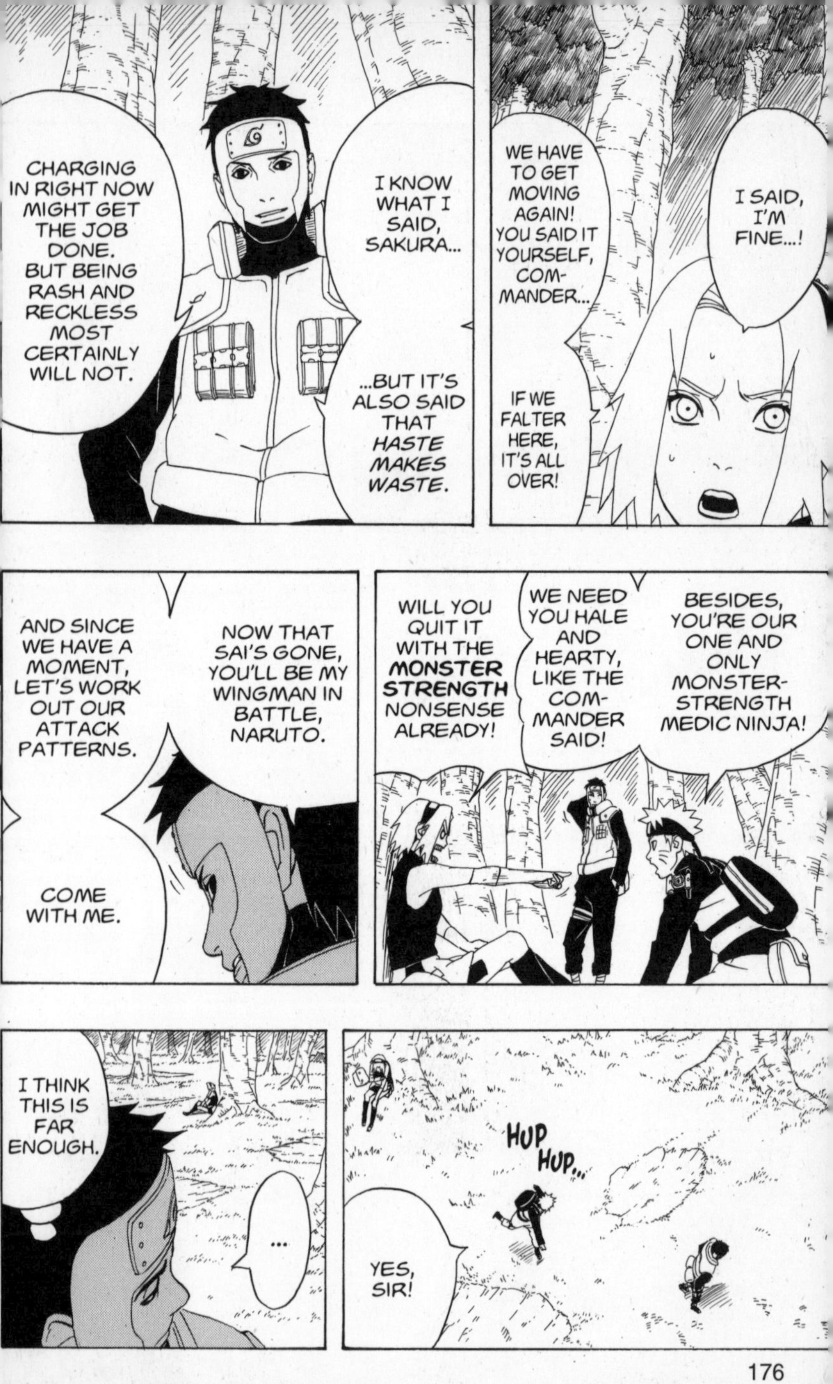
I SAID, I'M FINE...!
WE HAVE TO GET MOVING AGAIN! YOU SAID IT YOURSELF, COM-MANDER...
IF WE FALTER HERE, IT'S ALL OVER!
I KNOW WHAT I SAID, SAKURA...
...BUT IT'S ALSO SAID THAT *HASTE MAKES WASTE.*
CHARGING IN RIGHT NOW MIGHT GET THE JOB DONE. BUT BEING RASH AND RECKLESS MOST CERTAINLY WILL NOT.
BESIDES, YOU'RE OUR ONE AND ONLY MONSTER-STRENGTH MEDIC NINJA!
WE NEED YOU HALE AND HEARTY, LIKE THE COM-MANDER SAID!
WILL YOU QUIT IT WITH THE **MONSTER STRENGTH** NONSENSE ALREADY!
NOW THAT SAI'S GONE, YOU'LL BE MY WINGMAN IN BATTLE, NARUTO.
AND SINCE WE HAVE A MOMENT, LET'S WORK OUT OUR ATTACK PATTERNS.
COME WITH ME.
HUP HUP...
YES, SIR!
I THINK THIS IS FAR ENOUGH.
...

READ THIS WAY

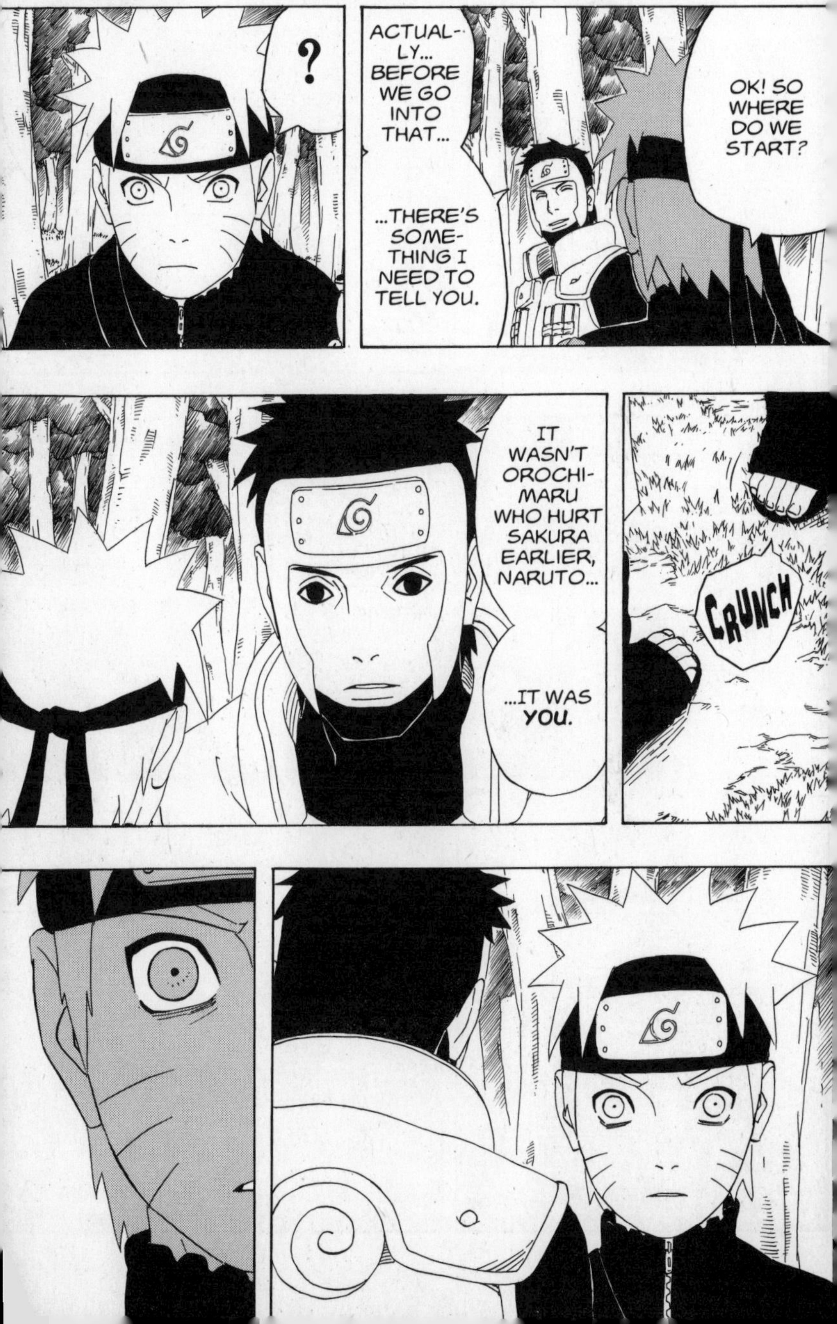
OK! SO WHERE DO WE START?
ACTUAL-LY... BEFORE WE GO INTO THAT...
...THERE'S SOME-THING I NEED TO TELL YOU.
?
CRUNCH
IT WASN'T OROCHI-MARU WHO HURT SAKURA EARLIER, NARUTO...
...IT WAS **YOU.**

...

...!

THAT'S RIGHT... I FORGOT...

TK TK TKTK

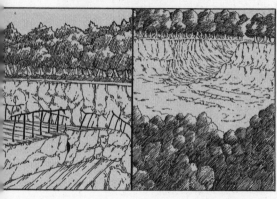

...REALLY DON'T REMEMBER A THING...?

NARUTO, YOU...

178

READ THIS WAY

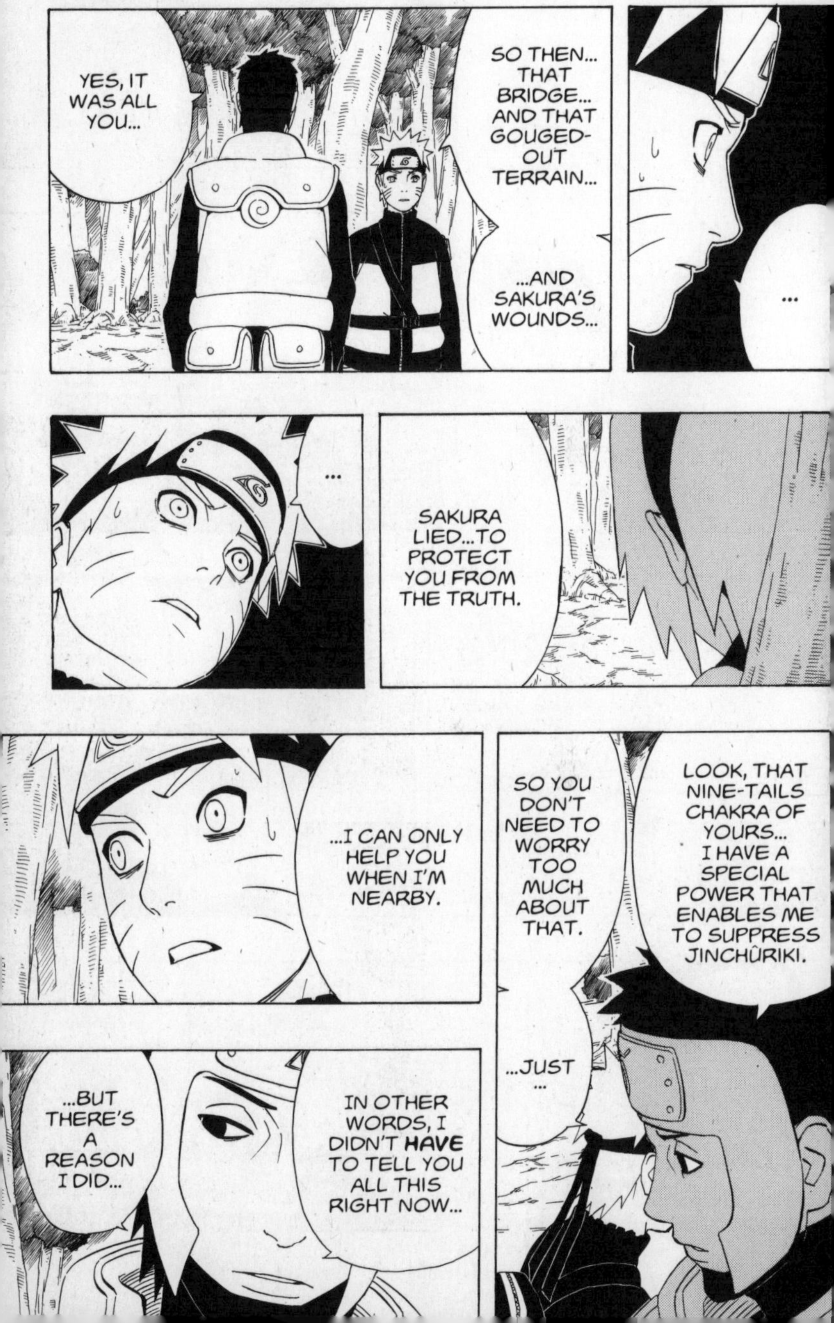
...
SO THEN... THAT BRIDGE... AND THAT GOUGED-OUT TERRAIN...
...AND SAKURA'S WOUNDS...
YES, IT WAS ALL YOU...
SAKURA LIED...TO PROTECT YOU FROM THE TRUTH.
...
LOOK, THAT NINE-TAILS CHAKRA OF YOURS... I HAVE A SPECIAL POWER THAT ENABLES ME TO SUPPRESS JINCHÛRIKI.
SO YOU DON'T NEED TO WORRY TOO MUCH ABOUT THAT.
...JUST ...
...I CAN ONLY HELP YOU WHEN I'M NEARBY.
IN OTHER WORDS, I DIDN'T **HAVE** TO TELL YOU ALL THIS RIGHT NOW...
...BUT THERE'S A REASON I DID...

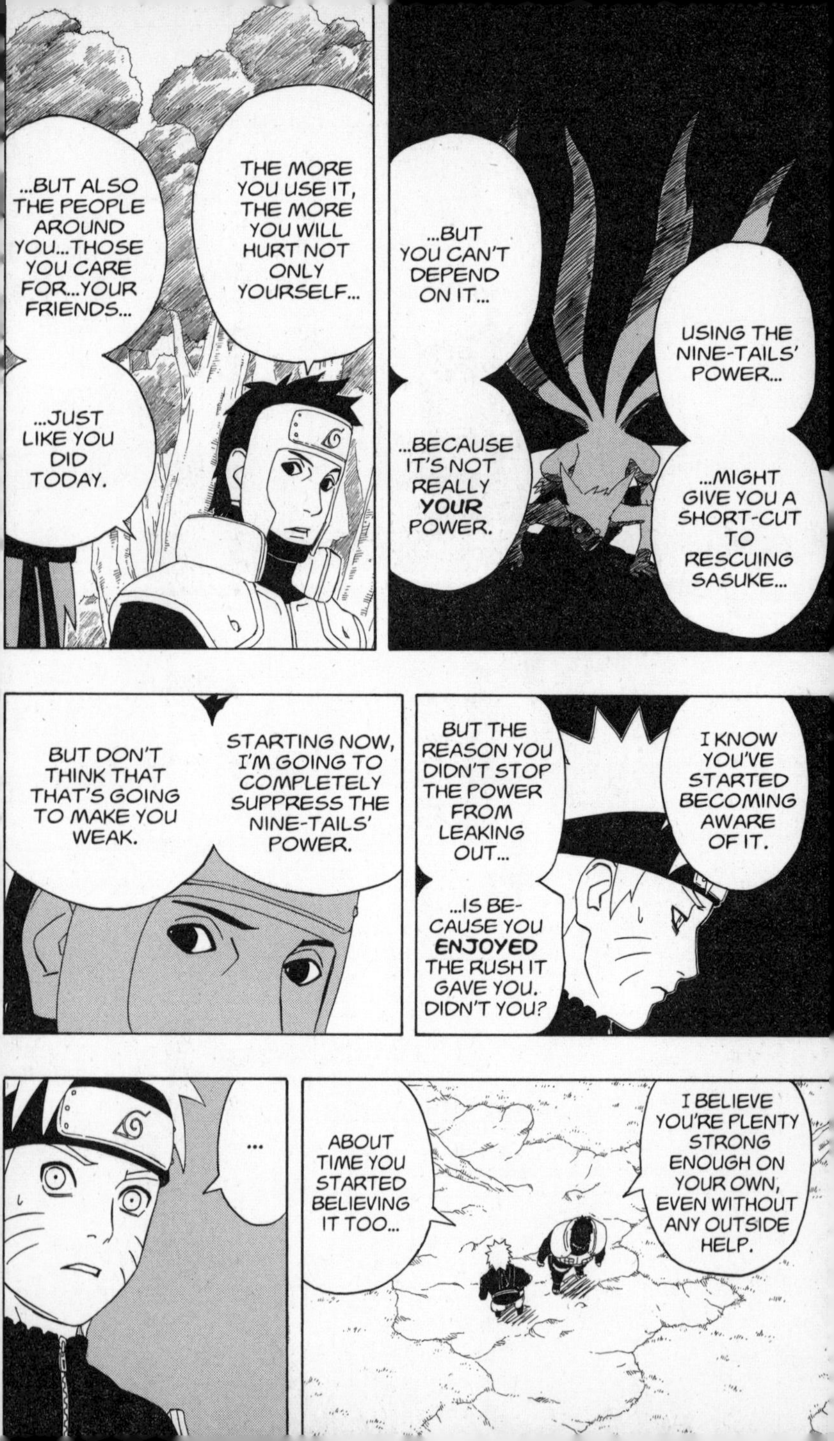
USING THE NINE-TAILS' POWER...
...MIGHT GIVE YOU A SHORT-CUT TO RESCUING SASUKE...
...BUT YOU CAN'T DEPEND ON IT...
...BECAUSE IT'S NOT REALLY **YOUR** POWER.
THE MORE YOU USE IT, THE MORE YOU WILL HURT NOT ONLY YOURSELF...
...BUT ALSO THE PEOPLE AROUND YOU...THOSE YOU CARE FOR...YOUR FRIENDS...
...JUST LIKE YOU DID TODAY.
I KNOW YOU'VE STARTED BECOMING AWARE OF IT.
BUT THE REASON YOU DIDN'T STOP THE POWER FROM LEAKING OUT...
...IS BE-CAUSE YOU **ENJOYED** THE RUSH IT GAVE YOU. DIDN'T YOU?
STARTING NOW, I'M GOING TO COMPLETELY SUPPRESS THE NINE-TAILS' POWER.
BUT DON'T THINK THAT THAT'S GOING TO MAKE YOU WEAK.
I BELIEVE YOU'RE PLENTY STRONG ENOUGH ON YOUR OWN, EVEN WITHOUT ANY OUTSIDE HELP.
ABOUT TIME YOU STARTED BELIEVING IT TOO...
...

READ THIS WAY

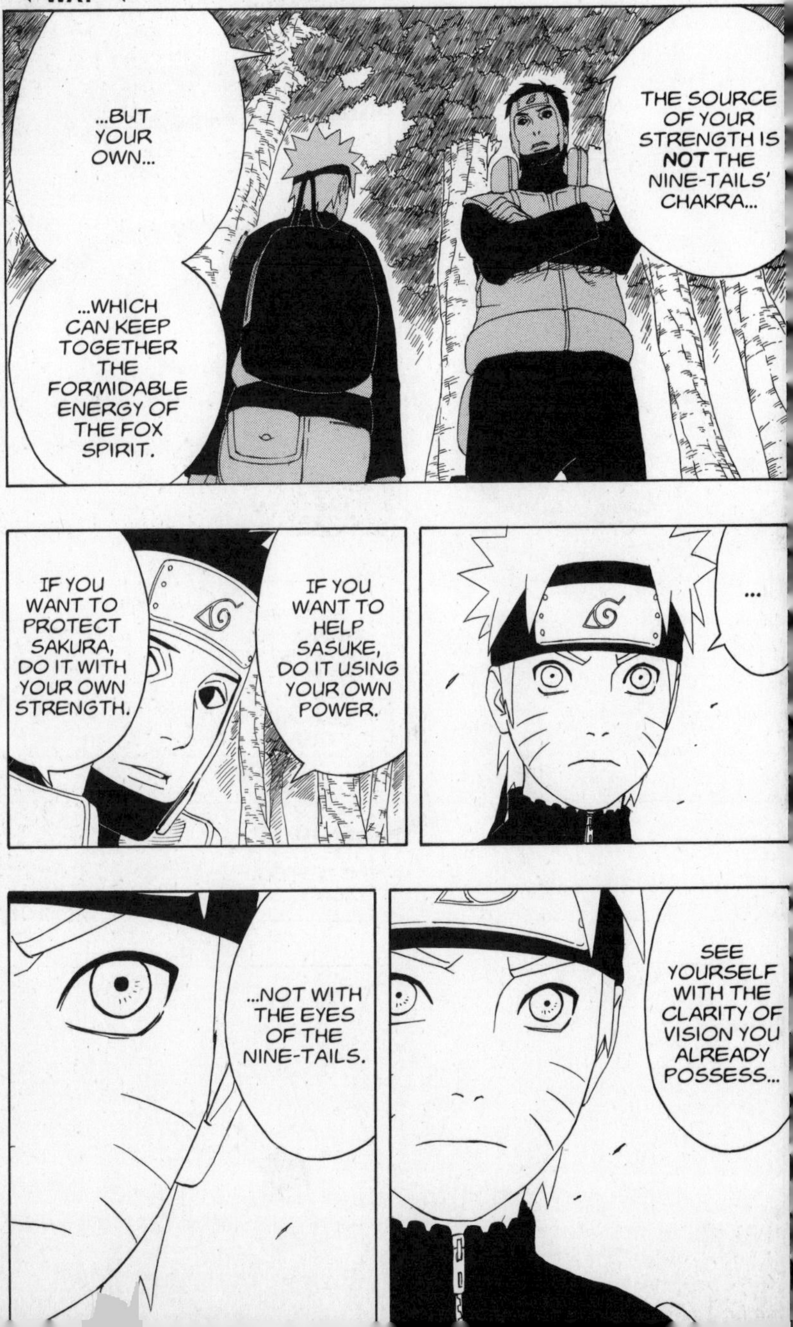
THE SOURCE OF YOUR STRENGTH IS **NOT** THE NINE-TAILS' CHAKRA...
...BUT YOUR OWN...
...WHICH CAN KEEP TOGETHER THE FORMIDABLE ENERGY OF THE FOX SPIRIT.
...
IF YOU WANT TO HELP SASUKE, DO IT USING YOUR OWN POWER.
IF YOU WANT TO PROTECT SAKURA, DO IT WITH YOUR OWN STRENGTH.
SEE YOURSELF WITH THE CLARITY OF VISION YOU ALREADY POSSESS...
...NOT WITH THE EYES OF THE NINE-TAILS.

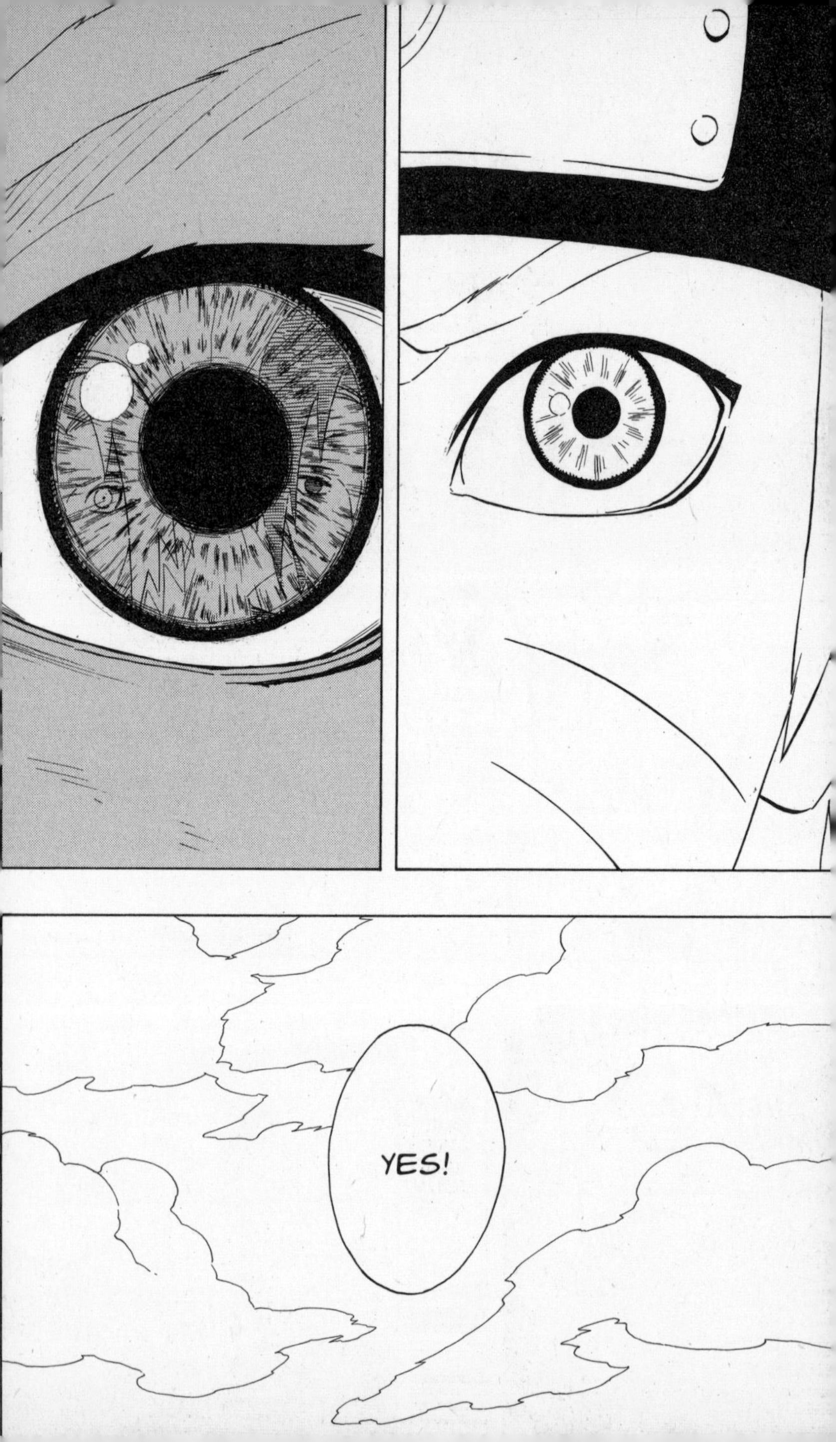
YES!

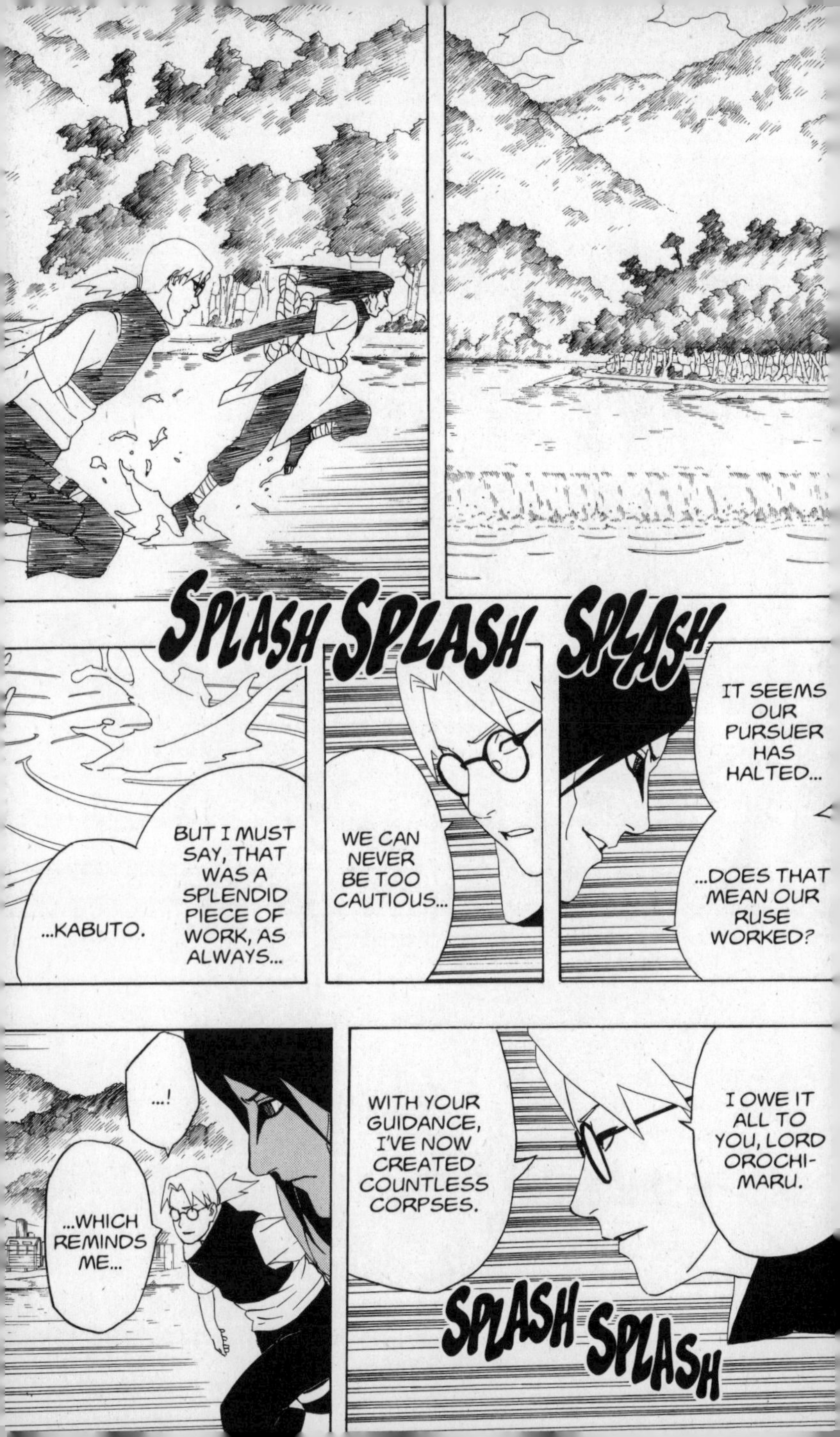
SPLASH SPLASH SPLASH
IT SEEMS OUR PURSUER HAS HALTED...
...DOES THAT MEAN OUR RUSE WORKED?
WE CAN NEVER BE TOO CAUTIOUS...
BUT I MUST SAY, THAT WAS A SPLENDID PIECE OF WORK, AS ALWAYS...
...KABUTO.
I OWE IT ALL TO YOU, LORD OROCHI-MARU.
WITH YOUR GUIDANCE, I'VE NOW CREATED COUNTLESS CORPSES.
SPLASH SPLASH
...!
...WHICH REMINDS ME...

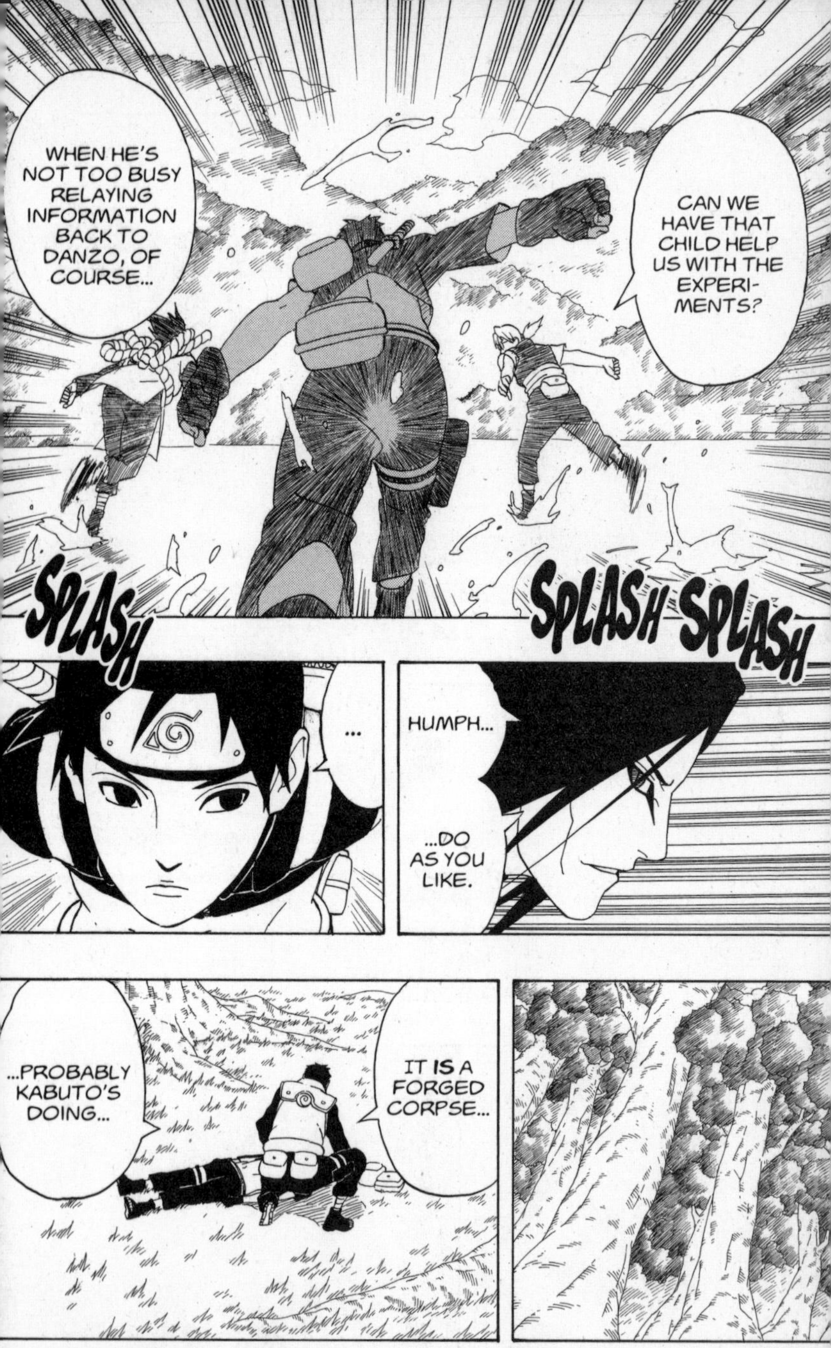
CAN WE HAVE THAT CHILD HELP US WITH THE EXPERIMENTS?
WHEN HE'S NOT TOO BUSY RELAYING INFORMATION BACK TO DANZO, OF COURSE...
SPLASH SPLASH
SPLASH
HUMPH...
...DO AS YOU LIKE.
...
IT IS A FORGED CORPSE...
...PROBABLY KABUTO'S DOING...

READ THIS WAY

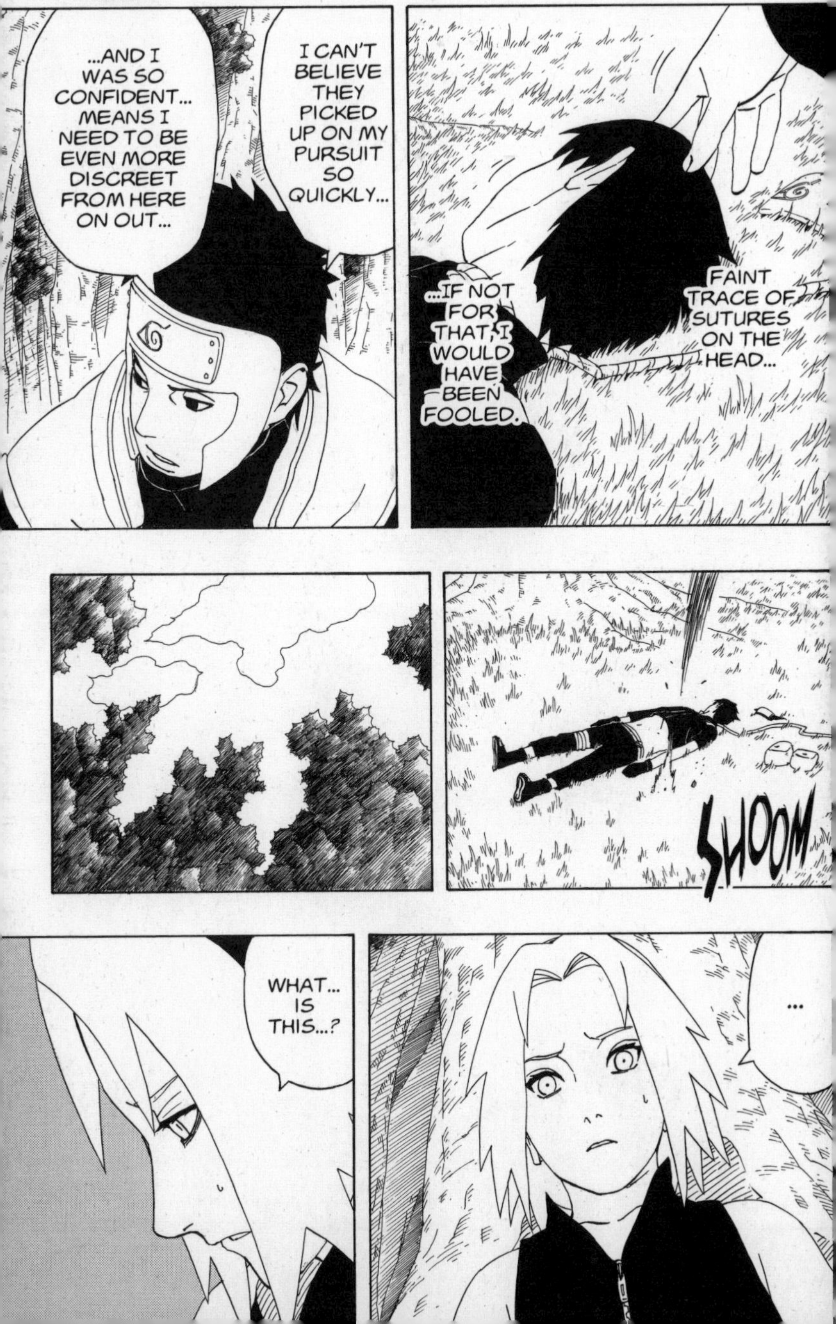
FAINT TRACE OF SUTURES ON THE HEAD...
...IF NOT FOR THAT, I WOULD HAVE BEEN FOOLED.
I CAN'T BELIEVE THEY PICKED UP ON MY PURSUIT SO QUICKLY...
...AND I WAS SO CONFIDENT... MEANS I NEED TO BE EVEN MORE DISCREET FROM HERE ON OUT...
SHOOM
...
WHAT... IS THIS...?

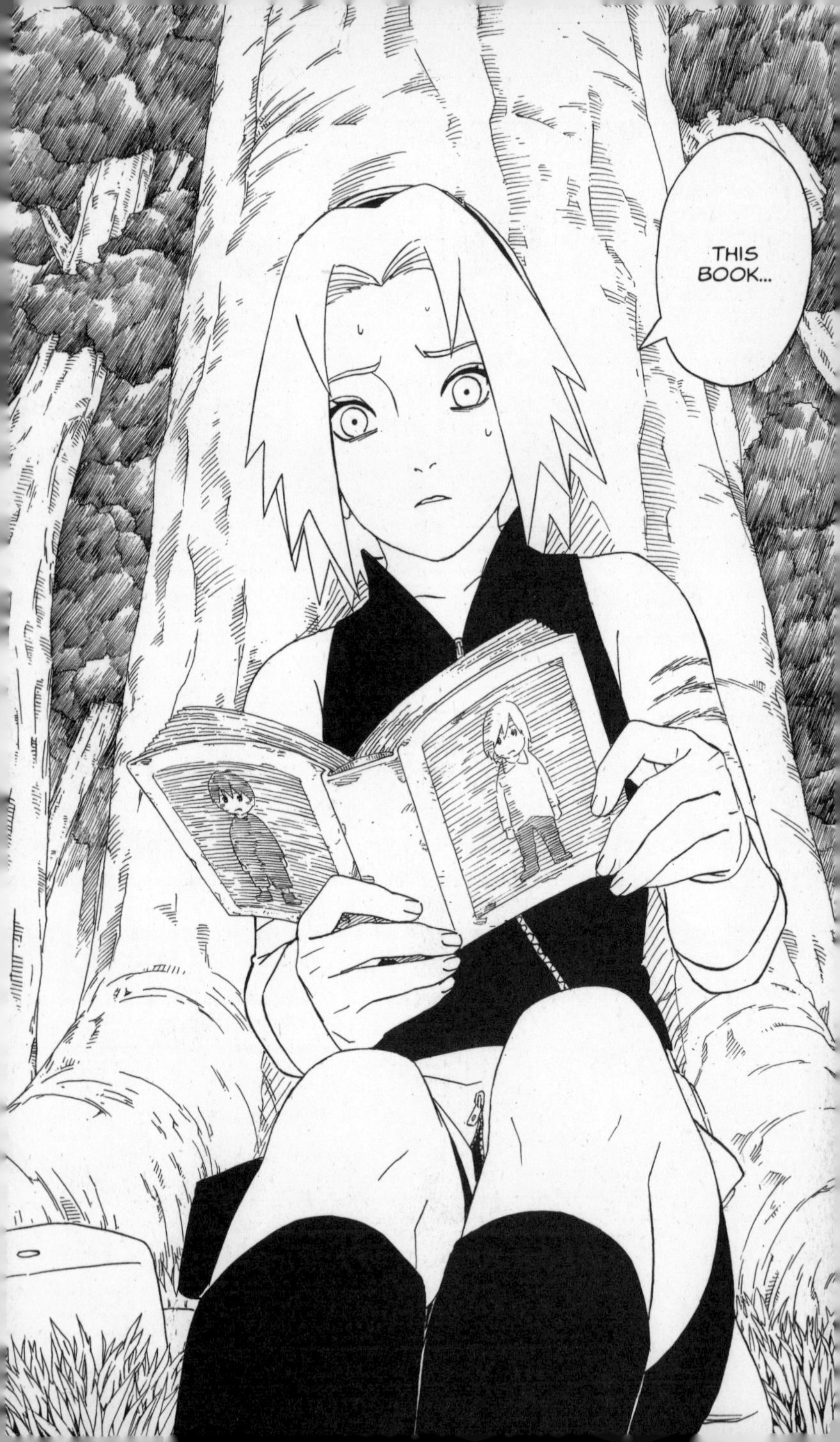
THIS BOOK...

READ THIS WAY

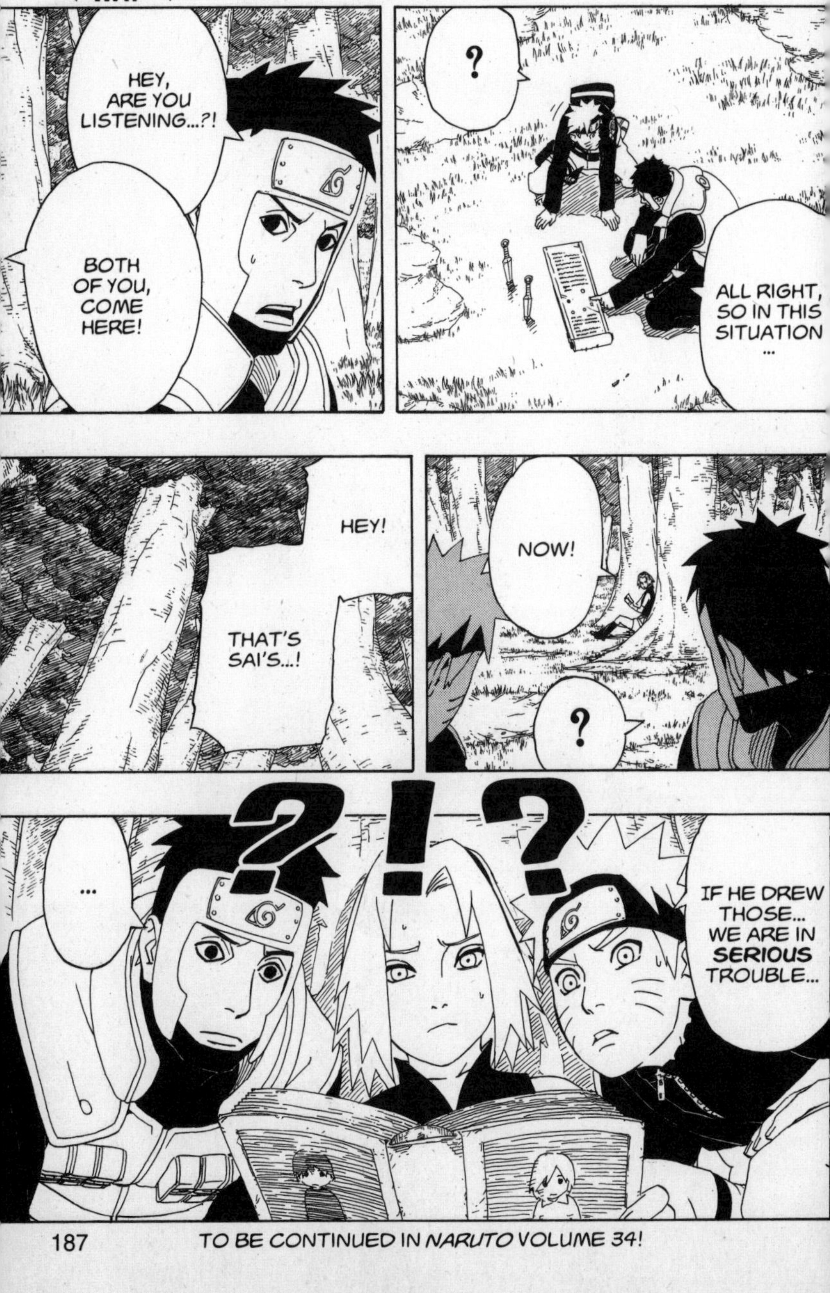
?
ALL RIGHT, SO IN THIS SITUATION ...
HEY, ARE YOU LISTENING...?!
BOTH OF YOU, COME HERE!
NOW!
?
HEY!
THAT'S SAI'S...!
?!?
IF HE DREW THOSE... WE ARE IN **SERIOUS** TROUBLE...
...

TO BE CONTINUED IN *NARUTO* VOLUME 34!

IN THE NEXT VOLUME...

THE REUNION

Naruto finally finds Sasuke! But Sasuke won't return to Konoha without a fight. This time it might take all of Team Kakashi to bring him down—and bring him back.

AVAILABLE MARCH 2009!
Read it first in SHONEN JUMP magazine!

When a dream of utopia becomes a **NIGHTMAR**
it'll take a ninja to set things right!

NARUTO The Movie 2:
Legend of the Stone of Gelel
NOW ON DVD!

GET THE COMPLETE
NARUTO COLLECTION
OF BOOKS, MAGAZINES AND DVI

ON SALE AT NARUTO.VIZ.COM
ALSO AVAILABLE AT YOUR LOCAL BOOKSTORE AND COMIC STORE

  © 2002 MASASHI KISHIMOTO © NMP 2005

Tell us what you think about SHONEN JUMP manga!

Our survey is now available online.
Go to: www.*SHONENJUMP*.com/*mangasurvey*

Help us make our product offering better!

THE REAL ACTION STARTS IN...

SHONEN JUMP

THE WORLD'S MOST POPULAR MANGA
www.shonenjump.com

ST ADVANCED

SJ

viz media

BLEACH © 2001 by Tite Kubo/SHUEISHA Inc. NARUTO © 1999 by Masashi Kishimoto/SHUEISHA Inc.
DEATH NOTE © 2003 by Tsugumi Ohba, Takeshi Obata/SHUEISHA Inc. ONE PIECE © 1997 by Eiichiro Oda/SHUEISHA Inc.

SHONEN JUMP

THE WORLD'S MOST POPULAR MANGA

12 ISSUES FOR ONLY $29.95*

THAT'S 50% OFF THE NEWSSTAND PRICE!

Each issue of SHONEN JUMP contains the coolest manga available in the U.S., anime news, and info on video & card games, toys AND more!

SUBSCRIBE TODAY and Become a Member of the ST Sub Club!

- **ENJOY** 12 HUGE action-packed issues
- **SAVE** 50% OFF the cover price
- **ACCESS** exclusive areas of www.shonenjump.com
- **RECEIVE** FREE members-only gifts

Available ONLY to Subscribers!

RATED T FOR TEEN
ratings.viz.com

VIZ media
www.viz

3 EASY WAYS TO SUBSCRIBE!

1) Send in the subscription order form from this book OR
2) Log on to: www.shonenjump.com OR
3) Call 1-800-541-7919

*Canada price for 12 issues: $41.95 USD, including GST, HST, and QST. US/CAN orders only. Allow 6-8 weeks for delivery.
BLEACH © 2001 by Tite Kubo/SHUEISHA Inc. NARUTO © 1999 by Masashi Kishimoto/SHUEISHA Inc.
GINTAMA © 2003 by Hideaki Sorachi/SHUEISHA Inc. ONE PIECE © 1997 by Eiichiro Oda/SHUEISHA Inc.

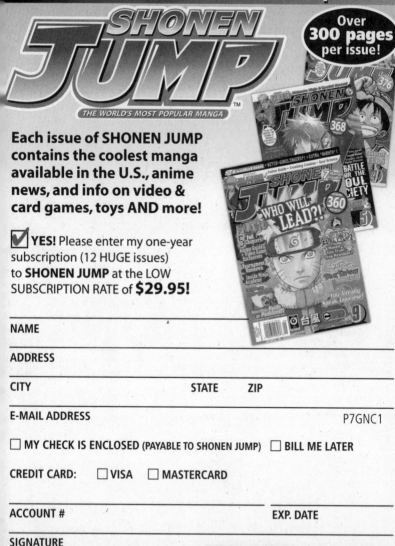

Save **50% OFF** the cover price!

SHONEN JUMP
THE WORLD'S MOST POPULAR MANGA

Over **300 pages** per issue!

Each issue of SHONEN JUMP contains the coolest manga available in the U.S., anime news, and info on video & card games, toys AND more!

☑ **YES!** Please enter my one-year subscription (12 HUGE issues) to **SHONEN JUMP** at the LOW SUBSCRIPTION RATE of **$29.95!**

NAME

ADDRESS

CITY   STATE   ZIP

E-MAIL ADDRESS   P7GNC1

☐ **MY CHECK IS ENCLOSED** (PAYABLE TO SHONEN JUMP)   ☐ **BILL ME LATER**

CREDIT CARD: ☐ **VISA**   ☐ **MASTERCARD**

ACCOUNT #   EXP. DATE

SIGNATURE

CLIP AND MAIL TO ➤

SHONEN JUMP
Subscriptions Service Dept.
P.O. Box 515
Mount Morris, IL 61054-0515

Make checks payable to: **SHONEN JUMP**. Canada price for 12 issues: $41.95 USD, including GST, HST and QST. US/CAN orders only. Allow 6-8 weeks for delivery.

BLEACH © 2001 by Tite Kubo/SHUEISHA Inc. NARUTO © 1999 by Masashi Kishimoto/SHUEISHA Inc.
ONE PIECE © 1997 by Eiichiro Oda/SHUEISHA Inc.

RATED **T** FOR TEEN
ratings.viz.com